Sonic Icons

ORTHODOX CHRISTIANITY AND CONTEMPORARY THOUGHT

SERIES EDITORS

Aristotle Papanikolaou and Ashley M. Purpura

This series consists of books that seek to bring Orthodox Christianity into an engagement with contemporary forms of thought. Its goal is to promote (1) historical studies in Orthodox Christianity that are interdisciplinary, employ a variety of methods, and speak to contemporary issues; and (2) constructive theological arguments in conversation with patristic sources and that focus on contemporary questions ranging from the traditional theological and philosophical themes of God and human identity to cultural, political, economic, and ethical concerns. The books in the series explore both the relevancy of Orthodox Christianity to contemporary challenges and the impact of contemporary modes of thought on Orthodox self-understandings.

SONIC ICONS

Relation, Recognition, and Revival in a Syriac World

SARAH BAKKER KELLOGG

FORDHAM UNIVERSITY PRESS
New York • 2025

The maps on pages 5 and 8–9 used by kind permission from Gorgias Press.

Parts of this book were previously published in different form: portions of Chapter 2 and Chapter 3 in "Ritual Sounds, Political Echoes: Vocal Agency and the Sensory Cultures of Secularism in the Dutch-Syriac Diaspora," *American Ethnologist* 42, no. 3 (August 2015): 431–45; portions of Chapter 2 and Chapter 5 in "Perforating Kinship: Syriac Christianity, Ethnicity, and Secular Legibility," *Current Anthropology* 60, no.4 (August 2, 2019): 475–98; and portions of Chapter 6 in "A Racial-Religious Imagination: Syriac Christians, Iconic Bodies, and the Sensory Politics of Ethical Difference in the Netherlands," *Cultural Anthropology* 36, no. 4 (November 18, 2021): 618–48.

Fordham University Press has no responsibility for the persistence or accuracy of URLs for external or third-party Internet websites referred to in this publication and does not guarantee that any content on such websites is, or will remain, accurate or appropriate.

Fordham University Press also publishes its books in a variety of electronic formats. Some content that appears in print may not be available in electronic books.

Visit us online at www.fordhampress.com.

Library of Congress Cataloging-in-Publication Data available online at https://catalog.loc.gov.

Printed in the United States of America

27 26 25   5 4 3 2 1

First edition

CONTENTS

A Note on Transliteration

Among modern scholars, Classical Syriac is usually transliterated into Romanized languages according to standardized conventions, yet throughout the global Syriac Orthodox diaspora it remains a vital artifact, subject to the vagaries of local linguistic influence. So, where scholars might transliterate the word for "liturgical teacher" as *malpana*, ordinary Syriac Orthodox might transliterate it as *malphono* or *malfono*, the "o" being a sign of dominant West Syriac pronunciations in the twenty-first century. Similarly, variations occur when transliterating cognates from different languages into English. For example, *Süryânî* is a transliteration from Ottoman Turkish, while *Suryānī* is a transliteration from Arabic. As an ethnographer, my primary purpose is to document local usage and contextual specificity. Thus, my field notes reflected these variations as my research participants Romanized key words for me according to their own phonetic intuitions, sometimes originating in Ṭuroyo, sometimes Arabic or Turkish or Kurdish, sometimes Dutch or German or Swedish, depending on the constellation of languages spoken by a given individual. I have tried to make my own transliterations as straightforward and readable as possible for an English-speaking audience while staying faithful to the patterns I encountered in the Dutch-Syriac diaspora.

PRELUDE

Just as from the small womb of Eve's ear
Death entered in and was poured out,
So through a new ear, that was Mary's,
Life entered and was poured out.
                St. Ephrem the Syrian (c. 306 CE–373 CE), *Church* 49:7

*   *   *

A young girl from the house of David, whose name was Mary, became the chariot which carried the Saviour of the world; she appears to me to be much greater than the chariot which Ezekial saw: that chariot had faces and wheels that spoke, but Mary has a mouth that sings praise to you, O Lord. Alleluia. May her prayer assist us. Artists gathered to portray Mary, but their paints were inadequate and they failed to portray Mary: they portrayed her as a virgin—but they found her with child; they portrayed her as a married woman—but her virginity was preserved; they portrayed her as wife of a husband—but the husband knew her not. O portrayer who [truly] portrayed Mary, have pity and mercy on us, and may her prayer assist us.

Hymn on the Virgin Mary, Part Five of the Prayer of Sanctification for Icons and Images of the Syriac Orthodox Church (quoted in Chaillot 1993, 102).

*   *   *

Illumine with Your teaching
The voice of the speaker
And the ear of the hearer:
Like the pupil of the eye
Let the ears be illumined,
For the voice provides the rays of light.

     St. Ephrem the Syrian (c. 306 CE–373 CE), *Hymn 37*

Sonic Icons

CHAPTER

1

INCARNATIONS OF THE WORD

"Christianity is the blood in my veins," she said, years later, over dinner, as she touched the tender flesh on her inner wrist. "This is what is so hard for others to understand. I could no more stop being Christian than I could change the color of my skin."

*   *   *

On the easternmost edge of the Dutch country-side, a red-brick monastery sits surrounded by farmland. Once an abandoned Roman Catholic convent, the cloister found new life in the 1970s as the Mor Ephrem Syriac Orthodox Monastery, when a group of Syriac Orthodox, or *Suryoye*, guest workers recruited from Turkey pooled their money and transformed it into a boarding house, eventually gifting it to the Church.[1] Entering the monastery grounds and walking east, visitors pass the cloister's main building with its dormitory, refectory, and receiving rooms on the left, the *grote kerk*, or "big church," at the center of the grounds, and a cemetery at the north end. Along the southeastern edge of the property, a parking lot is edged by pastures that extend to a line of trees marking the international border and the German village of Gronau beyond.

On any given day, the Mor Ephrem monastery is astir with activity and visitors from all over the world, as local and distant kin visit the bishop, the abbot, a handful of monks, nuns, and a rotating crop of resident students. The monastery regularly hosts community events and public lectures for the Syriac Orthodox faithful who have settled throughout the region, often attracting up to a thousand visitors at a time for the most important holy days of the year.

Today's event, however, was sparsely attended as only the most dedicated locals trickled in for a public lecture in honor of the New Year. Snow had fallen heavily through the night, and fewer than a hundred intrepid parishioners had dared to make the trek over the icy freeways. The event's organizers had hoped to move the public lecture into the smaller and more intimate dining hall in the adjoining building but were thwarted by a baptismal party planned later in the afternoon for a family who lived in the neighborhood. So, the small crowd settled in their pews, preparing to learn what the monastery's newly reinvented education and outreach committee had in store for them this year.

Elena,[2] a young *Suryayto*, or Syriac Orthodox woman, stood with some of her fellow committee members in circles around two lecterns in the space in front of the altar where deacons, cantors, readers, and others with sufficient knowledge of classical Syriac may stand to sing, chant, and read or recite their parts in the formal worship service, or liturgy, and to provide vocal atmosphere for public events like this. A quietly earnest twenty-four-year-old, Elena was a pillar among the community's youth leadership. She lived, in the period when I knew her well, with her parents in the small conservative town of Rijssen, working for a Dutch bank and spending her free time with the sometimes-thankless job of community organizing for the Syriac Orthodox Church of Antioch and All the East. As she and the women next to her chanted in unison with a low, rhythmic cadence, the voice of an unseen male deacon rose up from behind the proscenium-like fabric wall shielding the altar in a rich, wailing vibrato, breathtaking in its virtuosic, microtonal complexity.

Elena was a *mshamshonitho*, which might be translated as "deaconess," but is more often referred to in English and other European languages as "choir girl." Textual records of women singing crucial parts in the formal worship services of Syriac Christianity date as far back as the second century CE, in the late antique city of Edessa, once a major center of ecclesiastical learning in the eastern Roman Empire and now the site of the modern Turkish city of Urhoy. In the twenty-first century, women's liturgical singing is a central feature of Syriac Orthodox community revitalization, both in the global diaspora and in parts of Syria, Turkey, Lebanon, and Iraq where a few Suryoye communities remain.

Periodic episodes of violence since the nineteenth century—reignited in the twentieth century by the *Sayfo* (Syriac for "Sword"), the 1915 genocide against Syriac Christians in Ottoman Anatolia, as well as by the Turkish government's ongoing conflict with the Kurdish independence movement, the cascading effects of the American invasion of Iraq in 2003, and civil war in Syria—have largely emptied the region of its long-standing ethnoreligious diversity.[3] For most Syriac Orthodox Christians in the global diaspora, the disappearance of Syriac tradition from the Middle East is a source of everyday anxiety and grief; but these feelings are shadowed by a parallel fear articulated to me by a young priest, born in Turkey but raised and university-educated in the Netherlands: "The past is the past. We can't do anything about it. The real genocide is happening here, in the West. Western Christians have changed Christianity so much it's unrecognizable, and they want us to change too. How can we stop it when no one knows about us? Of all the peoples of the world, we are like a single strand on a head full of hair. Legally, in most places, we don't exist as *a people*, so what recourse do we have?"[4] For many of my interlocutors, cultural assimilation in Europe is as dangerous to communal survival as is political violence in the Middle East.

That is why Elena was here singing at the monastery at the beginning of a community event she helped to organize. Several years earlier, Elena had visited the monastery of Mor Gabriel in her family's ancestral homeland, near the city of Mardin in the highland region of southeast Turkey known in Syriac as Tur Abdin, or "the mountains of the servants of God." Having fled as a small child with her parents from violent conflict between the separatist Kurdistan People's Congress (formerly known as the Kurdish Worker's Party) and the Turkish government, she told me later, the experience of rediscovering the monasteries of Tur Abdin was like being "born-again." Before, she had had no interest in doing things for the church, but after she had spent time with the nuns of Mor Gabriel, learning from their sisterly sense of community, she realized that if Syriac Orthodoxy is to survive the twin dangers of political violence and cultural assimilation, it was up to her to save it. Yet the true nature of these twin dangers was not always entirely clear to her, she said, and thus not easily navigated, nor was the question of what part of being Syriac Christian, precisely, she was saving. These questions, in turn, raised deeper and potentially more destabilizing questions: What does it mean to be a "people" in any sense of the word? Which versions of *peopleness* form the basis of recognizable claims to minority rights, political autonomy, self-determination, or territorial sovereignty?

What does it take to be recognized as "a people" in secular regimes of recognition—national and supranational—and how does recognition, or a lack thereof, come to bear on a people's understanding of themselves as they discover themselves in new political contexts? And, perhaps most crucially for my research participants, how can one reproduce one's *peopleness* without recognition from a state? This book grapples with these questions and explores the answers that suggested themselves to me as I sang with Elena and her peers in parish churches and secular cultural choirs in this Dutch corner of the Syriac world, working with them to understand the logics of religious, ethnic, and racial belonging that systematically render their *peopleness* invisible, inaudible, and illegible on both the national and global stage.

The Syriac World

Syriac Orthodox Christians partake of a Christological and liturgical tradition historically viewed as heretical by the Western (i.e., the Greek and then later Latin) Church. This tradition is known as the West Syriac Rite, which dates from the earliest centuries of Christianity. The West Syriac Rite is distinctive not only for its continued use of classical Syriac in ecclesiastical and literary writings but also for its liturgical practices: the organization of worship services, festival calendar, prayers, hymns, and supplications comprising an aesthetic culture all its own. The term "Syriac" technically refers to the second century variety of Aramaic spoken in Edessa (now Urfa in Turkey), capital of the Roman client state of Osrhoene, but it was also commonly used to refer to several varieties of Aramaic spoken throughout the region, as is also the case now. The Edessan variant of Aramaic became, throughout late antiquity and into the medieval Islamic world, a transregional Christian literary language, ensuring its longevity where other variants died out. Present day congregational communities who trace their liturgical traditions to the ancient Syriac-speaking world include traditions of the West Syriac Rite—the Syriac Orthodox Church of Antioch, the Syriac Catholic Church, the Maronite Church, and various Malankara churches of India. Heirs of the East Syriac Rite, those Syriac-speaking Christians who parted ways with imperial Christianity even earlier at the Council of Ephesus in 431 CE, now include the Assyrian and Ancient Churches of the East, the Chaldean Catholic Church, and the Syro-Malabar Church in India.[5]

Regional Map with post-World War I Borders
Originally published in *The Syriac Orthodox Christians in the Late Ottoman Period and Beyond: Crisis then Revival* by Khalid S. Dinno (Piscataway, NJ: Gorgias Press, 2017).

The Syriac Orthodox Church formed gradually over the course of centuries into an independent hierarchy in the aftermath of the ecumenical councils of Nicaea (325 CE), Constantinople (381 CE), and Chalcedon (451 CE). At these councils, imperial and ecclesiastical authorities sought to determine what part of the essence and personhood of Jesus Christ was divine, what part human, and what the arrangement of these parts might mean for Mary's relationship with the Creator (Syriac *yoldath aloho*, Mother of God). Answers to these questions guided, in turn, Christian understandings of the relationship between visible humanity and invisible divinity more broadly, for centuries to come. These were political questions as much as they were theological ones, in that they determined the proper dispensation of ecclesiastical and political power throughout the Roman - Byzantine imperial era. Twenty-first-century social scientists interested in religion, ethnicity, and race have largely ignored the lasting influence of this founding moment in the marriage of Christianity to empire on later political structures, despite its influence on the ethnographic imagination itself. This enduring ethnographic imagination, as historian Todd Berzon (2016) argues, took shape throughout the third, fourth, and fifth centuries in the heresiological writings of imperial Christian writers identifying genealogy and territorially emplaced peoples with anti-imperial heresy (see also Buell 2005).

This was the period during which Syriac Orthodoxy emerged as an "ethnic" church in Patristic writings—the *Suryoye 'atiqe*, "the ancient Syrians" (Weltecke 2016), who were ethnically Syrian in the eyes of Greek and Roman Christians because of their non-Chalcedonian theological difference. They rejected the proceedings of the Council of Chalcedon and the language of its definition of Christ's dual incarnate nature, along with those congregations who would eventually identify as Coptic, Armenian, Ethiopian, and Eritrean Orthodox—although there is reason to believe that the original disagreement was largely grammatical, political, and linguistic-cultural rather than substantively Christological, as I explain in Chapter 2. One crucial outcome of these battles over the sociopolitical meaning of heresy was the expulsion of West Syriac congregations from Byzantine territory, many of whom took refuge in Persia and, later, in the Islamic caliphates, where centuries of dialogue with Jewish, Muslim, and East Syriac Christians left their marks on Syriac Orthodox thought and practice (e.g., Griffith 2008).

Since the nineteenth century, multiple waves of violence have spurred global Syriac Orthodox migration out of their ancestral villages and towns in Turkey, Syria, Iraq, Lebanon, and Iran, leading to new diasporic formations (Armbruster 2014; Atto 2011; Björklund 198; Cetrez 2011; Hager 2020; Jarjour 2018; Kiraz 2019; Mack 2017; Nordin 2023; Schmoller 2018; Schukkink 2003; Woźniak-Bobińska 2018, 2019). Since the 1970s, according to diocesan estimates reported to me orally, at least twenty-five thousand Syriac Orthodox Christians have settled in the Netherlands, especially in and around the cities of Enschede and Hengelo in the easternmost region called Twente. While they remain largely unknown to the rest of the country, the Syriac Orthodox are visible enough as an ethnocultural group in Enschede to merit dedicated liaison officers both in the municipal government and in the local police force. In the suburb of Wesselerbrink, they constitute the largest minority group in the district, which many young Suryoye of my acquaintance call the WesselerBronx, in playful reference to New York City and the US's history of racialization, immigration, and cultural production.

While disparate national histories of secularization throughout the Middle East have created regional differences among Syriac Orthodox self-understandings, diasporic Suryoye have nonetheless maintained a tight grip on collective memories of non-Chalcedonian history as the authorizing wellspring of ethnonational difference, whether defined as Assyrian, Aramaean, or just Syriac—a painful and polarizing "name-debate" I describe and analyze in coming chapters in terms of the mutual problem of political legibility and social reproduction. This persistent problem is rooted in an entangled process of identity formation I call "the ethics of recognition."[6] How they labor to make this non-Chalcedonian Christianity relevant to the programs meant to integrate them into the societies they now live in holds a mirror to the logics at work in Euro-American debates over immigration, racism, religious difference, and minority recognition and accommodation, and raises questions about secularization as both a political project and a cultural process.

When Elena performs her role in the liturgy, her tradition's complex, cosmopolitan history is embedded in the very sounds of the hymns and prayers she sings. Diasporic from the outset, Syriac Orthodox liturgical sound carries within it a history of recognitions and misrecognitions in diverse sociopolitical contexts. Elena and her peers understand their identity in the modern sense of the word as staked upon their relationship with this ancient tradition and its texts, rituals, aesthetic forms, literature, myths, and a distinctive genre of Syriac-language poetic-theology that is sung and chanted liturgically. The practice of sacred chant is in itself an embodied mode of doing theology and, as such, grounds Syriac Orthodox understandings of sociopolitical identity in liturgical history, even for the most secularist articulations of ethnonational identity among Assyrian and Aramaean political movements, the two dominant sociopolitical identifications linked to the West Syriac Rite.[7] Taken together, I conceptualize the connections among sociopolitical identity, liturgical history, and their ethnonationalist articulations as an ethnographic formation called the Syriac world, following historian Daniel King (2019). By world, I mean a globalized sociopolitical formation defined by a historical relationship with the liturgical traditions of both the West and East Syriac Rites, which connect a series of communal names—Assyrian, Aramaean, Chaldean, Syriac—to each other and to fourth-century Edessa, fifth-century Tur Abdin, thirteenth-century Baghdad, sixteenth-century south India, eighteenth-century Damascus, the nineteenth-century Hakkari Mountains, twentieth-century suburban New

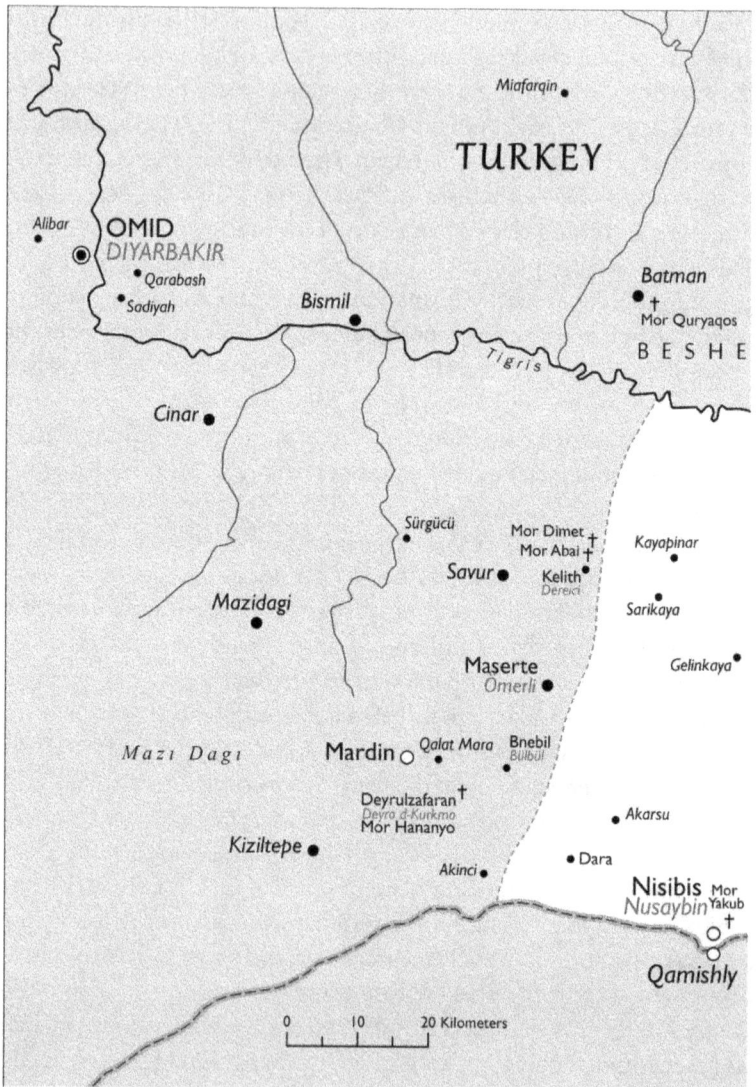

Left side: Tur Abdin and surrounding regions
Originally published in *The Syriac Orthodox Christians in the Late Ottoman Period and Beyond: Crisis then Revival* by Khalid S. Dinno (Piscataway, NJ: Gorgias Press, 2017).

Cities

Towns and villages

† Syrian Orthodox monasteries

Kurtalan

Siirt

RYEH

Raman Dağı

Seyhömer Dağı

Eruh

Baggöze

Yassı Dağı

Hesno d-Kifo
Hašankeyf

Karakas Dağı

Gürgen

Küreli Dağı

Sirnak

Gercüs Yardo
Yamanlar Dayro Daslibo Arbaye
Çatalcam Alayurt

Kafro Elayto Kfarburan
Dargeçit

Mor Mor Arıca Zaz Findik
Loozor Yakub Bote Izbırak
† † Bardakçi Derkube
Salah Bekusyone Karagöl
Habsus Barıstepe Achlah Hah Alagö
Mercimekli Narlı Anıtlı Bostanlı

Kizilsu

Midyat Urdnus Kfarze
Bağlarbaşı Altınas Beth Debe
Daskan Esfes
Yarbası

Inwardo Tulgali
Mor Abraham Gülegöze Mor Midun Dirsekli Azakh Gziro
Mozizah Gabriel Öğündük Beth Zabday Cizre Hassana
Anhel Dogançay Kfabre İdil Köşralı
Yemişli Güngören Dicle

Kartmin Bsorino
Kafro Yayvantepe Habertı Tepeköy
Elbegendi Harabale İstir Silopi
Uçköy Arbo Satıköy
Kaynak Taşköy Oyali
Mor Malke† Ehwo Beth Menan Duru
Sederi Güzelsu
Uçayl Badibe
Harabemishka Dibek Mor
Dağıcı Abraham (Kashkar)
Marbobo
Mor Augin† Günyurdu Birguriye
Balaban
Girmeli Gündükushükrü
Odabaşı

Izlo

Tigris

SYRIA

Faishkhaboor

IRAQ

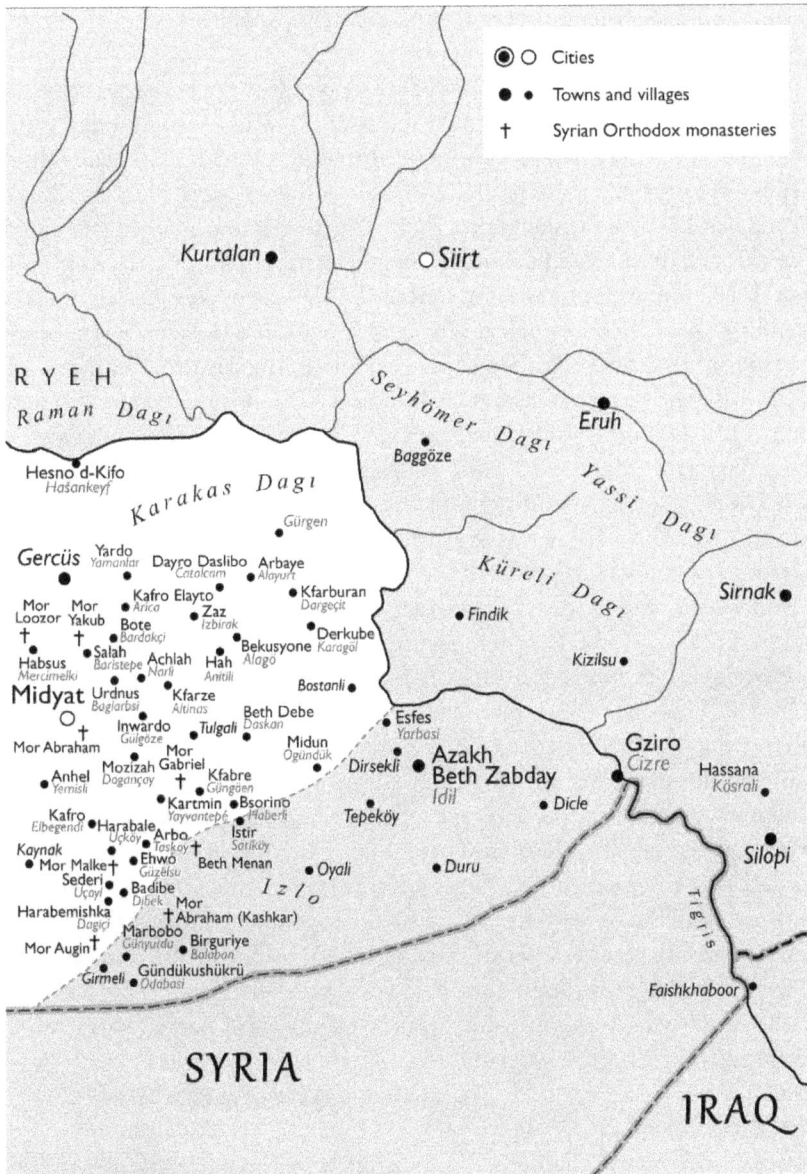

Right side: Tur Abdin and surrounding regions
Credits for each map: Gorgias Press, originally published in *The Syriac Orthodox Christians in the Late Ottoman Period and Beyond: Crisis then Revival* by Khalid S. Dinno (Piscataway, NJ: Gorgias Press, 2017).

Jersey and Los Angeles, twenty-first-century Sweden, and the Dutch-German border.

While a self-consciously defined anthropology of the Syriac world does not (as yet) exist, approaching my subject as a "world" accommodates the fact that the world in question could be understood in different terms depending on one's vantage point within it. Just as with the Islamic or Roman or Black Atlantic worlds, local experiences and interpretations of the global can vary widely while nonetheless together constituting that world. My argument focuses on Syriac Orthodox, or West Syriac, under-standings of their genealogical relationship with the broader Syriac litur-gical family, while recognizing that this relationship is often understood quite differently among East Syriac liturgical traditions (see Murre-van den Berg 2019). Historian Alda Benjamen (2022), for example, in her study of Iraqi Assyrians, characterizes this world in terms of ethnic relations consti-tuted among Assyrians throughout Mesopotamia over the course of cen-turies "through ecclesiastical organization, pilgrimage routes, and market networks, all of which predated the emergence of the new nation-states." These routes and networks facilitated inter-denominational marriage across the West and East Syriac divide despite putative Christological and ecclesiological differences separating the Syriac Orthodox Church and the Church of the East (Benjamen 2022, 22). What her view shares with my own is the observation that a historically enduring sociality furnishes the basis of an ethnic identity which is constitutively *Syriac* and *Christian*. There is a reason that the Suryoye never came to identify sociopolitically with, say, Armenians, despite sharing their Christology and being placed under the Armenian patriarchate's administrative jurisdiction by the Ot-toman regime for a lengthy period of time (Clements 2019). The reason for this, in my view, is a set of theologically significant historical attach-ments transmitted through both the West Syriac and East Syriac Rites.

Because there is so much history packed into this tradition's material forms, however, both textual and sonic, performing it raises as many exis-tential questions as it settles. My interlocutors have repeatedly said to me: "How can I explain to others who I am when I don't fully understand myself?" But rather than leading to fights over the purification and ho-mogenization of "tradition" under the influence of Protestantized notions of "true religion" (as many religious studies scholars assure us must inevi-tably happen to religious subjects in the modern world), these tensions and uncertainties lead my research participants in another direction. They are drawn, instead, to embrace the principle of unity-in-diversity conveyed by Syriac Incarnational theology, in which history itself *is* an expression of Jesus Christ's complex identity as both human and divine. This view of history-as-Incarnation resonates in secular political fights about how to translate that history into terms that powerful political audiences like the Dutch government and the United Nations—on whom they depend for political recognition—can understand. The problem is one of unstable categorical distinctions and conceptual mistranslations, which reverberate back into Syriac Orthodox self-understandings of communal identity, social reproduction, and the ground of belonging, a problem the following story demonstrates.

*   *   *

Later that year, in August's warm humidity, the Mor Ephrem Monastery buzzed with youthful energy. Several dozen young men and boys from Sweden, Germany, Belgium, and the Netherlands had recently arrived for their annual multi-week summer school training in Syriac language, liturgy, and theology.[8] Just before lunch, for some reason that had seemed urgent at the time, I'd gone looking for Father Yaqub, the monastery summer school's head teacher, resident polyglot, and unofficial public relations officer, in the upstairs dormitory chapel where monks and residents assemble for daily prayers. There, I stumbled upon a small crowd of students who had just been released from their morning lessons. Recognizing me from the bishop's earlier introduction, they murmured and pointed. A tall young man from Sweden called out to me in English: "Are you the American anthropologist? The bishop said you are here to do research with us."

"Yes, that's me!" I replied, smiling overbroadly to cover my self-consciousness at the unexpected attention.

Fixing me with a frown that made him look far older than he was, he shifted into interrogation mode: "Did you grow up religious?"

Brought up short by his probing, I paused and stuttered: "Y-es, I did."

"Good," he said with a curt nod. "If you are going to do research with us, you need to have been raised religious. You need to know how it feels; otherwise, you'll never understand."

Feeling oddly chastened, I tried to shuffle past the boys to get into the chapel, still looking for Father Yaqub, until another student, a boy of maybe ten or eleven, burst out:

"*Mevrouw! Wat is uw kultuur?*" [Ma'am, what is your culture?].

I turned to him, knowing my idiosyncratic accent when speaking Dutch can make me difficult to place, and cut straight to what I mistakenly believed was the chase: "*Mijn kultuur? Mijn vader is Nederlands en mijn moeder is Amerikaans.*" [My culture? My father is Dutch and my mother is American.]

"*Nee-ee!*" he huffed, voice frying with impatience at the willful obtuseness of adults, "*Wat is uw **kultuur**? Ortodox? Katholiek?*" [No-o! What is your **culture**? Orthodox? Catholic?]

"Ahhh . . . ," I hesitated, and then offered my usual cagey reply to inquiries about my relationship with Christianity. "*Ik ben Protestants opgegroeid.*" [I grew up Protestant.]

Satisfied with my credentials (or bored with the conversation), the students departed, leaving me alone in the chapel, with no Father Yaqub in sight.

*   *   *

What is this story in the chapel about? Is it about "religion," as the Swedish Suryoyo seems to suggest? Or is it about "culture," as the Dutch-speaking boy might insist? What is the difference? With the hindsight of many years, it has become clear to me that both young men were asking the same question, albeit in a different language, about *kinship*: the relations that made me who I am and shaped my ability to relate to them empathetically.

So, this is a story about kinship, a concept which overlaps with the idea of family but is not always the same thing. It is a story about how kinship gets made, about how we erect borders around who we imagine counts as our kin, and how we choose the words we use to explain and justify those borders. Kinship, often understood by anthropologists as the conceptual logics according to which humans imagine themselves to be related to each other, and family life, by which we usually mean the practical arrangements through which humans enact their sense of being related to each other, have both become key sites of political anxiety in a world dominated by the individualizing forces of secularism and late capitalism. Amidst the politics of religious and racial difference in Western Europe, a region often imagined to be the epicenter of something some people call "secular modernity," how new citizens of non-Western descent raise their children, treat their spouses, and care for the physical and psychological well-being of their relatives is subject to intense and often well-meaning scrutiny. For self-described progressive Western European states like the Netherlands, where this ethnography is set, doing family right is a litmus test of civilization itself. This is a test that immigrant families, especially those with origins in the Middle East and North Africa, are often accused of failing. How one understands what it means to be kin, what the responsibilities of kinship entail, and how one enacts one's sense of kin relatedness are inherently political questions. As such, they are central to the project of cultural assimilation in Western European states like the Netherlands. They are also, I argue, questions with deep roots in the history of theological controversy within Christianity and its unfolding relationship with states and empires.

Kinship, in this book, is an irreducible relation—that is, a relation that can only be broken with difficulty and trauma—produced through ethical, aesthetic, affective, and political practices anchored in sensory and material histories. These histories encompass ancient, medieval, and modern religious-political entanglements within and across Europe and the Middle East, entanglements that have made claiming, naming, and disavowing others as kin an exceptionally charged political act. This means that kinship is also linked to a problem of recognition, as the summer school students in the story above make clear: what we name the relations we think of as kinship (culture? religion? ethnicity? nationality? race?), as well as how others name them, is also part of the story of who we are. Such relations form the basis of our claims to peoplehood.

Kinship Is the History You Sing

In the following pages, I describe a corner of the Syriac world where young women and men who are committed to Syriac Orthodox Christianity address the past and the present by practicing kinship liturgically and liturgy as kinship. They do this, primarily but not exclusively, by participating in the *gudo*, a Syriac word often glossed in English as "choir." The gudo is made up of singers, cantors, and readers who feature prominently in the Holy *Qurbono*, or Sunday morning mass. The form and content of the Qurbono follows an *ordo*, or "divine order" (essentially a liturgical calendar), that shapes social life throughout this Dutch corner of the Syriac world. Community social events happen on feast and saint days, while the workweek is integrated into a schedule of fasting (a vegan-pescatarian diet on Wednesdays and Fridays), daily prayers at home and at church, and preparation for the Qurbono on Sunday mornings. The calendar follows an eight-week liturgical cycle marked by the microtonal modal system found in the *Beth Gazo*, the "Treasury of Song," a repertoire of hundreds of hymns compiled over centuries, possibly as far back as the third century, from the institutional memory of the church. Annual, weekly, and daily prayers and hymns are sung in different modes—meaning, one song may have multiple variations—depending on when in the cycle they appear. The tonal and melodic quality of each mode is meant to evoke a different feeling appropriate to the events commemorated in that week's Mass or that day's prayers, such as grief at the death of a martyr, joy at the birth of a saint, or longing supplication to the Mother Mary.

Although the Syriac Orthodox Church has a formal theory of sound elaborated by early theologians, few of my informants were aware of the official meanings attached to their singing practice, nor were they fully proficient in classical Syriac. It takes years to master each song with its multiple variations, so training begins as young as six years old and continues into adulthood. Hymns, chants, and prayers are taught orally, and the musical notation system devised for the Beth Gazo in Syria in the late twentieth century rarely, if ever, appeared in Syriac Orthodox churches in the Netherlands during my fieldwork.[9] In English, the variations are often referred to as "modes" and correlated with the Arabic and Turkish *maqām* systems. Yet, as ethnomusicologist Tala Jarjour has shown, there is considerable variation in scholarly and lay understandings of the mechanics of these modes, depending on the cultural context and musical assumptions of the theorist or practitioner in question. In Syriac, each melodic variation is called a *qolo* ("voice").[10] My interlocutors, in Dutch, referred to the *qole* (pl.) as *toonladders*, which is "scales" in English. Jarjour's own fieldwork among the ecclesiastical liturgical masters of the Mor Gabriel Monastery in Tur Abdin reveals that the conventional claim that there are eight musical modes corresponding to eight liturgical weeks is incorrect. In the Beth Gazo, each song's variation is distinctive enough that there are in fact 240 modes, not eight, which is why the repertoire can be challenging to master.

Those who sing, chant, and pray as part of the gudo generally learn by doing, beginning in early childhood. Participating in the gudo is a multisensory practice that habituates bodies from a young age into a coherent

A Syriac Orthodox women's choir in the Netherlands, chanting a liturgical hymn in presentational formation for a special feast day, overseen by the *yoldath aloho*, the Mother of God, with a television camera recording the liturgy for broadcast on an international neo-Aramaic-language satellite television station (photo by author).

sensory culture and ethnoreligious subjectivity that is recognizable in any Syriac Orthodox parish around the world, despite variations in local church aesthetics. Anthropologist Charles Hirschkind characterizes such a habituation process as ethical sedimentation, in which sensory practices like listening to a sermon or, in my study, singing in the Qurbono, train "the body's gestures and affects, its physiological textures and colorations, its rhythms and styles of expression" as well as the "ethical habits and the organization of sensory and motor skills necessary for inhabiting the world in a manner considered to be appropriate" (Hirschkind 2001, 637).[11] The organization of this process of sensory habituation can vary, however.

Some church choirs are more formal and use dedicated rehearsals, while others are less formal and participants come and go as they are able. On ordinary Sundays, singers and cantors stand in two circles, where they represent the voice of the congregation—some of whom might sing quietly along if and when they feel so inspired—in call and response with the priests and senior deacons throughout the liturgical service. On special feast days, the women's choirs—in some churches, they might be joined by a few men and boys—often differentiate themselves by standing in a presentational formation more reminiscent of Western choirs, sometimes in the front of the church, as in the photo below, or up above and out of sight on a balcony at the back of the nave, depending on the layout of the building and the preferences of their priests and teachers. Nonetheless, across the diversity of organizing strategies across the diaspora, the fundamental practice is the same: singing hymns and chanting prayers create relations, with others and with history. The function of these liturgical voices is self-consciously defined by the church as distinctively, if not uniquely, Syriac. The sound of these hymns and chants, when sung by members of the gudo, are sonic icons.

Sonic Iconicity

Icon veneration is ubiquitous in Orthodox Christianity. Yet one of many misrecognitions shaping Syriac Orthodoxy's relationship with imperial Christianity is the claim that Syriac Christian tradition, influenced by its Islamic context, is iconoclastic—that is, theologically opposed to imagistic representations of the divine. In his foreword to Christine Chaillot's study of non-Chalcedonian images and icon veneration, however, Syriac Studies scholar Sebastian Brock identifies this long-standing misperception for what it is. In Brock's assessment, non-Chalcedonian "iconoclasm" was only ever a matter of perceived contrast to the pronounced visuality of Byzantine Chalcedonian churches. In the iconoclastic controversies of the eighth and ninth centuries, he points out, icon veneration became a central piece of Chalcedonian Orthodox ecclesial identity as an expression of defiance during periods of imperial repression, when the Byzantine state sought to appropriate the social power of the visual on behalf of the emperor (see also Mondzain 2005). Non-Chalcedonians, on the other hand, were peripheral to these controversies, and so they were not provoked to the same degree of visual expression in their corporate worship practices.

This, however, did not mean that non-Chalcedonians were genuinely icon-oclastic, only that their iconographic practices remained understated and unregulated in comparison. After the ninth century, the non-Chalcedonian reputation for "iconoclasm" came to be associated with what Chalcedonians pejoratively called *monophysitism*, or "one nature" heresy.[12] This mistaken notion that Christological and iconographic differences are inherently linked in the ecclesiologies of Orthodox Christianity influenced inter-Orthodox relations until the late twentieth century.

Furthermore, the logic of the holy icon is not exclusively tied to visuality, as anthropologist Angie Heo's description of Orthodox iconicity makes evident: an icon declares "a holy person's death and safe passage into eternal life. Intrinsically temporal, the icon is therefore a technology that institutes a divide between earthly, worldly transience and heavenly, eternal permanence" (Heo 2018, 216). The icon creates a separation and a relation simultaneously; thus, the icon becomes iconic via the relation it establishes. This process is grounded in an understanding of Incarnational theology because "the icon captures the contemporaneous existence of the human with the divine enabled by Christ's incarnation—what is referred to as the *hypostasis*" (Heo 2018, 217). In the Coptic Orthodox case that Heo describes, the visual icon works like a window or door, enabling "ordinary people to reach the saints in the other world" (Heo 2018, 217). When a holy person dies, their translation to heaven leaves a trace or a pathway that could be visually conveyed in a painting or statue, through which living Christians might access the divine through prayer. The icon is neither medium nor mediator but rather an open space, a portal through which earthbound humans might gaze to open themselves to encounters with the divine, and its power in Orthodox thought is grounded in Incarnational theology.[13] The icon enables a relation, an intersensorial exchange that constitutes the human in the image of the divine, generating the relations that make us who we are. There is also nothing about this theological understanding of the icon that precludes it working through sound rather than (or in addition to) sight, especially when that sound gives voice, like so much of Syriac hymnography and chant does, to the Biblical women who were Jesus Christ's friends and family on earth and were thus integral to his Incarnate identity.

Yet iconicity also has a parallel set of meanings in secular linguistic theory. These secular linguistic meanings are generally assumed to be unrelated to the religious sense of the icon, whereas I see them as analogous and, at times, convergent. Throughout my analysis, secular and theological understandings of iconicity intersect in the premise that icons are sites of reproductive power where relations and identities are made. Sometimes, anthropologists write about iconicity as if it is a characteristically un-Western and, thus, a potentially decolonial mode of meaning-making. Iconic meaning-making, in such conversations, is often juxtaposed with *symbolic* meaning-making, that is, a semiotic process based on arbitrary linguistic signs, and is often characterized as uniquely modern and secular (e.g., Meyer 2009, 5, 43). As Angie Heo has argued, however, iconicity can saturate modernist sociopolitical imaginaries and exacerbate identitarian divisions, as it does among Egyptian Copts and Muslims (Heo 2018), where one may implicitly participate in iconicity's semiotic logic without explicitly espousing Orthodox Christian doctrine about icons. The sonic icon, I argue, is a distinctly West Syriac variation of Orthodox Christian iconicity, attested not in explicit theological writings of the Syriac Fathers but rather in the embodied practices and lived relationships of devout Syriac Orthodox Christians. Throughout each of the following chapters, I make the case that sonic iconicity is a way of *doing theology* in a variety of domains, inside and outside of church, that creatively and dynamically produces the relations that make the Suryoye *a people*, and in the process shape the Syriac world across space and time.

My interlocutors' voices-in-prayer are sonic icons through which they incorporate and reconfigure the terms of power of a given regime of recognition in service of liturgical kinship. Drawing on the theories of philosopher Charles Sanders Peirce—who himself publicly admitted to being influenced by Trinitarian theology[14]—I argue that iconicity is a semiotic process that produces meaning by virtue of a sign's embeddedness in reproductive relations. Devout young Suryoyo men and Suryayto women use their liturgical voices to produce and reproduce the Syriac world, integrating into their sound the powers of the past and the powers of the present from which they seek recognition, in order to secure the tradition's survival from one generation to the next. Communicative acts, I will argue, are acts of reproduction.

My key claim in this book, then, is that the liturgical voices of the young men and boys in the upstairs chapel are icons-in-training and constitute the more visible half of community renewal and liturgical revival: the liturgical voices of women like Elena, who were not visible in that particular scene, are also icons, and are central to the story, as is the very matter of their relative invisibility and, at times, inaudibility. Gender is key here because, as anthropologist Lucinda Ramberg argues, gender "is necessarily tied to strategies of and for relatedness. [. . .] a tool for producing certain kinds of humans endowed with particular obligations to and claims on others, social functions, and forms of value" (Ramberg 2014, 211). As sonic icons, these young women and men enact a gendered ethics of recognition not only to render their world perceptible to others but to reproduce and refashion that world—as well as to reproduce and refashion for themselves what it means to be Syriac Orthodox *in* the world.

In developing my argument, I work from two interwoven premises. The first is an ethnographic observation uncovered in fieldwork: in Syriac Orthodox tradition and practice, an icon is an intersensorial object that works as a site of reproductive power—that is, it enables acts of social reproduction to take place—and as such, it is inherently porous, fluid, and malleable. Unlike Eastern Orthodox traditions, the Syriac Orthodox Church does not officially regulate the icon's meaning or use. This means that while, in many ways, Syriac iconicity overlaps with Eastern Orthodox understandings and practices, it can also exceed and elude them. My second premise is enabled by the first and intervenes in theoretical accounts of political recognition, ethnicization, racialization, and secularization, each of which has a direct bearing on Dutch-Syriac experience in the twenty-first century. Rather than viewing them as inevitable forces of history, I analyze these processes, chapter by chapter, as modes of reproductive labor that intersect throughout the Syriac world. Syriac iconicity's very slipperiness as an embodied and unregulated theological discourse makes it useful for uncovering the struggle for reproductive power inherent in global processes of ethnicization, racialization, and secularization.

A Theopolitical Anthropology of Morality

This book offers a diasporic vantage point on the practices of producing and reproducing relations—with others and with history—that constitute the Suryoye as a people and Syriac Christianity as a world. But because *every* human is heir to multiple and, at times, contradictory histories, so too are the practices that materialize our relationships with these histories. The dissonance of living with a past too cosmopolitan to narrate in secular-modernist terms of primordial identity and territorial continuity accounts for kinship's political charge in modernist regimes of recognition. In such regimes, "history" is presumed to have something to do with "identity" and thus with the racially and ethnically defined possessive individualism and territoriality of the Western political imagination.[15] This book is thus an inquiry into the political charge of kinship in twenty-first-century religious and racial politics from the oft-ignored perspective of Syriac Orthodox Christians, whose experiences as new citizens in northwestern Europe are rendered invisible and inaudible by a reductive binary equating Europe with Christianity and Islam with the Middle East.

As a work of ethnographically driven social theory, this text engages Suryoye categories and concerns, as I encountered them while conducting in-person fieldwork in parishes and cultural organizations in the Netherlands and digital ethnography in the global Assyrian/Syriac public sphere between 2007 and 2020. These categories and concerns are products of particular times and places, and I make no claims about their generalizability to all Syriac Christians everywhere and for all time. Worlds, in my experience, tend to defy totalizing narratives (most of the time). Instead, my claims reflect my evolving relationships with a group of first-, second-, and third-generation Suryayto women and Suryoyo men and their families, whose experiences illuminate certain dimensions of European religious, racial, and ethnic politics in the twenty-first century. I bring these relationships into conversation with the social scientific study of religion and secularism, modern European studies, Christian theology, feminist theory, sound studies, and the history and historiography of the late antique, medieval, and modern Middle East. I draw these disparate-seeming strands together to pursue a theopolitical anthropology of morality capable of discerning the worldliness of the Syriac world in its localized forms.

The founding premise of a political anthropology of morality is the notion that moral sentiments are the bedrock of our common life. Our inclination to act in a political mode is both spurred and shaped not simply by what we think is right and good or wrong and bad but by what we *feel* is right and wrong or good and bad. Our moral sentiments often play out in politics before we ever find the conceptual language to put our feelings into words. A *theo*political anthropology of morality, on the other hand, excavates those sections of our moral bedrock that were formed by the histories of religious thought, practice, and conflict that preceded us. This book argues that kinship, in addition to whatever else it may be in a given historical setting, is a moral sentiment about our mutual relatedness that emerges from our sensory encounters with others and is given shape through long histories of theological reasoning about human nature.

The political charge of kinship animating European debates over migration, religious difference, and racism is structured not only by postcolonial political economies but also by moral sentiments about who we believe shares in our embodied relationship with a given history. For many, history makes an ethical demand. As scholars have often observed, the demands of the past trouble state- and nation-making projects in the present more often than they do not (e.g., Ballinger 2003; Bet-Schlimon 2019; Herzfeld 1982, 1991; Hirschkind 2021; Richardson 2006; Tambar 2014). Anthropologist Ashley Lebner (2019), building on the work of Talal Asad (2003), has argued that a particular kind of concern for history, as well as a related aspiration for public visibility in response to that concern, is a hallmark of the intensification of secularity. By the "intensification of secularity," she means not the rise of unbelief but the cultural condition of living with secularization, a set of practices that expand a conceptual-practical domain distinguished from religion, which may or may not include state-driven political secularism. My observation is that communal interest in history as a political problem is not *only* modern and secular. That well-spring of moral sentiment about the past is sometimes rooted in political problems *of* the past that continue to resonate in the present in surprising ways. This is an ongoing dialogical process I term "the ethics of recognition."

The Ethics of Recognition:
Or, the Intersensoriality of Social Reproduction

Tensions over migration, religious difference, and racism are often cast in terms of the affordances and limits of "recognition" as a political tool for administering relations between majoritarian and minoritarian populations (e.g., Markell 2003; McNay 2008; Taylor 1992, 1994). My understanding of recognition diverges from those influential theories rooted in the thought of the nineteenth-century philosopher Georg W. F. Hegel. In a Hegelian sense, recognition is a political struggle between sovereign subject and abject other. This approach tends to treat recognition as a binary political accomplishment in which one has either secured recognition (correctly) or not. I understand recognition, instead, to be an ethically complex and ultimately unfinishable process of communal self-fashioning. This self-fashioning process not only responds to being seen and heard by others but also folds others' perceptions into an always-emerging sense of self. This approach is informed by the semiotic theories of Charles Sanders Peirce, as well as by the linguistic philosopher Mikhail Bakhtin and the moral philosopher Emmanuel Levinas.

If identity is the aesthetic form of an ethical self, as social anthropologist Edmund Leach wrote in 1968, then community is the tangle of ethical relations—whether of care, obligation, authority, responsibility, or love— that bind some people together whether they like it or not. These relations are fashioned through the powerful call and response of recognition and sustained by the ever-emergent sensory work of everyday life. Anthropologists like Melissa L. Caldwell (2004, 2017), Ashley Lebner (2016, 2021), Mayanthi L. Fernando (2014), and others have shown that an ethnographic focus on the seemingly private domain of relations, especially intimate relationships like friendship and marriage, can yield unsettling perspectives on state power, its institutional logics, its tensions, and its limits. These relations are a key site for understanding recognition as both a political struggle and an ethical formation.

For my research participants, the West Syriac Rite is that which has endured in its capacity to cultivate a set of irreducible relations over centuries. The Rite's aesthetic features—in the Greek sense of *aisthesis*, or "our total sensory experience of the world and our sensitive knowledge of it" (Meyer 2009, 6; Meyer and Verrips 2008, 21; see also Morgan 2008)— lend it this power. Many scholars have argued that a "religious community" might then be better termed an "aesthetic formation," because, as anthropologist Birgit Meyer writes, "a community is not a preexisting entity that expresses itself via a fixed set of symbols, but a formation that comes into being through the circulation and use of shared cultural forms and that is never complete" (2009, 4; Luehrmann et al. 2018). In this approach to the social scientific study of religion, modern religious communities are *modern* because of a series of radical disjunctures structuring their understanding of the world: self is not the same as other; individual is not the same as society; form is not the same as meaning. These binary oppositions are understood as rooted in the separating effects of a referential view of language, exemplified by the thought of the nineteenth-century linguistic theorist Ferdinand de Saussure. Saussure's structural view of language assumed an arbitrary relationship between signs (e.g., words and other units of meaning) and the phenomena they signify. So, in a modern, referential model of language, the sounds comprising the English word "table" have no inherent formal relationship to any actual table in existence. This referential model of language is understood as an elemental dimension of all our lives and conditions our experience of "community." The gap between form and meaning derives, according to Birgit Meyer, from the ontic rupture separating divine truth from worldly power (2009, 5, 43). In light of this rupture, the question of how community becomes real in our experience—"felt in the bones," as she puts it—is a question of the sensory and affective labor that bridges that divide, materializing what is imagined and overcoming its arbitrariness. Speaking directly to Benedict Anderson's influential argument that political communities such as nations are imagined, Meyer asks how our imaginations become tangibly "embodied in subjects" (2009, 5). This demands attention to the role played by things, media, and the body in actual processes of community making.

Replacing the notion of an imagined community with that of an "aesthetic formation" allows for an approach to national, ethnic, and religious community that keeps the ongoing material and embodied processes of "binding," in Emile Durkheim's classic sociological sense of social solidarity (2008 [1893]), at the center of analysis. The emphasis on "formation" brings the interwoven, performative, processual, and ultimately unfinishable dimensions of crafting subjects and making communities to light (Meyer 2009, 7). Through circulating multisensory liturgical practices like chanted prayers and hymns, Syriac Christian community remakes itself over time. They labor to represent this formation as *a community* even as they run up against the modernist terms by which the concept of "community" is generally understood in national and supranational regimes of minority recognition. In these regimes, the exteriorized language of community is staked upon an interiorized and essentialized language of identity. Here, there is a subtle yet crucial tension between scholarly-constructivist and normative-liberal understandings of what it means to be a person, what it means to be a person in community, and what it means, by extension, to be a people. In dominant political regimes, a person is socially and politically recognized as a member of this or that community because of *who one already is*. As I demonstrate in the coming chapters, however, normative political projects of recognition depend on obscuring the "formative" part of the aesthetic formation in service of an essentializing view of identity. This places Syriac Christians—and most other marginalized and minoritized populations the world over—in a political and existential predicament.

This predicament, as I see it, lies within the black box of Durkheimian social solidarity. What exactly is this "binding," and how does it work? And how much does the binding process actually depend on the ostensibly modern "referential" view of language to function? These are interconnected questions. In my understanding, the "binding" of social solidarity is based on the foundational ethical relation that sculpts human subjectivity. This foundational relation sustains itself because it is, in what perhaps seems to be a paradox but, on closer scrutiny, is not, both produced through language and embodied prior to language because communication is a reproductive act. Language is learned through the intimate synesthesia of early infancy, through the touch, smell, sight, and sound of the caregivers on whom an infant is utterly dependent. From the earliest moment, language is a function of the face-to-face intersensoriality that reproduces life. Language is relational before it is referential. It is here, where language and body are yoked together, that the inextricability of the aesthetic from the ethical and the ethical from the aesthetic are revealed. As with language, so with chant. "Growing up in the church, listening to these hymns, learning these melodies," as one of my research participants told me, "a Syriac Orthodox Christian cannot help but be a musician." Nor, I would add, could they help but be Suryoyo, whether they articulate that relational identity in religious or ethnic terms.

My view of language as intersensorial, relational, and reproductive is grounded in Peirce's semiotics because his approach to communicative meaning-making engages an expansive sensorium through three categories of the sign: the index, the icon, and the symbol. For Peirce, none of these signs' meanings are contingent on the arbitrariness of language. Instead, they acquire meaning through a triadic relational process, characterized by qualities he calls *Firstness*, *Secondness*, and *Thirdness*. Meaning is created through the relational encounter between *Firstness*, the quality of possibility that exists *before* a sign comes into material being, and *Secondness*, the quality of actuality that exists *after* the sign comes into material being. The quality of *Thirdness*, which he calls the Interpretant, brings *Firstness* into relationship with *Secondness*. *Thirdness* is the connecting bond between sign-producers and sign-recipients when acts of communication occur. Communication requires an effort at meaning-making from both producer and recipient in order to work. A sign is thus anything that calls to mind something else and creates an effect in the observer; it is inherently relational. In Peircean semiotics, then, no sign can be *purely* referential or arbitrary; even the most abstract symbol depends on an interlocking process encompassing multiple communicators' experiences, perceptions, and contexts. What distinguishes one kind of a sign from another is the nature of the interior relation that produces its meaning.

So, an iconic sign is defined through a relation of formal resemblance: the icon looks or sounds like that which it calls to mind. Imagine the outline of a bicycle on a sign next to a bike path, telling cyclists where to ride. Or the emotionally expressive sound in a woman's voice as she chants a hymn dramatically reenacting a dialogue from the Bible in which Mary expresses joy over her pregnancy. The sentiment of the chant resembles the sentiment of the text. An indexical sign, on the other hand, is defined by a relation of co-occurrence: smoke does not resemble fire, but we consider it a sign of fire because we so often experience them together. Similarly, the singer voicing Mary's joy pitches her voice low, as I learned during a Syriac lesson in which my teacher taught me the hymn but then scolded me when I rehearsed it in too a high register. Singing high, he said, sounds sad, whereas the song is meant to convey joy. In his experience, growing up attuned to hybrid Syriac, Turkish, and Arabic musical aesthetics in diaspora, high pitches occur with sad songs, and so they mean "sadness," whereas in my experience growing up with Western musical aesthetics, they do not. The differences in our sensory histories had taught my teacher and me two different indexical meanings to the sound of a high note.

A symbolic sign, meanwhile, is defined through linguistic definition and social convention. The English word "cat," for example, refers to a general concept of *catness*. Until, that is, we say "that cat," at which point the word begins working indexically because we are essentially pointing at a particular cat in the material world with our words. Similarly, in practicing hymns for the Qurbono, my fellow singers debated the proper pronunciation and grammatical correctness of the Syriac language. Coming to agreement about how to sing was a matter of social convention, but these conventions were sometimes contested. Full proficiency in the classical language was rare, and liturgical teachers' level of expertise varied, influenced by where in the Middle East they were trained. My own teacher, Peter, was often infuriated by fellow singers who reacted negatively to his (in his view) "proper" knowledge of the classical language derived from diligent study of grammar books. A zealous lover of *Suryoyo kthobonoyo*, the book language, he had mastered classical Syriac under the tutelage of the monks at Mor Ephrem Monastery and through voracious reading of reprinted medieval texts. Often singing at the monastery with the many visitors who came and went, he regularly ruffled feathers by pronouncing words in an archaic fashion that his fellow cantors didn't recognize, disrupting local social convention.

Here, as in every attempt to signify, the symbolic sign of linguistic definition and social convention relies on the other two kinds of sign in its meaning-making process. Social convention dictated that liturgical meanings were produced through parish-specific habits of pronunciation—a complex ethnographic situation I examine in detail in Chapter 3. But Peter's pronunciations disrupted their symbolic value by insisting upon an iconic mimesis of an archaic sound that itself indexed an alternate set of historical memories than those valued by his fellow singers. While other singers reproduced the recent intimate histories of their parish sounds, Peter reproduced a history inscribed in ancient texts. Each history of meaning was embedded in the sounds of their collective chant. Because of the relationality within the sign—the *Thirdness* of the space between the signifier and the signified, producer and recipient, possibility and actuality—every moment of meaning-making builds upon past efforts at communication.

This is where Peirce's secular(ish) theorization of the sign converges with the Orthodox doctrine of the holy icon: the iconic sign's relation of resemblance mirrors the relational logic of the holy icon because "resemblance" so often indexes, in human experience, a sexually reproductive relation. Analogously, the holy icon indexes the *hypostasis*, the mutuality of divine and human being within the Incarnation through which humans are made actual in the light of divine potentiality. Ultimately, *every* act of communication is also an act of social reproduction. In the reproductive, relational, communicative act—in the space of *Thirdness*—meaning is co-produced in the relations among communicators. But these acts are porous and unstable. Attempts at meaning-making are not always received or recognized. Miscommunications happen. Meanings change. Reproduction encompasses adaptation and variation, and the consequences for relations are ethical.

Thus, if semiosis is a critical element in the aesthetic formation of national, ethnic, and religious communities, recognition is a critical element of that semiosis. As the mechanism for fashioning an ethical bond, recognition is the process through which attachments are formed and relations are sustained. Conversely, lack of recognition has the power to dissolve attachments, change meanings, and destroy relations. Ethics is the ground of the social, in my view, because it is that intersensoriality of reproduction that makes every other configuration of social and political life possible. Ethics is a *living for the Other* in a manner that need not be entirely ordinary nor exceptionally problematized to be ethical, as other anthropologists of ethics and morality have argued (e.g., Das 2012; Faubion 2011; Robbins 2007; Zigon 2009). This vision of ethics is most akin to the "face-to-face" encounter that Levinas (1985) describes as foundational to human Being, and from which sociality and moral systems develop. To add a Bakhtinian layer to this understanding of ethics, we might describe the foundational moment of intersensoriality as a "voice-to-voice" encounter: the enveloping, tactile vibration of mouth-to-ear or skin-to-skin—what Nicholas Harkness calls "the phonosonic nexus" (2014), although its tactility makes language learning accessible to deaf children as well—without which humans fail to fully form as recognizably socialized subjects.[16] When my research participants sing and chant and pray in church from earliest childhood, they are doing the ethical work of reproduction that makes their later social relations, political alliances, and moral debates possible. That dialogical encounter between teachers and learners of the liturgical tradition generates the relations that generate identities, face-to-face and voice-to-voice. Recognition is reproduction; reproduction is recognition.

Many anthropologists interested in ethics and morality resist what they understand to be a Durkheimian tendency in anthropology to absorb the ethical into a diffuse and deterministic vision of sociality, turning instead toward other traditions of thought like virtue ethics, phenomenology, or Ludwig Wittgenstein's philosophy of language (e.g., Al-Mohammed 2010, 2015; Lambek, Das, Fassin, and Keane 2015). My view of ethics as intersensorial and reproductive, on the other hand, is influenced by those anthropologists of sound who grapple with how music (or, indeed, any sonic production) *means* (Brenneis and Feld 2004; Blao 2002; Bull and Back 2006; Erlmann 2004; Feld and Keil 2005; Qureshi 2000; Samuels, Meintjes, Ochoa, and Porcello 2010; Turino 2008).[17] With these thinkers, I find a bridge to the phenomenological approach against which a semiotic approach to ethics is often contrasted (e.g., Mattingly and Throop 2018). As I see it, when humans learn language, they also learn the grammar of the relations *through which* they become communicating subjects, and in which they remain socially embedded. As an infant learns language synesthetically, they learn the grammar of the relations that shape them. This is where diacritics of identity like gender initially take shape (e.g., Butler

2006). As a child comes to recognize these relations and this language as their own, they become the person they are, replete with a sense of the rights, obligations, roles, values, aspirations, and criteria for judgment that define them. This gradual process of self-recognition is a mechanism of ethical self-fashioning, individually and communally, sedimented into the human sensorium over time, and it is far from static or predetermined. As an effect of reproduction, it is porous and open to change.

A semiotic process that exceeds language opens up not only our study of morality and ethics but also complicates the "aesthetic formation" and the assumption that modern religious communities operate within a referential model of language. This assumption is itself predicated, according to influential social scientific accounts originating in the thought of Max Weber (1974 [1946]; 1978 [1922]) and Emile Durkheim (2001 [1912]), on a presumed state of secular rupture saturating our globalized modernity. That is, it is the Divine's separation from the world that conditions the arbitrariness of the sign, a "disenchantment" that makes modern language, modern selves, and modern religiosity possible (e.g., Gauchet 1985; Taylor 1989, 2007). This is in itself a theological supposition concerning the nature of the divine and its relation to the human world, couched in secular linguistic and sociological theory.

Yet this presupposition of secular rupture is far from all-encompassing in modernity. A host of twenty-first-century religious communities configure relations with the divine otherwise, and so there is no inevitable logical inference to be made about the linguistic or theological models underpinning *any* given aesthetic formation (see also Eisenlohr 2006, 2009, 2011, 2018; Moll 2018; Sahlins 2022). The point here is not to reject the analytical language of the aesthetic formation but to modify its intellectual architecture slightly. While Syriac Christianity forms and reforms through aesthetic practices that generate that tangle of ethical relations called community over time, the underlying theological presupposition of this process is not one of secular rupture reflected in the arbitrariness of the linguistic sign. Rather, the Syriac world reproduces iconically, in the theological *and* Peircean senses of the word, through the circulation of communicative signs defined by relations of formal resemblance. These signs are, in turn, interwoven with a history of indexical and symbolic meaning-making. Although these reproductive acts of communication are open-ended enough to accommodate change over time, they are staked upon an underlying theological presupposition of history-as-Incarnation, or the divine's immanent, generative presence in the world. These iconic signs index kinship with each other and with the divine. This is as modern a way to be a person, or a people, as any other.[18]

Theological Politics

Theorizing the relationship among language, personhood, and community is one conceptual issue for thinking through the ethics of recognition for minoritized groups like the Suryoye. Grappling with what we mean by "religion" is another. Defining religion as a social phenomenon, analytical category, or ethnographic object is a well-documented epistemological problem in the social sciences (e.g., Asad 2002, 2012; Bialecki 2017; de Vries 2008). When talking to Christians and ex-Christians, it is an emic category that requires definition relevant to its local usage. For my purposes, "theological politics" serves as a more expansive way to conceptualize my object of inquiry, as it enables me to trace submerged connections that often (although not always) escape my interlocutors' notice, and its study requires a distinctive set of analytical tools. "Theological politics" is the terrain in which Christian understandings of the universe produce ethical, affective, and material attachments that then travel beyond the moment of their founding to shape worlds. These attachments carry some residue of theological reasoning within them, even when the specifics of Christian practice and belief have been forgotten. For me to call this residue "religious," the people I work with would need to think of it as religious themselves. Sometimes they do, sometimes they do not, even when in both situations their reasoning echoes ancient and medieval Christian thought about divinity's relationship with humanity. My approach to theological politics shares an affinity with the theopolitical anthropology articulated by Carlotta McAllister and Valentina Napolitano, which

> asks not only how theological categories permeate everyday life [. . .] but also how these categories participate in long histories of the body, affects, and material religion, and how these histories are lived in the constitution of peoples and commons. An ethnographic angle on these questions engages theology not as a set of propositions but as a matrix of affective and situated histories, imbued with life forms and materialities. . . . (2021, 7)

This understanding of theopolitics stands in contrast to Carl Schmitt's well-known conception of political theology, in which sovereignty is conceived primarily as the power of a state to constitute and suspend norms. Political theology, following Schmitt's claim that "all significant concepts of the modern theory of the state are secularized theological concepts," (2005 [1922], 36) privileges the state as the sole site of sovereign power by equating it with a secularized concept of the Divine. This unilinear narrative of secularization-as-rupture universalizes from a particular moment in early modern European history, as McAllister and Napolitano have observed (2021, 3). A theopolitical perspective, on the other hand, entails a richer engagement with the myriad, dynamic ways that Christian theology operates as an ethnographic object in its own right (see also Carroll 2017).

My focus on theological politics, meanwhile, attends to the intersection between implicit theological discourses—by which I mean ontological positions with theological implications—at work in self-described secular regimes, as well as explicit theological commitments that animate competing sites of power beyond the state (see also Boylston 2018) or that succeed in keeping the state at an ambivalent remove (see also Oliphant 2021). This approach to theological politics is especially important for understanding the place of kinship in transnational non-Chalcedonian Christianities and their engagement with globalized imperial formations. Candace Lukasik (2021), for example, explores differences in Christian theologies of kinship to draw attention to how twentieth-century Syriac, Coptic, Armenian, Ethiopian, and Eritrean Orthodox Christian leaders deployed their common non-Chalcedonian Christology to construct a postcolonial, "Oriental" Orthodox solidarity against the geopolitical maneuverings of Western evangelical and Eastern Orthodox Christians in Africa and the Middle East.[19] Looking even further into the past, I see theological politics at work in communal efforts to think through the ethical, social, and political implications of Incarnational theology in the late antique and early medieval formation of the Syriac world. Incarnational theology, a wide-ranging and contested discourse, grapples with what Christians understand as the relationship between divinity and humanity in Christ and, thus, by implication, the significance of Christ's human life on earth. My interlocutors implicitly and explicitly draw upon this discourse as they respond to the pressures of living as a racialized minority in northwestern Europe, even as those traces of the past bring them additional predicaments in the twenty-first century.

Thinking about theology's relationship to politics raises a set of thorny issues that must be carefully thought through when talking about Middle Eastern Christianity in Europe. Reductive binaries concerning Islam, Christianity, secularism, Europe, and the Middle East regularly stymie productive debate in academic as well as in popular and political discussion. The critical anthropology of secularism has offered one path forward with an especially rich body of work examining the mechanics of minoritization and the politics of religious diversity in Europe and the Middle East. Scholars working in this tradition have argued that the secular is an embodied mode of living in the world, entailing certain concepts, practices, and sensibilities concerning *how to be a person* (Asad 2003, 17, 67–99, 100–124, 127–158; Bakker Kellogg 2015, 2019; Göle 2010; Jakobsen and Pellegrini 2008; Mahmood 2005; Milbank 2012; Scott 2007; Valenta 2006). They have shown how the political practice of secularism depends on securing the secularity of subjects through the maintenance of boundaries between categories, especially between that of "religion" and those deemed "not religion" (Bowen 2007; Fernando 2012). Secular categories are themselves unfixed (Engelke 2012), as their power to shape a subject's sense of her own identity is an effect of inherent structural tensions, indeterminacies, and inconsistencies (Agrama 2010, 2012; Eisenlohr 2006a; Farman 2013, 753; Hirschkind 2011; Starrett 2010, 628). These studies have demonstrated how the discursive power of secularism, as a legal framework and political practice, both produces and depends upon secularity as cultural common sense. This cultural common sense, evident in recognition regimes like the United Nations Commission on Minority and Indigenous Affairs discussed in Chapter 5, can shift a population's perception of itself *as a minority* by redefining categories like "religion" and "politics" and staking particular kinds of rights and responsibilities upon them.

This tradition of criticizing secularism/secularity has limits, however. As historian Ussama Makdisi writes, "The criticism of Western secularity does not explain the nature of the sectarian problem in the Middle East" (Makdisi 2019, 15). For diasporic Syriac Orthodox Christian families maintaining strong ties to specific locales in Turkey, Syria, Lebanon, and elsewhere, this point is especially relevant. Makdisi observes that in critiquing "the secular," some scholars have essentialized the modern state's secular-resistant Others to a degree that religious identity appears monolithic and deterministic. My aim is to avoid such a binary view and think carefully about how traditions with ancient roots are continually reworked, resignified, and repoliticized in different contexts. This new context may be regime change within a territory or migration to a new country and translation into a new language. Across these spatiotemporal disjunctures, a liturgical tradition (and the sacred language in which it is reproduced) may serve as the material, transhistorical thread that defines and authorizes irreducible social relations. Nationally specific secular common sense weaves itself into local articulations of transnational and transhistorical liturgical kin relations like Syriac Orthodoxy. The liturgical ground of these relations may signify as ethnic in one context, as when the young men in the Dutch monastery's summer school are taught that learning Syriac makes them ethnically Aramaean. In another sociopolitical context, the liturgical ground might recede from public visibility to enable, say, the political commitments of a mid-twentieth century Arabic-speaking Marxist Assyrian in Iraq whose roots belong to the East Syriac Rite (e.g., Benjamen 2022). As Makdisi points out, "Religious identity does not automatically or necessarily dictate political belief. Ideological diversity is often far more important than ethnic or religious or sectarian diversity: one cannot merely equate being Sunni or Shi'i, Druze or Alawi, Maronite Christian or Jewish with having one predetermined communal outlook" (2019, 14). For transnational Syriac Orthodox maintaining strong ties to their home countries, regional variations in how their families and villages experienced the transition from the late Ottoman Empire to the post–Ottoman European Mandate system and then to Arab and Turkish secular nationalism have left lasting marks and complicated the relationship between their religious and political orientations.

In Makdisi's analysis, secular nationalism in the Arab world offered, in the late-nineteenth and early twenty-first century, the possibility of what he calls "an ecumenical frame" in which multireligious citizens may coexist *as openly religious* because they are united by Arabic language and culture. For Arabic-speaking Syriac Christians (not many of whom appear in my ethnography), this represents one possible configuration of the relationship between the religious and the ethnic in signifying liturgical kinship in the global politics of minority recognition. For neo-Aramaic-speakers, however, the ecumenical frame could not work in the way Makdisi describes without erasing the linguistic, cultural, and regional specificities of Syriac Christian historical experience, especially in their Assyrian forms. These specificities will return in upcoming chapters as I explore their theological and sociopolitical significance.

But this discussion raises yet another question: Who or what does secular power serve? Many scholars have more or less explicitly argued that secularism, wherever it may be found, serves a globalized Euro- and Christocentric world order that interpolates a nineteenth-century Protestant definition of "religion" into postcolonial legal frameworks where it does not belong and where it does much violence. Broadly speaking, I agree, but it is not the whole story. Mahmood suggested as much in her work on Egypt's Copts when she demonstrated how Egyptian secularism, while ostensibly aimed at protecting the religious freedoms of minorities, in fact, exacerbates their vulnerability by privileging the norms of the historical majority, which in Egypt's case is Sunni (2012, 2015). In that situation, the specifics of Sunni thought, practice, and history matter to the shape of Egyptian secularism and its norms.

Furthermore, the very notion of what constitutes a majority versus a minority is less easy to determine when a religious community's numbers are not reflected by the proportion (or the quality, or the strength) of the political, economic, or cultural power they may possess. Such is the case, arguably, in twentieth-century Lebanon, where Maronite Christian political and economic dominance belied their numbers. Such is certainly the case in the Netherlands, where Calvinists were politically dominant at the founding of the modern state, even though Roman Catholics were far more numerous. Twenty-first-century Dutch secularism/secularity consequently echoes a long history of Calvinist-Catholic negotiation in complex, even unpredictable ways (e.g., Verkaaik 2010). Ussama Makdisi's point that religious identity should not be constructed as a primordial attachment that predetermines a person's ideological position is well-taken. That said, the intersensorial ethics involved in practicing a liturgical tradition from childhood is a starting point. Liturgical kinship orients a person's ideological trajectory in one direction or another in a given sociopolitical context. It shapes a person's baseline sense of who they are and to whom they are related, even if their individual existential journey takes them far away from where they started. It influences their sense of where they come from, ethically and affectively, and how much of a sense of loss they experience the further away they travel from those origins. For many people, this early childhood enculturation into liturgical kinship is not easily unraveled. When it does unravel, it is as worth understanding as when it remains tightly knotted. And neither knotting nor unraveling should be assumed to be the default condition of modernity, Middle Eastern, European, or otherwise. And so, in Syriac Christianity, at

least, learning to chant, sing, and pray from a young age means an embodied immersion in Incarnational theology. This theology allows for multiple
possible configurations of the relationship between political and religious
life, which in turn may produce differently patterned networks of affiliation.
Nonetheless, across these variable patterns, a Syriac Christian interpretation
of Incarnational theology makes the bedrock claim that those who practice
and believe are kin.

Relational Ethics in Social Research

Thus the nonwritten law does not only refer simply to the oral tradition whose model is Christic teaching: it is that *paradosis sioposa,* that
mute tradition that is inscribed silently in the social body itself in order to impose what would henceforth become law and would therefore be sacred. (Mondzain 2005, 135)

Methodologically, this study is based on the principles of emergent
ethnography, an open-ended and collaborative approach to qualitative research that prioritizes adaptability and the trust that comes from long-term
relationship-building. Since the exchange with the monastery summer
school students described earlier in this chapter, I have encountered numerous echoes of those young men's insistence that I make myself legible
to them as a social researcher in terms of affective filial bonds—whether
among elders distraught that I was a young unmarried woman alone in
the field, or curious neighbors convinced I could only be so interested
in learning about Syriac Orthodoxy if I intended to join the Church and
marry a Syriac Orthodox man. Amidst that multilingual exchange outside the monastery chapel, the English-speaking Swede invoked the category of "religion," while the Dutch-speaking schoolboy used the word
"culture" in their efforts to render me legible. "Religion" narrowed the field:
I had enough of the right kind of kinship experience to relate to the pressures of Syriac Orthodox family life. "Culture" placed me more precisely
within that field: neither Orthodox nor Catholic, my Protestant family was
at least on their map of Christian relations. If I had had my wits about me
then, I would have asked the schoolboy what difference he thought it made.
The following chapters should illuminate why a Dutch and Syriac child
would link Christian denominationalism to the "culture" concept at all.

The effect of this response to my presence was that I centered relational ethics in my research design: I took a relational approach to ethnographic fieldwork that privileged achieving depth, trust, and intimacy. Maintaining the posture of a passive and neutral observer would have ended my research before it began. Thus, my fieldwork took the form of what Campbell and Lassiter (2015) call Observant Participation. While rooted in the anthropological tradition of holistic immersion and documentation (e.g., Malinowski 2014), Observant Participation entails an open-ended, dialogical, and collaborative approach to reworking our research aims and methods as we conduct fieldwork in light of unexpected experiences and encounters. In Observant Participation, as Campbell and Lassiter write:

> seemingly unrelated encounters can often turn out to be pivotal, especially as we move to couch various and diverse experiences as story. And so can doing ethnographic fieldwork, which requires much more of us than just watching and recording sights, sounds, tastes, and feelings as they occur: ethnographic fieldwork demands that we open ourselves to the process of observing experience itself, reflecting on that observed experience in the moment, and seeking out dialogue with others as this reflexive practice unfolds. (2015, 64)

To that end, I followed the lead of my interlocutors in the field to the greatest extent possible: singing, praying, and generally participating in the liturgical life of parish communities, as well as working to make myself a trustworthy friend and collaborator. Only after becoming a known presence in the community did I initiate a series of long-form semi-structured and unstructured ethnographic interviews. In these relationships, I had to be fully myself, sometimes foregoing a research opportunity when obligations to my Dutch family called me away to the other side of the country. If I had not, I would have shown myself to be less attuned to the ethical demands of Syriac Orthodox family life. With a focus on building long-term relationships, even friendships, I made myself vulnerable to people for whom structural vulnerability was a historical condition. While I did not imagine that this counted toward equalizing the power dynamics and social locations that separated me from my interlocutors' experience, I did this because family and faith were the terms through which we could reach each other—the neutral ground, in a sense, for rendering our respective differences intelligible to each other.

I struggled nonetheless with a profound discomfort at the gendered conservative religious norms that reminded me of my youth, which I had repudiated, along with my adherence to any particular church years prior. Beginning this project as a committed agnostic, I found that surrendering to the ethical demands of family, relationality, and my fraught history with my own faith tradition meant that as time went by, I recognized the ostensibly neutral "secular" ground of my social scientific inquiry less and less. Or rather, even within my secularity as a social researcher, I stood on ground shaped by my family's intertwined histories with Dutch Calvinism and American evangelicalism. I was not aware of how much I sought to transcend them until I discovered the extent to which they shaped my own sensibilities, perspectives, and research questions, as in my initial astonishment at some of my interlocutors' indifference toward understanding the classical Syriac words they sang every Sunday, "meaning" having been an essential value in my Calvinist upbringing. The role of Christianity in shaping that "secular" terrain on which social science is meant to be conducted became a central methodological problem because it prompted me to examine how my childhood Christianity, my early adult secularity, my gender, and my social location as a bicultural Dutch-American academic with a background in Classics and early Byzantine history shaped my access and my relationships. As I discovered the extent to which the young women I hoped to learn from had taught themselves *not* to speak about their own tradition with a posture of authoritative knowledge, and the extent to which the authoritative keepers of knowledge, the elderly priests, monks, deacons, fathers, and uncles, were uncomfortable teaching me these things because of my gender, I attuned myself to the thrum of tension running through their daily lives: studying their lessons with them, struggling to learn Syriac and memorize melodies with them, helping them with chores at home, and generally finding ways to support them in the daily grind of juggling work, school, exams, family obligations, church duties, community activism, and personal piety. I filled diverse roles that rarely looked like that of the "objective" and authoritative academic researcher.

This approach resonates with Elizabeth Freeman's notions of "chrononormativity" and "temporal lag" (Freeman 2010) and with Valentina Napolitano's methodology of the "trace" (2015). These tools enable the social researcher to investigate silence as a productive presence in history and ask how the gendered dimensions of liturgical theology might be understood as a submerged discourse. Such a discourse is bodily, relational, and implicit and is reproduced through rhythmic, repetitive, citational practices as much as through texts or explicit instruction (and sometimes more so). Discerning it entailed identifying connections among cultural, theological, and historical resources that might seem, at first glance, to be unrelated.

By learning when to ask questions, when to stay silent, when to make myself useful, and when to make myself scarce, I developed close relationships with some research participants (but by no means all) in a community with well-founded concerns that I might use what I learned to hurt their aspirations. For some, I was never able to move past the fear that I might be a spy for the Syrian government. For others, I was able to build lines of communication as long as I stuck to a delineated script of what a researcher is supposed to sound like, and my conversations with those people were often the most stilted and unproductive. My most successful fieldwork engagements were with non-elite young women, usually between the ages of sixteen and forty-five, who, after a time, came to see me as an ally of their goal to facilitate healing in their relationships with their families, parishes, and the broader community. In some cases, this resulted in long-lasting friendships that continue to this day. By necessity, this was an idiographic project focused on achieving depth and specificity over nomothetic breadth and generalizability. To pretend I was an impartial outsider with no effect on or personal investment in the well-being of my research participants would have been both an ethical and an empirical failure. This is "kinky empiricism," in Danilyn Rutherford's (2012) words, "an empiricism that admits that one never gets to the bottom of things." Rooted in the Scottish Enlightenment philosopher David Hume's understanding of "sympathy," it is

> the embodied outcome of proximity—occasioned by the placement of human bodies and artifacts in space and time—that leads people to share perspectives and passions. Sympathy is the outcome of inference, but with a twist. One witnesses an event—a gesture, a facial expression, an utterance—and one infers a cause, in this case the passion that led to this effect. Proximity makes the passion vivid, and one comes to feel what one imagines the other feels. (Rutherford 2012, 472)

Interpreting a smile or frown, an outburst or a stony silence, then, requires triangulating among multiple scales of context and comparison as well as something more. It requires friendship, a reciprocal vulnerability, and a heightened level of transparency about our own embeddedness as researchers in the social relations that make our work possible, as well as about the limits of our partial perspectives. Kinky empiricism, in its sympathy, ethics, and skepticism, bends back on itself not to center the researcher's experience but to illuminate the conditions that make certain insights possible at the expense of others.

Ethical empirical research for an anthropology of the Syriac world demands keeping an honest account of such relations, and the power dynamics, alliances, and exclusions they generate, as they complicated any straightforward boundary around my field site. This includes the historical entanglement among European and Euro-American academics and Middle Eastern churches, where Western-trained scholars with the material resources and connections to study ancient Christianity, classical languages, and theology in elite universities have become experts in ancient texts of the Syriac tradition. By virtue of their credentials, these scholars are often positioned as authorities on Syriac historical identity to Assyrian and Syriac communities themselves.[20] This relation of authority is often facilitated by the ecclesiastical hierarchy which has, historically, been closely allied with the field of Syriac Studies. Promising young Syriac Orthodox men advance their knowledge of Syriac language and theology by attending these elite European and American universities. A network of monasteries like Mor Gabriel Monastery in Tur Abdin and the Mor Ephrem Monastery in the Netherlands double as liturgical schools, publishing houses, and translation centers, where ecclesial scholars, seminarians, and educated laymen generate a vast corpus of texts, translations, calligraphic inscriptions, and exegeses on the histories and liturgical traditions associated with the West Syriac Rite for the benefit of the global diaspora. These monastic and ecclesiastically sanctioned scholarly activities function as a kinship practice in a gendered soteriological (that is, a salvific) system that operates on both a theological and a sociopolitical register. Syriac Orthodox women were rarely (with crucial exceptions) included or welcome in these ecclesiastically authorized sites of scholarly production as scholars unless as authorities on historical traditions. Rather, the Church offered Syriac Orthodox women other avenues of institutionally authorized engagement defined by their shifting position within their own family structure, as I document in Chapter 4. Many women embraced these roles while also experimenting with them, expanding or reconfiguring them to better address what they understood to be their communities', their families', and their own needs. Noticing these discreet activities called for me to attend to the undercurrents that drew women into connecting their liturgical practices with the rest of their social, political, professional, and intimate lives and to note the significance of absences, silences, and thwarted dreams. My position as a female researcher with no background in classical Syriac and an interest in current, rather than ancient, practices made me something of a conundrum for my ecclesiastical hosts, and gender figured centrally in my unfolding methodological design. I found myself in odd situations—academic visitors to the monastery were common but were inevitably established historians, theologians, religious studies and classical Syriac experts who were welcomed with a great deal of ceremony, while I lurked at the edge of the crowd or sat with a parish friend in the audience. Occasionally, I came to know these visiting academics if they stayed for the evening meal, and on one occasion I accompanied a Dutch history and religious studies professor taking her undergraduate students on a tour of the local Syriac parishes so they could experience daily prayers and the Sunday morning Qurbono in person.

In this relational field, I had to seek out Assyrian understandings of liturgical kinship at a remove from the center of ecclesiastical power in the monastery, where Syriac (and to a lesser extent Aramaean) perspectives dominated, underwritten by authoritative scholarship from the field of Syriac Studies. As a Dutch-American researcher who began this project interested in how Christianity, racial discourses, and secularity/secularism each contribute to shaping a Dutch, European, and global politics of minority recognition, I navigated relational barriers to access that emerged depending on whether I named my research interlocutors Assyrian, Aramaean, or just Syriac. In my preparatory work, I studied Arabic in the United States with an Assyrian-American teacher from Iraq. When I arrived for preliminary fieldwork in the Netherlands, I understood myself to be undertaking work with Assyrians, an impression that was validated that first summer by time spent interviewing local Assyrian political leaders who were then more frequently to be found on the monastery grounds shortly after the death of Archbishop Mor Julius Çiçek, a vehemently anti-Assyrian Aramaean. My first moment of disorientation occurred when I met a mother my age visiting from Sweden, who was residing at the monastery for the summer to help cook while her young son attended summer school. After I addressed her as an Assyrian, she gently but swiftly berated me: "No, no, no. We are not Assyrian! Assyrians are part of a different church. We are just Christian. That's it. That's everything. This monastery is our country—like all our monasteries. This is our homeland. We have nothing to do with Assyrians. They are heretics!"

This exchange, echoed by countless others over the coming years, as I encountered gatekeepers who would bestow or deny access depending on whether I acknowledged that I understood I was working with either Ara-maeans or Assyrians (using the word "Syriac," *Syrische*, or "Suryoyo" was usually enough to satisfy both factions, although not always, as I explain in later chapters). After I began attending choir rehearsals at an Assyrian cultural association in south Enschede, I was frequently upbraided for hav-ing been seen, somewhere, speaking to the wrong people: "You must not talk to ignorant people! There are many ignorant, uneducated people in our community!" This accusation, the belief in others' lack of proper knowl-edge, was levied on all sides—Assyrian, Aramaean, and Syriac. The con-troversy over "proper knowledge" led me to attend to regional and historical disparities in how Syriac Orthodoxy has been constituted as an object of knowledge by scholars and practitioners and how these epistemic tensions reverberate in the diaspora as part of the ethics of recognition.

My project thus evolved to account for the tensions I observed and nav-igated, and early on, I attributed them to the interventions of secular Euro-American categories and colonial constructs, in keeping with the arguments of recent scholarship on Western Christian missionary work in the Middle East. Deeper investigation complicated this story, as I grew troubled by the political, ethical, and epistemological implications of the claim that Assyrian/Syriac ethnicity was a wholly modern construct attributable to nineteenth-century Euro-American missionaries, archaeologists, and anti-Arab propaganda. The violent erasure of the peoples of the Syriac world, whether they identify as Assyrian, Aramaean, Chaldean, or simply Syriac, is real and pressing, and scholarly narratives that mark the beginning of these communities in the nineteenth century and attribute agency for na-tional awakening to Western intervention miss, I believe, the transhistori-cal sociopolitical significance of liturgical kinship (see also Donabed 2015; ter Haar Romeny et al. 2010).

That said, it is difficult to run against the grain of Benedict Anderson's ubiquitous thesis that national identity is an imagined community pro-duced by secular modern processes, technologies, media forms, and intel-lectual habits. Anderson's original point is, of course, vitally important:

minorities become so through a minoritization process that reflects unequal power arrangements vis-à-vis a state apparatus. But this point can be formulated in a way that obscures preexisting attachments, formations, and relations that are themselves subject to various powers and transformations, not all of which originate with the modern state nor fall within its purview. This observation can open one up to accusations of a naive primordialism—but I think that this accusation misreads the temporal horizon of the ethnographic situation. Before the transformations of the historical moment we call "secular modernity," the Syriac world underwent myriad transformations within different stages of Ottoman hegemony in Persia and South Asia, and before that, in the Mughal, the Sassanian, the Abbasid, and Byzantine and early Roman Empires, as well as, perhaps, the ancient city-states of Aram and the ancient Assyrian Empire, from whom twenty-first-century Syriac Christians inherit their modern living spoken languages. Each of these past transformations maintains some purchase on the present. What bridges these transformations?

Once we understand that the task of bridging these transformations—of making relations sociopolitically legible to more powerful Others—was never solely a modern one, we are compelled to ask: What enables Syriac Christians to reach across time and space, then and now, across linguistic, regional, and political differences, to recognize each other as somehow related, to identify with each other, and to claim each other as kin? In my view, the answer is *liturgy*. But this raises another question: How does liturgy possess such sociopolitical power? As I will show, the answer to that question lies in iconicity and the ethics of recognition.

Liturgical Kinship

Liturgy, in my analysis, is simultaneously a philosophical category, a ritualized practice of collective worship, and a set of social-emotional relationships infused with the power to shape political imaginaries, binding far-flung communities into a connected, coherent, global formation—the Syriac world. Writing about liturgy in the West Syriac tradition is difficult because it generally remains undefined in authoritative texts. As West Syriac liturgical theologian and priest Father Baby Varghese (2004) has observed: "The West Syrian fathers [sic] have not given a definition of liturgy. Perhaps it is felt unnecessary to define something self-evident, and so intimate to one's experience" (2004, 8). Instead, he offers from his own experience as a priest of the Malankara branch of Syriac Orthodoxy in south India and deep reading as the leading exegete of Syriac Patristics: "Worship is the vocation of man [sic], the very purpose for which he was created. He was created to live in communion with God, as a liturgical being" (Varghese 2004, 8).

This notion of "liturgical being" as essential to personhood informs my understanding of Syriac liturgy and its power to generate, reproduce, and reinvent relations extending beyond what secular social science conventionally names the "religious" domain.[21] For Syriac Christians like my interlocutors, liturgy makes kin, and knowledge of the liturgy is a step toward kin-making. In Syriac Orthodoxy, liturgy and kinship are co-constitutive forms of ethical personhood. The implications of this proposition are vociferously contested even though throughout much of European history, the Latin Christian tradition has reproduced itself through virtually the same premise, sometimes to devastating effect (e.g., Bynum 2007). How this premise is interpreted can vary widely, and the ways that secularist and Western Christian Europeans hide this history from themselves is instructive. Today, an Episcopalian Christian in the U.S. could happily claim that liturgical practice produces Christian kinship, but they would nonetheless mean something more metaphorical and less literally corporeal by it than a Syriac Christian would. That is to say, for an American Episcopalian, the moral or political obligations of generic spiritual relatedness are not *quite* identical to the moral or political obligations of consanguineous kinship. The spectrum of possibilities for articulating an analogy between biogenetic "family" and spiritual kinship in Western Christianity can vary widely, and as Todne Thomas (2021) has shown, this spectrum constitutes an ethical imaginary and a theological project to conceptualize what it means to be Brothers and Sisters in Christ in ways that can side-step, overcome, *or* reinforce racial, ethnic, denominational, and other sociopolitical boundaries—a labor she names "kincraft."

For Syriac Orthodoxy, the link is not analogical but substantive; it produces obligatory, rather than elective, affinities. For many Syriac Christians, the mere fact of participating in daily liturgical practice generates specific bonds and obligations that, in Euro-American thought and practice, are often predicated on blood-relatedness (see also Calder 2016, 2017). This modality of relatedness is irreducible in that my interlocutors consider it an inherent, rather than an optional, dimension of human personhood.[22] It is to this that Marta, my research interlocutor quoted in the epigraph at the beginning of this chapter, refers when she says, "Christianity is the blood in my veins." This way of understanding relatedness, generated by liturgical practice, entails obligations of care as well as deference to patriarchal authority. Iconicity explains *how* this generative process happens.

The force and complexity of these relations are not easily discerned by outsiders. Many of these insights only became apparent to me because I was sometimes mistaken for a young Syriac Orthodox woman myself, which led to encounters that would never have happened to, say, an older male researcher, such as being forcefully shoved by an elder at a church festival or being chased down a stairwell by a middle-aged woman outraged by how my long winter coat inadvertently fell open to reveal my legs while kneeling to photograph a liturgical choir in action. I take up the moral semiotics of such encounters in later chapters to address the gendered ethical demands of liturgical kinship, which the young women who participated in my study submitted to willingly, if not always without chafing. In embracing these ethical demands, my interlocutors practice what Saba Mahmood (2001, 2011) has described as a docile, in the sense of teachable, form of agency, and they understand these demands as the unavoidable price of the ethics of recognition.[23] For now, it suffices to say that there is a subtle distinction in the understanding and enactment of Christian kinship in different traditions, which sometimes only becomes apparent if one is drawn into such relations oneself.

Given the complexity of my research relationships, I had to make certain decisions about where my ethical priorities lay. Some of my research interlocutors kept secrets that would have been hurtful to them or to their loved ones to reveal. The community is small and tight-knit enough that careful readers could discern identities beyond pseudonyms. I saw and heard things I will not write about, even though these observations would furnish useful evidence of some of my claims; I do not believe it is the ethnographer's place to divulge secret knowledge, however valuable to social scientific knowledge production. Yet I have written about the Assyrian-Aramaean conflict even though some of my interlocutors are disappointed and even hurt that I do not support one faction over another. My purpose here is to diagnose the historical conditions that have produced the conflict in hopes that this conversation may aid in long-term community healing, a purpose I have discussed openly and extensively with the young women whose stories feature most prominently in the following chapters.

Perforations; Or, the Problem of Scale

One of the other central ethical knots that my research participants negotiate is the impulse of their Dutch Calvinist and Catholic Christian allies
to help them learn how to become *better Christians* when they themselves
see Western Christianity, at times, as a failed tradition that has been emptied of its ethical content. I explore this question of how to relate across
mutual misrecognition in Chapters 5 and 6, drawing connections with
Christianity's broader historical problem with pluralism, evident in the
tendency to burn or excommunicate heretics and in the very impulse to
evangelize. Such tensions are subtle and inchoate—as the relationship between salvation and annihilation is fraught with ambiguity—and are easily transposed into secularist anxieties over religious, ethnic, and racial
difference. My social location as a white, more-or-less Western Christian
sometimes triggered the conversations that revealed these tensions in ways
I did not plan. The encounter between my interlocutors' definitions and
my own Protestant and secularist definitions of the basic categories of social scientific thought runs throughout each chapter.

Chapters 5 and 6 are especially concerned with the secularity, and thus
theological implications, of concepts like ethnicity and race, and so I think
through iconicity and liturgical kinship in terms of the religious and racial
politics that intersect in my research interlocutors' lives across multiple
scales, from the municipal to the national to the supranational. Secularist
and Western Christian anxieties in Western Europe operate on a sensory
register, where incipient intuitions over what it means to be a person, whether
religious or secular, are rooted in differently configured theologies of cosmological intimacy. In many European Christian traditions, kinship with
divine power dictates certain rights and responsibilities that—as some scholars have argued in the tradition of Schmitt's political theology—translate
into secularized conceptions of moral citizenship. Kinship with the divine
is analogous to kinship with the sovereign, which in turn yields the blood-
and-soil metaphors of modern territorial nationalism (see Berlin 1973;
Holmes 2000; Linke 1999). These metaphors do not require active Christian belief or identification to maintain their purchase on secular political
imaginaries. Nor do they entail an isomorphic relation between secularist
norms and majoritarian religious histories. Instead, it is the conflicting
interpretations of these metaphors, themselves originating in the dynamic
and unstable field of theological politics, that underwrite secularist dis-

putes over the rights and responsibilities of citizenship in Europe today. Yet the dynamics of these disputes differ depending on the scale: demands made by the municipal government differ from those made by the national government or by the European Union or by the United Nations. Responding to these disparate demands affects Syriac Orthodox understandings of liturgical kinship in unexpected ways, an open-ended process I characterize in Chapter 5 as "perforation."

The Irony of Tradition

Finally, I aim to avoid playing the role of the "adjudicating anthropologist" who simply enumerates the ways that a minoritized community fails to measure up to the normative categories of modern political life. Charles Briggs (1996) has cautioned against the danger of this kind of analysis, in which pointing out the "invention of tradition" among a vulnerable minority exposes that community to even greater violence and dispossession by the state. My foundational premise is that every tradition, whether ritual of state or sacred chant, is constantly under construction and that the specific kind of labor that goes into its construction—ethical, aesthetic, epistemic—illuminates broader cultural, social, and political conditions. As Michael Herzfeld writes, "The irony of tradition is precisely that it cannot exist except in relation to a self-serving concept of modernity" (2004, 31). This is true for everyone, everywhere, especially those peoples whose claims to national sovereignty go unchallenged. The practices and performances I describe in this text constitute a set of deeply felt explorations in memory and belonging—in practices of relating—that are both destabilizing and generative. Describing these practices faithfully demands attention to their reproductive and communicative dimensions, as well as attunement to that which has been rendered invisible, inaudible, illegible, or unintelligible in the many histories of the Syriac world.

*   *   *

My argument is rooted in my reading of the history of imperial and anti-imperial Christian debates, whose legacies inform current debates over migration, religious difference, and racism in Europe. This inheritance becomes clearer when approached from the perspective of those marginalized Christians like the Syriac Orthodox who lost those ancient debates.

In Syriac Christianity, we may discern a liturgical understanding of history not as linear narrative but as the relational, cyclical, and enfleshed medium through which humanity is claimed as kin by the Divine; in my analysis, this is the prototype of the ethics of recognition. Recognition—a double-edged sword in its violence and ambiguous exclusions—is a theological claim upon Others. Categories like "secularity," "ethnicity," and "race," I will show, are theological concepts produced as outcomes of ethically complex processes and regimes of recognition, iconic processes of struggling for control over sites of reproductive power. In European political cultures strongly influenced by certain strains of Christianity, "traces" of theological reasoning linger in implicit intuitions about national, ethnic, and racial belonging. Valentina Napolitano (2015) describes the methodological affordances of the "trace" as ethnographic sensitivity to "the materials of knots of histories at the margins, as well as auratic presences" (2015). In Syriac Orthodoxy, such knots are evidence of an alternative conception of Christian kinship, in which "real" relatedness is the liturgical embodiment of complex and contested histories, as the sounds, smells, haptic tremors, and bodily rhythms of sung prayer materialize painful memories of the past, which diasporic Syriac Orthodox Christians reconfigure to address new predicaments in the present, in hopes of securing their future.

2

LITURGICAL MEMORY

The continuity is one of a rupture, of an impossibility, of a wandering and an excess that cannot be contained by the very tradition of which it is a part. (Hollywood 2012, 198)

Whose Memory?

Walking along one day, St. Ephrem encountered a woman doing laundry, who glanced up at him as he passed. Rebuking her brazenness, the saint shouted, "Woman, keep your eyes cast down to the earth from which you were made!" She replied: "Sir, it is you who should keep your eyes fixed on the earth, for you were created from it. Woman, however, was created from the side of man, therefore it is appropriate that I look upon you." Astounded and impressed, St. Ephrem wondered: "If the women of this place are so wise, is there any telling how wise the men and boys are?" (Amar *Syriac Vita*, chapter 11; cited in Amar 2011).

The late antique text in which this story is found was written many years after the death, in 373 CE, of the historical St. Ephrem of Nisibis and Edessa, the Syriac-speaking poet-theologian credited with founding the Daughters and Sons of the Covenant (*Bnoth* and *Bnay Qyomo*), a consecrated order of celibate liturgical singers and cantors among early churches of the West Syriac Rite.[1] It is an odd story because the saint's scornful attitude toward the washer-woman is unrecognizable from the attitude conveyed in his own attributed writings. St. Ephrem's warm admiration for women—real individual women, Biblical women, mothers, daughters, sisters, and women as a general category—infused his life's work. A celibate deacon, Ephrem wrote theological discourses in metrical verse to be sung in urban Syriac congregations by the Daughters of the Covenant. But there is no sign of this Ephrem who chastely loved and respected women in the *Syriac Vita*, a Byzantine creation which served as source material for later Syriac scribal elites' accounts of their own tradition's roots.

According to Syriac Studies scholar Joseph Amar, this story exemplifies the struggle for interpretive control between Greek West and Syriac East and a Syriac surrender to the cultural power of Greek language and thought (Amar *Syriac Vita* vol. 629, 64). In an effort to make the Syriac world legible to imperial Byzantine Christianity, the anonymous author of the *Syriac Vita* recast the creator of the Sons and Daughters of the Covenant as a proto-monastic of Western (i.e., Greek) tradition, holy in his denigration of women and earthly matter. And yet, despite imperial influence on the West Syriac literary tradition, traces of the Ephrem evident in his own writings lingered in the liturgical poetry chanted among West Syriac congregations from Antioch to Baghdad. In the time intervening, medieval and modern Syriac Orthodox historical memories have taken shape in that space of disjuncture between the Ephrem of liturgy and the Ephrem of literature. The multisensory interplay of their auratic presences in sound and text, to draw on Napolitano's language of the "trace," shapes the tradition, while their auras are, in turn, transmitted through it.

In this chapter, I examine my research participants' relationship to ancient tradition by tracing the dislocations of space and time through which imperial Christianity and its Others were formed. Running through this history of spatiotemporal disjuncture, I show, is the structuring omission of gender, which in anthropological theory is integral to understanding kinship, evidenced in the strategic forgetting of the saint's affections in the *Syriac Vita*. Gender, I argue, is the key analytic for understanding sonic iconicity in West Syriac tradition and for understanding Christianity's relationship to political and social life more broadly. In other words, gender makes liturgical memory.

At every scale and from every angle, gender has organized how people conceive of and practice Christian community. Throughout much of Christian history in Europe, a theologically grounded conception of gender as binary, patriarchal, and defined by complementary social roles mirroring the dynamics of sexual reproduction influenced secular-modern commonsense notions of what it means to be kin. That is to say that, following thinkers like Marilyn Strathern (2005) and Kim Tallbear (2013), in a dominant Euro-American tradition, "real" relatedness of the kind that grants you legal claims upon another person or upon land is based on blood and now genetic ties.[2] These claims are gendered inasmuch as the reproduction of these ties is sexed, and this tradition is often equated with a normative and globalized vision of secular modernity. In liberal regimes, the biological idiom of kinship thus authorizes every other scale and modality of relatedness, from marriage and adoption laws (e.g., Hayden 1995) to the concept of territorial sovereignty inherent to the nation-state system (e.g., Borneman 1992). In such regimes, this biological idiom shapes whether or not a given relation is legally recognized as *inherent* to someone's personhood, as in one's national or ethnic origin, or as *optional*, as in one's freely chosen religious affiliation. In both Syriac and Western Christianity's relationship with empire, as with secularist understandings of political identity, gender silently structures the relation and its practical implications.

Before mapping out certain key turns in the development of Christian liturgy's relationship with broader social and political forms, I first sketch out an ethnographic scene from my field site that illustrates the structuring omission of gender as both a methodological and an epistemological problem for the study of Christian kinship, empire, and history. The structuring omission of gender brings to light one of the central claims of this book: that liturgy is a sociopolitical formation and a site of reproductive power, in which irreducible relations and the political identities staked upon those relations are generated. In doing this, I reexamine a common theme in the anthropology of secularism/religion concerning the power of the state to define, regulate, and shape minor religious traditions. I suggest, along with other anthropologists of non-Chalcedonian Orthodoxy like Mark Calder (2017) and Tom Boylston (2018), that liturgical power demonstrates the limits of state power in how it creates spaces for alternate modalities of irreducible relatedness to take shape (see also Clements 2019). In making this argument, I have two objectives. First, I aim to clear several epistemological barriers that have inhibited the study of Syriac Christianity in the secular social sciences: (1) an overreliance on textuality-as-evidence at the expense of other sensory forms of the historical "trace," (2) a tendency of critical anthropology to reproduce the very modernist assumptions that are ostensibly under critique, (3) a siloed "area studies" approach to ethnographic contextualization, and (4) a secularist unwillingness to discern powers of dialogical becoming and boundary-production in sites other than in relations with a state. Bringing down these barriers, I hope, will make clear how it is that twenty-first-century Suryoye in diaspora might embody, reproduce, and reinvent their relationship with the theological and historical content of the West Syriac Rite through sonic iconicity—through, that is, the sensory and ethical labor of liturgical kinship. My second objective is to show how the structuring omission of gender constitutes a thread of continuity connecting ancient, medieval, and modern forms of Syriac Orthodox Christian identity and belonging to argue for the theological importance of Syriac Orthodox women's invisible labor. These aims intersect, as they each bear upon the fundamental connection between reproductive power and the ethics of recognition.

Where Is the *Malphonitho*?

By early May of 2010, I had been taking weekly lessons in classical Syriac at the Mor Ephrem Monastery for many months. Peter, my teacher, was a young man whose family lived a few kilometers away in the German village of Gronau. Peter slept at the monastery, taking the train over the border every day to attend a German Catholic secondary school where he was preparing to enter university to study biological sciences. Whenever we were tired of our lessons, we would either talk or sing. Peter would teach me songs with tremendous patience for my Western inability to hear, much less reproduce, microtones.[3] At that time, Peter was a Reader, two ranks below a full Deacon of the Church, although many said he should be promoted for the extent of his knowledge of Syriac language and music. Peter disagreed. He said a deacon should be a moral paragon, and at eighteen, he was nowhere near ready to live up to such a great responsibility. There are YouTube videos still circulating throughout the global diaspora of Peter singing solos during the Sunday morning Qurbono. He had a powerful voice and an impressive breadth and depth of knowledge, which is why the bishop assigned him to teach me to read the classical script. He was respected but also laughed at a little for his excessive enthusiasms. He favored wearing a long black cossack over his jeans and trainers, even though he was not yet in training to become a priest or monk—nor did he ultimately pursue that path after he graduated from university several years later, to the dismay of the ecclesiastical authorities who had invested time and money into his liturgical training. At that time, however, Peter was something of a zealot, a fervent 'umthonoyo—a man committed to serving the 'umtho, the Syriac people and their cause—and the pride of his elders. His calling, he often told me, was to master and teach kthobonoyo, "the book language," to other Suryoye in hopes that classical Syriac would once again become a living language and unify the dispersed Syriac Orthodox diaspora, which, he told me, was being torn apart by its tainted vernacular languages.

One Thursday afternoon, I arrived at the monastery just before 5 P.M. to meet Peter upon his return home from school. The weather was cool and cloudy, and elderly Sister Seyde let me into the building with an affectionate laugh at my frazzled state after a long train ride. She led me to the communal sitting room, where Peter sported a newly shaved head, one of his recent enthusiasms for spiritual fashion. Several other monks and nuns were watching an international Syriac Orthodox satellite station with a new boy I had never seen before. They were watching coverage of a live event in Sweden, with huge Aramaean flags and a crowd of priests and deacons, as Sister Seyde squinted at the television, commenting to no one in particular that she recognized a famous Syriac Studies scholar from Oxford University among the crowd. When the bell rang for Vespers, we trudged up the stairs together to the tiny chapel.

In the chapel, the readers, monks, and seminarians gathered at two lecterns on the left and right sides of the gudo. On the left, Peter's cousin, Matthias, from the German side, sang with a workman contracted to do some remodeling work on the cloister.[4] They were led by Father Yaqub, who was primarily responsible for teaching Syriac language and liturgy to the boys and young men in residence at the monastery. On the right, Peter stood with thirteen-year-old Afrem, also visiting from the German side. The bishop arrived a few minutes later, and after slipping his shoes off, he disappeared behind the curtain separating the raised altar space from the gudo. As the liturgical office progressed, the singing wavered. Without the abbot and Father Gabriel present, the forty-five-minute sung call and response began to be too much for Father Yaqub and Peter to carry on their own. From behind the altar curtain, the bishop called out lines of melody to help the young men discern what and how to sing. The texts in front of them were not notated, so the melody had to be sung from memory, and the ancient Serto script in which they were written had no punctuation, so the young men often lost their way without more experienced voices to guide them.

As prayers ended, I filed out with the nuns to wait on the landing until the men and boys finished singing. Peter and I spent the next half hour before dinner in a small office reserved for our lessons, recording a new song Peter wanted me to learn. The song, *Toyson wothyon*, is a hymn sung occasionally by women's choirs for Sunday Mass, honoring women of the Bible. I listened with a sinking feeling as Peter laughed in delight at his own bright idea to teach me this song "Because of your research, Sarah! It's perfect because it is about women! Now you can sing it for other people! You can sing it for the bishop soon, too. It's okay that you can't sing the notes [meaning the microtones] very well. What matters is what it means." Suspecting a plot between Peter and the bishop, I sighed inwardly at the prospect of being called upon by the bishop to sing poorly in front of visiting dignitaries, many of whom were academic colleagues from Dutch and Belgian universities (and indeed, in the coming months, my worst fears came to pass).

On our way to dinner after our lesson, we passed by the kitchen, where several women were eating with the nuns, having already prepared food for the monks and boys. Looking briefly in on the gathered women, all seemingly above the age of forty-five, I continued on with a pang of regret as they studiously avoided my gaze, taking my place next to Father Yaqub in the dining room. By this time, I knew that I would only cause embarrassment if I tried to join this cohort of women in the kitchen. The first and most difficult rule of fieldwork for me to learn was that the very relations of authority I sought to understand also shaped and limited my access—a contingency of how I first entered the community that left lasting marks on how my would-be interlocutors saw me. These relations bent and refracted around gender, generation, and knowledge: the bishop had long since made my status within the space of the monastery clear as both a (relatively) learned person and "not a Syriac Orthodox woman," and so any effort of mine to defy his intentions was upsetting to almost everyone I encountered in the proximity of the monastery. Even though I was there to study with the women's choirs, the gatekeepers of my access were determined that what knowledge there was to be gained about the choirs would come primarily from men, because the women did what they were told to do by their priests and liturgical teachers. The women sang but did not know what or why they sang, I was told. I was instructed repeatedly by various priests and *malphone*, the liturgical teachers, not to speak to people who did not possess the right knowledge, but none of these men were in a position to teach me themselves for various reasons. And, indeed, very

often when I would ask the women with whom I sang what we were singing and why, they would express embarrassment and tell me that I should
ask someone with proper training, like a priest or the bishop.

For many long months, these dynamics were a source of worry and frustration until I realized they were data. There is a broad historical context
for understanding this complex relationship between women's and men's
participation in the Syriac Orthodox Church's liturgical life, none the least
of which are the gendered exclusions of patriarchal authority. Significantly,
the revival of women's liturgical singing is relatively recent; the first
European archbishop, Mor Julius Çiçek, established the first women's choir
in Europe in the late 1970s, and so this is a gendered practice that women
under the age of forty-five (at the time of my primary phase of fieldwork
in the late aughts and early 2010s) only began learning from their fathers,
uncles, priests, and malphone, rather than from their mothers, who were
mostly illiterate and grew up keeping silent in church altogether if they
were from a village that permitted women entry into church at all. The
women of my acquaintance view their ecclesiastical elders with respect, deference, and a deep well of affection; they understand such deference as
essential to keeping Syriac Orthodoxy recognizably Syriac and Orthodox
in Western Europe.

Yet, there was also a less visible dynamic at work. The women I sang
with, women like Marta and Rebekah, the choir leaders of the church in
the nearby town of Hengelo described in later chapters, and my close friends
Mariane and Elizabeta, more or less embraced the conservative gender and
sexual norms of their parents and grandparents, while still engaging in profoundly transformative work that their ecclesiastical fathers did not always fully apprehend. Mariane and Elizabeta, in particular, went largely
unacknowledged as the masters of Syriac grammar and liturgical melody
that they were. Only after several years of witnessing Mariane and Elizabeta position themselves as eternal students of the various malphone who
taught in their parish *madrashto*, or church school, did I begin to discern,
despite their efforts to obscure the fact, that they understood more about
their lessons than some of their teachers did. That the young women's
knowledge was still patchy at best attested to how little mastery some of
their malphone actually possessed. Given the difficulty and vastness of the
body of texts and melodies constituting the West Syriac Rite, even partial
mastery of liturgical knowledge was a major accomplishment and a path
to widespread esteem and respect.

After my primary phase of fieldwork was finished, Mariane and Elizabeta both married and left their childhood parish. For several years after marriage, Elizabeta contributed to significant changes in her new parish, working with an organizing committee of like-minded reformers to develop spaces and mechanisms for teaching language and liturgy to children. Elizabeta's status and self-view as the passive recipient of patriarchal knowledge shifted so that she became a *malphonitho*, a liturgical teacher who is a woman, holding weekly lessons in classical Syriac for children at her husband's parish in South Enschede and developing outreach programs for an increasingly disaffected and even criminalized population of Suryoye teens in the neighborhood. Her neighborhood in South Enschede, Wesselerbrink, is over 99 percent Syriac Orthodox, and locals like Elizabeta refer to it with self-conscious humor as the Wesselerbronx. The racialized North American connotations of this nickname were intentional, as were its implications of economic precarity and petty crime. Her teaching and outreach with this portion of her community, Elizabeta told me during one of my return visits, was a new phase of her campaign for liturgical revitalization. Her aim was to transform the Church and, in the same motion, rescue Syriac families from social and political marginalization; except, few of her church elders could grasp what she was up to, nor did many of those who could grasp it appreciate it. These themes in our conversations will return in later chapters. For now, the pressing ethnographic question is, given her expertise and ideal social location, why was Elizabeta, despite eagerness to support my research, not assigned to be my teacher?

The answer to this question has everything to do with the way women's contributions—and the sociopolitical significance of these contributions—can be obscured by official ecclesiastical understandings of what liturgy and gender are in Christianity, from antiquity into the present. In simple terms, Elizabeta had no time. But this lack of time, I suggest, is not theologically simple. The gendered nature of her work for her church and family, in addition to her part-time job and full-time school work, occupied every waking moment. As liturgical historian Teresa Berger argues, the rites and institutions of Christian liturgical life in each of its historical trajectories have been produced by complex gender systems because "the foundational materiality in Christian worship is the bodily presence of worshippers" (2011, 2). This gender complexity extends far beyond binary, essentialized understandings of "men" and "women" operating within prescribed social roles. In 325 CE, for example, the bishops presiding at the Council of Ni-caea affirmed the biblical foundation for including in worship services male-bodied persons who had been castrated, with the exception of those who had been "self-castrated." Such a detail, however tiny, suggests that broader debates over embodied difference have been central to the formu-lation of Christian community from the Church's earliest moments. Com-plex understandings and experiences of gender inflect liturgical practice in a fashion that goes far beyond the question of "women's participation," for gender shapes the very conditions of possibility, the means of sexual and social reproduction through which liturgical practice unfolds (see also Merdjanova 2021).

Elizabeta's lack of time *is* the condition of possibility for the Syriac Or-thodox Church in the Dutch diaspora to survive. In this vein, my friend's rescue operation, her community organizing and teaching, is a silent rev-olution in liturgical kinship, shaping and reshaping the quality of social relationships produced through church membership and ritual practice. Her labor's invisibility and inaudibility to authority is, to a certain degree, necessary in order for it to be effective—any hint of disrespect or disrup-tion to patriarchal family and ecclesiastical relations could do more harm than good to her cause. To perceive the theological and sociological sig-nificance of her labor ourselves, we need to understand how these trans-formations cohere with centuries of complex relations among ecclesiastical elites and their congregations and from liturgy's place in the global history of Christianity.

What Is Liturgy?

In the simplest sense, liturgy refers to collective acts of worship. But what anyone means by "collective," "acts," or "worship" is far from straightfor-ward. Developed from the Greek *leitourgia*, the word "liturgy" has meant many things to many people as its root concepts have evolved over centu-ries. In English, liturgy is often rendered as "the work of the people" (e.g., Shepherd 1952) or, more recently, "public service" (e.g., Meyers 2010), de-pending on which dimensions of its genealogy theologians invoke. In combining *leitos*, meaning "public" or "concerning the people" and *ergon*, "work," according to liturgical theologian Ruth A. Meyers, *leitourgia* was originally "used for services rendered for the body politic. One might build a road or an aqueduct or supply equipment for the armed forces.

Gradually, the term came to be used more generally for an act done in the service of another, and even in the cultic sense of service to the gods" (Meyers 2010, 45). She writes:

> The New Testament use of leitourgia builds on this earlier usage. [. . .] In his letter to the Romans, Paul describes himself as a "liturgist" (leitourgos, sometimes translated as "minister" or "servant") to the Gentiles [. . .] (Rom 15:16). [. . .] A more explicit use of "liturgy" in reference to worship appears in Acts 13:2. A group of prophets and teachers at Antioch are engaged in a "liturgy" (leitourgounton, translated variously as "worshiping" or "serving"), resulting in a missionary call that sends Barnabas and Saul on a journey. Although "liturgy" eventually came to refer to Christian worship, particularly the Eucharist, the appearance of the word in Romans and Acts offers only a glimmer of this subsequent development. The term eventually fell out of use in Western Christianity for many centuries. (Meyers 2010, 45)

As an ordained priest of the Episcopal Church of America, Meyers draws on specific moments in liturgy's genealogical development to argue for a missional understanding of worship as "enacting and signifying God's love for the world." Understood in the context of twenty-first-century North American Christianity, this is a pointedly progressive statement about what Christian community is and should be and the role that prescribed forms of communal prayer and ritual practice should play in both shaping the ecclesial community and the nature of its relations with others outside the Church.

In other contexts, liturgy's genealogy yields further insights and questions for defining Christian worship and tracing its sociopolitical effects. The root of *leitos* is *laos*, or "people," which itself originates in an archaic Greek description of the followers of a military leader. The late Antique Greek translators of the Hebrew Bible, when faced with a range of possible terms for a "people" (e.g., *demos*, *ethne*, etc.), each conveying a different quality of relatedness among the people in question, opted to render the Hebrew *'am* (a cognate of the Syriac word *'amo* still commonly used among twenty-first-century Syriac Orthodox to refer to being Suryoye) as *laos* to convey the pastoral, mutually defining relation of the sheep to the Shepherd.[5] While the military sense of the relation defining the *laos* has faded in much Christian historical memory (with a few notable exceptions), the binding mutuality of the pastoral relation has endured. From that pastoral relation, intellectual historian Nicholas Heron (2018) argues, fifteen hundred years of Latin Christian liturgical development gave rise to the paradigm of impersonal, vicarious, bureaucratic power that defines secular modern governmentality (see also Foucault 2007 [2004] and Agamben 2011, 2013a, 2013b).

Writing from an Eastern Orthodox position, meanwhile, the theologian-priest Alexander Schmemann excavates two other modes of understanding *leitourgia* in Christian history and their sociopolitical implications. The first understanding is a scholastic tradition of conceptualizing liturgy as an *object* of theological inquiry, distinct from other domains of Christian experience and practice. The second is a patristic tradition in which liturgy is "the living source and ultimate criterion of all Christian thought" and therefore *not* something that can be objectified or defined externally (Schmemann 1990, 12–13). He saw in the history of Christianity a transformation of liturgical consciousness, from early "cultic" meanings—by which he meant "a sacred action, or rite, performed in order to establish 'contact' between the community and God" (Schmemann 1990, 16)—that presupposed a distinction between "sacred" and "profane" dimensions of existence to a non-cultic meaning in which such distinctions have been abolished. In the non-cultic sense, liturgy is not an action *within* the Church but rather the expression of the life *of* the Church, "a visible sign of the Kingdom which is to come, its anticipation in time and history" (Schmemann 1990, 17). For Schmemann, this expansive vision of liturgy understood as immanent and undifferentiated from "secular" or everyday life and demarcated by neither time nor space was the later, more progressive historical development (cf. Durkheim 2001 [1912]). It is striking that despite significant differences in tradition and context, these exercises in defining liturgy demonstrate a common interest in how the *nature of the relatedness* connecting Christians to each other within the Church should dictate the Church's relationship with all that exists outside of physical church walls.

While these thinkers reflect only the tiniest fraction of the diversity of viewpoints on the definition, regulation, and historical significance of liturgy, that diversity demonstrates that liturgy is as capacious and flexible an entity as Christianity itself because it is, in a practical sense, what Christianity *is*. Whether self-consciously invoking the term "liturgy" or not, self-described followers of Christ have met cyclically since the earliest decades after the death of Jesus to perform a series of actions that, woven together, define the character and scope of a given Christian community. Their actions—reading, praying, teaching, singing, confessing, baptizing, breaking bread and drinking wine, among others—are acts of worship. These acts are how Christians, when gathered into groups of two or more, become "a people." How these actions are woven together, how greater weight is given to some elements at the expense of others, who performs what role in the proceedings, and according to what logic, not only make a community Christian but also mark what kind of Christian that community is. In the millennia separating the Last Supper described in the Synoptic Gospels and Paul's first letter to the Corinthians from the present day, performing these acts as a community has driven Christians to ask two burning questions: "What is this work?" and "Who are these people?" Disagreements over how to answer these questions have shaped the history of Christianity globally, proliferating heresies, schisms, and restoration movements, as Christians have realized that differing answers to the first question often lead to differing answers to the second.

Liturgical developments have interacted with linguistic differences, intellectual orientations, cultural practices, social formations, and political structures across and among empires. The liturgical practice of ordination (i.e., making priests), for example, laid the foundations for the political structure of social life, which over time mingled with the political order of the empire in both its centers, Rome and Constantinople (see also Heron 2018). Similarly, the emergence of a liturgical theology of marriage laid foundations for regulatory understandings of kinship and sexuality enshrined in the legal frameworks of modern states. Sacramental theologies around penance, confession, and absolution laid the foundations for patriarchal control over the disciplinary regimes that defined the boundaries of an ecclesial community, eventually influencing modern biopolitical and economic conceptions of sovereign power (Agamben 2011; Heron 2018; Mondzain 2005; Singh 2018). The sociopolitical consequences of these tightly knit theological themes of authority, kinship, and community unfolded gradually over centuries but followed different trajectories in the western and eastern reaches of the Roman Empire, well before the official schism between the Latin and Greek Churches in 1054 CE and the centuries' long process of severing communion between them.

This history shows a pattern of spatiotemporal disjuncture: meanings shift as theological conversations embed themselves in different contexts in dialogue with diverse social and political interlocutors, which, in turn, produce new social formations. And yet, questions endure across traditions as ecclesiastical authorities rework the thoughts of their predecessors and rivals both inside and outside the faith. Liturgical history is kaleidoscopically complex; some texts, traditions, and practices attest to efforts at disciplining and standardizing, while other texts, traditions, and practices attest to fragmentation and pluralization (see also Bradshaw 2002). These spatiotemporal discontinuities fertilize the ethical ground in which social change, religious transformation, and political revolution occur, as unfolding theological conversations create new contexts for liturgy to pose the moral and existential question, again and again: What is it to be a Christian?[6] As conversations and practices move through time and space, they are not transformed but transposed: conceptual terms are rearranged, discursive forms are lent new significance, and ecclesial structures are turned inside out.[7] In the process, the question *What is church?* becomes a sociopolitical, world-making utterance.

Liturgy and Power

Christian liturgy's complex relationship with broader sociopolitical formations, whether the Holy Roman Empire or the late Ottoman millet system, is in part an effect of global migration and conversion, and in part an effect of the generative problems of communication, translation, and reproduction. Such a problem spurred the earliest tensions between Greek-speaking and Syriac-speaking Christianities, leading to a bifurcation of Greek and Syriac liturgical worlds. From a Western Christian perspective, the Council of Chalcedon in 451 CE marked the end of the early Church's fragmentation and put to rest the rumblings of heresy throughout the empire, while from a West Syriac perspective, Chalcedon marks little more than the political achievement of the Sees of Rome and Constantinople in establishing imperial Greek and Latin Christianity's political dominance and cultural hegemony at the expense of the Sees of Alexandria, Antioch, and Jerusalem.

The Councils of Nicaea (325 CE), Constantinople (381 CE), Ephesus (431 CE), and Chalcedon (451 CE) were intended to settle a number of disputes among the leaders of what would later be distinguished as "Western" and "Eastern" Churches over the relationship between the divinity and humanity of Christ, the divinity of the Holy Spirit, and the relationship between imperial and ecclesiastical authorities. The Chalcedonian Definition,

the imperially approved Christological formulation, speaks of "a single concrete existence that both unites but holds distinct the human and divine
natures of Christ." Proponents of this definition won the debate at Chalcedon and became associated with the imperial Orthodox Church (with occasional interruptions by unsympathetic emperors), which centuries later led
to a schism between the Latin "West" and the Greek "East." The dissenters
(those now retroactively called "miaphysites"[8]) objected to this definition
because they felt it was too "dyophysite," that is, it emphasized the duality of
Christ's identity too much. Those who dissented, while not a unified faction,
came under pressure from imperial Byzantine authorities and, with the
crackdown instigated in the sixth century by emperors Justin I and Justinian
I, sought refuge with their followers in Persian and Arab lands. Anti-
Chalcedonian writing was forbidden and suppressed in Greek but could be
safely translated and circulated in Syriac and Coptic (Ashbrook Harvey 2018
[1990]). Over the course of centuries, through missions and the circulation
of texts in west, central, and South Asia, as well as East Africa, congregations
reading these texts formalized their hierarchical structures to become what
are now known as the Syriac Orthodox, Armenian Apostolic, Coptic Orthodox, Ethiopian Orthodox, and Eritrean Orthodox Churches, as well as the
Mar Thoma Syrian Church of Malabar and the Malankara Orthodox Syrian Church of south India.

    Yet there is little uniformity among these traditions today in how they
understand what was, precisely, at stake at the Council of Chalcedon and
what the theological grounds of their ecclesiological differences may be.
The diversity of views among these churches has been over-simplified and
anachronistically mislabeled by later Western Christian commentators,
who have tended to characterize the proceedings of the Council of Chalcedon in terms of a pre-existing Christological factionalism among "Nestorians" (a pejorative term for those congregations who rejected Ephesus
and eventually became known as East Syriacs, or the Church of the East),
"miaphysites" (the current preferred term for the Syriac Orthodox among
modern religious scholars), and Chalcedonians. This tendency reifies and
projects current ecclesiological divisions and interpretations onto a situation about which we understand very little, but which extant written sources
suggest that dynamic human relationships were perhaps as or more fundamentally at stake than clear-cut Christological dispute.

    Convened by the Byzantine Empress Pulcheria and her senator husband
Marcian, the Council of Chalcedon formally agreed that Christ's identity

was both fully divine and fully human while also insisting that his divinity was of the same essence as that of the divine Creator. This definition was credited to the writings of Bishop Cyril of Alexandria, although it represents a compromise between the competing theological traditions of Alexandria and Antioch, with influence also from Pope Leo I of Rome. These were not homogeneous Christological "factions" per se, but rather intellectual communities animated by diverse and dynamic currents of thought.[9]

Problems developed decades before Chalcedon in the so-called Nestorian Crisis, which fissured Byzantine relations with Syriac-speaking congregations in Persia and Mesopotamia and is thus considered the founding moment of the Church of the East's distinct ecclesiological identity. The "crisis" seems now to have been more a matter of Cyril of Alexandria's over-interpretation of a single, poorly thought-out comment by Nestorius, a theologian associated with the Catechetical School of Antioch, during a sermon given when he was briefly bishop of Constantinople, in which he spoke of Mary as the *Christotokos*, Mother of Christ, not the Mother of God. Going on the attack, Cyril took down not only Nestorius but also Nestorius's teacher, the widely beloved Theodore of Mopsuestia, and many fellow theologians associated with Antioch. The pugnacious Cyril, being Cyril, would not let it go, and so the crisis culminated in the Council of Ephesus (431 CE), at which *both* bishops were excommunicated. Cyril bribed his way back into office while Nestorius returned to his monastery, living just long enough to see his ideas, but not his name, vindicated by the Chalcedonian Definition twenty years later (Young 2010).

Yet widespread debate over the implications of Nestorius's sermon about Mary failed to die down. While the Trinitarian creed developed at the first council at Nicaea in 325 CE had defined the relationship between God the Son and God the Father as *homoousious* ("consubstantial," meaning of the same "essence"), questions lingered about the relationship between Christ's essence and his mother's essence, and how Mary should be addressed in liturgical prayer. The rub here is that much of Nestorius's writings appear to be not particularly un-orthodox, according to some twenty-first-century Chalcedonian theologians (e.g., Green 2004). This has been the claim of the Church of the East for centuries. By refusing to repudiate Nestorius's name, they were called by others "Nestorian," but they themselves consider this to be a pejorative term because the dyophysite Christology attributed *by* Cyril *to* Nestorius does not accurately convey what they themselves believe Christologically. East Syriac difference appears as such now, from a Western Christian perspective, only through the lens of a long history of cultural, political, and linguistic separation from Greek Christianity's sphere of influence.

The so-called miaphysite position is difficult to discern in all this, as the relationship between language and Christology is especially obscure in the case of the early formation of the Syriac Orthodox Church. In this early conciliar period, ordinary people in the eastern provinces spoke Syriac while Greek remained culturally and politically dominant. Many elite families from whom ecclesiastical leaders were drawn were bilingual in Greek and Syriac. After the Council of Chalcedon, it took well over a century for language and a sense of Christological difference to bind themselves to each other. Historian Fergus Millar (2013) details this gradual binding in the formation of a Syriac-language "orthodox" scribal tradition, in which the term "orthodox" is the only consistent term these writers used to distinguish themselves from supporters of Chalcedon. Millar writes, ". . . what we can see with absolute clarity, as is made possible by a mass of concrete evidence, is, first, the progressive transfer into Syriac of 'orthodox' works originally expressed in Greek; and, second, the creation in Syriac of a distinct historical tradition of the experiences of the 'orthodox' and their sufferings at the hands of their opponents" (Millar 2013, 90). This is a process that began in earnest in the late fifth century, decades after Chalcedon. Understanding this process, as well as acknowledging the limits of what we know about it, is crucial for grappling ethnographically with the theological materials that constitute the living tradition through which twenty-first-century Syriac Orthodox Christians make sense of their lives. My interlocutors, whether university-educated or not, take late antique and medieval Syriac patristic traditions deeply seriously and find creative ways to interpret and integrate them into their everyday lives.

A related issue for grappling with these ancient materials as sources of liturgical memory is that early Christian polemicists used a panoply of terms, expressions, and heresiological accusations against any bishops, priests, monks, monasteries, or congregations who rejected the legitimacy of Chalcedon. The diversity of these terms reflected the fact that those who opposed Chalcedon were not particularly unified. The commonly used pejorative "monophysite"—a heresiological expression meaning "one-nature"—appeared in the second half of the seventh century sporadically and then became a preferred Chalcedonian name for non-Chalcedonians after the arrival of Islam (Millar 2013, 51). Alternate terms like *akephalos* ("headless ones," i.e., dissidents) and "Those around Severus" were used variously in letters and histories recounting the life of Severus, Patriarch of Antioch from 512 to 518 CE. These references were possibly the earliest evidence that associated being "Syrian by birth" and "the sound of chanting the Psalms in the Syriac language" with accusations of "one-nature heresy" (Millar 2013, 54), even though Severus himself wrote exclusively in Greek. Similar terms of the sixth and seventh centuries included the *Diakrinomenoi* ("Those who hesitate") to refer to followers of Dioscorus of Alexandria, who had also been condemned at Chalcedon (Millar 2013, 53), and the term "Jacobite" to refer to followers of Jacob Baradaeus, who was Bishop of Edessa from 542 CE until his death in 578 CE.

The currently preferred term "miaphysite," meanwhile, came into use only in 1997 as a substitute for "monophysite," in recognition of the fact that many centuries of Chalcedonian polemic describing Syriac-speaking "orthodox" as believers in a "one-nature" heresy mischaracterizes their Christology entirely.[10] Until the late sixth century, neither the "Chalcedonian" nor "orthodox" (to follow Millar's terminology) factions constituted a stable, coherent, distinctive collective body. Rather, writer by writer, bishop by bishop, congregation by congregation, monastery by monastery, competing ecclesial structures peeled away from each other to then consolidate and form separate church hierarchies founded upon disparate attitudes toward the legitimacy of Chalcedon. From the 520s onward, there seemed to be a gradual shift from Greek-Syriac bilingual congregations loosely connected by their opposition to Chalcedon into a distinctly Syriac liturgical community. What little generalization one can make across the diversity of writings, writers, and their followers of this period seems to be a thread of concern for the legacy of Cyril of Alexandria and whether the Council of Chalcedon dealt with his Christological thought appropriately. While a vast corpus of early non-Chalcedonian writing in Greek *and* Syriac remains untranslated and unanalyzed, several foundational theologians of the "orthodox" tradition, like Severus of Antioch, articulate the crux of their theology with reference to Cyril's earlier writings. The gap between positions, to the extent that there is one, appears to be between an anti-Chalcedonian "orthodox" attachment to early Cyril and a pro-Chalcedonian "Orthodox" attachment to late Cyril.

The bishops assembled at Chalcedon relied on the later writings of St. Cyril to develop the Definition of Christ's nature, essence, and personhood. Later theologians and bishops of the "orthodox" tradition, like Severus of Antioch, meanwhile, cited St. Cyril's earlier writings to argue that the Chalcedonian bishops had strayed from Cyril's true meaning. Specifically, in an early letter, Cyril used the phrase *mia physis tou theou logou sesarkomene* ("one enfleshed nature [*physis*] of God the Word"), arguing *against* "the Syrians" of the School of Antioch ("the Syrians" seeming in this case to mark a regional identity rather than a linguistic or Christological one). With the term *mia physis*, Cyril was not designating a communal position or doctrine but was instead describing "a metaphysical mystery of a vast cosmic order having taken place in the coming of the Word into history by means of an incarnation as a Man" (McGuckin 2017, 38). As the grammatically feminine Greek word for "one," *mia*, here modifies *physis*, or "nature," in contradistinction to what some might consider the "strong" masculine formulation of the Chalcedonian Definition (Millar 2013, 52). However—and this is the crucial point—in later writings, Cyril shifted from using the word *physis* ("nature") to *hypostasis* ("being" / "essence" / "substance") to refer to "the underlying reality of a thing" (McGuckin 2017, 38). Early Cyril's *physis*, here, is semantically equivalent to late Cyril's *hypostasis*. Describing Severus of Antioch and his followers as believers in Christ's one nature, then, is to accuse Cyril of Alexandria himself of monophysitism.

These early debates matter ethnographically because they are the authoritative ground upon which twenty-first-century efforts to define and distinguish boundaries among traditions are staked, and because Christological discourse speaks to pressing existential questions across traditions. According to womanist theologian Eboni Marshall Turman (2013), what is essential about the Chalcedonian Definition is the way it resolves the problem of the temporality and materiality of personhood—that is, the question of the relationship among history, identity, and embodiment posed by the birth, life, death, and resurrection of Jesus Christ—by allowing a *both/and* approach to complex identities. The Chalcedonian Definition affirms that a human is defined by more than what happens to her in her life because Jesus is defined by more than what happened to him living on Earth. In Cyrillian Christology, first, the word "physis," and then the word "hypostasis," conveys this integration of different parts into a cosmic, spiritually significant wholeness. Gender and other socially produced traces of a human's life history on Earth, like culture, race, ethnicity, and language, are central questions for Incarnational theology.

Yet, even though no faction at Chalcedon called themselves miaphysite, the term has become a commonplace self-designation among non-

Chalcedonian Orthodox Churches in the twentieth and twenty-first centuries, as church leaders seek ecumenical reconciliation by finding common kinship through the texts of patristic figures like St. Cyril (they are called Church "Fathers" for a reason). The grammatical gender of the word *mia* suggests a carefully modulated emphasis on *oneness* that falls just short of calling Syriac Orthodox Christians monophysites (Millar 2013, 52), who, as McGuckin wryly observes, "have largely existed between the covers of heresiology books" (2017, 33). In Syriac, *physis* is usually translated as *kyono*, while *hypostasis* is usually translated as *qnomo*. Even though these terms do not carry the same shades of meaning in Syriac as they do in Greek, today the Syriac Orthodox Church delineates how these terms figure into the Church's application of Trinitarian orthodoxy:

> The three being of one Essence, of one Godhead, have one Will, one Work, and one Lordship. The special aspect of the First Person is His Fatherhood, that of the Second Person His Sonship, and that of the Third Person His Procession.
>
> The Syriac Orthodox Church believes in the mystery of Incarnation. That is, the Only Son of God, the Second Person of the Holy Trinity, took to Himself a body and became man. It further believes that at the time of Annunciation, when the Angel Gabriel was sent to the Virgin Mary, the Holy Spirit came upon her and cleansed her of all natural impurity, filling her with His grace. Then the Only Son of God came down and entered her immaculate womb, and took to Himself a body through her, thus becoming a perfect Man with a perfect Soul. After nine months, He was born of her and her virginity was maintained contrary to the laws of nature. It further believes that His true Godhead and His true Manhood were in Him essentially united, He being one Lord and one Son, and that after the union took place in Him, He had but one Nature Incarnate, was one Person, had one Will and one Work. This union is marked by being a natural union of persons, free of all separateness, intermixture, confusion, mingling, change and transformation. (Source: https://www.soc-wus.org/ourchurch/ourfaith.htm)

The church's statement highlights how Christ's personhood matters for understanding his relationship with his mother, Mary, who, in Syriac, is addressed as *yoldath aloho*, the Godbearer. These theological questions are not mere abstruse wrangling over grammar. They are corporate efforts to grapple with the question of humanity's kinship with the divine and what the implications of such kinship might be for identity, authority, and the temporality of Incarnation; in other words, for history. If Mary is only the mother of the human Jesus, who is of a separate substance from the second Person of the Godhead, then the Son is fragmented and subordinate to the Divinity of God, which would suggest that there was a time when God the Son was not, which means that either Christ was *only* human, or that there is more than one God, which would be, at least from the perspective of conceptually precise Greek speakers, the logical collapse of either Christ's claim to being the Messiah or of the monotheistic claim entirely.

Settling these questions bore implications for understanding Christ's place in liturgical prayer, as different traditions conceptualized his role and the nature of human-divine relatedness differently. Syriac Orthodox tradition lays a claim to the integrated wholeness expressed in Cyril's description of *mia physis*. One consequence of this is that certain elements of liturgical prayer, such as the *anamnesis*, the commemorative statement within the Eucharistic prayer, address the Incarnate Christ's divinity directly, rather than "to God *through* our Lord Jesus Christ" as is more common in Latin traditions. In Latin Christianity, greater emphasis on Christ's humanity frequently positions him in the role of mediator between the created world and the First Person of the Godhead. In Syriac tradition, however, "Christ is the co-receiver of the prayers along with the Father and the Holy Spirit" (Varghese 2008, 111). This emphasis on Christ's divinity means he does not occupy the same kind of mediating space between visible creation and invisible creator. Rather than Christ serving as a bridge across a vast chasm of separation between human and God, it is Mary who comes more frequently to the fore, as her complex maternal relation to Christ's divinity becomes an icon of the created world's immanent relation with the Creator, a relationship of mutuality conveyed through the Syriac concept of ʾiḥidoyutho.

ʾIḥidoyutho as Christological Icon

ʾIḥidoyutho has been an important Christological concept for Syriac Christians since St. Ephrem and carries within it a host of meanings. This concept is in no way at odds with Cyril's thought, nor does it signify a reduction of Christ's complex divinity and humanity. Rather than denoting an individual, 'iḥidoyutho evokes a deep relationality—a singleness of mind, heart, and purpose in the disciple's relationship to the community. In Syriac-speaking circles of the first through seventh centuries, echoes of Jewish discourses on sexual and social discipline appeared in connection to emerging Christian ascetic practices, linking multiple connotations of the word "singleness" to Christ (Brown 2008, 41). This "singleness" was central to the identity of the Bnoth Qyomo, the Daughters of the Covenant, whom my research participants look to as the precursor to their liturgical revival.[11] Both the words *qyomo* and *'iḥidoyutho* communicate the notion of a "covenant"—a holy pact between humans and the divine defining the faithful as God's chosen people. It conveys the holiness of discipleship, and it designates singleness in relation to family and marriage (as in Christ the Only-Begotten Son). It evokes the singleness of mind, heart, and purpose appropriate to a spiritually mature disciple, and it evokes that disciple's oneness, in the sense of "unity," with Christ. In embodying 'iḥidoyutho, one may become an *'iḥidoyo*, a person who follows and imitates Christ. The 'Iḥidoyo *is* the Christ, the first Icon, whose humanity is iconic of his divinity, and the disciple becomes an 'iḥidoyo by imitating Christ in service to community. Running through classical Syriac writings on 'iḥidoyo and qyomo is an understanding of the theological significance of sexuality for dedicated discipleship (Kathanar Koonammakkal 2010 [1999]; see also Griffith 1991). For late antique Syriac-speaking congregations, the soteriological function of such a single life was delegated to the Bnoth and Bnay Qyomo, who served the urban congregations in which they remained socially embedded despite their dedicated celibacy. Thus, the "singleness" of this Christological concept of 'iḥidoyo encompasses the sociality and relationality of family and community. This is a Christological discourse that took shape *through* and *as* a liturgical, poetic, aesthetic, ethical, and relational communal practice and continues to be reflected in the invisible labor of women like my friend Elizabeta.

Thus, in my view, Syriac Orthodox tradition is less defined by a relationship to any clear-cut Christological faction at Chalcedon than by a long-standing linguistic, cultural, epistemic, and practical orientation toward *thinking* and *doing* theology. What we understand of the scribal tradition of the third through eighth centuries supports the view that Syriac-speaking Christians' emergent self-definition in opposition to Chalcedon was inflamed more by deeper problems of incommensurability among languages, literary traditions, and the publics these languages and literatures brought into being, than by disagreement about whether Christ's personhood is comprised of precisely one nature or two (Amar 2011; Mellon St. Laurent 2015; Palmer 2015; ter Haar Romeny et al. 2010). This is not to say that Christological differences do not matter to ecclesiology, nor that ecclesiastical hierarchs of later centuries did not rely on the authority of their precursors' writings to legitimize boundaries among their congregations. Rather, this is to say that predominantly Syriac-speaking Christians had different practices and forms of celebrating liturgy than predominantly Greek-speaking Christians before and during the centuries of Christological controversy—indeed, from the very start of Christianity—and these practices and forms of liturgy did more to shape communal subjects than the Christological disputes of bilingual ecclesiastical elites. These practices and forms are not identical to current practices and forms, but their auratic presences are transmitted through textual traces and sonic echoes, shaping liturgical memory in the space between.

Imperial Vicissitudes

Falling out with Byzantine imperial authority was not the only major sociopolitical situation to leave a mark on Syriac Orthodox liturgical memory. For decades after Chalcedon, many Syriac-speaking Christians sought refuge from Byzantine persecution in the Persian Empire for similar reasons as those Syriac-speaking congregations who later welcomed Arab Muslim caliphs in formerly Byzantine lands. As politically subordinate yet protected People of the Book, Syriac Christians were relatively safer in the caliphate than in the Byzantine Empire. In the early medieval period, Syriac Christian ecclesial communities flourished in Baghdad, Alexandria, and other urban centers of Islamic civilization, while their scribal elites engaged in mutually generative dialogues with Muslim theologians and became an important part of cultural and political life (Baum and Winkler 2003; Griffith 2006; Wood 2013). Yet spatiotemporal disjunctures are evident in textual and archaeological studies of this period as well, as in the writings of Patriarch Michael the Syrian (d. 1199), a "Jacobite" Patriarch who was himself interested in seeking continuities with a pre-Christian past to resolve certain political and theological tensions of his own time. It was Patriarch Michael who decided that whoever spoke Aramaic was a forefather of his, whether that be the ancient Assyrians or the ancient Aramaeans, in a time when political alliances were becoming as important as theological differences in producing communal boundaries (ter Haar Romeny 2010, 50).

In contrast, Bar ʿEbroyo, a famed and still-much-loved thirteenth-century Syriac Orthodox bishop and polymath, wrote ecclesiastical histories modeled off Patriarch Michael's within the Abbasid and then the Mughal Empire. In his new imperial context, Bar ʿEbroyo dropped Patriarch Michael's explicit references to the ancient Aramaeans. Instead, he used terms like "ancient Syrians" (*Suryoye ʿatiqe*), "our people" (*ʿamo dilan*), and "our faithful" (*mhaymne dilan*) to establish a historical precedence for a local "eastern" Jacobite Christian liturgical identity within the bounds of the former Abbasid Empire, as he worked to make his congregations legible to new rulers. Bar ʿEbroyo's historical narrative linked the Syriac Orthodox to the political and social legibility of the erstwhile influential Church of the East, even as he repudiated it for its alleged two-nature Christology (Weltecke 2016, 310–323). Such historicizing maneuvers entailed constructing a spatiotemporal link with specific pasts in specific places and rejecting theological language perceived as heretical. Both the Assyrian Empire and the ancient Aramaean city-states furnished late antique and medieval Syriac Christians with ancestral narratives that could position them as linguistically, territorially, or theologically legible to more powerful audiences. Aramaean ancestry offered a spatial orientation toward Syria in the "West," where Aramaic-speaking city-states like Antioch and Edessa were among the very first converts to Christianity, while Assyrian ancestry offered a spatial orientation toward Mesopotamia in the "East" to the cities of Nineveh, Takrit, Baghdad, and Celeucia-Ctesiphon. The reason *why* such spatiotemporal maneuvers had any purchase in the first place had to do with the way imperial Christian ecclesiastical writers like fourth-century historian Eusebius of Caesarea had already established a textual tradition for incorporating pre-Christian peoples and empires into linear, chronological narratives serving the self-image of the Byzantine state (Grafton and Williams 2008). Far from being a uniquely secular modern way of constituting national identities and nationalist discourses (cf. Asad 2003, 193–194), we can discern in these histories how the linear textualization of world history became a hegemonic mode of either authorizing or delegitimizing minoritarian positions within imperial domains. This mode of textualization obscured the far more complex social realities of persistent spatiotemporal disjuncture, as ordinary people married, migrated, and spoke multiple languages across doctrinal and political boundaries.

Thus, there are certain structuring omissions in the testimony of ancient and medieval scribal elites evident in the gaps between the ecclesiastical and world histories of the likes of Patriarch Michael and Bar ʿEbroyo on the one hand, and the material evidence provided by artistic and archaeological records, on the other hand. Ecclesiastical authorities wrote of adherence to the West Syriac Rite as if it operated as a stable, continuous, communal boundary in their sociopolitical worlds. Their writings provided a material thread of liturgical memory for later generations to link up with, but the solidity of their claims was not necessarily mirrored in other media forms of the same period, as attested in this account of medieval interreligious material culture found throughout Syria and Mesopotamia:

> The wall paintings [in churches and monasteries] in the area of present-day Syria and Lebanon show intensive contact between Orthodox, Maronites, and Syriac Orthodox, whereas there are also Crusader and Muslim influences. And neither the style nor the iconography of the art of Mosul suggests that Christians and Muslims had different artistic traditions. [. . .] [T]he reality of everyday life in the small towns of the Middle East necessitated contacts between the various communities to a much higher level than the keepers of the tradition, the clergy, may have wanted. (ter Haar Romeny et al. 2010, 51)

Historical texts speak to carefully policed boundaries between traditions, which are in turn contradicted by the evidence provided by visual culture. How do we interpret such contradictions and their significance to the "aesthetic formation" and reproduction of Syriac Orthodoxy? What these contradictions suggest to me is that sensory cultures are fluid and porous; what happens in one sensory register may or may not be reflected and reinforced in another. Aesthetic practices become sites of reproductive power only in dialogical tension with broader regimes of recognition and, as I explain in the next chapter, there were specific sociopolitical reasons that the visual was deprioritized in Syriac Orthodoxy while the textual and the sonic developed a special affinity in articulating West Syriac distinctiveness. The key point, for now, is that reproducing human relations can be messy, and we can only discern so much from the evidence offered up by the past. My research participants work with what they have.

Ottoman Bureaucracy, European Imperialism, and the Rise of the "Ethnonational" Idea

We know very little about Syriac Christianity in the transition from the medieval caliphates to the early Ottoman Empire. What we do know is that under the Ottoman *millet* system, differences among religious traditions were politicized in new ways. Within a hierarchical system of Islamic supremacy, Muslims, Christians, and Jews were permitted separate courts to adjudicate within the realm of personal law. Personal law covered matters to do with marriage and family, and thus with gender and kinship. In this imperial regime, to be a Christian ecclesial community was to be a political entity with legal rights and responsibilities; they were subordinate but also protected (Masters 2001; Quataert 2005). While differences among Muslim traditions were treated as largely equivalent by the ruling regime, Christians received a relatively nuanced degree of political recognition for their ecclesiological distinctions up to a point. Churches who qualified for millet status were large and visible; they included, for example, the Greek Orthodox Church. Yet Syriac Christians were never numerous enough to constitute a millet of their own until 1883 when, under pressure from Western Christian colonial powers, the Ottoman state designated the "Ancient *Süryânî*" pillar (Atto 2011, 86). Before 1883, "Jacobite" West Syriac Christians were represented by the Armenian Patriarchate or were otherwise periodically classified through the Ottoman bureaucratic concept of *ṭāʾifa*. This minor category indicated a group that was smaller than a millet; at times, it could mean a religious group or sect. There were still other times when a ṭāʾifa was not even a religious community; it could be any kind of communal organization—blacksmiths' guild, for example. Archival evidence suggests that in some times and places in the Ottoman Empire, West Syriac and East Syriac Christian communities shared the same ṭāʾifa, while in other times and places, they did not (Masters 2001, 61–65). The millet system, more of an ad hoc set of administrative tactics than a "system" per se, was flexible, differentially distributed across the empire, and frequently reconfigured in response to shifting political conditions on the ground.

From the sixteenth century on, these on-the-ground conditions were increasingly destabilized by the rise of European imperial power. The seeds of an entirely new genre of imperial vicissitude were sown when the Ottoman Empire, at the height of its power, bestowed a special diplomatic status, known as the Capitulations, on certain favored trading partners like

France and the Italian city-states. A capitulation created a special exempt status for Ottoman Catholics. Initially created to protect Christian pilgrims traveling to holy sites, the capitulatory system gradually expanded to provide protection for an extensive network of French Catholic missions, orders, and missionaries throughout Ottoman lands. Capitulatory status exempted Catholic Christians living in Ottoman lands from taxes and customs duties. In this period, from the seventeenth to the eighteenth century, a number of West and East Syriac Rite congregations came into communion with Rome while maintaining their traditional liturgical practices and languages and developing their own ecclesiastical hierarchies. These congregations became the Syriac Catholic (branching off the West Syriac Rite) and Chaldean (branching off the East Syriac Rite) churches. As the Ottoman state gradually weakened and European imperial powers strengthened, the capitulatory system came to be seen as a growing threat to Ottoman sovereignty. In 1673, Sultan Mehmet IV granted Louis XIV guardianship of the Church of the Holy Sepulcher (Chatty 2010, 49). By the eighteenth century, other European nations had also negotiated their own capitulations, and by the nineteenth century, non-Muslim Ottoman subjects could apply, if they had sufficient money and the right networks, for a certificate of exemption from Ottoman taxes, customs, and courts. The Capitulations were unpopular among Ottoman Muslim producers and tradesmen. In regions and cities where the system enriched local Christians at the expense of their Muslim neighbors, a class divide emerged that belied the theopolitical hierarchy of the Ottoman Muslim state, creating crosscurrents of economic tension and political resentment across religious lines (see Chatty 2010; McCarthy 2001; Robson 2016, 2017; Makdisi 2019).

In the nineteenth century, the Ottoman government was aware of its weakening power, the growing divisions among its subjects, and a globally circulating discourse of equal citizenship and national belonging. Between 1839 and 1876, Ottoman officials attempted to transform the state's administrative service, educational system, economy, public health, and all aspects of public life (Chatty 2010). Known as the Tanzimat Reforms, these transformations attempted to redefine Ottomanism as a source of public identity and belonging across the empire that would guarantee equality before the law regardless of religious identity. From the perspective of most historians, the Tanzimat Reforms ultimately failed because they were overwhelmed by too many obstacles coming from too many different directions. From the corrosive effects of European imperialism and missionary influence to the regional instabilities of administrative control in the outer reaches of the empire to the Orthodox Patriarchs who did not want to lose their long-standing political status or social clout to European Catholics to the rise of ethnonationalist separatist violence, the Tanzimat Reforms were for many Ottoman subjects too little too late, and for others, entirely unwelcome (Chatty 2010; see also Makdisi 2019).

Perhaps most damage to the new Ottoman project was done by the Russian Empire, who, in addition to funding the Greek, Bulgarian, and Serbian wars, sought to expand its own imperial borders in regions that continue to be disputed today, initiating an era in the nineteenth and twentieth centuries when mass dispossession and population expulsion became the standard international response to disputes over territorial sovereignty.[12] Even as peasant economies were starting to stabilize under the Tanzimat Reforms, ethnonationalist sentiment spread, albeit unevenly, leading to internal divisions within many Christian groups and, ultimately, very different historical trajectories in various parts of the empire. In the northern part of the empire, the Balkan Wars of Independence led to an extended period of intense warfare, forced migration, and mass death among Muslim *and* Christian populations that bled into Anatolia and the formation of the modern Turkish state. The transition from Ottoman Empire to modern state was punctuated by the end of World War I and a systematically planned genocide against Anatolian Armenians and Assyrian/Aramaean/Syriac Christians. The southern, Arabic-speaking part of the empire, on the other hand, was spared the homogenizing violence of ethnonationalist separatism and its extreme imperialist backlash, giving rise to a pan-Arab nationalism that could ostensibly embrace Muslim, Christian, Jewish, and other religious differences within its Arabic-speaking populations (Makdisi 2019). Similarly, the urban-rural divide meant that ideas circulating among Ottoman Christian elites in cities within the imperial core failed to penetrate rural areas like Tur Abdin and the borderlands of the Hakkari Mountains, where Kurdish and Assyrian tribes had coexisted (although not always peacefully) within their own semi-autonomous political framework for centuries (Robson 2017).

In the late nineteenth and early twentieth centuries, evangelical European Christian missionizing lit a fire among Assyrian communities in the areas around Lake Urmia, Van, and the Hakkari Mountains in the borderlands between the Ottoman and Persian Empires. American Protestant missionaries, in particular, influenced Assyrian adherents of the East

Syriac Rite in northwest Iran during the nineteenth and twentieth centuries (Becker 2015). In the missionary encounter, an Assyrian nationalist printed public sphere emerged in dialogical tension with Protestant Christian epistemological reforms. By promoting a "purer" form of Christianity, Protestant reformers insisted upon conceptual distinctions between religious, ethnic, and national identity, distinctions which proved more persuasive among East Syriac communities in Iran and Iraq than among West Syriac Christians in Tur Abdin. This Assyrian public sphere continues to operate globally in publications like the Assyrian International News Agency and the Assyrian Star, reproducing links between Assyrian ethnonationalism and an ecumenical vision of Syriac Christian unity that encompasses West and East Syriac Rites, as well as Syriac Catholic, Chaldean, and Maronite Churches. Yet twenty-first-century diasporic Syriac Orthodox participation in this global public sphere is partial at best, as the ecumenicism of this Assyrian political orientation makes those Syriac Orthodox Christians who understand the West Syriac Rite to operate as an ethnic boundary deeply uncomfortable, if not outright angry. To quote my Syriac teacher Peter, a devoted Aramaean, who often stewed despondently on the fact that one of his musical and linguistic heroes of the early nationalist period, Naum Faik, identified as Assyrian: "You must be careful, Sarah! If you speak of being Assyrian to an Aramaean, you might get hit!"

Early Syriac Orthodox participation in the rise of ethnonationalist discourse in the late Ottoman period was complex, and historians dispute how to interpret the available evidence heavily. By the late nineteenth century, while Western Christian missionaries were insisting upon clear-cut distinctions between "religion" and "ethnicity" in Iran, the already geographically dispersed Syriac Orthodox were reinterpreting these notions and weaving them into complex local configurations of sociopolitical and liturgical identity.[13] Only after meeting in the North American diaspora, according to historian Aryo Makko, did Ottoman and Persian adherents of each branch of the Syriac liturgical tradition come to think of *each other* as *also* Assyrian—that is, until Patriarch Barsoum had to back out of the arrangement in the 1930s out of a reasonable fear for the Patriarchate's safety in French Mandate Syria and the regionally destabilizing effects of the 1932 Massacre of Simele[14] in Iraq, instructing Syriac Orthodox Christians throughout the global diaspora not to think of themselves as Assyrian, but as Aramaean.

While Assyrian self-ascription was evident among some villages in the Syriac Orthodox heartland of southern and eastern Turkey, according to Assyrian historian Sargon Donabed, even in areas that had never encountered Western missionaries or British archaeologists, and although the famed Assyrian nationalist Naum Faik was a Syriac Orthodox Christian of Tur Abdin, most ordinary Süryânî villagers in Anatolia were rarely exposed to Assyrian nationalist writings, and so an Assyrian ethnonationalist political imaginary never fully took hold.[15]

Some commentators have insisted that Aramaeanism is a secularist artifact concocted as a response to the equally secularist artifact of Assyrianism, invented by British archaeologists and Assyriologists working on Assyrian ruins in the Plains of Nineveh in northern Iraq, and leveraged by Western colonial powers to sabotage anti-colonial, pan-Arab nationalism. The picture is, of course, far more complicated: as we have seen, evidence of conflicting claims to Assyrian and Aramaean ancestral lineage among Syriac Christians goes back centuries and reflects complex, ongoing reconfigurations of Syriac liturgical tradition in relation to other modalities of relatedness either authorized or undermined by more powerful political authorities, whether that of the Byzantines, the Sassanids, the Abbasids, the Ottomans, or modern secularist nation-states. For Arabic- or Turkish-speaking Suryoye, the "ethno" part of ethnoreligious identity is a more difficult proposition than for neo-Aramaic speakers, but not impossible, as I will show in later chapters. For the ancestors of the Syriac Orthodox of Tur Abdin, now heavily represented in the Dutch-Syriac diaspora, it is conceivable that Assyrian ethnonationalism presented a particular danger, given that in the bloody aftermath of the Balkan Wars, the formerly Ottoman military officers who founded the modern state of Turkey violently enforced Kemalism, a form of secularism that, at many points in the twentieth century, set out to extinguish visible signs of ethnoreligious or ethnonationalist difference among its non-Turkish speaking subjects, sometimes with complex and contradictory effects on minority self-understandings (Atto 2011; Erol 2015; see also Sheklian 2017; Stokes 1994; Tambar 2014).[16]

Reproducing Disjuncture

One of the enduring legacies of this history of spatiotemporal discontinuity and conceptual translation is the tension that now wracks the Syriac Orthodox diaspora with a painful, inward-focused ethnic politics, which

materializes in a widespread disagreement over the distinction and relationship between the Greek-derived terms *ethnos,* a people, and *ekklesia,* a
church. As I have argued elsewhere (Bakker Kellogg 2019), the liturgy of
the West Syriac Rite produces the Syriac *'amo,* the people, through several
different interwoven modalities often translated into English as "religion."
One such modality, for example, is *tawditho,* the Syriac rendering of the
Hebrew word *todah,* which means confession, praise, thanksgiving, and
doctrine, and is always understood as a relational, performative utterance
toward the Divine. *Deḥlo,* which renders *abodah* from the Hebrew Bible,
captures the affective dimensions of the liturgy by conveying the sense of
fear and awe in worship. *Qurbono,* the word my research participants most
often used for the weekly Sunday morning liturgy, denotes the dimension
of offering, oblation, or gift-giving, as an act of drawing near to the Divine. All these words are saturated with the notion of *rozo,* literally translated from the Greek *mysterion,* "mystery," but weighted with a distinct
understanding of the relationship between materiality and signification.
Rozo is simultaneously a materialization *and* a symbolization of liturgical practice as partaking of the mystery of Incarnation (Varghese 2004,
37–38). The liturgy teaches theology to the people while also incorporating them into the Body of Christ. My research participants work with a
theological understanding of the liturgical production of the Church in
the world as an expression of the Incarnation. Their service is, in the words
of Father Varghese, "a relationship based on love and trust." It is intimate,
affective, moral, and generative: as sonic icons, their voices materialize their
irreducible relationship with the Divine and, in the process, generate an
irreducible relationship with those assembled.

   A parallel term, *'umtho,* often translated as "nation," is in some ways a
more politicized and secularized conception of "the people" than the *'amo,*
but my research participants disagreed with each other on the meanings,
boundaries, and political implications of these words, and some would use
these terms interchangeably. For my Syriac teacher Peter, the *'umtho* was
coterminous with the *'amo.* For him, *'amo* meant "Suryoyo" and *'umtho*
meant "Oromoyo (Aramaean)," and both were defined by the sacredness
of the Aramaic language—"the language God speaks," he told me. As far
as he was concerned, the *'umtho* was only different from the *'amo* inasmuch as the word carried a connotation of mission: the *'umtho* is that dimension of the *'amo* which summons nationalist feeling and demands
learning and teaching classical Syriac as a vital mode of nation-building

across the diaspora. This is even though, in his usage, both words referred to the same set of relations and shared the same boundary. The emphasis, for him, was on being an ʾumthonoyo, someone who works fervently, in a manner comparable to a nineteenth-century nationalist, on behalf of the people. My friend Elizabeta, on the other hand, described the ʿamo and the ʾumtho as fundamentally different entities. The ʿamo, she told me, refers to being Suryoyo. The ʿamo resides inside of church walls, and while this makes her who she is culturally, religiously, and ethnically, it nonetheless is ontologically distinct from the ʾumtho. For Elizabeta, the ʾumtho was both broader and more political than the ʿamo. Only much later, after my fieldwork ended, did she begin to use language (at least around me) suggesting that she equated the ʾumtho with Assyrian nationhood. Yet despite their difference of opinion regarding the meaning and boundaries of the word ʾumtho, Peter and Elizabeta both believed that the ʿamo came first, conceptually and experientially, because it was made in and through participation in the Syriac Orthodox Church. Without liturgical kinship, there would be no ʿamo to make public as an ʾumtho.

Saving "Our Faithful"

These liturgical developments compel serious consideration of spatiotemporal discontinuity and its relationship with gender as a characteristic feature of living at the margins of empire. Spatiotemporal discontinuity has both theological and political implications for Syriac Christians living in the twenty-first-century global diaspora. In Euro-American social scientific thought, the very premise of "identity" is based on presumptions of spatiotemporal continuity. That is to say, for a collective identity to be politically salient in secular modernity, for a group to make legitimate claims to a degree of political autonomy or self-determination, they must prove a continuous, long-term relationship—preferably one of residence—with a particular place. This kind of coherence and continuity is a normative ideal but, in practice, is not particularly true for *anyone, anywhere.* The tension here for any claim to indigeneity in the Middle East is the role played by early theopolitical controversies in producing mass phenomena of forced migration, conversion, and a host of imperial vicissitudes across centuries, if not millennia.

These disjointed histories play out in the twenty first century diaspora in how Peter, Elizabeta, and the young women I will describe in the upcoming chapters practice liturgical memory. These historical disjunctures accrue layers of meaning in how they are narrated and transmitted. What matters is which monks, priests, liturgical teachers, fathers, and uncles these historical narratives and orientations were learned from because the distribution of these narratives throughout the diaspora bear a complex relationship to the global distribution of kinship networks, which are themselves intertwined with the ritual power of the ecclesiastical institution to form kin relations. But this history of spatiotemporal disjuncture fractures Syriac Orthodox liturgical memory in a way that manifests in a fraught disagreement among Syriac Orthodox Christians themselves about whether they are, in terms secularist audiences can understand, ethnically Aramaean, part of the Assyrian nation, or "just Suryoyo—just Christian," as the mother at the monastery summer school insisted in Chapter 1.

Epistemologically, these disjunctures are a problem for secularist social scientists who reproduce claims about the tradition from a single standpoint within it, as in the claim that Syriac liturgical song is a straightforward folkloric expression of ethnonational identity or that Assyrians are "secular" while Aramaeans are "pious" (as it happens, I know many deeply pious Assyrians, and plenty of Aramaeans who are less so). Situating such claims within the broader history of spatiotemporal disjuncture helps make sense of the work these claims do. For my research participants, adopting these historical narratives is more about reproducing the moral and affective relationships that generated a young Syriac Orthodox person's political subjectivity than it is about any provable genetic link to ancient Assyria or the Aram city-states. Elizabeta and Mariane's brother-in-law put the matter vividly during one Sunday afternoon visit with the family when he joked disdainfully (accompanying his words with a rude gesture representing male genitalia): "*Who cares?!* No one *knows whose [—] their ancestors actually came out of!*"

What Elizabeta and her peers are trying to "save," then, is not a biologically essentialist notion of ethnonational identity but a moral community that takes shape around their parish's liturgical memories and the authorizing discourses that situate their parish among broader kinship networks. This is evident, for example, in the relationship between the sisters Elizabeta and Mariane and their paternal cousin, Marta, also a choir leader at another parish as well as a globally prominent Aramaean activist and one of the central figures of the next chapter. Despite their family connection, they disagreed on the question of whether their liturgical practice is linked narrowly to the history of the West Syriac Rite or to a broader ecumenical vision of Assyrian unity across (ostensible) Christological divisions separating East and West Syriac traditions.

Elizabeta and Mariane lived in Enschede and saw their cousin Marta's Aramaean activism as odd for someone from their extended family network. Although they were all from Tur Abdin, and their fathers and uncles had been trained to perform the liturgy as children in the monastery of Mor Gabriel, Marta's nuclear family had experienced a great deal of hardship after moving to the Netherlands. Marta had grown up somewhat distantly from her paternal kin and was absorbed socially, in school and at church, into her co-director Rebekah's kinship network, an influential family in local parish affairs. Learning to sing the liturgy from Rebekah's uncle as a child, Marta adopted the same parish-bound sense of "our village, our church, our sound" that most of my research participants describe as a distinct feature of Syriac Orthodox socioreligious life. The right, authentic sound, as well as the right, authentic historical narrative, is defined situationally in terms of who taught you, even if you know full well that what your teacher taught you is not quite what his teacher taught him. So even though Marta and Elizabeta are related to each other, and they recognize the official significance of paternal cousin relationships (i.e., traditionally, paternal cousins may not marry each other, while maternal cousins may), they see their primary sense of affiliation in terms of parish-bound practices of liturgical memory and community: their liturgical teachers, their deacons, and their priest.

Marta's strong identification with Aramaeanism was deeply enmeshed in the affective and moral entailments of mastering the liturgy of the West Syriac Rite in the style of her parish malphono, Rebekah's uncle, even as this relationship provides the foundation for the formal innovations I describe in the next chapter. Meanwhile, Mariane and Elizabeta identified as *just Suryoyo*—although in the years since my primary phase of fieldwork was completed, Elizabeta is increasingly inclined to identify herself publicly as Assyrian. This reflects a nested, situationally defined but powerfully generative understanding of the historical, political, and social identity of the Syriac Orthodox as "our faithful," an understanding that echoes the spatiotemporally delimited sense that Bar 'Ebroyo used it to refer to the "eastern" Syriac Orthodox of thirteenth-century Takrit. When Marta and her peers seek political recognition to "save" (in order to reproduce) Syriac Orthodoxy, what they are trying to make legible is the ethical and affective bond with the ecclesiastical authorities who authorize the spatiotemporal boundaries of their affiliations—even when these authorities do not fully grasp or appreciate their labor.

Liturgical Activism

Their voices working as sonic icons, the Daughters of the Covenant in antiquity were a crucial site of reproductive power, bridging and strengthening relations between the ecclesiastical institution and the broader urban communities they served until, at some point in the medieval period, they did not. The last extant reference to Syriac-singing deaconesses that I am aware of is an untranslated thirteenth-century text by Bar 'Ebroyo (Weltecke personal communication). We do not know what happened to them, when they disappeared, or precisely why, but their omission from late medieval and early modern liturgical memory is without question a function of Christian empire's—and later, Islamic empire's—power to recast other histories into its own image.

Two key premises are at stake in this story of the structuring omissions of liturgical memory. The first premise is that behind hegemonic theorizations of personhood lies the might of empires. The second premise is a history of debate over the proper dispensation of ritual and political power. According to literary theorist Gil Anidjar (2014), the symbolic-ontic status of blood in Christian sacramental thought and practice, grounded in imperial understandings of Christ's personhood and Incarnation, is responsible for the history of national violence, colonial subjugation, racist exclusion, and genocidal slaughter that has shaped so much of European Christianity's relationship with the rest of the planet. This violent relation is dictated, he suggests, by the very nature of the relatedness that constitutes Christian communities as Christian. This is a view worth taking seriously; *and* it coexists awkwardly with its own counterpoint—the view of womanist theologians like Eboni Marshall Turman (2013) who see within Chalcedonian Christology the hermeneutic tools to integrate the fragmentation of identity and embodied difference that underlie persistent problems of misogyny and racism in Western Christianity. These two opposing perspectives emerge from the open interpretive space at the center of Christological thought and materialize in the disjunctures of liturgical history: to conceive of irreducible relatedness in terms of likeness to the Divine Family, whose substance and personhood are Three-In-One, does not inevitably lead to any one configuration of political authority or belonging.

These histories—of translational incommensurability, of interreligious dialogue, of competing imperial horizons, and of gendered bodily practice and reproductive power—make this interpretive open space, this structuring omission within liturgical memory, an endlessly renewable resource for experimentation. It is this final point—the history of gendered bodily practice and reproductive power—that accounts for why Elizabeta was so reluctant to put herself forward as a malphonitho, and why Peter became my teacher despite his lack of pedagogical training. Elizabeta's silent revolution, her experiment in saving Syriac Christianity, authorizes itself by working through, rather than against, Syriac Orthodox liturgical memory. She is, in a sense, a liturgical activist, reshaping her world through her sometimes-invisible liturgical practice.

Liturgical memory is an embodied form of historical knowledge, in which the question *"What is it to be a Christian?"* is also a question about the meaning of Christ's Incarnation. While the later scribal tradition commemorating a Hellenized St. Ephrem is accessible to scholars, it is Ephrem the Syriac-speaking poet whose hymns and prayers voicing and praising Biblical women in the cosmic drama of salvation left a legacy in liturgies sung weekly among congregations around the world. It is the Ephrem of liturgy who inspires so many of the women I work with to liturgical activism. To them, St. Ephrem is a poetic visionary whose melodies made their church famous. Through their vocal practices of singing and chanting, twenty-first-century Syriac Orthodox women reproduce an embodied relationship with this history and strive to live out the Christological concept of 'ihidoyutho, singleness of mind in service to their community, through their liturgical practice, in memory of Ephrem and the ancient Daughters and Sons of the Covenant. Their vocal practice is an expression of faith and an imitation of Christ's nature, and it is to the complexities of that practice that I now turn.

CHAPTER

3

THE VOICE IN THE ICON

Christ's icon does not refer to a higher reality, one that is more authentic; that would be the reality of an exterior model, invisible and distant. The distance is rather inside the icon itself, and it allows us to hear the echo of a voice within it. (Mondzain 2005, 107)

More Than an Image

As category, concept, and object, an icon belongs equally to pop culture, semiotic theory, art history, and Orthodox (both Chalcedonian and non-Chalcedonian) Christian doctrine and practice. In the semiotic theories of Charles Sanders Peirce, popularly cited among social theorists of non- and extra-linguistic modes of meaning-making, an icon is a communicative sign that depends upon a formal relation of resemblance to generate meaning. An icon might be, for instance, the image of a bicycle on a street sign communicating to bikers where to ride. The sign communicates meaning because the image resembles the model. Yet equally important is the iconic sign's location in time and space and the social processes that lead to the sign's placement: the image of a bicycle means one thing on the side of a street, another inside of a bike shop. The icon, like all signs according to Peirce, has a fundamentally dialogical character. The icon of a bicycle needs a bicyclist for it to work iconically; the icon facilitates an unspoken dialogue, a communicative relation, between bicyclist and street-planner, and with cars, and with pedestrians. The voice of the city-planner echoes silently within the icon: *Please stay on the bike path, biker!* The icon hails the viewer, and in being hailed, the bicyclist responds to the icon, facilitating a set of interlocking relations that, hopefully, prevents dangerous collisions. The icon thus requires both a material form and an act of imagination to interact in the communication, an interior relation of meaning-making within the sign Peirce called *abduction*.

According to philosopher and Byzantinist art historian Marie-José Mondzain (2005), the ontological foundations of the Orthodox icon were forged amidst the theopolitical controversies of the early Byzantine Empire, and evidence of their pervasive influence on modern political imaginaries is widespread. In the writings of Nikephoros I (c. 758–828), Ecumenical Patriarch of Constantinople, a philosopher, political theorist, and major iconophile apologist, the icon is central to the workings of sovereign power, and early iconoclastic controversies emerged as imperial authority sought to usurp the icon's social power. As numerous recent theoretical accounts of modern sovereignty demonstrate, this power is deeply implicated in a historically Christian Incarnational imagination (Agamben 2011; Heron 2018; Mondzain 2005; Singh 2018). For the iconoclasts and iconophiles of Nikephoros's time, the icon was a site of power for the production, reproduction, and control of the meaning-making process itself. The icon constituted the symbolic order upon which both ecclesiastical and imperial powers depended for their legitimacy, from imperial coinage systems to painted likenesses of Christ and His Mother on church walls and mosaics in public spaces. Whosoever controlled iconicity within the empire controlled the terms through which its subjects understood themselves *as* participants of the divine economy. While these iconic systems were predominantly visual, visuality is not the only register in which iconic power might operate.

In this chapter, I develop the concept of the sonic icon as an intersensorial object to explore the reproductive power of my research participants' vocal practices when participating, or preparing to participate, in liturgical kinship. Considering the historical circumstances that have constrained the development of a strongly visual iconic tradition in Syriac Orthodox Christianity, I examine evidence that suggests the West Syriac Rite nonetheless possesses a tradition of icon production and use that is more readily discernible in a sonic idiom, in addition to the visual. This is to recognize the distinctive social and spiritual power of sacred chant in

Syriac Orthodoxy, as well to emphasize icon-*ity* as a relational process over icono-*graphy*, the latter of which is but one of several possible mediatic practices through which the relational process of iconicity may take material-aesthetic form. This is also to expand upon an Orthodox definition of the icon as *more than an image*.

I begin with an ethnographic moment from my fieldwork, a Friday night choir rehearsal in a Syriac Orthodox parish in the Netherlands that exemplifies what I mean by the social and spiritual power of liturgical sound to generate kin relations. I then contextualize this scene in Syriac Orthodoxy's distinctive liturgical history and theology, paying special attention to the tradition's historically diasporic condition. I then offer a comparative perspective on another theological orientation to Christian congregational music-making, specifically the Calvinist strain that influences my research interlocutors' current social context, in order to highlight the distinctively iconic contours of Syriac liturgical song. Throughout this discussion, I situate the differences I have observed in liturgical practice and innovation in different regional and national histories of minoritization in the modern Middle East, asking how these histories intersect with singers' efforts to seek recognition in a European context. In light of these contrasts, I show that my interlocutors' vocal practices are sonic icons in that they work as a mechanism of reproductive power; that is, they shape subjects as both Syriac and Orthodox while simultaneously creating openings for innovation and experimentation. Ultimately, I suggest the sound of Syriac Orthodox chant is iconic in a sense that shows the overlap between Orthodox theological meanings and secular semiotic meanings because it makes perceptible the imperceptible, yet Incarnationally significant, relations that make Syriac Christians in all their historical, linguistic, geographical, and sonic diversity.[1]

"Do You Hear What I Hear?"

It is the coldest Dutch winter in decades. I am in a provincial town near the German border, trudging through the snow to a Syriac Orthodox Church near the city center. I have been attending Friday night choir rehearsals for several months. Choir practice is sparsely attended this evening. The young women in attendance range from twelve to twenty-three years old. The two choir directors, Marta and Rebekah, are university students studying to become a lawyer and a schoolteacher respectively. Tonight, they are working with the girls on confidence-building exercises and rehearsing hymns for the Passion Week. We begin the evening with a special melody sung only on Palm Sunday, Tubo Lyalude, *"Blessed are the children," an ode to the young women and children who crowded joyfully around Christ upon his entry into Jerusalem. The cheerful, upbeat song is meant to evoke the sound of jubilant crowds shouting Hosannah and beating tambourines, a mood the singers are having trouble channeling this evening. We sing in classical Syriac:*

"ʾUshaʿano brawmo, ʾushaʿano labreh d-Dawid, brikh detho bash-
meh dmoryo"
[Hosanna in the highest! Hosanna to the Son of David! Blessed is
He who comes in the Name of the Lord!]

As we work through the Hosanna refrain, I realize with a start that I know this hymn, and yet do not know it. I have been practicing it with the Mor Afrem Choir singers, a self-described "secular" choir, at the Assyrian Mesopotamian Cultural Association Enschede (AMVE) in another town. Here in the parish choir, we sing the song in a lower register, at a slower tempo, and with fewer microtonal flourishes; I thought it was a different song altogether. This feels nothing like the choir days of my youth, as my Dutch/American ear's incapacity to hear sonic intervals smaller than a quartertone is confounding me yet again. At the AMVE, under the direction of a professional musicologist from Aleppo trained in the tradition of Syriac Orthodox chant known as the School of Edessa, the Hosanna refrain is light and bright, with a youthful staccato energy appropriate to the biblical characters given voice by the chant, and the Syriac is transcribed phonetically for the predominantly Arabic- and Dutch-speaking choir.

But here, in the parish choir, the young women's voices strain to catch the microtonal melisma of the ʾushaʿnoʾs drawn-out second syllable, which falls and then rises and then falls again, landing on the—no, which then immediately lifts in a lilting run once more: oooo sh-a-a-a-a-a no-oh. Singing without notation and struggling to read the untransliterated Serto (West Syriac) script, the choir's directors and older singers rely on the memory of their ears to locate the relative pitches and pronunciations required to execute the melodic line with any faithfulness to the sonic conventions of the School of Tur Abdin, the tradition of Syriac chant that developed over centuries in their grandparents' villages in the monastery-studded highlands of southeast Turkey. The younger singers scramble to find the proper pitches and pronunciations at all, and I scramble to keep up with them. After an hour, their energy flags. They sit down, one by one, with headaches, dizziness, and exhaustion. Everyone is busy and anxious about school and exams, and they have been fasting—eating a vegan, low-protein diet—for weeks. By the time we pause for a break, my throat hurts, and one of the young women begins to cry from stress and weariness while another sits and holds her head, feeling faint.

Taken aback by my failure to recognize a hymn I thought I knew, I wait anxiously while Marta and Rebekah attend to their young friends. After they have calmed the girls, given them water, rubbed their backs, and pep-talked them with the gentle confidence of older sisters, I approach Marta and Rebekah.

"I think I know this song," I say, hoping they will help me make sense of my disorientation. "But I am not sure. I think I learned it differently."

"Where have you heard it?" Rebekah asks.

"I have been singing it with the Mor Ephrem Choir," I reply, with mounting trepidation at the looks on their faces as they absorb the fact that I have been working with people at the Assyrian cultural center.

"We thought the Mor Ephrem Choir didn't meet anymore," Rebekah frowns. At my querying look, she remarks with studied neutrality: "What you need to understand, Sarah, is that that choir is part of the Assyrian faction."

"Yes," Marta explains, "we are Aramaeans because we speak Aramaic, but there are some others who call themselves Assyrian, even though they are also Syriac Orthodox."

*"There **are** real Assyrians out there who speak Assyrian," Marta continues, "but they are different." I ask if she means Swadaya speakers—those Syriac Christians who speak an eastern branch of neo-Aramaic, also called neo-Assyrian, found in northern Iraq. Neither Marta nor Rebekah knows what this means. I try: "East-Syriac?" referring to the liturgical language of the Church of the East. They debate momentarily whether Assyrian is a dialect of Aramaic or an entirely different language. Marta is sure it is a dialect, but Rebekah says, "I don't really know." They appear flustered. Is that a fluttering of irritation on their faces? Or embarrassment? I hesitate to press them further. It was never my desire to interrogate them about the ethnic politics wracking their church community. They have bigger problems: parents, friends, jobs, exams—lives of scrutiny and pressure in a country obsessed with whether or not they are, as women of Middle Eastern descent, properly "integrated" into Dutch society. But I have heard stories of fights breaking out in church parking lots over the Assyrian-Aramaean question, and I fear that I have angered them.*

The break is over, and they offer no resolution to my confusion. Marta and Rebekah call the girls back together and we sing again.

*   *   *

The creativity, contingency, and relational complexity of liturgical singing in Syriac Orthodox tradition is fully evident in the story described here and features at least two auditory dimensions that evoke the social and spiritual powers of the icon. The first auditory feature is the problem of the anthropologist's un-enculturated ear: her own failure to perceive a hymn she thought she knew and how the difference between the two versions of the Ṭubo Lyalude illuminates a theologically grounded understanding of both historical migration and aesthetic innovation. The second auditory feature is the strain in these young singers' voices, attesting to their emotional labor in listening, teaching, and learning as they reach for sounds that materialize a relationship with their parents' histories, making perceptible the imperceptible relations that make them who they are. These auditory features illustrate the main ethnographic theme of this chapter: the echo of past voices resounds within these young women's voices in diaspora. In this moment of teaching and learning, the history of intimate relationships with parents, grandparents, teachers, and priests who have brought them to this moment leaves sonic traces on their vocal practice.

The strain in their voices comes from the effort required to reproduce a sound that imitates the sound of their precursors with some faithfulness despite growing up in a European country with very different musical and religious aesthetics (e.g., Vogel, Klomp, and Barnard 2022a; Vogel, Klomp, and Barnard 2022b). Hymns like the Ṭubo Lyalude are drawn from the *Beth Gazo,* the "Treasury of Song," a repertoire of hundreds of hymns compiled over centuries, possibly as far back as the third century, from the institutional memory of the church (Aydin 2017). This compendium of liturgical hymns that furnishes the melodies and meanings of the liturgy is not any isolable object that exists in any specific place, nor is it conveyed through any specific privileged medium. In this respect, it is like many sacred texts whose effects proliferate transmedially beyond the circumstances of their initial writing. There was once, I have often been told, a complete and authoritative book of liturgical hymns, although no one is quite certain where or what might have become of it. There are numerous abbreviated versions that circulate in some parts of the globe, whose primary purpose, according to my research participants' memories of their teachers' teachers in Tur Abdin and Syria, is to serve as an aid to advanced practitioners who rely on the memory of their ears, cultivated since early childhood. They, in turn, relay cues to less advanced practitioners.

Although the most complete versions of the Beth Gazo reside in the heads of senior deacons and priests, it is generally understood that the mastery of even the widely esteemed monks of Mor Gabriel Monastery in Tur Abdin is partial at best and that the relative differences in style and content of the Beth Gazo as it is known and sung across far-flung corners of the Syriac world echo centuries of regional migration and fragmentation—this is part of the story of why I failed to recognize a hymn I had learned at the Assyrian cultural center when we sang it in the parish. Many centuries of crossing and being crossed by shifting political borders has had a fractalizing effect on Syriac Orthodox conceptions of authority and authenticity in the performance of the Beth Gazo. The story sounds similar everywhere, yet the "source" of authority and authenticity at the center of each story differs slightly. For my Assyrian research participants like those at the AMVE, the earliest Syriac Orthodox poet-theologians of antiquity, hymnographers like St. Ephrem, adapted preexisting pagan melodies to Christian texts to evangelize to the Syriac-speaking populations of late Roman Syria, Mesopotamia, and Persia, producing an aesthetic bridge with the cultural forms of ancient Assyria. For my Aramaean research participants, like Marta and Rebekah, St. Ephrem's melodies were original compositions written to woo congregations away from heterodox Christian factions like the Edessan followers of Bardaisan (154–222 CE). These narratives about the origins of the chant are geographically and temporally oriented by disparate ancestral narratives. The former establishes a religiously authorized continuity with pre-Christian Assyrian ethnonational identity, while the latter links Syriac Orthodoxy to an ethnic understanding of Aramaean peoplehood rooted in biblical references to Laban the Aramaean and the politically autonomous city-states of ancient Aram. As I and others have argued elsewhere, these ancestral narratives are no mere modernist fabrications spun out of thin air but are sociopolitically distinct articulations of a shared Syriac Orthodox Incarnational theology with a complex genealogy (see also Calder 2016, 2017; and Jarjour 2016, 2018). This practical theology interprets history Incarnationally; that is to say, history is not composed of empty, homogeneous time but of the cyclical "drama of salvation" (Ashbrook Harvey 2001, 2005). This means that historical events, archaeological remains, ritual practices, textual traces, and sonic echoes of the past incarnate a spiritual, affective, and moral relationship with Creation that animates even the most secularist claims to sociopolitical belonging. Chanted hymns like Ṭubo Lyalude work iconically to reproduce embodied memories of the distant past as an intimate and deeply felt part of the present.

Another crucial point of auditory disjuncture between the two versions of the Ṭubo Lyalude was the fact that in the parish, the choir was singing in the style of the School of Tur Abdin, while the choir at the cultural center was singing in the style of the School of Edessa. By "School," the Church refers to the eight regionally distinct stylistic traditions of performing the Beth Gazo that have developed over centuries among congregations of the West Syriac Rite: the School of Tur Abdin in southeast Turkey, exemplified in the sounds of the monks of Mor Gabriel Monastery; of ancient Edessa, now of the Urfalli parish of St. George's in Aleppo; of Diyarbakir, also in southeastern Turkey; of Sadad, in southwest Syria; of Kharput, now called Elazig in eastern Turkey; of ancient Takrit, now sung in and around Mosul in northern Iraq; of Malankara in Kerala, India; and of Mardin, the Patriarchal School originating in the Monastery of Deyr el-Zafaran and now centered in Homs, Syria. Together, these eight Schools constitute a sonic map of ancient migration and contemporary loss that cuts equally across Assyrian and Aramaean ancestral narratives. In the parish church where this Friday night rehearsal took place, congregants with roots in and around the province of Midyat, whose long-serving priest was born in the tiny village of Hah, sang in the style of the School of Tur Abdin. They sounded, I was frequently told, like their fathers' grandfathers: low, rough, farmworkers' voices, heavy and laborious with an even, staccato cadence that evoked the hard repetitiveness of rural life in the impoverished highlands. Meanwhile, at the cultural center in south Enschede, singers in the Wednesday night "secular" choir were mostly recently arrived Arabic speakers from the Syrian border town of Qamishli, where several well-known musicians from Aleppo had become prominent liturgical teachers and folklorists (see also Zeitoune 2015). Although the Assyrian singers also had ancestral ties to the villages of Tur Abdin, their families had lived for several generations in Syrian cities like Qamishli, Aleppo, and Damascus. These urban environments influenced the aesthetic quality of their voices, which were more evocative of the sounds of Arabic *tarab*: higher pitches, tight vocal control, technically elaborate improvisational solos, and often accompanied by an accomplished violinist.

The Memory of the *Malphono's* Ear

From some scholarly perspectives, such stylistic variations between the Assyrian choir's and the parish choir's rendition of the Ṭubo Lyalude might be analyzed in terms of the relationship between right practice and right belief and how this relationship is recast and negotiated in shifting sociopolitical conditions such as one might experience after migration from Turkey and Syria to northwestern Europe (cf. Engelhardt 2015; Luerhmann 2018; Hann and Goltz 2010, 15–16). For my research participants, however, getting the sound "right" was not part of any explicit effort to give voice to right "belief" per se. No one I know speaks of their own School as the *truest* or *most correct* school relative to any of the others in a doctrinal or dogmatic sense because they understand these schools to reflect the cosmopolitan diversity of the late antique and medieval Syriac world.[2] If anything, many of my research participants in the parish choirs would admit that the Edessan sound of the AMVE was most beautiful purely to listen to, but they did not aspire to imitate it themselves because they did not belong to that School of Edessa. The theological resonances of this approach to liturgical sound differ somewhat from choral traditions where hymns and sung prayers exist on a spectrum from standardization across the denomination (as in notated hymnals) to individualized creativity (as in a one-off arrangement where the arranger is identified by name on sheet music). In the Syriac Orthodox context, my research participants have neither totalized standardization nor individual creativity in mind. Rather, what they insist upon is proper pronunciation of classical Syriac within the conventions of their own School and of melodic lines reconstructed from their liturgical teacher's, or *malphono's*, memory.

The malphono's memory is the source of authority and authenticity for a given parish sound within a particular School's historical trajectory because the malphono embodies a personal relationship with a specific past in a specific place. My research participants understand that memory works like a game of telephone, where sounds alter slightly in their transmission over time and distance. This is natural, and so Marta, Rebekah, and their peers acknowledge and celebrate the sonic rightness of their tradition's diversity of styles precisely because each stylistic variation materializes a theologically significant diversity of relationships with a diversity of pasts. No one I know expects the congregations of, say, Mosul, Iraq, or Kerala, India, to sing in the styles found in southeast Turkey; in my observation, diasporic Suryoye are far more likely to share video recordings of these disappearing traditions online with pride and delight at the richness of their Rite and its history. Nor, in turn, would they aspire to imitate these other Schools in their own parishes. Marta and Rebekah themselves, in a later conversation at the Friday night choir rehearsal, admitted the beauty and skill of the Assyrian choir's performances and respected the director's faithful interpretation of the sounds of the School of Edessa. Their consternation was fixated solely on the cultural association's claim that the Syriac Orthodox are Assyrian rather than Aramaean.

The sonic differences between the two choirs' arrangements were theologically acceptable because they reflected different migration trajectories across multiple generations of a kinship network, a reality my interlocutors pragmatically acknowledged. Much more recently arrived in the Netherlands, the Assyrian choir was connected to a professionalized Syrian musical scene that understood the chants and hymns of the West Syriac Rite to be part of a broader ecumenical—yet still liturgically Syriac—world. The young singers of the parish, on the other hand, strained to embody the vocal technique of their fathers, uncles, teachers, and priests from Tur Abdin against the grain of their own Western musical sensibilities (Marta and Rebekah's favorite singer happened to be Mariah Carey, and vocal warm-ups and cool-downs sometimes spun off into singing portions of her greatest hits). Rather than being concerned with right sound as an expression of right belief, my interlocutors were concerned that their sounds reproduce their relationship with a specific regional history saturated with feelings of love, longing, and loss. My parish friends reproduced a relationship via ecclesiastical fathers and monastic uncles to the villages and monasteries of Tur Abdin, while my AMVE friends reproduced a relationship of refugee teacher to refugee student with the lost city of Edessa, via Aleppo and Qamishli. These histories, in turn, are the embodied human traces of an intimate yet complex relationship with divine Incarnation, an incarnation whose diversity is a sign of the Trinitarian God's expansive, infinite, and irreducible Mystery, the mystery that is called in West Syriac *rozo*. Faithfulness to the sounds of particular parishes and Schools of liturgical chant enacts the richness and complexity of Incarnation.[3]

The strain in my choir friends' voices is also a sign of the ethical dimension of social reproduction—they fashion themselves and each other as both Syriac and Christian in trying to master the sounds of their teachers and fathers and priests. As they work to train their bodily capacities to produce that sound, they participate in something similar to what Rebecca Bryant (2005) has called "empersonment" and what Eitan Wilf describes as an "open-ended and regenerative embodied practical mastery" (2010, 578) in absorbing the aesthetic values of a given sonic tradition. In Bryant's and Wilf's ethnographic settings, Turkish folk musicians and American jazz musicians navigate a tension between a modernist discourse of rationalist learning necessary to master the art form, on the one hand, and a Romantic idealization of spontaneity, individuality, and creative liberation and expression on the other, working to hide the mechanical nature of the first to foreground the second (for a nonmusical example of a similar modernist tension, see Brahinsky 2012). For my choir friends, there is neither opposition nor tension between learning and expression: Syriac Orthodox values of iconic continuity (i.e., the transgenerational game of telephone) encompass an understanding that individual differences cannot help but creep in to shape the sound of a specific parish. This is known and accepted because human specificity is part of "liturgical being." The aesthetic value of a liturgical performance is a function of the ethical achievement of reproducing a relationship with history.[4] Their voices are iconic in this moment because the icon works through that open-ended reasoning process called abduction, what Peirce described as an inferential relation akin to an informed guess or imaginative speculation about a material, formal fact of resemblance. Playing with inherited materials, "there is always a plenitude of ways in which likenesses may be interpreted; the iconic sign is always open to conjecture and disputation" (Hughes 2003, 143). The interior relation of Firstness that defines the icon is the relation of potentiality and possibility and variation, and it is precisely this indeterminate open space that makes it a site of reproductive power.[5]

Kinship with the Saints

Another key contour of Syriac chant's iconicity is evident in how it enables singers to revoice the founding saints of Syriac tradition, like St. Ephrem and St. Jacob of Serugh, whose writings were frequently concerned with explaining and disseminating orthodox Incarnational theology. For example, in St. Ephrem's *Hymns on the Nativity*, the Virgin Mary "carries the weight of explaining the mystery of God's salvific work in the Incarnation of his Son, wholly God and wholly human" (Ashbrook Harvey 2001, 105–106).

Theologies of the Incarnation played a role in the formulation of prayers within the historical Church's liturgical order, and these required distinct vocal roles to impart the lessons of Christ's life on earth in the form of dramatic dialogues. According to the fifth-century Rabbula Canons, male and female choirs would sing antiphonally, where the ancient Sons of the Covenant would chant the Psalms while the Daughters of the Covenant (Marta and Rebekah's model for their own women's choir) chanted the *madroshe*, the stanzaic poems that explicitly taught correct doctrine, as well as the *soghitho*, a genre of dialogue poem that reenacted Biblical scenes in the weekly liturgy. In this dramaturgical tradition of staging the voices of important characters and interactions from the life of Christ, Syriac singers in antiquity wove ritual and social life together through biblical narrative. Through their vocal practices, they animated the parallels between past and present that shaped the liturgical order of days, weeks, and years into a cyclical pattern of infinitely renewable social healing and spiritual salvation. As Susan Ashbrook Harvey writes, "The dynamic interplay of voices allowed an inclusive representation of the gathered church to take place, as conflicts of gender as well as ecclesiastical (social) hierarchy were intoned in harmonious performance. Exchange, negotiation, and reconciliation were embodied by the participating voices, male and female, clerical and lay. What one heard was more than words" (2001, 125).

In the twenty-first century, diasporic choirs like the one led by Marta and Rebekah link their practice to their ancient precursors by singing a repertoire of hymns and prayers attributed to the early and late Syriac Fathers, from the sixth-century Mor Jacob of Serugh to the twentieth-century Mor Philoxenos Yuhanon Dolabani, Bishop of Mardin. None of these poet-saints are more beloved in the Dutch-Syriac diaspora than Mor Ephrem, who wrote, taught, and (according to later tradition) directed the earliest Bnoth and Bnay Qyomo in fourth-century Edessa and Nisibis.[6] Following an eight-week cycle in which a given hymn may be sung in one of eight different melodic variations, according the emotional "mood" of that week's liturgical drama, Marta, Rebekah, and their peers sing in classical Syriac, St. Ephrem's language. This is despite their sometimes-hazy understanding of the hymns' meanings, with a strongly articulated view that an intellectual grasp of content, while not unimportant, matters far less than sonic fidelity—within their ability and to the best of their knowledge—to the meaningful chain of relationships that link their voices back to St. Ephrem's voice. This revoicing is a kinship practice because it embodies sensorially an intimate relationship with the founding moment of Syriac Orthodoxy's distinct sociocultural, liturgical, and ecclesiological identity, and it is reinforced by other kinship practices like naming. Dutch Syriac Orthodox, like Suryoye in other parts of the world, named their local monastery, choirs, cultural organizations, and many of their children after Ephrem, lovingly remembered as "the Harp of the Spirit," and attribute to him all that is most essentially and authentically Syriac.

The epistemologically tricky historian's question of whether the "real" St. Ephrem actually founded and led real women's "choirs" or whether his relationship to the Daughters of the Covenant (who unquestionably existed) was fictionalized by later writers is beside the ethnographic point. St. Ephrem is as theologically real as he needs to be to reproduce the chain of transmission around which Marta, Rebekah, and their peers define themselves as kin to the founder of their tradition. This mutuality is a hallmark of iconicity, and it is a mutuality that the historical author of Ephrem's vast corpus of theological poetry would recognize. Such iconicity is also recognizable in other orthodox traditions, as Angie Heo has shown in the mutually constitutive relationship between saint and icon in the case of the Coptic Orthodox (2018, 216). In the Syriac Orthodox situation, the sonic icon enables an intersensorial relation with the saint. Voicing the songs of the saint enables faithful singers and listeners to connect with him. The chant, like the visual icon, implodes space and time by virtue of the hypostatic union within the Incarnation, which enables congregations, as well as the deacons and cantors leading them in prayer, to participate in salvation by revoicing their saintly and biblical precursors.

This is an expansive understanding of what an icon can be. People may become icons by imitating Christ, Mary, and the saints. Here, imitation means a holy mimesis, denoting an active, consecrated participation in Christ's divine life, bringing the cosmic realities of the salvific economy into the daily rhythms of social life through liturgical practice. The Bnoth and Bnay Qyomo of antiquity were frequently written of in such language: as imitators of Christ and servants of their urban communities (Ashbrook Harvey 2005; Griffith 1991; Koonammakkal 1999). Icons are created by imitating earlier icons, reaching back to the "the first Icon," Christ himself.[7] While this can also be said of other Orthodox traditions, much of Syriac literary tradition attests to a heightened multisensory and multifunctional understanding of the icon, from the Teaching of Addai's foundational account of King Abgar of Edessa's iconic image in the early fifth century to the extensive iconographic wall paintings of the late-thirteenth-century monastery of St. John Bar Nagare in Bar Telli, near Mosul, Iraq, in which the entire drama of salvation is animated in a distinctively Syriac aesthetic style of vibrant color contrasts and paired figures. This striking visual aesthetic mirrors the aesthetics of much theological poetry found in liturgical texts, Gospels, and lectionaries, with incongruent image pairings highlighting the confounding mysteriousness of the Incarnation (Loosley 2019; Vesa 2017). This harmonization of visual and textual elements proved valuable with the coming of the Umayyads and subsequent empires, as the Islamic prohibition on religious images periodically inspired destructive raids on church properties and their visual arts. Syriac Orthodox instead began to paint icons into books, which could be easily hidden when necessary, while the voices of those depicted by the icons could be memorized and spoken (or chanted) aloud.[8]

Such connections among biblical narrative, liturgical dramaturgy, and the Incarnationally significant chain of kin relations residing in the icon are also found in the Syriac Orthodox Church's official prayer of consecration through which images become icons. In thirteen steps, the prayer stages a dialogue, or perhaps more accurately, an interaction, between the assembled congregation and the divine. In this prayer, the priest invites the Holy Spirit to reside in the icon as it did in "the Tabernacle over Moses, Aaron, Samuel, and the Prophets, the apostles at Pentecost and John the Evangelist, in continued charismatic succession" to the present assembly. Following the prayer with unction, the icon is "marked, imprinted, and sealed," and the assembled congregants are invited to commemorate and imitate the saints in their own daily lives. As the priest and deacons process around the church, singing special songs for the Virgin Mary and other saints who knew and loved Christ during his life on earth, the congregation reconnects with the Mystery of Incarnation as a profoundly intimate relationship that collapses space and time. One of the elements of this consecratory prayer is the hymn quoted in the prelude of this book, sung in the melody, or *qolo* (lit. "voice") associated with poems of the Incarnation, which highlights the gendered, reproductive, and relational aspects of the Mystery by exalting Mary's mysterious paradoxical condition as both virgin and mother. The vocality of this moment is essential as the icon is constituted as a relational, intersensorial object: both gaze and utterance, window and ear.

Incarnation, Now: Tensions in the Dutch-Syriac Diaspora

The iconic contours of Syriac chant also become discernible when compared with other Christian conceptions of what congregational singing and
liturgical practice might be and how they might work. For Marta, Rebekah,
and their peers, Dutch Christianity presents an alternate commonsense understanding of what church-singing *is* that can make it difficult for them
to explain their sensibilities to others. To make matters more complex, the
Dutch context has woven itself into their experience and understanding
in sometimes unexpected ways.

Within the past fifty years, with migration and growing access to education and wealth, Syriac Orthodox women's liturgical choirs revived after
centuries of suppression and forgetting in the towns and villages of Tur
Abdin. In the Netherlands, the late Archbishop Julius Çiçek, the first Syriac
Orthodox bishop in Europe, established women's choirs among his growing parishes, founding the first European parish in the city of Hengelo in
1977. The archbishop actively encouraged and supported teaching young
girls to sing the liturgical melodies and to read the *Serto*, the West-Syriac
script; his sponsorship was essential to gaining widespread acceptance
among those congregations from villages where women's presence, much
less vocal participation, in church was frowned upon.

Ayfer, an acquaintance I met frequently at public events at the monastery, was one of the original members of this first choir in Hengelo. Having moved from southeast Turkey with her family as a very young child in
the early 1970s, she was an active member of this early generation of liturgical singers until her marriage. In the period when I came to know her
well, she was a busy lawyer and the mother of teenage boys, as well as an
active volunteer for her local parish and the diocese. When I visited Ayfer
in her tidy rowhouse in a Hengelo suburb, she reminisced with me about
her time in the choir, telling me how important the bishop had been to
the revival's success. His vision, will, and determination; his far-reaching
activities to develop Syriac Orthodox ethnic consciousness in the global
diaspora; and his loud insistence on the importance of the women's choirs
to Syriac Orthodox community and identity were indispensable to their
growth and success throughout the 1970s and 1980s, she told me.

Ayfer looked back fondly, showing me pictures of when the bishop took
them on a trip to Rome to perform at a concert for choirs of many different Christian traditions hosted by the Vatican. Suddenly pensive, she said,

"I do wish we had learned the meaning of what we sang, though. But of course, that would have been moving too far, too fast for many of the men in our community. . . ."

She trailed off, and then came back to herself:

". . . but we sounded good! And we felt valued. We knew we were an important part of the church. We knew we were an important part of the tradition."

When I asked her about the present and the future of the choir, she paused and measured her words carefully:

> Without Çiçek's forceful personality, there is less support for the women's choirs today, and everyone is so busy with other things, so it's diminishing a little. When I was a girl, the thought of doing anything else in the evenings or the weekends was unthinkable. All we had was church! All we were allowed was church. So, you know, we practiced a lot. We sounded good! Now girls can do other things . . . and so . . . it doesn't always sound so good. The choir directors now have beautiful voices and work hard, but there are forces working against them.

Ayfer shared these thoughts with me at a very particular moment in the history of the Dutch-Syriac diaspora. The archbishop had unexpectedly passed away shortly before my arrival for preliminary fieldwork, in a traumatic event that left the diocese somewhat in disarray. Because of this, I could not speak to him or anyone very close to him to learn more about his role and relationship to the revival of the women's liturgical choirs. Initially, I was alarmed at what seemed a sudden halt to organized and sustained activity across the Dutch parishes and by the widespread sentiment that things were falling apart, according to those I met in those early days. In retrospect, the aftermath of the bishop's death was a period of widespread distress and mourning but also a pause for breath, when parishes, families, and community leaders took time to regroup and reflect on the future, especially with the arrival of the bishop's successor, the youthful, multilingual, and Princeton-educated Mor Polycarpus Augin Aydin. As I would discover over the following years, my friends, acquaintances, and interlocutors were beginning to lay the foundations for a newly invigorated period of revival that built on Archbishop Çiçek's legacy while also exploring new possibilities for innovation and experimentation.

During Archbishop Çiçek's time presiding over the formation of the Syriac Orthodox diaspora in Western Europe, the Syriac Orthodox had made significant gains in education, wealth, and access to information about ancient Syriac traditions. These developments coincided with a growing awareness of the dangers of political invisibility within the politics of Western nations, as anxieties over assimilation into European societies mixed with fear that the already-attenuated Syriac tradition would disappear from the Middle East entirely. For this reason, despite some lingering cultural misgivings in some corners about women's active liturgical participation, the revival of Syriac Orthodox women's liturgical choirs re-emerged out of a combined impulse for both dialogical recognition and existential self-discovery.

This is the spirit in which Marta and Rebekah drilled their younger choir members in confidence-building techniques and vocal strength and shared their thoughts about how to comport themselves as choir members: how to speak, how to handle conflict, and how to cultivate humble hearts so that their songs would serve, rather than detract from, the spiritual health of the congregation. Many of their moral ideas and aesthetic sensibilities came from their Dutch environment, especially from their publicly funded Christian schools, teachers, friends, and television. Yet they walked a delicate line in sorting out what was an improper interpolation and what was a necessary, beneficial change in service of their faithfulness. Agreement on where to find this thin line was rare.

While I unpack more of these discussions in Chapter 4, one dimension I will focus on here is an aesthetic one highlighting a contrast with other Christian approaches to congregational music-making. The Dutch aesthetic culture that these young women were immersed in is influenced by Calvinism, although many of its explicitly theological undertones have been forgotten.[9] In Calvinist thought, music has a clearly articulated role in worship, a role which itself reflected a synthesis of medieval European Christian and Platonic thought. Church music, according to Calvin, could only be drawn from the Psalms, which he considered the divinely provided songbook, and should be audible, intelligible, and simple enough for all to sing without specialized training or knowledge. Calvinist church music is readily recognizable for its uncomplicated metrical, monophonic (i.e., without harmony) and monosyllabic (i.e., one note per syllable) structures. Such strictures grew out of medieval European Christian understandings of musical metaphysics, where music was embedded in a mathematically calculable cosmic order (although early Reformers disputed the precise nature of the sacrality of sound). While for Martin Luther, himself an accomplished musician, music possessed its own kind of agency to drive away evil (Begbie 2013, 34), Calvin was suspicious of this line of thinking, maintaining a strict boundary between divine agency and music's capacity to do *anything* on its own.

Liturgical sound, in Reformed churches, served a distinct purpose in configuring egalitarian social relations within congregations as they sought to bring about a newly horizontal understanding of the Church as the Body of Christ in the world. Melodies, in this context, do not convey or produce specific emotional states. Nor do they transmit relational histories or materialize correct belief. Whatever agency music might possess, in Reformed thought, it requires the presence of language, the divine language of the Word of God spoken and heard in a living language, to animate and activate it. In this view of sensory materiality, I see traces of Calvin's interpretation of the Incarnation, in which he understood and preached that Christ's life on earth was tied directly to a particular understanding of atonement. For Calvin, Christ's life on earth was God's response to humanity's fallen, sinful nature. Humanity, being lowly and depraved, needed only Christ as a mediator (rather than priests, deacons, or anyone with special knowledge). The nature of that mediating relation, however, was substitutionary, transactional, and focused on Christ's death; in other words, his humanity was important for its mortality, a practical necessity for taking our place in suffering divine judgment (Hall and Lillback 2008). Incarnation's soteriological purpose was meant only for the chosen few predestined for salvation rather than for all of humanity. Such a view of the Incarnation's significance could only ever—at least in my view—constrain theological conceptions of materiality and sensoriality, a point that has been widely documented and debated among scholars since Max Weber first discerned Calvinist Christianity's outsized role in producing capitalist modernity (e.g., Keane 2002; Seligman 2009).

Versions of the Reformed conviction in the importance of understanding God's Word are so globally widespread in the commonsense notion of modern sincerity that it is now one of the most thoroughly analyzed concepts in religious studies and the anthropology of Christianity. Even so, it made Marta, Rebekah, and their peers—just as it did Ayfer's generation—decidedly uneasy. While the sacrality of classical Syriac remains undisputed, in some corners of the global diaspora, portions of the liturgy are translated into modern vernaculars like Arabic or English, although not without local controversy. Here in the Netherlands, my research participants stopped short of ever demanding that the liturgy be translated to facilitate their understanding (although once in a while, the bishop would invite one of them to give the Gospel reading in Dutch during a major festival service, which made some of them happy and others among them terribly nervous and enraged more than a few elders in the pews).

For their part, the young singers sought resources from the parish governance board (an uphill battle everywhere) for training in the classical language and liturgical theology. For a brief time, they received it in the Dutch school system. Many parishes responded by offering language training for children, and some offered sporadic additional training for older women, but this usually depended on the availability of a willing and qualified malphono, often a close friend or brother. The dearth of sustained institutional support for women's advanced instruction reflected a complex social and cultural situation described further in the next chapter. The point I wish to highlight here is how contrasting musical metaphysics in Calvinist and Syriac approaches to congregational music reflect a deeper incongruency in the interpretation and application of Incarnational theology and their distinct understandings of materiality, agency, and the social life of sound. While each tradition shares a common view of music's pedagogical value, their take on music's aesthetic power differs. Calvinist thought stipulates a theology of music-making that might be described as aniconic: its aesthetic qualities are meant to be radically dis-embedded from its social relations. Anyone, anywhere, can and should be able to sing the same hymn in the same way, in principle. The materiality of sound is theorized away despite its unavoidability in practice, an empty and temporary vessel for God's grace to work through, and is *emphatically* a one-way street: God reaches down to us. We do not reach up to him. The mutuality of the iconic gaze is absent. In Syriac music-making, on the other hand, the materiality of sound is a trace of Christ's Incarnation inscribed in real, living, human history and lays a claim on the humans who reproduce these sounds. Through these sounds, in which the divine is present by virtue of the mystery of the *hypostatic union*, the human may also reach for God. While Calvinist and post-Calvinist Christian music-making in the Netherlands may not, in practice, be so indifferent to the social dimensions of sound as my characterization suggests (e.g., Vogel, Klomp, and Barnard 2022a; Vogel, Klomp, and Barnard 2022b), Calvinist tradition does nonetheless take a clear theological position on how materiality *shouldn't* matter, and how much an individualizing, intellectual understanding *should*, in the liturgical crafting of Christian subjects.

Liturgical Practice as Ethical Reflection

Another way that the Dutch context folded itself into Dutch-Syriac tradition is in how it inspired many of my interlocutors to make liturgical practice into a site of explicit ethical reflection and debate. The sisters Mariane
and Elizabeta are among my closest friends in my field site, so much of my
analysis emerges from my observation of their efforts to develop liturgical
practice into an occasion for cultivating a renewed sense of Syriac Christian community and identity in response to the pressures they feel in their
Dutch social setting. As consistent members of the gudo in their parish
church in the center of Enschede, they exemplified the "lead-from-behind"
approach to community revitalization shared by many Syriac Orthodox
women in the diaspora. The greatest source of heart-break for these two
sisters, they told me, was observing a growing resentment and alienation
among their peers toward the church establishment and the liturgical choir
functioning at the center of church life. This they attributed to the effects
of growing up in the Netherlands, where public religiosity is interpreted
as either a sign of an unassimilated, anti-modern, and frankly scandalous
quality of Middle Eastern-ness associated by Islamophobes with Dutch
Muslims or of the historically anachronistic neo-Orthodox Calvinist minority seen as relics of the Dutch religious past (see also Taussig 1997).

In alliance with several core liturgical singers, the sisters petitioned their
church board for a youth group, which was an unfamiliar concept at that
time. At first, the board resisted their efforts because of a sense that it might
affront the patriarchal order in which "village" leaders dominated the
political and financial affairs of the parish. Fortunately, their priest was a
kind, moderately conservative father of university-aged daughters himself.
With his support and the election of new church board members, several
of whom were fathers to girls in the group, Mariane, Elizabeta, and their
allies were successful.

Sunday night madrashto became an expansive space for discussing the
challenges of living as a Syriac Orthodox Christian in the Netherlands. A
mixed-gender group of singers, cantors, and sub-deacons between the ages
of thirteen and thirty would meet to study classical Syriac grammar under
the direction of a malphono, usually a deacon or sub-deacon. After the
grammar lesson, the malphono, at that time, a young man named Matthias, who often played an electronic keyboard accompaniment to the
hymns of the Qurbono on Sunday mornings, would read a lesson from a

Bible study guide translated from Arabic into Dutch, originally written by the Coptic Orthodox Pope Shenouda III. While he had chosen the guide because Coptic Orthodox theology is closer to Syriac theology than other traditions, it was unclear if he had any official authorization to read from this text. Nor did the students in his class always seem persuaded by what they heard. Conversations would often wander away from the didactic point of the initial reading as students discussed among themselves the concerns that were uppermost on their minds: the relative importance of adherence to church rules, of the details of fasting and ritual observance, of domestic arrangements and familial obligations, of professional and political commitments, and of sexual conduct and interpersonal relationships. Open dispute was as rare as open consensus. My research participants often spoke obliquely to avoid offending, but feelings were strongly held. Matthias's reading of Pope Shenouda's words against divorce, for example, went largely unheeded, as many of the young women and men in that room would go on to be married more than once. This space for liturgical practice became an occasion for developing a deeper appreciation of holy texts and how to benefit spiritually from performing their role in the liturgy. Members of the *gudo*, a rotating cast of characters who came and went as their schedules and personal life circumstances allowed, sought deeper knowledge of classical Syriac, sharing the belief that mastery over grammar would facilitate a more meaningful relationship with what they sang, and they inquired deeply with each other into what the moral content of their Suryoyo identity should be. Gathering on Sunday nights with other singers and cantors in service of deepening their understanding of the liturgy, madrashto became a safe space for exploring an expanding set of ethical questions about being Suryoyo in a complicated world.

Since my departure, the youth group associated with the gudo has grown and begun to organize activities, outings, and Bible studies, extending the function of liturgical practice not just to leading Mass but to reinforcing the West Syriac Rite's affective and ethical purchase among the young with newly invigorated intellectual and social pursuits. What was striking here, especially in contrast to the singers I describe in the following section, is how the sound of their voices in Holy Mass seemed to be an afterthought, receiving far less conscious attention than transforming the moral comportment and social relations among the singers themselves. These concerns reflect their commitment to the idea that the future of the West Syriac Rite rests on a foundation of solidarity among singers that is as social as it is spiritual. Their efforts produced frictions nonetheless, as when, during a youth group outing to an amusement park on one of my return visits, Elizabeta was reduced to tears by a handful of participants who refused to eat lunch with the organizing committee, taking it as a profound failure of her mission toward liturgical revitalization. The ethics of liturgical kinship, for Elizabeta, took material form in the social bonds it was meant to consolidate within the parish. Here, the religious and the ethical cannot be distinguished from the social. The work of organizing community relationships required activation through practice: families eat lunch together. But the sisters' position was not one that goes without saying. They had to work against the grain of Dutch secularity, which insists upon certain modes of religiosity, wherever it still exists, being as invisible in everyday social life as possible. Quite a number of the young people on the amusement park trip, after eagerly participating in the Syriac-language sing-along on the bus journey there, surreptitiously scattered to the wind once out in public despite Elizabeta and Mariane's efforts to keep everyone together. Elizabeta and Mariane maintain that a secular Dutch distinction between "the religious" and "the non-religious social" does not apply to being Dutch Suryoye, but how they perform this non-distinction takes characteristically Dutch forms—amusement parks, formal debate parties, regular brunches, and other activities common among secular Dutch social clubs and cultural associations. All of this is in service of strengthening the bonds of liturgical kinship first established through the chant.

Liturgical Practice as Aesthetic Experimentation

Elizabeta, Mariane, and their fellow parish singers in Enschede approached liturgical practice quite differently from Marta, Rebekah, and the singers of a different Syriac Orthodox Church in the nearby city of Hengelo. During my fieldwork, a steady group of approximately fifteen young women met on Friday nights to rehearse the coming Sunday's hymns separately from the men and boys in an effort to improve and experiment with their sound. The vignette described in the opening of this chapter occurred during one of these Friday night rehearsals. The girls would stand in a circle around the lectern holding the liturgical texts and prayer books to rehearse, just as they stood during the Sunday Mass, where singers are divided into two groups who sing antiphonally, in call and response, the women and some men on the left, and men exclusively on the right.

The young women who attended Friday night rehearsals took the view that while in principle what they were doing as singers was praying, in practice, they were performing for the benefit of their audience in the church congregation. They were there, they told me, to create a spiritual atmosphere for the congregation through their song: they provide a pastoral service for their community. The girls had all studied classical Syriac in primary school from an esteemed senior deacon, Mr. Çelik, in the period before 2004, when the Dutch government ended teaching native immigrant languages in public schools. Rehearsals took place under the direction of Marta and Rebekah, both university students with a self-taught gift for singing and a deep love for late-'90s-era R&B.

Marta and Rebekah sought to create a cohesive group of performers who could sing professionally at Syriac weddings and special events. Although Marta and Rebekah had learned to sing in the style of the Tur Abdin School from Rebekah's father at a young age, they aspired to make their choir singing more "interesting," as they were inspired by the musical ideas they heard on MP3s, Facebook, and YouTube clips from Sweden, Syria, and Lebanon. In choir rehearsals, they drilled the girls on singing together in tune and with confidence. They experimented with the aesthetic qualities of texture, tone, dynamics, breath control, vocal technique, and the structural layering of their voices over one another. They taught the girls the difference between head resonance and chest resonance and encouraged them to use their chest voices, as it provided a deeper, lower, stabler-feeling sound. This was a variety of experimentation I never observed during my time at the church in Enschede.

At times, Marta and Rebekah would attempt their own melodic innovations. Once, inspired by a video clip of a Syriac Orthodox choir competition in Sweden, they attempted a harmony. While Marta and Rebekah were admired in the community for their beautiful voices, their innovations were often met with disapproval, and their attempts to create a cohesive sound during Mass were thwarted by other singers who did not share their vision of the gudo as a formal choir and refused to attend weekly rehearsals. But by rehearsing their parts in the liturgy, Marta and Rebekah staked out a set of claims through their singing and their choir direction, intending to make a point to those they perceived as dilettantes, trying to push them out with the sound of their voices and to make their voices strong enough to withstand resistance. To a degree, they were willing to stray ever so slightly from their church's accustomed sound, learned from

Rebekah's own father, in service of a vision of the gudo's potential to become an outward-facing representation of Aramaean liturgical identity. At the same time, Marta and Rebekah would instruct the young women with whom they rehearsed to sing in a manner that embodies their conservative conception of Syriac Orthodox womanhood. They would say: "You must learn to sing with your own voice; sing with strength, but also dynamic subtlety; comport yourselves morally, in your outward behavior and your inward sensibilities . . . the feeling in your heart matters, the spirit in which you sing matters."

Since my long-term fieldwork ended, Marta and Rebekah have successfully formed their professional choir from among a core cohort of liturgical singers, which includes several boys and instrumentalists. They travel as an Aramaean choir to festivals showcasing other Syriac Orthodox liturgical choirs who have repurposed themselves for nonliturgical performance contexts, often broadcast by Suryoyo Sat, the international satellite television dedicated to aligning Syriac Orthodoxy with Aramaean ethnicity. They, and others like them, have created their own performance context, broadcast into the living rooms of Suryoyo households throughout the diaspora.

The young women's experiments occur in relation to the standards of twenty-first-century "art" music pervasive throughout Western Europe, in which they have been immersed since childhood. When Syriac Orthodox liturgical singers form themselves into choirs and perform at festivals representing their tradition, they rearrange how they occupy space. While performing the ritual during the Holy Qurbono, they stand in two circles in front of the altar where they can hear the buzz of each other's voices in their ears (as Marta told me in practice once, "When I get a headache, that's when I know it sounds good!").

In presentational performances, however, the singers stand in orderly lines, four to five rows thick, facing the audience, even when performing in a Syriac Orthodox church. During the liturgy, women are forbidden to step upon the altar, whereas, in the festival performance, they may be positioned, headscarf-less, on the altar steps. A choir might perform in the same space on the same day during Mass and then in an entirely different formation for a community festival following Mass. This is a recent innovation.

As in other Western European regimes where the constellation of religious practice, belief, and identity has been politicized in new ways, public expressions of religious conviction can cause widespread discomfort in the Netherlands, as decades of political debate over headscarves, mosque-building, and Muslim visibility attest. But there is a way of performing "religious tradition" publicly without causing discomfort. There is, after all, a commercial market for the aesthetic enjoyment of sacred music. Here, the music's aesthetic dimensions are highlighted at the expense of any ethical or ontic demands the music might make upon the listener, and the aesthetics of such a performance, when it occurs, is meant to provoke an artistic or emotional response.

Sacred music provides an "atmosphere," as Marta and Rebekah describe it. Even if experienced as a spiritual action by those performing, it is possible for those listening not to participate in the same way. Singers and listeners may have a different relationship with the identity of the performance. In the Netherlands, where it is common to be "spiritual but not religious," sacred music is often valued for how it "moves" the listener without any reference to the conditions of its original production. Aesthetic appreciation is disconnected from the relations of authority, discipline, and doctrine through which the music was composed, unless this appreciation is configured as a mournful secularist sense of "loss and longing" (see Klomp et al. 2018). Singing the liturgy as the "sacred music of the Aramaean people" follows this presentational logic (see also Turino 2008). Their presentational performances retain a pastoral aura that renders their liturgical practice commensurable with the sacred music of the world in hopes of occupying what we might call, following Kapchan (2008), the "festive sacred" slot. This festival audience was almost always other Syriac Orthodox, not outsiders. Yet not all other Syriac Orthodox were convinced.

The sisters Elizabeta and Mariane, for example, were deeply uncomfortable with what they saw as the political divisiveness of aligning Aramaean ethnicity with Syriac Orthodox liturgical performance in this way. That Marta was their paternal cousin only highlights the complexity of the relations among singers in their efforts to negotiate such claims vis-à-vis the boundary between the ethnic and the religious as they work to make their tradition recognizable to others. Elizabeta and Mariane's discomfort with their cousin's approach to presenting Syriac Orthodox liturgical music as ethnically Aramaean lay in two tacit intuitions: first, that it brings a certain kind of "politics" into a domain that it should not penetrate, and second, it allows that politics to coexist visibly in the public presentation of the liturgical. These practical anxieties devolve from dissimilar conceptions of what counts as political and what counts as ritual. In the sisters' political-religious sensibilities, ethnicity ought to be subsumed within and effaced by the moral, social, and spiritual bonds activated by liturgical practice. The politics of ethnicity should disappear within liturgy rather than publicly align with it. The tension between the cousins' different approaches to understanding and practicing liturgical kinship formed through the ethics of recognition: inherited voices and understandings resound discordantly within their sense of themselves and the meaning of their practice as they rework and reinterpret inherited materials to make sense of their situation.

The Assyrian Mesopotamian Association

I discovered another seam of tension when my parish friends, especially those who identify as Aramaean, became aware that I was attending rehearsals of the Mor Afrem Choir at the Assyrian Mesopotamian Cultural Association Enschede (AMVE), a self-described "secular" choir led by a professional, university-trained musical director from Aleppo, Syria. Most members of this choir had fled to the Netherlands within the previous fifteen years and spoke more Arabic than Turoyo or Dutch. The group was made up of roughly twenty-five people who would come and go as their schedules permitted, most of whom were born in either Aleppo or Qamishli.

The walls of the AMVE are papered with maps of ancient Mesopotamia and posters of Assyrian carvings housed in the British Museum—the visual dimension of a sensory culture in which Assyrian Christianity originates in the Ninevah Plains of northern Iraq. In an Assyrian Christian sensorium, these connections are existentially self-evident and historically self-authorizing (Atto 2011; Donabed 2012). The singers of the AMVE choir contend that their liturgical music was Assyrian before it was Christian and that all other forms of the Middle Eastern *maqam*, or modal system, derive from it.

This choir sang the Beth Gazo one evening a week for fun and companionship while smoking and drinking tea and coffee in the AMVE hall, which shared a building with the local Italian Cultural Association in south Enschede. When they could get the money together, the director arranged public concerts for Dutch audiences and, in 2009, took the choir on tour to England. Hanna, the director, took pains to explain to me how important it was that they sing in the most original and beautiful way, following the style of the School of Edessa (*Urfa* or *Urhoy*), which was sung with a lighter, more delicate, and lilting vocalization and more vocal flourishes than the School of Tur Abdin, evoking the tremulous, high-pitched wail that sounds, to my ear, like Arabic *ṭarab*. Hanna told me that the Edessan style was the oldest and, therefore, most suitable for European aural consumption of Syriac liturgical singing styles.

Many of my parish friends, mostly born of parents from the Turkish side, were suspicious of this choir and expressed indignation that they sang Syriac hymns and songs from the Beth Gazo outside of church—that is, in non-Syriac Orthodox spaces, such as city concert halls, for non-Syriac Orthodox audiences. At AMVE, they sang the Beth Gazo in a way that might lead one to categorize it as folklore if one was not careful. Such a view of the AMVE's singing practices would discern only that there is a traditional body of Assyrian folk songs, some of which were adapted to liturgical use centuries ago, and that their performance "expresses" Assyrian identity irrespective of audience or context. This is not to say that secular Assyrian folk songs with provenance outside the church tradition do not exist; only, rather, that the status of the liturgical repertoire *as folk heritage* is up for debate.

For the liturgical repertoire, the category "folklore" is problematic because the dichotomy between "ritual" and "folklore" obscures the basic indeterminacy at the heart of any definition of *leitourgia* as "the work" of "the people." Over time, I learned that the director wanted to perform for the rest of the Dutch-Syriac community at the monastery but was prevented by the governance board of the archdiocese, which was dominated by people from Tur Abdin and Aramaeans. This situation complicates any conventional expectation that the Mor Afrem Choir sings the Beth Gazo as folklore for secular audiences, while the parish churches sing it as religious expression for an exclusively religious audience. Even though several individual choir members are church deacons active in their parishes in other parts of the region, the AMVE was prohibited from performing for their own ecclesial community, in ecclesial spaces, as a secular choir. The rationale was rooted, I was told, in the Patriarchate's early-twentieth-century prohibition on using classical Syriac for nonliturgical music. The political origins of this prohibition were deeply convoluted. What matters now is that the prohibition continues to resonate for everyday Suryoye in the Dutch diaspora: allowing the Assyrian choir to perform *as an Assyrian choir* would have undercut the boundaries drawn by the current regime in power of local diocesan affairs around what they understand as the essential core of Syriac Orthodox *peoplehood* and the conviction that this core is sufficient to intelligibly furnish the grounds of their public identity. The liturgical repertoire of sacred chant, according to the Aramaean faction in charge of the decision, produces "a people" constituted and defined by adherence to the West Syriac Rite alone.

I gradually became aware of how tense the disagreement between the Assyrian and Aramaean sides could be. Beyond the firestorms that would light up online chat rooms on the websites of cultural organizations, there were reports of violence against religious leaders across the diaspora, of riots in Sweden between rival Aramaean and Assyrian soccer fans, and of grants from the Dutch government lost because the community would not coalesce under a single organization to represent their interests. Aramaeans were blamed for their inflexibility and autocratic hold on the archdiocese, while Assyrians were blamed for impiety and the rise in crime (and thus a bad reputation) among the public housing estates of south Enschede.

One evening at the AMVE, I discussed these issues with Rachid, an elderly gentleman who traveled every week from a distant town with his wife, daughter, and son-in-law so that they could participate in the choir while he sat and chatted with whomever else came and went in the hall. Rachid had studied Assyriology at university in Syria, and he was eager to answer my questions about the tensions I observed among factions. The issue, he told me over tea, came down to the difference between being an immigrant from Tur Abdin and an asylum-seeker from Syria. He told me that the Turkish side resents the Syrian side for their relative indifference to Church authority, which stems from the fact that in Syria religious minorities had more opportunities to develop a life and an identity outside of church, whereas in Turkey, the highland villagers relied implicitly on the ecclesiastical hierarchy for political protection and guidance in social life. At the same time, the Syrian members of the community suffer from a paradoxical condition. They are more educated, coming from developed urban areas, but because they are recent migrants to the Netherlands, they are poorer than their more established but less educated Turkish counterparts. While there is no tidy correlation between Syrian nationality and Assyrian ethnonationalism, the history of secularization in Syria is different from that in Turkey, making it more imaginable to disarticulate religious identity from political identity for these more recent arrivals.

Whether invested in the name Aramaean or simply Suryoyo, my parish friends could not relate to a sensory culture in which the line distinguishing ethnicity from religion made room for such famously pagan ancestral roots as the Assyrian Empire, for such an ancestry makes it perfectly possible to *think* being Assyrian without the West Syriac Rite, utterly undoing the ethical and affective attachment to Syriac Orthodoxy-as-kinship-practice so dear to descendants of those who arrived from Tur Abdin.

The problem I am describing here differs from that described by Kabir Tambar (2010, 2014) for Alevis in Turkey. Alevi ambivalence about the folklorization of *cem* ritual is due to the destabilizing effect on the ritual's religious significance and, thus, the political legibility of Alevi religious identity. There is a subtler tension for Syriac Christians in the gap produced by divergent secularization processes in Turkey and Syria. The AMVE's effort to perform Syriac Orthodox liturgical music as "secular" Assyrians— though in their minds they are as devoutly Christian as any Aramaean— is an effect of the interplay among distinct political situations taking place throughout Turkey and Syria in the twentieth century.

After World War I, the Syriac Orthodox Church's protected position under the Ottoman millet system collapsed when the patriarch failed to claim recognized minority status for Syriac Orthodoxy at the Treaty of Lausanne. Theories vary as to why. Some sources tell me that the patriarch wanted to reassure Ataturk that they were "loyal Turks." Others say that the patriarch was sabotaged by members of his delegation or that he was excluded from the treaty talks by Western powers who cast aside the Ottoman Christian minorities they had once targeted with their missionizing. Whatever the reason, the Syriac Orthodox lost their chance to exist on paper as a legally recognized minority. As Marta explained to me one night after choir practice while describing her work as a legal research intern for the Universal Syriac Alliance, now renamed the World Council of Aramaeans: "Legally, we don't exist. It feels bad."

These political machinations brought about a seismic shift in non-elite conceptions of Syriac Christianity's identity vis-à-vis the state, however, that identity was understood in diverse parts of the Middle East. Questions circulated: *Who, and what, are we? Are we a political or ethnic or religious group?* My friends in the choirs said to me over and over again: "We cannot explain to people who we are because we barely understand ourselves. But we are not fictional—we do exist. We are a *people*! [Dutch *volk*, Syriac *'amo*]." These questions continue to circulate rather than dissipate into post-migration assimilation or a settled notion of *Yes, we are indeed an ethnic group* or *No, we are simply a religious community* because the political significance of those categories in the states the Suryoye resided were not the same: to be a certain kind of religious person in Syria is not the same kind of political problem that it is in Turkey. Nor is it the same kind of problem to be a certain kind of ethnic person. This raises another question: In what ways might a "religious" identity be more or less politicized as a problem than an "ethnic" identity?

Studies in folklore (ironically) provide us with a clue. Folklorization has a long history as a tool of nationalists and nation-builders (Herzfeld 1986; Hobsbawm and Ranger 1983). Kabir Tambar (2010, 2014) shows that in the Turkish context, folklorized Alevi ritual is that which is domesticated and non-threatening, whereas others document how the piously worn head-scarf is deemed a discursive challenge to the secular authority of the state (Scott 2007). In the former situation, secularism depoliticizes religious difference by transforming the ontological ground of its intelligibility (i.e., what it *is* changes); in the latter, secularism politicizes religious difference by controlling its symbolic weight (i.e., how it is *represented* to the state and in public).

Ethnic claims attached to liturgical identity became more politically potent when early Assyrian composers wished to use the classical language to compose new songs about nonreligious topics. The patriarchate initially forbade it precisely for the ethnicizing effects it would have. The ecclesiastical hierarchy understood their structural dependence on first the Ottoman state, then the Turkish state under Ataturk, and then the Syrian state from 1933 onward. Saba Mahmood has similarly diagnosed the dangers of over-drawing the lines of ethnoreligious minorityhood against a national majority among Coptic Christians in Egypt (2012, 445–446). But as with everything related to the politics of the patriarchate, reports are conflicting as to whether this actually happened and why.

Reflecting on the Turkish context, we can infer that Syriac religious difference was a political challenge only inasmuch as it was fused with the perception of possible ethnic or national difference. This is because, historically, Turkish secularism is one of the faces of intense and symbolically excessive statism (Navaro-Yashin 2002). Secular state practices produced Turkish national identity in constitutive tension with Islamism, erasing any other form of difference from public life. In Turkish statism, the ethnoreligious is the kind of difference that poses a challenge to the sovereign state's

discursive power to ground ethnic Turkishness in culturalist conceptions
of Islam. One neutralizing response is to take out the religious by folklor-
izing it to make a community purely ethnic, or to take out the ethnic and
make it purely religious, defined by private, unobtrusive belief.

The effect of Turkish secularization was to impel the Christians of Tur
Abdin to engage in a radical privatization: church services, the use of Syriac, and the instruction of children had to be done in absolute secrecy. The
fervency of rural Turkish nationalism in its heyday pushed the Christians
of Tur Abdin to worship underground (often quite literally in chapels
carved into caves). To this day, the Turkish-born nuns at the Mor Ephrem
Monastery in the Netherlands cover their habits with black robes, while
the Syrian-born nuns do not. Teaching Syriac liturgy was periodically forbidden and so could be reformulated as neither strictly religious nor strictly
folkloric. Without a state audience to recognize the grounds of Syriac Orthodox difference, liturgical identity was illegible, invisible, and inaudible.
But, ironically, the closely enmeshed relationship between the villagers of
Tur Abdin and the ecclesiastical hierarchy enabled many young boys to
receive full-time liturgical education without attracting undue notice from
the state, a practice that continues in monastic summer schools throughout the global diaspora.

On the other side of the border, the tightly controlled pluralism of the
Syrian *Ba'at* Party created a space for Syriac Christian public identity that
was in some ways more open and, in other ways, more restricted. Ritual
mastery was more difficult to attain precisely because of Syriac Christians'
equal standing with other religious groups in the eyes of the state. More
consistent integration into public and economic life also resulted in, ironically, less time for liturgical education (Loosley 2009, 242) and less economic incentive for well-educated youngsters to become priests. A secular
Syrian sensory culture steeped in pan-Arab cultural and aesthetic practices
aimed at producing a distinctly Arab-Islamic musical modernity (Shannon 2006), as well as authoritarian state practices monitoring competing
ethnic claims (White 2007), shaped a religious sensorium in which sophisticated knowledge of the Beth Gazo was more likely to come from professionally trained musicologists than from semi-literate local priests. This
sensory culture opened a space for folklorization under conditions of complex countermovements of Arab and Assyrian ethnonationalism.

The danger was in declaring secular Assyrian ethnonationalist identity
too loudly. A politically developed form of Assyrian nationalism migrated

into Syria from northern Iraq after the Massacre of Simele in 1933 by the Iraqi army. Originating as displaced Assyrian refugees from the Hakkari Mountains who had been denied the right to return to their homelands by the League of Nations, this community settled in the Khabur River Valley of east Syria. Their experiences as stateless refugees in British-run camps in and around northern Iraq through much of the early twentieth century had cultivated a strong nationalist consciousness that informed their community-building efforts in Syria. The establishment of this Assyrian community in Syria was followed shortly by the Patriarchate, forcibly removed from Tur Abdin by the new Kemalist government. Not wishing to attract the ire of the newly formed Syrian state, the Patriarchate distanced itself from the ethnic discourse articulated by the Assyrians of the Khabur Valley and compelled many established churches in the global diaspora to change their names from the Apostolic Assyrian Church to the Syrian Orthodox Church (Makko 2010). The shift was later justified on epistemological grounds in a pamphlet written by Patriarch Mor Ignatius Ephrem I Barsoum in 1952 called "The Syrian Church of Antioch: Its Name and History," in which Syriac Orthodox Christians were informed that they would be excommunicated if they called themselves Assyrian.

Nonetheless, ethnonationalist discourses were reinvigorated by the Assyrian Democratic Organization, founded in Syria in 1957, and the spread of a global diaspora in the latter half of the twentieth century. Migration released many Syriac Orthodox Christians from structural dependence on the Turkish and Syrian states, emboldening them to follow the example of Armenians, Copts, and Kurds in articulating their sense of liturgical kinship and communal belonging in terms of ethnonational political identity. But, by that point, the rift between Assyrian identity and Aramaean identity was sedimented into people's sense of themselves and reproduced throughout the diaspora.

This complex history partially accounts for why using liturgical music for secular public performances disturbs many parishioners. When she found out about my research with the Mor Afrem Choir, my friend Sophia in Hengelo wanted to know, somewhat angrily, why the Mor Afrem singers never came to church. Sophia did not know for certain whether they actually attended church (she was wrong, as several young men in the secular choir were in fact sub-deacons at the church in south Enschede, where an Assyrian family dominates the politics of the parish). Nor was that knowledge really the point. Her anger, which was shared by Rebekah and Marta, indexes something deeper at work. It points to a difficult-to-articulate unease with performing the Beth Gazo in ways and in spaces that suggest other boundaries between the ethnic and the religious than they feel are real.

Syriac Orthodox experience suggests that minority recognition is conditioned by the organization of sensory practices in which domains of experience are constructed as separable. Attention to the dynamics of the subject-sensorium-sensory culture nexus deepens our understanding of the politics of minority recognition by showing how secular political practices operate as culturally productive aesthetic practices rather than merely proceeding *from* the cultural condition of secularity. The effects of secular state practices as different as the Syrian and Turkish regimes are woven into the fabric of Syriac Orthodox tradition through the ethics of recognition, while digital distribution makes this dissonance audible across the diaspora. The liturgical subject hears more clearly the discord among multiple modes of singing and being within the liturgical tradition and asks, "What can this mean?"

Vocal practices produce sounds that shape the sensorium, while listening practices ascribe and contest their meanings. If, as Saba Mahmood wrote (2005), there is an architecture to selfhood, then the sensorium is not only the laboratory of the self but the scaffolding through which the constant work of construction is undertaken. Crucially, the self and the scaffolding can be equally worked upon by the same tool: the voice. Being both *of* the body and emanating *out from* the body, the act of vocalization resonates within the subject's embodied sense of self in the very moment that it creates sounds for others to hear. But this points to a complex problem: there can be a difference between the way people sing and listen and the way they *think* about singing and listening. That Mariane and Elizabeta do not explicitly theorize what they are doing with their voices does not diminish the centrality of the voice in their practice; by reproducing the sounds of their grandparents' village in the style of Tur Abdin, they authorize themselves to explore new possibilities for embodying and inhabiting their sense of liturgical kinship. For them, the ethnic resides *within* the liturgical, which equals the village-based kinship network. On the other hand, Marta and Rebekah use their experiments in vocal technique to consolidate their position that their religious and ethnic identities are coterminous. The ethnic belongs in religious spaces because the ethnic *is* a religious space. Aramaeanism is the West Syriac Rite—the West Syriac Rite is Aramaeanism. The singers of the AMVE perform liturgical songs in a mode that subsumes Syriac Orthodoxy within a broader political category: the Assyrian nation. This category aligns with both West Syriac and East Syriac Rites so that it includes members of the Church of the East, as well as the Syriac Catholic and Chaldean Churches. It is "secular" in principle yet constitutively Christian in practice. Together, these disparate voices shape a diasporic sensory culture, heterogeneous in their analyses, intentions, and effects. This historical complexity materializes in Syriac Orthodox debates over the meaning of "politics," "religion," and "ethnicity." Such categories are deployed by secular power to keep ostensibly separate domains separate. But the voices in my study demonstrate a complex agency with profound political implications: the capacity to change the way the body inhabits these categories in real time. The power of the voice to be simultaneously internally and externally directed gives it this distinct agency. The material voice of the liturgical singer is a site of reproductive power where the ethics of recognition are worked through, as voices past and present resound discordantly in the effort to shape the future of the tradition and the relations it authorizes. In the abductive interplay between inherited materiality and open-ended imagination, their voices are icons.

The Iconic Voice

In this chapter, I have argued that the reproductive relation lies at the heart of iconicity and that this relation is what was at stake in both the struggle of my research participants to reproduce the microtonal melisma in their Passion Week hymn and in the confusion I experienced learning the same hymn situated in two distinct genealogies of authoritative Syriac Orthodox liturgical knowledge, one originating in the School of Edessa and the other in the School of Tur Abdin. In each choir, the singers strove to shape their sound in a relation of formal resemblance to invisible and inaudible precursors: their teachers' teachers and those teachers' teachers, in a chain of transmission all the back to St. Ephrem. I see this as analogous to the relation of formal resemblance, a relation requiring an interplay of materiality and imagination to create shared meaning that defines iconicity as a communicative process. The icon is the nexus of reproductive power, whether of God's infinite, redemptive plan for humanity or of the earthly sovereign's multisited governmentality or of the enduring community of the faithful. In Orthodox Christian doctrine and practice, the social process that emplaces the icon in incarnate history includes relations with the Divine. Creator and created are irreducibly bound together. Given an Incarnational economy in which the Divine unfolds their plan for the universe through geographical space and historical time, the icon is a site of reproductive power where divine and human agency commingle in the ongoing drama of human salvation.

Iconicity entails an exchange of gazes, a mutual recognition, between the human and the Divine claiming each other as kin. But in this case, we are talking about a vast and vibrant tradition of *sonic* iconicity, even if it is not explicitly named as such. As feminist anthropologists have long noted, the materiality of a human voice contains within it the histories of speaking and listening—the imaginative work of commemoration—that make a voice audible and intelligible to others. Amanda Weidman argues, for example, that a particularly gendered kind of power relation shapes how any of us "come into voice" and the kinds of voices any of us can assume (Weidman 2003, 195). The voice has multiple histories, contexts, and materialities and thus is a site of reproductive power through which the social relations that precondition social meanings are produced and transformed.

This iconic understanding of voice as a cultural object that is both productive of and produced by complex histories is linked to what Mikhail Bakhtin (1981) conceptualized as dialogism: human becoming is an effect of dialogue with others, and others' voices resound within our emerging sense of ourselves. In Syriac Orthodoxy, vocality is a practice of relating, of producing that irreducible relation we call kinship, and it depends upon a moment of recognition. To know that we are *of* each other and *belong* to each other, whether we understand that relation in religious terms or ethnic terms or in a sense that defies the secularist distinction between the two, we must perceive something *about* each other that *feels* familiar: we must recognize something of ourselves in the other in order to claim each other as kin. And so, the sensoriality of the voice is inescapably bound to its social significance, textured and trained and shaped as it is by the sociopolitical conditions that precede it (Dağtaş 2020; Eisenlohr 2018; Engelhardt 2015; Fox 2004). As Kristina Jacobsen-Bia writes, "Voices represent the meeting point between the individual and the social" (2014, 402). To this, I would add that the iconic voice represents the meeting point between the social and the Divine.

Another way to say this is that through chant, Syriac Christians soni-cally inscribe specific histories onto their bodies and into their hearts. In this way, the political charge of kinship, its anxieties, conflicting defini-tions, historical narratives, linguistic differences, regional disparities, and competing configurations are all audible within the sonic textures of the chant itself—in the strain to revoice the voices echoing silently in mem-ory. As the key site of reproductive power—the site where recognition is sought, established, and authorized—across the Syriac world, these voices materialize fragmented histories and make them available to generate new relational formations, which in turn give voice to their part in the mystery of Incarnation and salvation.

INTERLUDE

"WE GREW UP IN THEIR FEAR"

Field notes
July 13, 2010
Enschede Zuid, *De Posten Zorgcentrum*, in the neighborhood
Wesselerbrink
10:30 A.M.–1:30 P.M.

I take the train and the bus to Enschede from Hilversum. The transition from North Holland [the province] to Twente, on the eastern edge of province Overijssel, is subtle. Twente becomes a little less crowded, a little more spaced out. Taking the number 1 bus from the station to the last stop in Wesselerbrink, next to the *Zorgcentrum De Posten*, a publicly funded eldercare center, on a sunny, beautiful July day, I notice the nicely ordered neighborhoods with yellow and grey brick row houses from the '70s, '80s, '90s, followed by tenement high-rises, with lots of potted plants and flowers on the stairwells and balconies, colorful awnings, and surrounded by green trees and grassy spaces.

I arrive at De Posten, and Ester is waiting for me. She waves me over as I walk from the bus stop and welcomes me warmly. When she was young, Ester had been a regular member of her church choir. Now, she has grown children of her own and has turned her attention to eldercare. For the past three years, the Suryoye of Enschede have been permitted to operate a special *dagopvang* program, a daytime care service for Syriac Orthodox elders, which she runs. Families pay approximately 140 euros to the program to have their parents or their grandparents spend one, two, or three days a week at the care center, where they get to chat, play cards, and eat lunch. The Tuesday group is only women. Most women in the community, as with many others, have outlived their men. She chose this group for me to meet because they are particularly lively and still independent. Other groups, although more mixed, have more limitations and can be difficult to talk to.

The women are very friendly and express delight at my basic Turoyo. I employ both the phrases *taudi sagi* and *taudi rgh'elebeh* (different ways of saying thank you) and ask (knowing full well the answer) if they mean the same thing. Lots of happy nods, and Ester says yes, but *taudi sagi* is *ietsje meer netjes* ("a little more proper"). Most of them only speak a few words of Dutch, but two or three of the women make a point to speak to me entirely in Dutch without Ester having to translate. For the limitations described, as being of a generation that didn't have access to education and are generally isolated, these women speak impressively well.

There are eighteen women there in total, some drifting in a bit late. We sit around a large table, filling it up, with a few extra full chairs along the wall. Ester suggests I introduce myself, and she translates for me. Ester and I are quickly on the same page in understanding that these women won't even try to be orderly discussants and that we'll improvise as necessary. Before I even begin asking questions, the women are talking animatedly, often over each other, to tell stories.

We begin to go around the room as the women tell their names, their home village, and how long they have been in the Netherlands.

I ask them how life has changed for Suryoye women over the years and how their lives in Syria and Turkey were different from those of Suryoye women today in the Netherlands.

They tell me that they feel like their daughters are benefiting from opportunities they never had in Syria and Turkey. One of them had a sister who had gone to school, but almost all of these women were illiterate in any language, despite speaking four or five, and had never seen the inside of a school. When they were growing up, the Turkish and Syrian states were starting to establish schools in the remote villages, but not many, and as women, they generally couldn't go, either because their families felt they didn't need to be educated or because there was too much work to be done for the family and the farm. Some of the women tell me they didn't know there was such a thing as school growing up.

Ester sums up the rising discussion among the women: (1) in those days, it was very clear that women had less to say and weren't allowed to say it in front of men; (2) they had more duties; and (3) that while they had enough to eat, they had to work very very hard for their family's basic subsistence. They say it was *altijd erg angstig* ("always very scary"). They lived in constant, daily fear, especially of the Kurds, but of Muslim Turks also, who they felt were a danger to their girls and would steal their cattle.

One woman gives an example of her sister, who was able to attend the local school. The teacher fell in love with her and made advances, so her family pulled her out and sent her younger sister in her place. "My sister was smart and stayed home." At that time, in that place, one daughter from the household was required to attend school, or the family would be fined. This came from the *overheid*, the government.

The women talk about how they choose to keep their traditional clothing, headscarves, and long skirts because it is what they know and who they are. They don't mind their daughters and granddaughters dressing differently . . . several women, in fact, say, "If we were their age, we would do the same!" But . . . "*te bloot vinden wij niet normaal*" [too naked, we don't think is normal]. (*Normaal* = morally correct in Dutch cultural terms.) But, they continue, "we know things change with time, and its normal to adapt to the place where you grow up."

I ask about *madrasse*, church school, or what my friends also call *madrashto*, and they tell me that it was extremely difficult for them to attend because they had no rights then, and it was strictly forbidden by the Turkish government. Ester tells me that she received lessons in secret for three months from her parish priest and had to carefully hide her notebook showing the Syriac script in it. She once accidentally let her Turkish teacher see it when she was at public school, and he got very angry with her and ripped her notebook up, telling her never to do it again.

The women made sure to clarify that regular Sunday church attendance was allowed, just that learning anything outside of that wasn't allowed. This meant the girls had to do the best they could memorizing the words and melodies they heard in church on Sundays. For the older generation, though, they knew they were needed to work at home anyway, so learning at *madrasse* wasn't a high priority. There was a gudo for the men and a gudo for the girls, but mostly deacons were boys and men. In Ester's time, there was more stimulation and encouragement to join the gudo than in the older generation. Ideas among the church hierarchy were changing. They explained that in their time, women couldn't speak when men were around. . . . "We adopted the culture of our neighbors, like the clothes, and much more," one woman says. And so they are glad to have come to the Netherlands where their daughters and granddaughters have *meer vrijheid* ("more freedom"). Several interject sharply, though, saying: "*de mannen hebben meer moeite met de vrijheid van meisjes vandaag!*" ("The men have more difficulty with the freedom of girls today!") There is some chuckling and knowing, rueful glances. One woman, the only woman in the room, apart from Ester and her assistant Mona, not wearing a headscarf, looks at me intently and speaks to me in quite passable Dutch, repeating several times over the next ten minutes, piercing through the sound of the rambunctious chatter of the women around her with passion: "It's good this way, I like it much better! The girls should have freedom and opportunities! I am grateful to Europe! *Ik zeg dank je wel Europa!*" ("I say thank you, Europe!")

Ester interjects, saying, "In that time, women were supposed to be submissive (*onderdanig*). Marriage decisions were only made by the father—regardless of what the daughter or female members of the family felt or thought." One woman pipes up saying, "I was married when I was fourteen! Can you imagine?" The woman next to her says, "I had never met my husband before I married him." I ask them how they felt about all this at the time. The answer comes back to me: "Well, we didn't know anything else, so we just accepted it."

I then ask them: "But if it was normal to you, was it a shock to come to the Netherlands and see things done so differently?" To this, there is a bit of shrugging: "If our children can live with each other well, we're happy. It's fine." As an afterthought, one woman remembers something: "When I was young, all the women in our village would meet together in a certain place in town to socialize, and a man was outraged and tried to break us up and send us all home. We didn't listen!"

To them, adapting to the local cultural norms is part of their historical experience and identity: "In Turkey and Syria, we had to adapt to those around us . . . and now we are adapting to the Europeans. It's what we do." The scarfless woman speaks up again, expressing her gratitude to Europe.

Some of the women are getting restless, as it is approaching lunch time, but Ester asks me if I have any more questions. I tell her that I'd like to ask them about "*geloof*" (faith/belief), and she says, "Oh I think that geloof is everything to these ladies." I hear the word *mohimyo* a lot in the conversation that follows. Faith, for them, they tell me, is essential. They are happy to be Christian and that, in the Netherlands, they are free to express that. Before, they could only keep their *geloof* "in their hearts." The scarfless Dutch-speaking woman says, "There was a sword [*zwaard*] against us for our Christianity." (Sword = Sayfo in Syriac, and is the word to refer to the genocide also directed at the Armenians.) "This is what made our faith so strong," she says. "It's not something we can describe," another woman says.

But mentioning the Sayfo shifts the mood of the conversation . . . this is the generation that lost their parents, siblings, aunts, uncles, and cousins. Everyone lost someone, and everyone here still wants to talk about it. One woman said, "There were fifty-five people in my family before the Sayfo, then there were only ten after, and then they were enslaved by our neighbors in Turkey."

Someone said . . . "We had a fair amount of land that was ours, but almost all of it has been taken away." Someone else said: "Our identity is *geloof* [belief/faith] . . . we have nothing else. And so we're happy to be in the Netherlands because we can keep it here. Everything else has been taken. So many were murdered for what they believe . . . especially the beautiful girls" (*mooi meisjes*). Someone brings up Mor Gabriel; "For centuries it was ours! And they are still trying to steal it!"

I think it might be noon now, because several women have gotten up from the table and have started standing or sitting facing the eastern wall to pray. Their murmured prayers are audible through the conversation still going on at the table [*about their faith! The ironies, I note silently in my jottings, and then remember, writing these field notes up afterward, that there is no reason to assume these noonday prayers are universally obligatory. The praying women might simply be tired of my questions.*] and they repeatedly make the sign of the cross. I ask the remaining women at the table if the younger generations in the Netherlands now understand what they went through and experienced. The answer comes back mixed. Some feel they do, some feel they don't. . . . It depends on the young person.

Ester says, of her own four children, two of them are very actively involved with their identity as Suryoye, while one of them doesn't care at all, and feels it is all in the past. But, someone says, it is exactly now, because they are here, the young people CAN learn about their identity and history in a way that wasn't available to them in Syria and Turkey. Here they have the *mogelijkheid*, the possibility. This word keeps coming up, over and over again. The idea of what is possible and impossible is important.

Mogelijkheid en vrijheid! Possibility and freedom!

Someone says, "These things are still happening in the Middle East! It's happening in Egypt, against the Christians, it happened to family members of one of the women just fifteen years ago, who still lived in a village in Turkey, when the whole family was killed, including a young pregnant mother."

Another woman says, "I had an aunt who was stabbed seven times in an effort to get her to convert to Islam, and yet another woman had an uncle who was murdered six months after his wedding."

Another woman told a story of a long conversation she had with her washing machine fix-it man, who, when he saw the crosses in her house, started asking her about her Christianity. She told him the story of their persecution, and he mentioned that in Europe, Protestants and Catholics fought each other for centuries. She said to him, "Well at least they had an equal go at it! For us it was always one-sided, and we were never able to fight back!" He felt bad after that and didn't charge her for repairing the washing machine.

Another woman told a story of her mother-in-law, who had been kidnapped by a local Muslim man and had three children with him. After some years, Mary came to her in a dream, telling her to flee to another village or she would die. She did so, leaving her three children behind.

The women say: "Our parents endured terrible things, and we grew up in their fear."

It's hard, they tell me; these stories are only in their hearts. They aren't written or documented anywhere. There are no photographs, no films, no books . . . nothing about it, and that's what makes it so hard, they say.

Toward the end of the conversation, one woman turns to me and asks Ester to translate: "She wants to make sure you understand and don't have the wrong idea: we don't hate Muslims because they are Muslim. We just don't trust them because of what they've done."

"*Gelukkig zijn wij in Europa.* [Luckily we are in Europe.] We're glad our children are getting educated and getting jobs . . . *dat geeft ons voldoening* [That gives us satisfaction]. *Voor veiligheid zijn wij hier gekomen* [We came here for safety]." Ester says, "This generation of women gave everything of themselves to others, trying to save their families, and never did or took anything for themselves. So they've earned this. This is why we have a *dagopvang* for them. They grew up as intensely social, interconnected people, so the least we can do is try to give them a space where they don't have to be isolated and alone, and where we can take a bit of care of them and pay them some attention." Ester tells me that her *opa*, her grandfather, had to flee after he lost his entire family in the Sayfo, and when he arrived in the Netherlands, he kissed the ground and said thank God we are in a Christian country. More women tell me about family members lost in the Sayfo. . . . These are the children of the few who survived and escaped: *Here we don't have to worry about our children and whether they'll make it home alive on any given day.* One uncle and cousins were *gedwongen om Moslim te worden* [forced to become Muslim] but they refused and were killed and thrown onto the snow to be trampled by horses. Another woman's aunt was killed on her rooftop.

The voices and stories keep coming and I can't write it all down fast enough.

The conversation starts to break down as the women are hungry and lunch is arriving. While Mona starts to set the tables, Ester takes me to the front desk to get copies of the books they've put out on the life stories of elderly people at the eldercare center. I meet several of her Dutch co-workers in different departments. The front desk lady is friendly and accommodating, as are others. The center is very modern and nice, beautifully designed and with a good feeling about it.

A young Dutch man in a plastic hair covering brings a large cart with lunch on it. They serve ground pork wrapped in bacon, or beef in sauce for a few individuals, braised red cabbage with apple, and instead of the potatoes that are served to other clients of the center, Ester and Mona serve bulgur they have prepared themselves in their own little kitchen. This is accompanied by poached pears and little containers of *vla*, a Dutch dessert distantly kin to American-style pudding. The room has a door opening to a small patio and the grassy lawn, and contains two large tables and several comfortable chairs, some small couches, a desk with a computer for Ester, and a small kitchen with a stove, sink, and amenities for making coffee and tea. I help distribute the meals and then sit at the smaller table with Ester, Mona, and two of the older women. While we eat, I ask about the tattoos many women have. It turns out that they were once a fashion in Tur Abdin, which some parents disapproved of, just as it is now. The women simply did it because they liked how it looked, although a small number of women received more elaborate tattoos on their inner forearms when they went on a pilgrimage to Jerusalem. The two women at the table with us show me their arms: one has a tattoo of the Virgin Mary with Child, and the other has a tattoo of the crucifix.

While we eat, I ask Ester about the Suryoye experience of the Netherlands and Dutch people, pushing somewhat on the "integration" discourse
I hear everywhere. Somewhat reluctantly, Ester admits that there is a no-
ticeable pressure and lack of understanding among Dutch people about
how hard it is for this generation of women to learn Dutch. Most of them
never went to school and wouldn't know how to even start learning. The
women *wish* they could speak Dutch . . . they feel bad that they can't, but
it's very, very difficult for them. Circumstances have not been conducive,
and it took a lot for them to just get to a point where their children could
survive. One of Ester's colleagues walks in the room just as we have fallen
silent on this subject, and we remain quiet, looking at each other with sudden strange mutual consciousness that we both know not to talk about
this in front of white Dutch people. It's as if we're both holding our breath
until her colleague leaves the room.

After lunch, the lady who often stands by herself outside and seems to
be a bit of an outcast sits down next to me at the table, while other women
are starting to nap or play cards. She speaks better Dutch than any of the
other women except for the scarfless lady, though she is still difficult to
understand. As she talks to me, she starts to cry. She tells me (I think) that
she has lost a daughter, a son, a brother, her parents, and her husband, and
that she lives alone. She is very lonely. She is the woman who lived in Rijssen for many years before coming to Enschede. She says it's better in Rijssen than in Enschede because they are better Christians there (it is famous
for being a holdout of strict conservative Dutch Reformed communities).
She tells me she has people buried in Syria, Turkey, Glanerbrug, and Arbo,
and she has little contact with her grandchildren. She says words that are
difficult for me to understand, but it seems to be about domestic violence,
the neighbors, the police, and the crime and youth in Enschede. She is very
upset.

She notices and is angry that the other women in the room are starting
to whisper about her. She says, "I know what they're saying! I can hear
them! They're saying, oh look at her, she's getting warm talking to Sarah!" As
we go outside, she says, "*verdomde vrouwen* [those damned women]!" Coming to the senior center doesn't seem to help much with her loneliness. She
seems deeply angry, and I can speculate about the circumstances of her
life which would lead plenty of people to angry conclusions. She stands
out on the grass as I walk toward the bus stop. When the bus picks me up,
we wave goodbye to each other as I ride away from her.

Later, when I get off the bus stop at the station to walk to the Tuesday market for cheese and vegetables, I observe a man on a bike angrily shouting about something that someone now out of my view has just done. I only pick up the last words of his angry tirade: *Belachelijke Surinamers!* [Ridiculous Surinamese!]

The scene is disconcertingly familiar. Where have I heard this before?

And then it comes to me: a few months prior, the day after Easter, when the entire community congregates at the monastery to visit their dead in the cemetery. Thousands of people pass through in one day, with cars and bikes piled up on the narrow country lane. As I was arriving myself, I witnessed a road rage incident, where a white Dutch woman passing by on a bike began shouting furiously at the crowd: *Wat zijn jullie belachelijk!* [How ridiculous you all are!]

CHAPTER

4

DAUGHTERS OF THE COVENANT

Outsiders who see rules and not the love that runs through them are often too ready to label other people as "prisoners." (Murdoch 1978, 60)

Mary and Martha

That summer, during midday prayers at the monastery, two Greek Ortho-dox nuns came to visit at the bishop's invitation. After prayers, the visiting nuns joined us for lunch. Among the party were the bishop, Father Yaqub; several other monks; my friend Elena, the choir singer from Chapter 1; Peter, my Syriac teacher; a small crowd of summer school boys; and me. The Greek Ortho-dox Mother Superior was Dutch-born, we learned, while the younger nun was a Greek national by birth, and they addressed us in English, the most commonly spoken language in the room. The Mother Superior was raised, we learned, in a nonreligious household in The Hague, where she began attending a Russian Orthodox Church as a teenager. She then found the Greek Orthodox Church and became a nun at twenty-one. The primary reason for her conversion to Orthodoxy, she told the assembled eaters, was the ancientness of its traditions.

"Having an ancient tradition is everything!" she declaimed with a piercing glance at every young person in the room. ". . . But translating and under-standing that tradition is everything too!"

"In which language do you pray?" asked the bishop politely. "Do you pray in Greek?"

"Oh, in Dutch, of course! Although sometimes we perform the Mass in different languages when we are with nuns and priests from different parts of the world, but we always know where we are because we know the melody and because we understand the meaning of what we are praying."

As the conversation progressed, the bishop gently prodded the summer school students into asking questions. Fourteen-year-old Gabriel asked the same question that, I learned later, was also on my friend Elena's mind: "Didn't your parents have a problem with you becoming a nun?"

"Well, yes," the Mother Superior replied, "but what could they do? I was twenty-one, so I was free!" As the Greek nun spoke, I became aware of Elena and Peter beside me, their mood shifting, consternation creeping over their faces. Elena was speechless. Later, she told me, she couldn't think of what to say because it hurt so much to hear God and faith and family spoken of in this abstracted, disconnected way. Peter, meanwhile, knew exactly what he wanted to say. "But . . . what happens to the language of the liturgy?!," he sputtered. "If you translate it and only think about understanding, you lose the language!" The Mother Superior was matter-of-fact: "Do we all learn Hebrew to understand the Psalms? No! Did Christ speak Greek? No! But the New Testament was written in Greek for a reason, so people could understand!"

Peter's expression hardened at the uncomfortable reminder that no part of the earliest versions of Holy Scripture were written in Syriac, while the nuns continued to describe their work painting icons and translating liturgical texts. In all black, with no visible adornment of any kind, the Greek Orthodox women were a striking contrast in their open, easy confidence and self-possession to the Syriac nuns who could appear, to many outsiders, as silent and subservient. I noticed, then, Sister Simona, the Syriac nun in charge of housekeeping, silently fuming at the doorway as we continued to talk in the dining room well after we had finished eating. She had a cleaning schedule to keep but couldn't clear our plates to wash up until the bishop departed. Finally, he rose, signaling the end of the meal, and we all walked over to the big church at the center of the monastery's grounds to watch the summer school boys give their final examination performance in front of parents and extended families, as Sister Simona slammed dishes in our wake.

*   *   *

Earlier that day, before our lunch with our Greek Orthodox visitors, Elena had suggested to me that we help one of the other nuns, Sister Marina, prepare the aula, *the event hall attached to the main church building, for that evening's goodbye party. Sister Marina was younger than Sister Simona and so was often assigned the most physically arduous housekeeping tasks. As Elena and I helped Sister Marina lift tables and set out chairs, we could hear the summer school boys playing outside in the courtyard through the open windows. Suddenly, the courtyard went quiet, and Elena said, "Oh, lunch must have started!" I suggested that we should go, but Elena wouldn't stop what she was doing, laying plates and silverware on the tables. After a few minutes, knowing from experience not to keep the bishop waiting, I decided to join the others, hoping she'd follow me, but she didn't—not until everyone had begun eating. When I entered the cloister from the courtyard, a harried-looking Father Yaqub came bustling down the corridor in search of Elena and me. He cried out in Dutch, "Where were you this whole time, Sarah?! Where is Elena?!" I told him, "We were helping Sister Marina in the aula! Elena is still there."*

"But it is time to eat now!" he said. "Hurry!" I rushed to the dining room where everyone but Elena had already taken their seat. As I sat, the bishop leaned toward me and asked in a low voice: "Where is Elena?" As I explained her tardiness, I said, in hopes of defending my friend in terms he would appreciate: "It is a bit of a Mary and Martha situation, you see."

With a small smile, he looked away.

∗ ∗ ∗

In previous chapters, I have argued for an understanding of the sonic icon as a nexus of recognition, reproductive power, and ethical self-fashioning, a site where kin relations are generated and where they may be safely experimented upon under the cover of authoritative tradition. In Chapter 2, I explored the history of Christian liturgy and its interface with imperial theological politics and sociopolitical formations as embodied memory. The memory of the senses, transmitted as much through the structuring omissions of gendered social reproduction as through material, mediatic, and ethical practice, is a wellspring of relational reinvention. In Chapter 3, I examined some of these practices in detail. My central premise, thus far, is that the voices of young diasporic Syriac Orthodox Christians like Elena, a stalwart choir singer in her parish and community organizer for her diocese, and Peter, a widely respected *qoroyo* (Reader, two ranks below a deacon), are sonic icons. With their voices-in-prayer, Elena, Peter, and their peers reproduce and reinvent the

relations that make Syriac Orthodoxy a living tradition and a sociopolitical form. When juxtaposed with the vocal practices and political orientations described in the previous chapter, this story of a devout and devoted
young woman working at cross-purposes with her bishop, an ecclesiastical authority she regards with high esteem and deep affection, raises a
question about the intersection of different sites of reproductive power in
generating liturgical kinship in diaspora. These stories demonstrate both
the obscurity and the centrality of gendered affective labor in processes
of reproduction. In Marta and Rebekah's confidence-building vocal exercises in the previous chapter and in Elena's defiant care for Sister Marina's workload in this chapter, each woman navigates conflicting pressures
and constraints as they labor to reproduce their varying interpretations
of what they see as the core ethical relationships without which, in their
words, Syriac Christianity will simply cease to be.

There are several triads of tension immediately apparent in the ethnographic scenes described above, which highlight a series of quandaries about
how to configure relations among families, parishes, and monasteries,
among liturgies, classical languages, and spoken vernaculars, and among
the visibility of some kinds of reproductive labor (e.g., scholarship, translation, icon-painting) and the invisibility of other kinds of reproductive
labor (e.g., cleaning, cooking, setting up for events). These triads converge
in Elena's defiant loyalty toward the Syriac nuns, expressed through her
domestic labor and in the connection between Elena's and Peter's feelings
about the Mother Superior's indifference toward family and the sacrality
of Syriac. I argue that these triads of tension reflect broader gendered patterns in a Syriac Orthodox soteriological system—that is, a metaphysical
economy of salvation rooted in Trinitarian Incarnational theology—but
they also contain further complexities within them that point to the problem of multiply-scaled audiences and contexts in producing the relations
that produce the Syriac world

One of the central predicaments of diasporic Syriac Orthodox daughterhood and motherhood is the pervasiveness of modernizing discourses
that link religious reform to the "emancipated" speaking subject,[1] a religious subject who understands, intellectually, the doctrinal ground of her
faith practices. This is a subjectivity that, I suspect, the bishop was hoping to
steer Elena toward by engaging the Greek Orthodox nuns that day. Yet this
hope ran aground on Elena's commitment to the very relations of liturgical kinship in which he, too, is embedded and to which he, too, is com-

mitted. These relations are organized around a gendered distribution of pastoral care and soteriological agency, leading to divisions of labor, knowledge, and authoritative speech among families.

Authoritative theological knowledge of the kind the Greek Orthodox nuns displayed that day is highly uneven among women throughout the Syriac world. There are a small handful of *malphonithe*, women liturgical teachers, mostly in North America, Sweden, and Syria, who are in possession of an ecclesiastically authorized understanding of Syriac Orthodox women's liturgical presence and purpose. Otherwise, most are left to their own devices to reformulate their sense of what they are doing when they perform their liturgical role in the West Syriac Rite from the materials they have inherited, both inside of church and outside: sonic forms from their fathers, uncles, priests, and senior deacons and ethical forms from their mothers, aunts, grandmothers, and friends. They bridge these forms through affective labor, doing the work to reproduce and maintain intimate relations that weave families, parishes, and cloisters together into a tightly knit fabric. That they rarely theorize or theologize these practices explicitly, however, does not mean that they do not bear theoretical or theological weight, nor that their practices of ritual, social, and sexual reproduction belong to separate domains. Rather, their ritual practices materialize a theology of kinship that becomes heightened and, therefore, more perceptible to outsiders like me, in moments when their affective and ethical practices rub up against other models of reproductive labor—such as, in the cases I explore in this chapter, the gendered and racialized Dutch discourse of "minority" motherhood and its fixation on the "emancipated speaking subject."

Because my methodological focus on theological politics does not distinguish between "everyday life," "ritual," or "theology" as separable analytical categories or ethnographic entities, I seek in this chapter to illuminate how different understandings of reproductive power—which I see as a coherent yet contested practical theology of gender and kinship—emerge at the intersection of established Syriac covenantal theology, of Dutch immigration politics, and of recent histories of violence and displacement in the Middle East. I explore the lingering effects of violence, displacement, and intergenerational trauma further in the next chapter; here, I attend to Syriac Orthodox women's engagement with the gendered dimensions of Dutch "minority" integration policies and the effects of these policies on how they interpret and enact a practical theology of kinship. I show how they weave disparate sources of authority into their understanding of what it is to have a "voice" in a sociopolitical sense and how their "voices" become iconic sites of reproductive power even when they deliberately silence themselves. I situate their gendered affective labor within the diasporic circulation of the Incarnational concept of *ihidoyutho*, or "singleness," a common topic of the bishop's public teaching, to illuminate the soteriological tradition that frames their labor. In what follows, I show how Syriac Orthodox women interpret that soteriological tradition and their ethical obligations to reproduce it in variable ways as mothers and daughters, aunts and nieces, and sisters and wives.

Soteriology and the "Single" Girl

Elena's affective labor takes place against the backdrop of a soteriological tradition—that is, a tradition of theorizing how salvation works—that foregrounds the gender of Incarnate reproductive power in the unfolding of God's plan for human redemption. This soteriological system links the politicized vocal practices of the previous chapter to Elena's defiant domestic labor at the monastery in this chapter. The contours of such a logic appear vividly in a story recounted by Tala Jarjour (2018) in her ethnomusicological study of Syriac Orthodox chant at St. George's Church in Aleppo, Syria, which both demonstrates the global reach of this logic and clarifies what I mean by a liturgical role, a ritual location, and a theology of kinship. Jarjour describes a woman she calls Farida who, despite her masterful liturgical expertise equaling or exceeding that of fully ordained senior male deacons, is forbidden from participating in the foot-washing ritual of Holy Week. Despite her liturgical role as a mshamshonitho and malphonitho, Farida is forbidden to occupy the ritual location of one of the Twelve Apostles whose feet Jesus Christ washed before the Last Supper prior to his Crucifixion, because the bishop of Aleppo, standing in the position of Jesus Christ in the ceremony, would be reduced to washing the feet of a woman. This would amount to such an unthinkable transgression against patriarchal authority that it is repeatedly invoked as grounds for denying Farida her claim to be ordained as a full deaconess, as many fourth-century Daughters of the Covenant are believed to have been. Instead, Farida retains the liturgical status of a child Reader (like Peter), despite the respect and deference she otherwise commands for her liturgical expertise (Jarjour 2018, 150–159).

This prohibition might be attributed to culturally patterned gender norms or to the bishop's sexual modesty, but in my view there is a deeper ritual logic to parse out in this limit on who can participate in the liturgy and how. The reason a woman cannot represent one of the Twelve Apostles during the Passion Week is, in this analysis, because Syriac Orthodox ritual works generatively as well as symbolically and performatively. In one sense, the ritual of the Twelve Apostles works symbolically, in the tradition of Syriac poetic theology conveyed by the term *rozo*, or "mystery," which is as much a materialization of divine power in the immediate present as it is a metaphorical mode of storytelling. In another sense, the ritual works performatively in that it proceeds through a citational, iterative process to produce effects—in this case an emotional response to the story of Christ's Passion that is doctrinally prescribed for this moment in the liturgical cycle. In a third sense, the ritual works generatively in that the intersensorial dimensions of collective singing and listening sediment the affective and ethical bonds that reproduce relations among the Urfalli congregation in Aleppo as an ethnically bounded community—by identifying the story of Christ's Passion with their recent memory of forcible removal from their ancestral homes in Urfa, Turkey. The symbolic, performative, and generative logics of the liturgy work simultaneously to create states, relations, and persons through the affective labor of women and men who voice distinct parts in the cosmic drama of Christ's Passion.

In this context, the ritual enactment of the foot-washing would generate a new kind of relation between the bishop and Farida, fundamentally altering the material substance and function of his patriarchal authority in relation to her, which would transgress the broader soteriological tradition—an economy of salvation in which each part depends on each other part to sustain the whole—through which the congregational community understands itself ethnically as well as theologically.

This broader soteriological tradition further demands that parish priests the world over must marry, for the pressures and strains of pastoral care require that a priest be sexually fulfilled and emotionally cared for by a wife. A holier and higher status bishop, whose attention must be directed to loftier affairs than that of everyday parish life, must be ordained from the order of celibate priest-monks who are disciplined, often from a very young age, into the rigors of ascetic life under the supervision and support of a dedicated community. Even here, however, the gendered and sexual dynamics of ritual power are closely monitored and policed and can be seen as devastatingly disruptive when disregarded. This is why, in retrospect, Elena's subtle defiance of the bishop at lunch so unnerved me. But her defiance was not straightforward: Elena used silence and avoidance strategically on behalf of the relations she found essential to the integrity of the whole.

This dynamic became clearer to me in discussion with the sisters Mariane and Elizabeta Mansur, who revealed one day how relations with ecclesiastical authority have—ironically, in their eyes—complicated their experiments in liturgical revitalization. They told me the story of their older brother. I had wondered for many months why the older brother of some of the most energetic and dedicated liturgical singers in the parish seemed so utterly indifferent to church. It seemed out of character for a member of this family. One day, years before my fieldwork began, they told me, Gabriel Mansur had co-organized a popular series of Bible studies and church parties (*hafle*) throughout the region. In fact, it was at one of these Bible study meetings that their oldest sister Ilona, described below, had met her husband. These events were so well-planned, informative, and fun that young people from other Syriac Orthodox parishes throughout the province began to attend regularly. The Bible study series was held in a different church every month and was led by three young, Western-educated monks who had grown up in Germany but had sought monastic orders at the Mor Ephrem Monastery. After some time, several church board members grew discontented with the popularity of these events. Soon a rumor spread that the monks were behaving inappropriately with young women throughout the parishes—by taking their confessions. It came to light that many young men and women were uncomfortable going to their own parish priests for confession because their priests had been raised and trained in the monasteries of Tur Abdin and thus had little understanding or empathy for the realities of everyday life among young people in Europe. Many young men and women turned to the monks of the Bible study for confession instead. Eventually, word got around to the ecclesiastical hierarchy that these monks were speaking to young women in private. They were excommunicated by the patriarch, which put an end to the Bible studies and church parties.[2] The monks left the country and joined a South Indian jurisdiction with connections to the Syriac liturgical tradition, while many previously devoted young people were left traumatized and disillusioned. Gabriel was devastated. Feeling betrayed by the church authorities, even today he no longer attends weekly Mass. Yet he still prays and fasts in solitude and with his family. No one among them, as devout and devoted as they are, holds his absence from public liturgical events against him; his housebound practice of ritual and filial piety suffices.

What was striking about this series of events was that the key controversy that led to the downfall of the excommunicated monks, from the Mansur family's perspective, was a disagreement over authorized forms of speaking and listening within a theologically ordered set of embodied relational ethics. Elizabeta and Mariane's father explained to me that the monks had been excommunicated for good reason. Only priests may receive confession from women, he said, precisely because priests are married, and so their bodies and minds are cultivated to contain and manage whatever sexual implications may be in the confession. Monks, in contrast, are not married, so it is understood that they cannot handle taking confession from women. They make for excellent cousins, uncles, and grand-uncles, but they lack the relational skills, emotional resources, and bodily disciplines to maintain appropriate boundaries and fatherly dispositions toward those who would confess to them. Their primary obligations lie elsewhere, particularly in various forms of authorized knowledge transmission and dissemination, from teaching liturgical forms to young people, to calligraphy and bookmaking, to scholarly research, translation, and publication, all activities which are seen to have a pastoral and liturgical function in ensuring the well-being of the Syriac tradition and its faithful. Father Yaqub explained it this way when we were discussing a major sex abuse scandal in the Dutch Roman Catholic Church that had just erupted in the national news. Father Yaqub felt that the scandal was evidence that the Roman Catholic Church really needed to start permitting its priests to marry. "Celibacy is a challenge," he said,

> you cannot be single-handedly responsible for the well-being of a parish when you do not have the support of the marriage relationship. It is different for monks. We are a community, so we give each other the support necessary to manage the challenge of celibacy. If you are a celibate priest on your own and you are dealing with all the personal problems of your congregation, it is too hard. You need to have a wife and a family to manage it.

Raised in Turkey at an age young enough to have been educated in the secular school system and to have served in the military, Father Yaqub's take on the sexual politics of priestly and monastic pastoral authority was clear that the point was not a question of women's sexual danger to men *per se*, which is how conservative Christians often justify gendered social roles. He was concerned, rather, with how the community as a whole distributes responsibility for managing the different kinds of tensions that inevitably arise in a tightly knit kinship network.[3]

For Syriac Orthodox women, this distribution of pastoral labor can mean several things. When it comes to liturgy's dramaturgical mechanics, a mshamshonitho's ritual location is offstage, away from the altar, where she is not permitted to stand. From the perspective of ecclesiastical authority, her voice should be audible, but her body should be invisible.[4] In the parishes of the Netherlands, there is disagreement as to whether the Daughters of the Covenant ought to be virgin girls who then leave the choirs once they marry. Many young women I know choose to follow that path. In giving disembodied voice to the biblical mothers, daughters, and sisters of the eternal and ongoing story of Salvation, *mshamshonithe* occupy a specific ritual location that exists on a continuum of the liturgical drama, fulfilling a pastoral role that complements, but does not replicate, the pastoral roles of priests and monks. This point was brought home to me in a conversation with Mor Polycarpus, during which the usually unflappable bishop surprised me with the heat of his anger on the subject of singers who imagine they perform the liturgy for their own benefit, or worse yet, for the admiration of others. The purpose of women's participation in the gudo, he insisted, is pastoral and soteriological: it is a vital service toward the salvation and well-being of the broader community as a whole. Following this logic, when a Daughter of the Covenant marries and bears children, she moves to another ritual location in the drama of salvation, where her care for the community shifts into a maternal register, and many of the women I describe below do view their maternal and domestic labor in this sense—but not all.

From many Western Christian perspectives, the pastoral and the soteriological belong to distinct domains; they may be related, but they are often conceptualized as discrete theological categories, as soteriology has to do with salvation, eternity, and eschatology, while the pastoral has to do with the everyday here and now. In the tradition I am describing here, the pastoral and soteriological are coterminous. The extent to which different Christians understand these two domains as having anything to do with each other depends on where they stand on the enduring theological questions of time and agency. As West Syriac liturgical theologian and church historian Fr. Baby Varghese (2004) observes, for Syriac Orthodox Christians, eschatology is not necessarily "future-oriented" as it is for those traditions within Christianity for whom salvation in the future remains an open question, as it depends on either human agency, Divine agency, or some complex configuration of the two. Mor Polycarpus tried to explain the difference to me as diplomatically as he could: "In Syriac Orthodoxy, we understand God to be less of a judge in the way that Latin Christianity does, and more of a physician." He checked himself momentarily and said, "It is not that it is wrong, that way of thinking—justice is important. But for us, the emphasis is on healing and restoration. It happens over and over: every day, we need to be healed and brought close to God again. Every day, we need salvation anew."

This theological discourse of daily, cyclical renewal, of individual healing bound up with the healing of the collective Body of Christ in the world, draws upon the ancient Christological concept of *ihidoyutho*, "singleness," a point first brought to my attention by Peter in Chapter 2 when explaining his reluctance to be promoted to the next rank of the diaconate. In terms of his knowledge of the texts, the grammar, and the melodies of the Beth Gazo, Peter was more than prepared for promotion but refused because he was not, in his words, prepared to be an *ihidoyo*, a moral paragon of Christian virtue, an imitator of Christ. He came to this conclusion reading the medieval theologian Bar ʿEbroyo's theological treatises and listening to Mor Polycarpus's homilies and public lectures.

Liturgical practice gains a new salience with this perspective on the convergence of the daily and the eternal into a cyclical pattern of salvation as restoration and healing. It relies on an economy, in the ancient sense of the *oikonomia*, in which sexual and social reproduction are connected to notions of holiness for both the individual and the community. The enduring salience of such a connection, even as it is reconfigured over time, is attested in both medieval and late-antique Syriac Orthodox texts. In early Syriac tradition, this discourse of singleness was central to the Bnoth Qyomo, the fourth-century Daughters of the Covenant. Both *qyomo* and *ihidoyutho* convey the notion of a "covenant," which in English denotes a holy pact between humans and the Divine, defining the faithful as God's chosen people. This pact is generally understood by Christians to have originated in the Old Testament account of God's covenant with Abraham, Isaac, and Jacob, and to have been replaced by the new covenant of Jesus's Incarnation, Death, and Resurrection. Yet even in English, how

Christians understand what is entailed in the notion of "covenant" is far from straightforward or uncontested, as I explained in Chapter 2.

'Ihidoyutho undergirds the notion of the living icon—of becoming, literally, the embodiment of God's promise of salvation in the sense that my teacher, Peter, also meant. This literalness, the transformational logic of rozo, the Divine Mystery, is one possible interpretative response to Paul's writings on the theological significance of the human body, elaborated in a cultural milieu that shared more in common with Jewish views of marriage and community than with Greek or Roman views. Historian Naomi Koltun-Fromm has argued that despite early Syriac authors' faith in the revolutionary transformation of Christ's Incarnation, Death, and Resurrection, they integrated their understanding of the New Covenant with a contemporaneous Jewish view of the connections among holiness, sexuality, endogamy, and heredity, such that children could inherit holiness from holy parents (2010). Out of this long and complex tradition of interpreting scripture, a view of the relationship between asceticism and married life emerges not as a spiritual hierarchy or opposition, as it has in much of Latin Christianity, but as complementary modalities of soteriological agency. Within such a tradition, it would make sense then why the medieval ascetic Bar 'Ebroyo, Peter's favorite writer, considered the practical questions of monastic living and wifely virtue to be equally under his jurisdiction and suitable subjects for the same written treatise; within such a soteriological system, they belong to the same domain. Much more recently, Father Varghese has put the relational ethics undergirding the logic of salvation in somewhat more general terms, allowing for greater interpretive space among his transnational, twenty-first-century Syriac Orthodox audience: "Liturgy is a relationship, liberation from individualism and egoism and therefore it is a means of salvation" (Varghese 2004, 171). Yet his position—the view that liturgy is a pathway of salvation because it generates the relationships that alleviates the problems of living for oneself rather than for others—contains echoes of earlier Syriac covenantal theology.

But in this relatively open interpretive space around the relational conditions of soteriological agency, a new fissure appears. Some women increasingly believe that following this trajectory from virginal mshamshonitho to married mother puts the survival of the women's choirs at risk by leaving them in the hands of inexperienced girls with little skill and waning interest in the institution's historic significance. Such women have begun returning to the choir after marriage and childbirth to strengthen its sound and the social fabric that connects the choirs to the broader community. Those that follow this path find other ways to configure the relationship between their ritual and kin locations in their understanding of the soteriological significance of their reproductive labor. In transposing their ritual and kin locations, they seek to remain faithful to an embodied theology in which their role in a reproductive economy of salvation is inseparable from their sonic contributions to performance of the West Syriac Rite. Elena's obligations as a liturgical singer demand that she support Sister Marina with her housekeeping duties in preparation for a major event in the liturgical life of the community, much to the bishop's chagrin. Those that follow a different path, meanwhile, find other ways to transpose the relationship between their ritual and kin locations, as they respond to demands placed upon them by the Dutch state's interest in managing "minority" motherhood, a function of its broader concern with the "integration," or *inburgering,* of racialized new minorities. I map out some of these varied pathways in the second half of this chapter, after a brief interlude in which Elena asks us directly to consider how the Dutch state inadvertently intervenes in the relations among cloistered women and the girls who care for them.

Elena Reflects

That same summer evening, after the summer school boys' public examinations, Elena and I talked in her bedroom, a tiny monastic cell adjoining my own, to reflect on our time with the Greek nuns. Sister Simona's barely contained fury was only the tip of the iceberg of what had been wrong all day, and much of Elena's defiance of the bishop, however mild and oblique, was rooted in her concern for Sister Marina, who had been tasked with far too much labor for far too high stakes an event than she could handle on her own. This reflected what Elena saw as a broader problem of the inequitable distribution of labor among the nuns, which led to interpersonal conflict and no clear "manager" to handle a very challenging set of relationships and personalities. She said:

"I think I should talk to the bishop about it. It's not supposed to be like this. I visited Mor Gabriel Monastery in Tur Abdin a few years ago. That is actually why I do this volunteer work for the diocese now and why I recommitted to my parish choir! I spent time with the nuns, and it was so beautiful. Their relationships were beautiful. They were a community. They took care of each other. They had their own Mother Superior to manage them and make sure everything was fair. That was my spiritual awakening! That was when I really started to feel responsibility for the Church. I felt the love and the care when I visited the nuns and it made me want to take better care of the Church here. I began with trying to teach basic classical Syriac to the children in my parish in Rijssen. But so many of the elderly men were constantly angry and complaining about it, so I started to feel frustrated, and I gave up and felt like, 'Who am I to be doing this? I am just a girl!' But then, this is why I am so happy with our new bishop! (Did you know he is my cousin? We come from the same village originally!) He respects women. He listens to us and cares what we think. He is trying to make things better for us. So many of the old men—they were farmers and villagers in the mountains. In their world, the women stayed in the kitchen and that was it. In some villages, women were not even permitted to enter a church at all. Then things changed so quickly for them when they were forced to flee. People say girls now have too much freedom; they are liberated too quickly here in Europe. It is confusing for the older generation, and the younger generation cannot communicate with them very well—it is unusual what a good relationship I have with my father. I even told him that there is a man I like who likes me. He wants to marry me, and I told my father about it. That does not happen very often."

"He is a little bit older than me," she interrupted herself; then, brightening momentarily, "He's from the German side. He is such a good communicator!" As we paused our serious discussion to bask in the delight of her new romance, I was struck suddenly by a thought I dared not utter out loud: What will the bishop think? I wonder why he was so eager for Elena to talk to the Greek Orthodox nuns . . . ?

She composed herself, and continued: "I have turned down a lot of marriage offers and I get comments and pressure from everyone all of the time. I am twenty-four. That is old for me not to be married. People do not like it. But my parents, thank God, are patient and want me to be happy. They support my decisions, so I am okay."

I asked her then if she was furthering her study in classical Syriac at the monastery so she could become a malphonitho, and she said: "I wish I could become a malphonitho, but I am far too busy! It is hard being a Suryayto. Anything you might want to do has to be secondary to your household duties. Cooking. Cleaning. Preparing for social and family events. And they happen *all—the—time!* Sometimes it feels like something is happening every day! And we are responsible for all of it!"

At home in the town of Rijssen, Elena was a bank teller by day. She longed for a time, like so many of the young women I met and spoke with, when they might have the hours, the energy, and the financial resources to learn classical Syriac in earnest and study theology; they want to be like Mary, sitting next to Jesus in the story to listen to him speak, but they are also Martha in the kitchen, for that is the work that makes the conversation in the front of the house possible. Staying at the monastery during her summer vacation, she was taking classical Syriac lessons with the bishop, whom she admired deeply but also recognized as being caught between conflicting imperatives of his own.

"The nuns," she said, "are run off their feet because the monastery is doing work that the cultural organizations should do." She continued:

"The nuns work so hard. Too hard. It's not right. But when the Dutch government eliminated funding for teaching minority languages in the Dutch school system, it's now left to the monks to teach us our historical language and organize public events. No one else can or will do it. The cultural organizations do some things, but not enough. But now the monastery is too involved with the worldly affairs of the community, so the nuns are doing all this extra work to make it possible for the monastery to do what it does. Sister Marina wanted to become a nun to devote herself to God, not to clean up after every single event that other people in the community should be taking responsibility for!"

She paused, reflecting, both sad and angry, but mostly sad.

"I hope you write about this, Sarah!" she said suddenly. "The effects of the government's policies on us. They are trying to assimilate us so much, taking away resources from the cultural associations, from the schools—it is forcing the Church to be responsible for everything. It's too much!"

"Integration" and Autonomy

Elena's analysis of the unintended consequences of the Dutch state's "integration" policies on the configuration of relations among monastery, parish, and family life is supported by other Syriac Orthodox women of my acquaintance, especially young mothers. As Dutch sociologists van den Berg and Duyvendak (2012) argue, there is a pronounced national obsession in the Netherlands with the role of mothers in the "production of moral citizens" that takes shape in a variety of targeted interventions toward women because of an explicit understanding of the gendered nature of social reproduction. Mothers are assigned responsibility, they argue, for producing citizens who are properly "autonomous" in a manner that is particularly challenging for women like Elena to navigate, given their commitment to revitalizing and reproducing Syriac Christian kinship. The Dutch "normalizing offensive," as it is called in bureaucratic documents (e.g., van den Brink 2004), mandates interventions targeted at reshaping minoritized women's subjectivities, especially their religious subjectivities, for the express purpose of teaching them how to "emancipate" their children, to become fully "free" autonomous subjects (van den Berg and Duyvendak 2012, 2–3). This practice, the authors argue, is situated in an unbroken line of continuity back to the seventeenth century in the Dutch conception of the role of mothers as autonomous within the domestic sphere. Amplified in an explicit "civilizing offensive" (now echoed in the state's "normalizing offensive" language) in the nineteenth and twentieth centuries aimed at the Dutch lower and middle classes in the same period that it was targeted at colonized subjects in the Dutch East Indies (see also Stoler 1995), the institution and ideal of autonomous motherhood and the radical nuclear family survived the culturally and socially transformative effects of second-wave feminism, which is reflected in lower rates of female participation in the labor market in the early twenty-first century, relative to other northwestern European societies (van den Berg and Duyvendak 2012, 5–6).

Twenty-first-century Dutch motherhood is thus implicated in what van den Berg and Duyvendak call a "paradox of paternalism," that is, "the idea that the government should intervene, yet people should remain autonomous subjects" (2012,7). The paradox is resolved by applying paternalistic policies to very specific groups of citizens who are understood to be "not yet" autonomous; in other words, mothers of non-Western, or "allochthonous," descent (van den Berg and Duyvendak 2012,7; see Chapter 6 for detailed analysis of Dutch "allochthony" discourse). The explicit moralism of teaching children how to become ethical citizens by becoming autonomous was configured after the 1960s as Dutch society grappled with the aftermath of World War II. Citing the postwar German cultural critic Theodor Adorno's writings on moral education after the Holocaust, the Dutch state and its proxy organizations asserted that teaching children to be autonomous was essential to "prevent another Auschwitz" (van den Berg and Duyvendak 2012, 8). Thus, throughout the twentieth century, the rise of Dutch feminism and the decline of active religious identification led not to a breakdown in the theologically Calvinist Christian tradition of paternalistic thinking about motherhood and nuclear families but reconfigured them in relation to a particular conception of the "emancipated and autonomous" subject.

Although targeting the education of women is a global phenomenon found in nationalist projects and NGO strategies everywhere, the Dutch project identifies itself with secularist progressive cosmopolitanism (Lechner 2008) such that its nationalism is obscured by a rhetoric of universal humanism, even as it functions as a tool for the state:

> integration policies focus on mothers *as a vessel* for the development of their children into citizens and for their children's integration into society as a whole. The idea is then that women should teach their children and families how to behave, think and feel Dutch. The mother is in such instances an entry point into communities. (van den Berg and Duyvendak 2012, 12–13)

These state interventions (especially in the form of municipally run parenting classes) focus on teaching mothers how to talk to their children about sex by intervening "in the most private sphere of the home and the family: mother love, sex talk and marital communication" (van den Berg and Duyvendak 2012, 18). An even more pointed intervention into the domestic relations of the family centers on social workers' preoccupation with teaching women how to emancipate themselves from their (presumably) illiberal, sexist husbands. I encountered examples of this in my fieldwork on several occasions. At a women's committee meeting at a Syriac Orthodox cultural association in Enschede, for instance, the alderwoman of the local Christian Democratic party lectured the first- and second-generation Syriac Orthodox women in her audience at length about how they should speak to and manage their husbands to secure some independence for themselves, with explicit remarks about how this would benefit their children. Similarly, at a large community meeting hosted by the Enschede city police department and several intercultural social work organizations geared toward immigrant families, speakers described their concerns that Syriac Orthodox families were even more resistant to interventions from police, social workers, and schools than other local immigrant communities, as when a police liaison complained to the room at large:

> we have many Turkish and Moroccan officers on the force, but never a single Suryoyo! And Suryoyo families are always so closed and hostile to outsiders! It is impossible to work with them!

The consensus of those presenting was that the key to opening up the insular Suryoye was to find a way to get fathers out of the room and to talk to the mothers.

The Dutch state's explicit interest in managing "minority" motherhood comes to the fore in the lives of two mothers I spoke with frequently: Ilona and Nahrin, who both expressed a sense of personal responsibility *as mothers* for the reproduction of what they understood as the historical liturgical identity of Syriac Christianity, yet their commitments entailed contrasting interpretations of how that tradition generates kinship, and vice versa, and their respective commitments echo the tensions of Elena's affective labor in the monastery.

The Ethics of Motherhood

Consider Nahrin, who has no time. When I first met her in her early thirties, she was somewhat unusual for having begun singing with the parish choir *after* marriage. Named after Beth Nahrin, the Aramaic word for the stretch of ancient Mesopotamia that lies between the Tigris and Euphrates Rivers, she described to me one day what the weight of that history feels like in the daily rhythms of her life, as her overloaded schedule takes her from home to her day job, to church, to her child's primary school, and to the monastery, nearly every day. In conversation, she speaks with gentle introspection. On the occasions when she is caught up in the excitement of a thought, words come quickly and warmly, but then she looks abashed as she catches herself being hasty and forceful. Her fashion sense, modest and chic, conveys an understated authority. She is the abbot's niece, and cousin to many prominent community members. As softly as she speaks, when she does, others listen. She works full-time for the municipal government; when she works with the public, she is perpetually conscious of how others perceive her. She tells me that she is always careful about how she comports herself so the Dutch people she meets in city hall learn that Suryoye are respectful and will be respectful to her in return, aware of the stakes of how she is seen. She throws her disciplined energy into her family and the church. Every morning for fifteen minutes, Nahrin and her nine-year-old son work on their classical Syriac homework in preparation for Sunday night madrashto, which they attend together as students. She spends much of her free time checking up on her elderly aunt Sister Seyde, the abbot's sister, driving her to the doctor's office from the monastery to translate between Dutch and Țuroyo, the neo-Aramaic spoken language of Tur Abdin.

Nahrin is an organizer for her parish church's youth committee, where she develops educational programming and social events, and she chants the liturgy every Sunday in the Holy Qurbono, one of several mothers at the church in central Enschede who participate in the women's choir after marriage. She does all this while maintaining a clean house, a well-stocked kitchen, the resources to entertain visiting kin who might drop by on a moment's notice, and an affectionate husband, a distant Lebanese cousin whose great-grandparents came from her village in Tur Abdin. With an embarrassed laugh, she admits to reaching her limit when it comes to exercise: her husband teases her for throwing away money on a gym membership she never has time to use, but she will not give up her membership because, she says with an exasperated laugh, "you have to have a gym membership. Dutch people exercise!"

Nahrin and I became friends after I began singing in her parish choir on Sunday mornings and attending Sunday night madrashto. Whenever I return to the Netherlands, I visit her at home, where she cooks me dinner and fills me in on the progress of the youth committee and parish affairs. After my long stint of fieldwork in 2010, she joined the diocesan committee at the monastery, where Elena also volunteered, to develop programming for young adults throughout the Netherlands. Nahrin described her work not simply in terms of living by example but in terms of embodying a relational ethic to which others can respond and be drawn in:

> It is my responsibility to show my son the importance of how to live as a Syriac Orthodox Christian, in all the different ways. This means caring for my family. It means participating in the church community. It means following church rules, and studying the ancient language, and singing the liturgy in the Holy *Qurbono* every Sunday. It is also my responsibility to show Dutch society, the people I help at city hall, what it means to be Suryoyo, and what it means to be Christian.

Living by example, straining to become a moral paragon, is a common motif in Orthodox Christian expressions of piety (e.g., Boylston and Bandak 2014). Just as in Vlad Naumescu's study of Syriac Orthodox pedagogy in south India, the different forms of instruction Nahrin involves herself in are oriented toward developing moral character: hers, her child's, and her community's. Yet her labors also index the sense of the sacral, sacrificial potential within the mundane, thankless work of everyday life found in Christianity more broadly. As Maya Mayblin (2014) points out, recognition is an ambivalent element of the structure of sacrifice in this mundane register, as such actions must not draw attention to themselves, and yet they must also be *known* by others to become socially significant as sacrifice. Similarly, recognition is a key theme in Nahrin's ethical and reproductive labor: others are needed to see, hear, and affirm who she is, not only sociopolitically, but morally—but not for her individual soul's eschatological sake, but for the integrity of the ʿamo, the people, and for the salvational economy that defines the ʿamo as the people of God. There is danger here, however, for in the context of the politically charged Dutch immigration debates, Nahrin's labor might be recognized in secularist terms as the ideal embodiment of the elusive subject called forth by Dutch multiculturalism discourse—a hybrid model of both pious Syriac motherhood (humbly vocal, selflessly hardworking in the home, visibly devout), and of the "emancipated" Middle Eastern feminine *émigré* to the Netherlands (humbly vocal, selflessly hardworking in the labor market, visibly worldly)—and then weaponized against her Muslim neighbors. Like many of her peers, she works with Muslim colleagues who are, like her, viewed with scrutiny and whose lives are similarly taken as a sign of some broader cultural or religious failure or success. Whether taken as a sign of the ancient church's survival or the Dutch state's integration policy, her work on herself is an Other-oriented vocation on behalf of others. This vocation has both an ethical and an aesthetic dimension: she is aware of herself as a visible and audible sign of matters she cares deeply about and for which she feels personally responsible. And yet, in another sense, her project of revitalizing liturgical kinship is completely illegible to her secularist and Western Christian neighbors and to many of her elders within Syriac Orthodoxy, and aligns her conservative self-characterization with the piety practices of other, more marginalized religious minorities in the Netherlands.

In the context of the Syriac tradition and the many transpositions it has undergone to secure recognition and thus protection from imperial and secularist states in the past, Nahrin's presentation of self is a form of pastoral labor. This labor echoes the historical ʾiḥidoyo's singleness of purpose, mind, and heart in service of community. She enacts soteriological agency on behalf of her kin as she works to facilitate others' relationships within and without the boundaries of her parish. The temporal rhythm of her days catches others—her son, her husband, her younger peers, the broader congregational community—up in its beat, creating conditions of possibility for their individual and collective restoration and salvation. She strives to produce, sustain, and reproduce relationships of a certain quality: stripped of its theological weight, you might call this "community-building." With 'iḥidoyutho circulating in the spaces where she does this work, her mundane labor appears less as sacrifice or moral exemplar than it does a mode of becoming-for and becoming-with as part of the theo-economy of Incarnation. In this spiritual economy, she constructs relations across sites that enable others' relationships to emerge: (1) madrashto, where she facilitates her son's relationship with the liturgical language of antiquity; (2) the parish choir, where she facilitates social relationships among her younger peers within her parish; (3) her office, where she strives to improve relations between the Suryoye and their neighbors; and (4) the monastery, where she organizes for a committee devoted to facilitating relationships across parishes.

Vernacular Intimacies

Ilona, the oldest Mansur sister, is very different from Nahrin. Ilona left her parents' church in the city center to join her husband's church in a southern suburb of Enschede when she married. Ilona told me:

> I am a married woman! So the choir is no longer mine. It is not *for* me. And even if it were, I would not have the time! Anyway, the singing is a little different at my husband's church. If I stood up in the gudo now, I would not know what to sing.

Liturgical singing at her husband's church has been learned from a different lineage of priests and deacons than at her parents' church in central Enschede, so the melodies, while technically the same, are performed differently enough that she does not recognize them. Instead, she devotes her energies to teaching her children to speak Ṭuroyo as their first language. This, she tells me, is the key to preventing Syriac Orthodox Christianity from disappearing from the world, even though this view puts her at odds with her children's Dutch school teachers *and* the ecclesiastical and lay elite who dream of making classical Syriac a living language at the expense of Ṭuroyo.

Ilona lives in a row house with a concrete patio and a children's playground just outside the back gate in a middle-class neighborhood near her parents and sisters. She is twenty-eight, with two young children and a pleasant, intelligent husband she adores. She works, officially, three full-length days a week at an office design company, which she spreads out across four days so that she can pick up her children from school and spend the afternoons with them. She works a full day on Wednesdays when her husband takes off from his job as a property tax analyst for the municipal government in Hengelo so that he, too, can spend time with their children. When I visited Ilona in her home, she made a point to tell me how pleased she was to show me what "Syriac motherhood is really like." As we spent the day talking and playing with her children and walking with her toddler son to pick up her five-year-old daughter from primary school, Ilona described her experiences with the Dutch school system. According to the teacher, her daughter's Dutch was not progressing as it should, so she was falling behind her peers in her ability to communicate in class. When the teacher summoned them to school for a conversation, she was shocked to learn that both Ilona and her husband speak flawless, unaccented Dutch. The teacher, Ilona said, had never imagined the possibility that parents might willingly choose to speak only Ṭuroyo with their children at home if they were capable of speaking Dutch. Ilona explained to the teacher that as a first-generation immigrant, she had learned Dutch exclusively at school and that her own parents did not speak a word of Dutch when she was growing up. Nonetheless, because her daughter was not progressing in some areas in class, Ilona and her husband finally agreed to help her with Dutch at home. After some initial tension, she told me, she felt her attempts at being reasonable and open with the teacher were met with equal openness and reasonableness, and together, they could help her daughter progress. Despite the additional time she takes to work with her daughter on her Dutch, however, she remains committed to ensuring that her children speak Ṭuroyo with native fluency. She tells me:

> We are not like other groups in the Netherlands. I understand that the teachers are worried about children growing up in the Netherlands without ever mastering Dutch, but we have no country of our own where Ṭuroyo is the national language. We have no government to fund language-learning programs in the diaspora. If we do not teach

our children to speak Ṭuroyo fluently, it will be a dead language in less than twenty years.

Despite their different priorities, Ilona and Nahrin both construct a strong ethic of motherhood that is tied to a sense of obligation toward multiple audiences and ethical demands. The problem of recognition shapes their sense of their task to save Syriac Orthodoxy in subtly distinct ways. They express personal responsibility, *as mothers*, for the survival and reproduction of what they understand as the historical identity of Syriac Orthodox Christianity. But the way they configure and orient their sense of responsibility is different. Nahrin focuses on cultivating her own and her son's liturgical voices by studying to master the classical Syriac in which the liturgy is sung while simultaneously creating a sense of community out of the group of regular singers who participate in the liturgy, whereas Ilona's efforts center on ensuring that her children's mother tongue is Ṭuroyo, because Ṭuroyo is the language of the home, of intimate relationships with grandparents, aunts, uncles, and cousins, and of the regional history of Tur Abdin.

Ilona's and Nahrin's contrasting commitments entail two disparate yet related interpretations of how the liturgical tradition generates kinship and vice versa, neither of which is particularly legible to secularist and Western Christian audiences. For Nahrin, the essential, ethical core of being a Syriac mother is participating in the liturgy, but this is not simply a matter of teaching by example and reproducing what she already knows and grew up with herself. In fact, Nahrin was prevented as a child from learning to sing the liturgy by her own parents. Because her parents moved too far away from their church for them to feel comfortable allowing her to travel to madrashto alone, and no one could drive her, Nahrin was forced to quit the choir at a very early age. As an adult, she rejected the norm that female liturgical singers should be composed of young unmarried women and has gained acceptance from the larger congregational community by strengthening the visible connection between liturgical performance and the pastoral labor of the youth committee, as she brings her professional experience and poise to the group of organizers who have, since my departure, reinvigorated interest and involvement among young people in the church community. Drawn in by her kind and unassuming leadership style, more young women have decided that they, too, will return to the choir after marriage.

Ilona, on the other hand, is far more concerned with keeping Ṭuroyo a living, spoken language, which flies in the face of the Dutch state's insistence that mastering the Dutch language is the first criterion on which cultural citizenship is based (Ghorashi and van Tilburg 2006; Mosher 2016), and thus is the highest priority among integration policies and practices targeted at new minorities (Vasta 2014). That an otherwise "perfectly well-integrated" mother who already speaks flawless Dutch would *choose* to speak another language with her child is, as the teacher's reaction and my conversations with my own Dutch family attest, *shocking.* These observations are not incidental. They get to the heart of Dutch anxieties about ethical personhood in the multicultural state and the national preoccupation with minority motherhood.

Not surprisingly, such discourses have the effect of reifying nationalist self-conceptions of white women as "us" ("progressive native Dutch") in opposition to "them" ("conservative migrant mothers"). Migrant mothers are "held accountable for caring work and collective responsibilities while being addressed as potentially autonomous subjects, symbols of progressive nationalism" (Berg and Duyvendak 2012, 18). In this way, they do double duty both as vessels of integration and as the constitutive Other of the nation itself. For Suryayto mothers like Nahrin and Ilona, the difficulty is this: in their conversation and self-presentation, they seek to embody the Dutch state's ideal of the "integrated" and "emancipated" minority woman. They are aware of the ways in which they are racialized and how this racialization is inflected with Islamophobic discourses with which they themselves have an uneasy relationship, given the intergenerational traumas of their parents' and grandparents' migration stories. Many (but by no means all) of these women are educated, employed, fashionable, and even inclined to progressive politics and sensibilities in certain situations, as when Ilona confides in a gleeful, mischievous whisper that she cannot live without her yoga class, is "a little bit feminist," and that her husband is a much more natural parent to their small children than she is. But they bring into dialogue two distinct models of ethical personhood that seem to share a common pathway directed toward different aims. The first is the Christological conception of singleness as the intimacy of relatedness, a theological discourse in which individualism and atomism are sources of suffering from which to be liberated, while a gendered ethics of reproduction and kin relatedness materializes God's salvific plan for the whole of humanity. The second is a secularist understanding of human personhood that reworks earlier Calvinist Christian understandings of domestic family life (cf. Houkes 2009; Kennedy 1995; Stoler 1995; van der Laarse 2009; Taussig 1997) in relation to anxious memories of the Holocaust and the Nazi occupation of the Netherlands. Splicing together classically Liberal and post–World War II corporatist visions of moral citizenship, this model undergirds a technocratic vision of the individual's relationship with society so that the state and its authorized proxies are held responsible for shaping moral individuals capable of autonomous thought. Such a moral person is educated to think and reason without reference to binding traditions or social pressures, even as a great deal of state-directed attention is poured into forming subjects capable of such thought. And yet motherhood is, in both cases, the pathway to either integration or salvation, and this mirroring effect reflects a deeper connection to fragmented histories of Christological thought.

At first glance, we may seem to be dealing with two axes of the enduring question of the individual's relationship with society (or the obvious point that the social reproductive labor of motherhood is as easily assumed as it is invisible). But it would be a mistake to equate these perspectives with a "liberal" autonomous versus an "illiberal" porous subject characteristic of influential theories of the secular (cf. Taylor 2004). This is because secularist and Western Christian Dutch sensibilities are themselves a hybrid array of Enlightenment and anti-Enlightenment sentiments, of Calvinist theocratic notions of the family, and of gendered autonomy haunting a Liberal project of religious "emancipation." We might rather think of these traditions as dynamic weather patterns, colliding, interacting, and reshaping each other as climate conditions change. Extending the metaphor, we might also think of climate conditions as the ethico-aesthetic conditions of possibility for given models of sociality and moral citizenship to emerge. What is key is that both models make a parallel set of ethical demands on motherhood to enact either a literal (in the Syriac Orthodox case) or a metaphorical (in the ex-Calvinist secularist case) soteriological agency on behalf of others. How Dutch-Syriac women balance and weave these ethical demands together is illuminating for our understanding of the aesthetics of ethical life in constituting gender as a site of reproductive power. In what remains of this chapter, I turn to the question of daughterhood and how Dutch conceptions of "emancipation" become folded into young Syriac Orthodox women's perspectives on what it means to have a "voice," especially in their strategic use of silence to reconfigure relationships within their families.

Strapless Party Dresses

Ilona's younger sisters, Elizabeta and Mariane, self-consciously inter-weave the ethical demands of Syriac covenantal theology and Dutch integration discourse in their understanding of what it means to save Syriac Christianity. Nineteen and twenty years old, respectively, at the time of my primary phase of fieldwork, they were pillars of their liturgical community. Even then, with their experience and expertise, they could have taught madrashto and led choir rehearsals if their youth and gender did not disqualify them in their own eyes and the eyes of their peers and elders. At that time, they both lived at home with one older unmarried sister, Evelien, who had no interest in participating in the choir (she was busy enough, she told me, working one hundred hours a week teaching other Syriac Orthodox children at a local Catholic primary school and being a very involved aunt to her nieces and nephews).

One Sunday after morning Mass, I spent the afternoon with the family, as I often did. As I helped the girls prepare lunch, I began to pick up on just how self-conscious and isolated Mrs. Mansur, Elizabeta and Mariane's mother, felt about her difficulty speaking Dutch and how frustrated her daughters were with her over this. The girls had been encouraging her to try to study Dutch more—or perhaps more accurately, were giving her a hard time about it—but Mrs. Mansur had become convinced that she could not learn. When I sympathetically shared my own mother's struggle to learn Dutch when I was a child, Evelien asked, "But could your mother read and write in English?"

When I replied that she could, Evelien responded, "Well, there is a big difference then. She had the basis for learning another language formally."

With a look of tired, strained resignation, Mrs. Mansur turned to me and haltingly said, "When my daughters speak Dutch to each other, I cannot understand them." Her weak smile and deep sigh suggested a weariness echoed in a later conversation with Elizabeta, who also spoke of the strain of not being understood by her mother. The strain was not only a matter of mere comprehension but of radically different outlooks on life that stem from the fact that her mother is illiterate, while she herself is engaged in advanced study at university. Because her mother was too old to start school when the Turkish government established public schools in the villages of Tur Abdin, she had never learned to read or write, even though her younger brother and sister did. Elizabeta told me that she feels the

difference is sometimes a vast chasm. Nonetheless, she values her education more when her mother tells her that she wishes she could have gone to
school. Mrs. Mansur is nothing but supportive of her daughters' educational aspirations, which is not a universally shared sentiment among the
community, as I often heard complaints from young women that the more
educated they become, the more they feel despised by elders and prospec-
tive marriage partners alike.

Despite occasions of deep misunderstanding and frustration, Elizabeta
worked hard on her relationship with her mother. Compared with other
young women in her parish, she believed their relationship was very good
because Elizabeta kept no secrets from her. She attributed her success in
life to this openness, unlike many of her friends whose mothers, they say,
are only concerned about shame and social control and so frighten their
daughters into silence. Elizabeta said to me once:

> I have a friend who has not told her mother she has been dating a
> boy for an entire year! It's terrible! But also not surprising. People
> really disapprove of relationships among young men and women in
> this neighborhood.

Despite gaps in worldview and the emotional strain of their unequal capacity to comprehend each other, Mrs. Mansur is Elizabeta's most important interlocutor on the subjects of morality and ethics. Elizabeta had
decided to stop attending weekend hafle because she learned from her
mother that attending these parties as a young unmarried woman meant
that people would think she was on the hunt for a husband. At nineteen,
with her education to finish, she had decided she was not. In conversation
with her mother, Elizabeta contemplated the moral semiotics of a strapless
party dress she once desired, determining just how much skin she was willing to bare at weddings and formal occasions.

"To here," Elizabeta said, holding her hand up to her collarbone, "and
it should at least have shoulder-straps!" It was in conversation with her
mother that Elizabeta decided that she wanted to continue singing in the
choir with her sister Mariane, working extra hard to provide logistical support for the choir's special feast day performances and to keep Sunday
night madrashto going, even when it was unpleasant and tiresome. Her
mother and father both would have preferred their daughters to work less
hard on the choir because they were tired of seeing each of their five
children, one by one, burn out on giving all to "save" the church, only to

then feel let down by the church board, the ecclesiastical hierarchy, and the
larger community. Instead, Mr. and Mrs. Mansur wanted their children to
take some time for themselves, to focus on their education, their part-
time jobs, and their home life (the girls worked very hard to help their
mother keep house and prepare for regular extended family get-togethers,
much as Elena did for her own family), and to get some rest occasionally.
Nonetheless, Elizabeta and her sister determined that they would continue
fighting to make the choir a strong, cohesive community of voices, and
their parents expressed pride in all their daughters did. Even though they
no longer learned anything new, the sisters continued attending Sunday
night madrashto to encourage younger students to attend. As with Nahrin, and echoing the bishop's explicit teaching, their practice was something
they did for others, not for themselves. By modeling desirable behavior,
others would benefit because it would strengthen the relations animating
their parish against the myriad pressures that might unravel them. At
this point, with nothing left to learn and getting very little back in return,
only their faith that their efforts would ensure the survival of the choirs
kept them going. And yet Elizabeta and Mariane wove into this commitment another thread drawn from Dutch discourses of the ethics of the
speaking subject, which they repurposed for their own liturgical ends—
most especially in reconfiguring the character of patriarchal authority within
their families and the broader parish community.

The Ethics of the Silent Subject

One day, when Elizabeta and I were having an unrelated conversation,
I asked her what sorts of things angered her, and she said, "Being disre-
spectful." I was surprised when she brought up her father as an example,
as I had always observed what I interpreted to be a habit of immense
deference to her father's authority. She recounted for me the history of her
relationship with him, which she described as a history of teaching him
how to speak to her.

> When I was younger, my father would say things like: "Get me
> water"—he would demand it, and not respectfully. So I would get
> out a glass and a bottle of water and place them on the table in front
> of him, folding my arms and looking at him without a word.
> I wouldn't pour the water. I communicated silently, so gradually, he

adapted. He learned to speak to me more gently. He was stricter [*strenger*] when I was younger, but now he is much better about communicating more respectfully with me. My older sisters would never have challenged him in this way. But I think I also benefited from the fact that he worked around Dutch people for so many years. It has changed the way he thinks, and it has brought some Dutch ideas into our family.

Dutch ideas in general, she said, are suffusing the community. She expressed this with ambivalence, admitting to a long-standing feeling of anger toward her father, but also love, compassion, and sadness for the myriad ways he is inaudible to those around him and for the violence, disrespect, and prejudice he has suffered both in Turkey and in the Netherlands.

Throughout my fieldwork, I spoke to few fathers other than Mr. Mansur, and almost no grandfathers beyond polite formalities. As a young woman, it was generally considered inappropriate for me to engage in close conversation with older men. So, instead, I learned to see them through the eyes of their daughters, granddaughters, and nieces. These relationships loomed large in the way the women I worked with theorized their positions in the church and in Dutch society. As others have argued, the experience of migration and diaspora must inevitably produce fissures among generations (Atto 2011; Bjorklund 1981; Schukkink 2003), but there is something to the gendered reconfiguration of generational hierarchy here that calls for closer attention. Young women like Elizabeta and Mariane rework elements of both Syriac theology and contemporary Dutch politics in how they silently rearrange the patterns of speech that define their relationships with their fathers. This repatterning is especially significant for the transmission of liturgical knowledge, which diasporic fathers like Mr. Mansur now take upon themselves to share with their daughters and nieces when their own fathers and grandfathers never would have.

I learned from Mariane that their father was quite knowledgeable in theological matters, especially of St. Paul's demands on moral Christian behavior, having studied in a monastery in Tur Abdin when he was a child. It was in conversation with her father, for example, that Mariane concluded she wanted to wear her headscarf in church because he showed her where in the Bible Paul says it is necessary to show respect for God when praying. This is how she decided that she must wear the headscarf while singing in Mass and during daily prayers, while it is permissible to sing the same song bare-headed at special events. Her cousins, she remarked, do not agree that the instruction to cover their hair while praying applies to them, although her father showed them the passage as well. But Mariane wondered whether, in the final analysis, the headscarf was a requirement or a choice because she was not quite sure whether the headscarf is, in practice, really showing respect for God or more about shielding men from female sexuality and thus not distracting them from prayer. When she asked me what I thought, after so much honesty, I told her what I felt, unable in that moment to contain or critique my own sensibilities, saying,

> I am always happy to wear a headscarf while in the Syriac Orthodox church, but that might be because I am a guest. I do not know how I would feel if I had grown up with it as a requirement, because as an outsider, I can leave whenever I want to.

I admitted to feeling that if a man cannot control himself such that he cannot handle even being in the same room as a woman, then that is his responsibility, not the woman's responsibility. Mariane nodded at my response, "Yes. My sisters think that way too. But I do not agree." This disagreement between Mariane and Elizabeta, who otherwise operated in near lockstep in their commitments to the Church, is crucial to understanding the fissures forming within the twenty-first-century reinterpretation of Syriac covenantal theology—although for Mariane and Elizabeta, these fissures would not manifest for several years. By 2016, Elizabeta had married and divorced, taking up a position within her ex-husband's parish in south Enschede as a malphonitho, developing and teaching a new classical Syriac language program for young children in the parish. In her capacity as malphonitho, she liaised with a local nonprofit organization working to develop broader-based programming for the increasingly disaffected and (according to many in the neighborhood) criminalized population of Suryoye youth in the southern district. Mariane, meanwhile, also married and, until the birth of her first child in 2017, began working in her husband's family's snack shop franchise. In this period, they have both put long-standing aspirations on the back burner: after gaining her credentials to be a social worker, Elizabeta earned a spot to study theology at the Radboud University of Nijmegen, her lifelong dream (also like Elena). Without the funds to pay for student rooms in Nijmegen, however, she found it impossible to keep up with the demands of her school work, family obligations, and her part-time job while commuting daily to Nijmegen from Enschede, so she was compelled to quit the program within the first year. Mariane, meanwhile, has distant aspirations to work in politics, daring even to dream of becoming a politician to counter what she sees as the incoherent right-wing anti-immigrant positions of people like Geert Wilders and his Freedom Party (*Partij van de Vrijheid*), but her hands are full for now, caring for her infant and supporting her husband's business.

Mariane and Elizabeta's primary commitments are to their families and, by extension, their churches. The girls respect their father's knowledge, even when they disagree with him, and they are conscious of how he is regularly silenced by the Dutch preoccupation with integrating minority mothers. After coming to the Netherlands in the 1970s to flee violent conflict between the Kurdish separatist movement and the Turkish government, Mr. Mansur worked for many years as a custodian and handyman at a local institution of higher education. On one of my visits, he spent a long afternoon telling me about a trip he had taken to his home village in Tur Abdin (which is now entirely Kurdish) by himself because his wife had been too frightened to return with him. He felt awkward at first when he was berated for saying good morning in Turkish instead of Kurdish, but in the end, he enjoyed himself, conversing pleasantly with several local residents. He told me that while it is true that Turkey is a place of discrimination, he had to admit that the Netherlands can be as well. He had been out of work for over a year because he discovered that his employers were paying him far less than other employees who were Dutch. They were not treating him fairly, and this put tremendous financial pressure on his children to support the household.

Elizabeta and Mariane's approach to their own life's work is haunted by the fantastical figure of the emancipated speaking subject, the sign of successful integration into Dutch society, which they see as a cruel joke on their parents. In Tur Abdin, there is nothing left for their parents except memories of violence. The villages that once were theirs are now ghost towns in deserted highlands, and they have been struck from the nationalist record of Turkish history. There is nothing for them in the Netherlands either, where their language, experience, and identities are entirely inaudible to those around them. Again and again, Mr. Mansur told me, "I am so sad that I cannot write about it." His children model good Suryoye behavior and are devoted to their obligations as daughters, Christians, and liturgical singers. Everyone is sweet, good-natured, thoughtful, and kind but tense and anxious. They roll from moment to moment with laughter and familiar teasing to intense irritation. This is like every family, of course. But there is something more. The girls fall into a stony silence when their father begins to soliloquize, longing as he does for a listener, feeling, in turn, unheard by him. They express a deep ambivalence with their mother, scolding her angrily for minor irritations, frustrated by her lack of comprehension of basic Dutch common sense. They are angry with their parents just as everyone is angry with their parents, especially in a multilingual diaspora, where migration produces vast generational chasms. But these experiences shape how Syriac Orthodox Christians in Western Europe perceive their task: saving Syriac Christianity means addressing, in some way, the conditions that have made their parents and grandparents inaudible to themselves and to others. As a student of social pedagogy, Mr. and Mrs. Mansur's youngest daughter, Elizabeta, was trained in Dutch theories and methods of socialization, education, and fashioning a particular relationship between the individual and society. Trained and authorized to speak in specific ways and to elicit speech from others, she struggles to elicit such speech from her mother and father, and sometimes her methods entail strategic silence, a silence strongly reminiscent of Elena's oblique refusal of the bishop.

Similarly, Ilona described her life as emblematic of a common transformation among Syriac Orthodox families in the Netherlands in the way her primary speaking relationship is not with her parents but with her husband. Yet she attributes this to the positive influence of her husband's father, not to any particular efforts of the Dutch state to "fix" their family dynamics. She insisted,

> My father-in-law was already unconventional before he came to the Netherlands. He likes to cook, he is not afraid of doing "women's work," and he is open and worldly in a way my own father never was growing up.

Ilona's relationship with her husband exceeds and inverts the logic of one of the central tropes of Dutch integration discourse, the belief that immigrant women from the Middle East and North Africa need to be "emancipated" from their husbands, fathers, and religious authorities (Berg and Duyvendak 2012, 14–15). Ilona met her husband at a church Bible study organized by her brother, and they married without significant delay. Her relationship germinated and grew according to proper religious conceptions of Syriac Orthodox romantic and family relationships. She has reconfigured the role of the extended family network in her life. She still expected to spend Sunday afternoons with her parents, her sisters, and their families. However, unlike her sisters (even after their eventual marriages), her primary emotional speaking relationship was with her husband. Ilona does not "emancipate" herself from Syriac Orthodox kinship but pragmatically reconfigures it so that her marriage relationship, which is influenced by Dutch notions of sexual partnership, is at the center of it. At the same time, she reconfigures Dutch ideals of the radical nuclear family and maternal autonomy to share her parenting load more equally with her husband, sisters, and extended family, while social life continues to center on church festivals and ritual prayer. Her parenting objective is not to produce Dutch citizens whose moral identities are defined by secular freedom, but Syriac Orthodox Christian children whose first language is Ṭuroyo and who organize their lives around their obligations to church and extended family through ritual practices like fasting, regular prayer, singing Syriac songs, and moral self-discipline.

What comes into view through the gendered affective labor of Elena and her fellow liturgical activists is an ethical subject whose agency is distributed across relations and enacted on behalf of another's becoming. Motherhood and daughterhood are locations in a liturgical world order, one in which helping nuns with their chores is as theologically significant as mastering classical Syriac or teaching children Ṭuroyo. Kin relatedness is a soteriological tool, which is to say, a pathway through which the Divine's plan for human salvation materializes in the world through affective labor enacted on behalf of another. Liturgy brings ritual and kin-based pathways into alignment. How such an alignment is possible and why these women feel ethically bound to maintaining this alignment through experiments in love, singing, mothering, and daughtering becomes clearer if we think of this labor as an embodied Incarnational theology that is always subject to the dialogical processes and politics of the diasporic condition— to the ethics of recognition—whether ancient or contemporary.

Transpositions

In this chapter, I have mapped out several experimental pathways through which many Suryayto women I know enact a practical theology of kinship and gender, and I have explored how this theology interacts with the discourse of the "emancipated speaking subject," a centerpiece of Dutch "minority integration" policy, to generate new configurations of the West Syriac iconic voice as a site of reproductive power. In sketching out these experimental pathways, I have shown how such experiments transpose kin locatedness and ritual locatedness into new patterns while affirming gendered and generational norms that they understand as indispensable to ethical personhood. Such transpositions are dialogical; they arise in a diasporic situation where multiple audiences and ethical demands are at work in the same moment, a consequence of disparate yet interwoven national histories of state secularism, feminism, immigration politics, and ritual knowledge.

When women like Elena, Elizabeta, Mariane, Ilona, and Nahrin say that they seek to "save" Syriac Christianity, what they seek to save are the ethical and affective relations that define Syriac Christianity as both Syriac and Christian; the key site of their labor is, in each case, their own "voice," whether silent or speaking. Covenantal theology and immigration politics are but two threads in the weave. They account for the shape of some of these pathways but not all because they are woven into broader patterns of the spatiotemporal reconfiguration of kinship. These reconfigurations happen at the interface among municipal, national, transnational, and supranational politics, where many of the Daughters of the Covenant have begun to realize they must turn their attention, and it is here that the problem of recognition as the ethico-aesthetic precondition of mutual becoming becomes especially charged. In the backdrop of these processes and politics are intergenerational traumas, as tensions among children and their parents bring recent memories of violence, displacement, and migration into the picture of Dutch immigration politics and this account of liturgical kinship. It is to the theological and sociopolitical afterlives of earlier generations' experiences in Turkey, Syria, Lebanon, and Iraq that I now turn.

CHAPTER

5

THE THEOLOGY OF ETHNICITY

No one, not even his mother, who was afraid to ask him whether he still believed in God, understands his religion or his broken alliance. (Caputo 1997, xvii)

F ive years after the choir rehearsal described in the opening of Chapter 3, Marta appeared before the Thirtieth Session of the Human Rights Council at the United Nations in Geneva. As the Secretary of the World Council of Aramaeans (Syriacs), formerly the Universal Syriac Alliance, she spoke near the end of a session reviewing a report by the UN Special Rapporteur for the Rights of Indigenous People to plead the case of Aramaean Christians, who had been fleeing the Islamic State in Iraq and then Syria since early 2014. Reading in a low voice from her prepared comments, she addressed the assembly in English:

Syria's indigenous Aramaean Christians face complete annihilation. Jihadists have seized thousands of their homes. Since last month, another 255 Aramaeans from Homs were kidnapped and others fear the constant attacks by militant Islamists. This is nothing new. Just last year, 160,000 Aramaeans from Mosul fled their homeland when the Islamic State captured it. Since then, they live scattered across the region with little support or humanitarian aid. [. . .] The ongoing crimes against humanity in Iraq and Syria amount to ethnic cleansing and genocide. And yet the resulting refugee crisis was long ignored until a young refugee boy tragically washed ashore. [. . .] Although Aramaeans are not recognized and have no legal status in their homelands, they are the indigenous people of southeast Turkey, Syria, Iraq, and Lebanon. [. . .] Mr. Vice President, we must act now and create this special UN fund. By preventing the near death of Aramaean Christianity the ethnoreligious mosaic, cultural diversity, and pluralistic coexistence of the new Middle East will be guaranteed.

In her speech, Marta asked a provocative question: Where was Western European concern for thousands of displaced Syrians and Iraqis before the highly visible death of Aylan Kurdi, the three-year-old boy who drowned during passage from Syria to Greece in 2015? She lodged her request for recognition within a broader critique of Euro-American indifference to the Middle East's religious, ethnic, and linguistic diversity. When she spoke of Aramaean Christianity, Marta employed the ethnicized form of the word "Aramaic" to signal a distinct spatiotemporal configuration of liturgical kinship. "Aramaean" is the "secular" ethnic corollary to her Syriac Orthodoxness. One cannot do without the other, and it is the grounds on which she seeks recognition within the globalized category of indigeneity, whereas for many of her Assyrian-identifying kin, like her cousin Elizabeta, Syriac Orthodoxy is but one liturgical branch of the broader ethnoreligious family tree. It is a bureaucratic as well as an existential problem, because for every Aramaean organization lobbying the local municipality, the national government, the European Human Rights Council, or the United Nations, there is a mirror Assyrian organization speaking on behalf of the same population, often with different political aims.

In the five years that elapsed between our choir rehearsal and her speech before the United Nations Human Rights Council, Marta refined her understanding of the ethnopolitical status of Syriac Orthodoxy as she engaged myriad pressures from the Dutch state, her local municipal government, and the world stage on which the transnational politics of minority recognition play out. Marta's speech before the United Nations foregrounded the question of violence at the heart of Syriac Orthodox confrontations with different regimes of recognition. The shape of Syriac Orthodox kinship in the twenty-first century emerges from the radical fractures of nineteenth- and twentieth-century mass violence, population transfer, and partition, and from its subsequent re-politicizations, first in the Mandate period after

World War I when the British controlled the newly formed Iraqi state and the French controlled the emerging Syrian and Lebanese states, and then in these states' anti-colonial movements and nationalization programs after World War II. In parallel with these struggles in the Arabic-speaking world, twenty-first-century Syriac Orthodox kin relations were shaped by the silences of the mid- and late-twentieth-century Turkish state as it attempted to assert, often violently, a homogeneous secular national identity over a far more ethnically and religiously diverse population than official discourses would admit. These histories produced regionally disparate understandings of what it means to be an ethnic or religious minority, as extended families separated by war, ethnic cleansing, and forced migration found themselves on opposite sides of newly constructed political, social, cultural, and linguistic borders. This is a story of complex, and at times conflicting, regimes of recognition intersecting with each other, as nascent states throughout the Middle East, from Syria to Lebanon to Iraq to Turkey, undertook different approaches to defining and configuring the political relationship among religiosity, ethnicity, and nationality as legal, bureaucratic, and social categories. These legacies continue to play out in twenty-first-century conflicts throughout the Middle East and across the Syriac world.

Although social scientists have long recognized the complex interpenetrations of ethnic, religious, and linguistic identities among diverse populations around the world, a globalized Euro-American regime of recognition nonetheless maintains a legal, bureaucratic distinction among these categories. These distinctions are grounded in a set of presuppositions about what it means to be related to someone. Euro-American conceptions of ethnicity are deeply entwined with Euro-American conceptions of kinship: both are rooted in what anthropologists of ethnicity call the "aura of descent," an understanding of genealogy defined by what Marilyn Strathern (2005) terms the "biological" idiom of kinship.[1] In Euro-American thought and practice, to be "really" related to someone means that you are of the same blood, or, as we now think of it, the same genes. This biological idiom authorizes every other scale and modality of relatedness throughout the polity by determining whether a particular relatedness is considered inherent to someone's personhood (such as one's national or ethnic origin) or as optional (such as one's freely chosen religious affiliation). Crudely stated, this view holds that ethnicity is of the body, while religion is of the mind.[2] Such a notion makes it difficult to imagine, in the halls of global power, linking the religious dimensions of communal identity or the embodied dimensions of religious experience to any degree of political self-determination. For this, my interlocutors have discovered, you need an ethnicity.[3]

Out of necessity, liturgical activists like Marta have learned to deploy a distinction between religion and ethnicity in their political advocacy in ways that sometimes belie how they understand and practice Syriac Orthodoxy as liturgical kinship. Disagreements among Syriac Orthodox Christians about how to most effectively make their tradition visible and intelligible to various levels of secular authority—a disagreement that unfolds as a political battle over whether Syriac Orthodox Christians are ethnically Aramaean or part of the Assyrian nation—also reverberate in debates about what disarticulating ethnic from religious identity means *theologically* for being Christian in a Syriac way. In this chapter, I focus on these theological reverberations.

Heeding Brackette Williams's caution never to "mistak[e] the concept [of ethnicity] for its use" (1989, 428), I situate my research participants' activism and advocacy in ongoing community debates over the theological and moral requirements of Suryoye-ness. The debate among Syriac Christians about the kind of political legibility they seek for their practice of Christian kinship is the consequence of a multiscaled, multidimensional process that I call *perforation*. *To perforate* refers to poking a series of tiny holes into something, like a piece of paper, so that the pieces hold together but become easier to pull apart. These perforations are not only conceptual but relational as they reorient peoples' sense of what liturgical kinship entails both theologically and morally. Perforation adds to our understanding of the sonic icon as a site of reproductive power because it illuminates the openings and instabilities within the very moments of transmission when the voices of powerful Others enter in, mixing with inherited voices of the past, to create and recreate tradition. Unlike the commonly invoked binary paradigm of secular rupture versus religious continuity, perforation as a metaphor describes how the act of reproducing tradition contains both openings and closures. The patterns of these openings and closures—the shapes made by the holes in the paper, as it were—may differ widely in different times and places, and where secular powers may exert their rupturing force, those committed to a liturgical understanding of kinship might work to suture the tears.

Because liturgical kinship is intertwined with family relationships, my interlocutors are heavily preoccupied with intergenerational dynamics as they grapple with their parents' and grandparents' trauma, dispossession, and displacement. How unspoken trauma resurfaces in their relationships with their elders shapes how they understand the theological and ethical requirements of being Suryoye, as well as the political aspirations informed by these requirements. My key claim in this chapter is that the intergenerational trauma of unrecognized genocide and its twentieth-century aftershocks echo in the diasporic theopolitical imagination through a series of perforating questions: what it means to be a people, what it means to be Christian, what it means to be a people defined as Christian, and what kind of freedom-in-belief liturgical kinship may afford. In the stories that follow, the theological resonances of these secularist fights become clearer: to distinguish among "religious," "cultural," and "ethnic" identity is itself a theological claim about history-as-Incarnation.

Freedom and Responsibility in a Christian *Ethnos*

During my extended fieldwork at the Mor Ephrem Monastery, I attended several public events hosted by the diocese to bring the Syriac Orthodox community together to discuss questions of identity, integration, and what it means to be Christian in Western Europe. One of these events shed light on a key dimension of the struggle to reproduce Syriac Orthodox liturgical kinship, as it exposed the theological knot of Christian freedom and responsibility, common topics of discussion for Christians of many denominations, among second- and third-generation Dutch Suryoye.

This event was a public lecture called "Making Choices for the New Year," which was intended to offer intellectual growth and spiritual guidance to those Syriac Orthodox faithful who long for such things and to instill such longings among those who do not. The parishioners in attendance were a mix of young, middle-aged, and elderly men and women who sorted themselves into their pews by gender, with head-scarved women on the left and men in suits on the right, as is customary in this conservative corner of the diaspora. Rare exceptions could be found among small clusters of glamorously dressed and made-up women from Syria who, bareheaded, preferred to sit on the right side of the church with their men, eliciting occasional dark looks from their more rural kin from the Turkish side. A couple of cameramen from the Sweden-based satellite television station Suryoyo Sat roamed about the nave, filming audience and altar alike, as they do whenever there is a public event of note.

The speakers were Dutch-trained theologians and religious philosophers who were either Syriac Orthodox themselves or possessed expertise in ancient Syriac theology. The first speaker was a young Suryoyo man who was among the first generation of Syriac Orthodox to grow up and be educated in the Netherlands. He had earned a PhD in philosophy from a Roman Catholic university and was in the process of writing a book on Nietzsche. Reading from a prepared paper, the scholar expounded upon the concept of freedom in Western Christian thought. His central argument for the evening was that "Freedom is both a blessing and a burden. It means not just getting a choice, but also *having* to choose." Reminding his audience of the harshness of life in the old country, where most of life's decisions were constrained by some other power, he said, "Now, in Western Europe, there is a new freedom, a freedom that brings new burdens and new questions: 'What should I study? What should I do with my life? Who should I marry? Where should I live?' The freedom of these questions is so burdensome," the scholar said, eliciting a knowing chuckle from the crowd, "that it is no wonder half the Dutch population is on anti-depressants: they are the most 'free' people on earth—of course they are miserable!"

Peppering his talk with references to Augustine and Kierkegaard, the scholar explained that freedom in Christianity does not simply equal "modern emancipation" popularly understood. He said,

Freedom is a pressure, and we humans must think carefully to understand what it is we are doing when we act on our freedom. Most importantly, we must understand that the duties and customs of being a Christian are part of freedom itself, though we have to come to our belief without coercion. This is the freedom that defines our humanity.

This final point—belief without coercion—disturbed his audience, and chuckles soon turned to audible consternation as the implications of his words sank in. When the time came for questions and answers, the scholar received multiple variations of the same question. Over and over, members of the audience stood up to ask: "How do we reconcile this insistence that Christianity is something we can choose with the understanding we all grew up with that it is a tradition into which we were born and to which we are tied by bonds of kinship and social belonging?" Audience members recounted personal traumatic experiences in their struggle to answer these questions; they described fights with grandparents and parents, doubts about what to teach their children, and experiences of what could be called an existential crisis. They asked: "Where is freedom in the idea that I am a Christian and have to be a Christian because it is my identity? If I have always thought that who I am is based on a hereditary Christian identity, but you are telling me I am not Christian until I seek, discover, and choose to believe, then who am I?"

One young man formulated this question in a particularly incisive manner, pushing the conversation to a deeper theological terrain that seemed to elude even the event's organizers. Tellingly, he quoted the automaker Henry Ford, in English: "It's like the old saying: 'You can choose any color of car you want, as long as it is black!' This is really a problem for us, right?" The crowd laughed, and some rolled their eyes and clucked their tongues in disapproval at his levity, but at some level, he had hit upon a core theological tension presented by the concept of "belief." His question exposed a logical knot at the heart of theological discussions of freedom within monotheism's exclusive truth claim: What is there to choose when there is only one true God? And yet, in response, the young scholar ended the conversation by reasserting his central claim: "I do not think you *are* a Christian," he said, "I think you *become* a Christian." This met with audible gasps across the hall as his audience exchanged dark looks.

Cosmological Intimacies

The tensions within the affective and ethical commitments underlying the congregation's dismay echoed in a conversation I had later that year with Marta and Rebekah, the two college-aged choir directors from the church in Hengelo described in earlier chapters (and the same Marta who addressed the Human Rights Council in this chapter's opening). On a warm afternoon in the middle of June, we sat in the television room on the ground floor of the monastery for a recorded interview. Up until that point, our conversations had occurred spontaneously during and after choir practices at their church. When we felt ready for a formal interview, the young women suggested that it would be both cozy and fitting to record their thoughts and feelings about life in the Dutch-Syriac diaspora at its spiritual and emotional center. As we talked, we were constantly interrupted by curious nuns and visiting families with rambunctious children, despite my having prearranged with the abbot that we would have this quiet time for our talk. Indeed, the elderly father checked in on us repeatedly, first to ask Marta and Rebekah about their families, later to give us his blessings, and then finally to give us each a church-branded Jesus key chain. Meanwhile, the abbot's younger sister, the nun Sister Seyde, sat down next to me to monitor our tea and cookie consumption and admonished us whenever she thought we were not eating and drinking enough. It was disruptive, but Marta and Rebekah were right: the chaos of the monastery space—with its mix of ritualized, patriarchal authority and domestic, familial intimacy—*was* an ideal space, cozy and comforting, for this conversation. So amidst the chaos, Marta, Rebekah, and I discussed their work as political activists, how and why they were developing their secular "Aramaean" ethnic identity, and their work leading the women and girls of the church choir in the weekly liturgical cycle. It was important, they told me, for Syriac Orthodox Christians to learn that they also have a secular, ethnic identity, not just a religious identity. "You cannot *just* be a Christian," Rebekah said. "You have to have an ethnicity too!" A person without an ethnicity does not exist politically. This is a problem for the effort by Suryoye to claim funding for culturally sensitive programs and services from the Dutch government, to assert land rights to their monasteries in southeast Turkey, and to gain global recognition for the Sayfo. They described their feelings of confusion and grief that bubbled up sometimes because of what this work required of them, emotionally and intellectually, as they actively tried to split their sense of inherited, kinship-based Christian identity, which encompassed all of social and political life, into distinct, separable spheres. It felt both necessary and wrong. Marta spoke emotionally of the longing she felt for the kind of intimacy and community her mother, aunts, and grandmothers experienced by living, sharing, and caring for each other as an extended family. She thought this was a way of life the self-consumed, individualistic, Dutch nuclear family could learn from.

At the same time, Marta and Rebekah said that even as they want to learn how to have an ethnicity, they also want their church to teach them how to become better Christians. Specifically, they want to know the meaning of what they sing every Sunday, the reasons for the rituals and rules they follow, and the spiritual significance of the liturgical order that organizes family and community life. If their religious identity must lose some of its character, they would like it to be enriched in other areas. But it is difficult, they said, because the church is so entrenched in old habits and dominated by old men who do not speak Dutch and do not see the value in teaching these things. As we discussed the tension between communal identity and individual belief, I asked whether questions about Syriac Orthodox identity were similar to questions about Jewish identity. Rebekah paused and said, "Yes, but there is a difference. You cannot be a secular Suryoyo yet, like you can be a secular Jew. In thirty years, yes; right now, no. If you stop believing in God, you just are not a Suryoyo anymore."

Rebekah's comment suggests that a taken-for-granted link between kinship and theology is becoming increasingly *less* taken for granted in the Syriac Orthodox diaspora. The young women's sadness and anxiety suggest that the process of ethnicization, however politically necessary, was destabilizing to their sense of liturgically mediated and kinship-based continuity fundamental to a Syriac Christian sense of community and identity. The idea that belief and identity can be separated is imaginable but not yet socially real. It has been perforated, but not yet split apart. For the moment, in this corner of the Syriac world, being Syriac Orthodox is something a person is born into, not something a person chooses to become. Conversions to Syriac Orthodoxy, while not unheard of, could be met with skepticism and derision unless the convert was willing and able to master the liturgical knowledge necessary to become a malphono, which two of my Dutch-born friends have managed by being highly trained experts on Syriac liturgical tradition and history, as I describe below. But marrying out of the faith, and thus out of the extended kinship network, is generally considered cause for disinheritance. With one or two noteworthy exceptions I describe later, the handful of people who defy these strictures eventually give up on maintaining their bond with the Syriac community, allowing themselves to become "assimilated" Dutch and thereby causing a traumatic rupture with their families.

Another choir woman pointed out the seriousness of this rupture to me. Elena, the young woman who sang in the monastery's gudo in Chapter 1 and who defied the bishop to help her friend, the nun, with her chores in Chapter 4, was a pillar of community organizing for the diocese, but she worried about Marta and Rebekah's style of overt political activism. Elena saw the debate over ethnic identity, and especially the fight over Aramaeanism versus Assyrianism, as deeply destructive. Instead, she dedicated herself to helping the archdiocese develop outreach and educational initiatives for young people in the church. According to Elena, these programs are meant to educate and help Syriac Orthodox become better Christians. Her mission puts her at odds with many in the older generation who feel these sorts of educational initiatives disrupt the structure of gendered moral authority that ensures the continuous reproduction of Syriac families and tradition. Like Marta and Rebekah, Elena longs for deeper, richer understanding of Syriac theology and shares their fear that the relationship between kinship and liturgical identity is growing increasingly tenuous and that this is cause to grieve. Elena cried when she told me the story of her aunt, who had left the Syriac Orthodox Church to join an evangelical Protestant church. Her aunt was no longer considered part of the family, and Elena had not seen her in years. She described her crushing sadness at the thought that the Syriac Orthodox Church had not been enough for her, but she knew, she said, that having left, her aunt simply was not Suryayto anymore. Unlike Rebekah and Marta, who see the political necessity of developing a public identity that is legible to secular audiences, Elena sees hope within the ecclesial community itself, if only it can be reinvigorated through education and spiritual guidance. But the three women agree that things cannot go on as they have; something radical must change in the way Syriac Christians go about being Syriac and Christian or they will disappear, either through violence or assimilation.

Mere "Religion"

So, in addition to their work as directors of the women's choir at their church in Hengelo, Marta and Rebekah were members of the Dutch Aramaean Federation, the national affiliate of the global World Council of Aramaeans (Syriacs), which had recently changed its name from the Syriac Universal Alliance. At the time of our first formal interview, Marta worked as a legal intern for the WCA but later rose through the ranks to become a highly visible spokesperson. In that capacity, she frequently addressed the United Nations Human Rights Council, requesting humanitarian aid for Syriac Orthodox Christians in Iraq and Syria. Marta co-wrote an important document posted in 2012 on the WCA's website explaining the logic behind the federation's name change and outlining their new strategy for securing recognition from various political bodies. This text illuminates how Marta and her colleagues understood the way the UN and other powerful political audiences see or, as the case may be, fail to see them:

Today, with a fresh generation of dedicated young men and women, we believe [. . .] that the rebranding of our name and logo are significant steps forward. Among others, they highlight our peoplehood and go beyond our linguistic, religious and cultural identity—more specifically, it stops reducing us to a "religious community." [. . .] we firmly believe that the new name and logo will help us raise more effectively the neglected voice of the Aramean [sic] people in the media and in political platforms and arenas like the United Nations, Council of Europe and the European Union.

This distinction between peoplehood and religious community mirrors a distinction made by the United Nations itself. Article 4 of the United Nations Human Rights Council's Declaration on the Rights of Indigenous People, for instance, predicates the possibility for corporate political autonomy upon recognition as a "distinct people," while Article 7 of the United Nation's Resolution on the Elimination of All Forms of Religious Intolerance stipulates the state's unambiguous sovereign prerogative over the exercise of religious beliefs and practices. In short, what makes "a people" of the sort that merits a measure of self-determination relative to the sovereign state cannot be "mere religion." Nonetheless, in this text the WCA immediately reclaims the religious grounds of their peoplehood by rooting it in the sacral language of the liturgy:

> The term "Syriac" was kept to ensure the synonymous meaning of "Aramean" [sic] and remind the world of the indisputable and fundamental truth aptly summed up by today's Syriac Orthodox Patriarch: "The Syriac language is the Aramaic language itself, and the Arameans [sic] are the Syrians themselves. He who has made a distinction between them has erred."[4]

By invoking the patriarch's position that the Syriac language is synonymous with the Aramaic language, the WCA authors echo a commonly asserted metonymic equivalence among (1) the vast family of Aramaic languages that have proliferated for millennia throughout the Middle East, (2) the first-century Jewish Palestinian Aramaic likely spoken by Jesus Christ, and (3) the seventh-century Syriac dialect of Aramaic still used as a liturgical and literary language throughout the twentieth- and twenty-first-century diaspora. This triple metonymy invests classical Syriac, what they call *kthobonoyo*, "the book language," with a multilayered sacrality. According to Peter, the young man who attempted to teach me classical Syriac at the monastery, it is the language God speaks and the only language that can unite the geographically dispersed and politically divided Suryoye, who are otherwise torn apart by their tainted vernaculars. Turoyo, in particular, was a target of Peter's disdain because it was so heavily mixed with Kurdish, Turkish, and Arabic that it bore, in his view, almost no resemblance to the language of liturgy.

Yet, in practice, classical Syriac's symbolic power to transcend regional disparities and unify the diaspora politically is limited because those very same regional disparities have created highly uneven conditions for teaching and valuing Syriac. In Iraq, as Heleen Murre-van den Berg (2015) has shown, Syriac had waned for centuries as Christians of the Church of the East, the Syriac Orthodox Church, and the Chaldean Church were linguistically and culturally incorporated into an Arabic-speaking world. Only in the twentieth century were they permitted to teach classical Syriac in schools in northern Iraq's Kurdish region. In that same region, in the Mandate period, British colonial authorities placed neo-Aramaic-speaking Assyrians (of the Church of the East) who had fled the Hakkari Mountains during World War I in refugee camps where they ensured classical Syriac would be taught. This was done in an explicit effort to develop the refugees' political consciousness in preparation for being resettled in an independent Assyrian state or territory, a dream that ultimately went unrealized (Robson 2017).

Syriac Christians in Tur Abdin, meanwhile, had been so marginal for so long that Syriac maintained as important a position in the liturgical life of villagers as it did for monastics. Their marginality, in some ways, saved the Syriac language until the Turkish government took active measures to suppress its teaching as part of its ongoing battle with what it perceived to be widespread separatism throughout the Kurdish-dominated region of southern and eastern Turkey. The WCA's assertion that the classical Syriac language defines Aramaean ethnicity because of its liturgical sacrality thus reflects a fragmented global field of power in which the legibility of the term *Syriac* to other Syriac Christians has been shaped by widely differing political conditions in their individual countries (see also Hanish 2008; Loosley 2009) and trajectories of migration across the diaspora (see also Hanoosh 2019). These other Syriac Orthodox Christians, according to the patriarch and the WCA, have erred, and the consequences of such error, from Marta and Rebekah's perspective, threatened to be cataclysmic for Syriac Orthodox liturgical kinship.

The extent to which political illegibility has bedeviled Syriac Orthodox kinship is further highlighted by the WCA's reaffirmation of the patriarchate's jurisdiction over Syriac's symbolic value and the ethnic boundary staked upon it. The text refers to the patriarch's position on the correct label for Syriac Orthodox Christians, which dates to a twentieth-century tract by Mor Ignatius Ephrem I Barsoum (1887–1957) addressed to congregants in the United States. In his "Declaration of the Syrian Orthodox Patriarchate of Antioch about the Nestorians," Barsoum forbade his church from uniting politically with the Church of the East—also known as Nestorians, East Syriac Christians, or (if you ask Marta and Rebekah) "real" Assyrians—by threatening his flock with excommunication (Barsoum 1947, cited in Makko 2010, 11–12). Yet when it was expelled from Turkey and sent into exile in Syria in the 1930s, the patriarchate was compelled to embrace pan-Arab nationalism for its own safety.

The Aramaeans and Assyrians I worked with were well aware of each other's conflicting narratives, and tempers frequently flared as a result. They disagreed not only about how to make Syriac liturgical kinship legible politically but about what modality of irreducible relatedness *to make* legible. The difference was partially a matter of scale. For the Aramaeans I worked with, the West Syriac Rite operated as a parish-level ethnic boundary. This position scales the relationship between the ritual and the political in terms of intimate, affective relations ordered around ecclesiastical authority. The Assyrian position, on the other hand, scales the relationship between the ritual and the political in broader ecumenical terms—participation in the West Syriac Rite is not the only criterion for membership in "our people."

Crucially, neither of these positions can be accounted for through the logic of secular rupture, as some scholars have claimed. Aramaeanism and Assyrianism are, instead, both signs of perforated kinship because the power of liturgy remains indispensable to both political orientations. Neither faction, in this corner of the Syriac world, has signed on to the secularist premise that ethnicity is of the body and religion is of the mind. Where they differ is in how that liturgical power articulates with political authority. Assyrian nationhood is staked upon a distinct set of geographically dispersed historical memories linked to the broader family of Syriac language liturgical traditions. For example, an internationally prominent Dutch Suryayto named Semela explained her commitment to Assyrian ethnonationalist activism in these terms: "My community has a history. I have an obligation to that history, or Syriac Christianity will disappear from the world." She paused for a moment, remembering: "It is when I hear the hymns especially. I sang in the choir when I was a young girl.

When I hear the singing now, I feel . . . emotional. I cannot let all that beauty disappear."

Early in her career, Semela relied on the Syriac Orthodox Church's ecclesiastical hierarchy to help her accomplish her political aims despite her private doubts about the existence of God, or at least, she says, the kind of God described in her childhood church. This was the reason for our meeting at the monastery that first summer in 2007, where the recently installed bishop had introduced us and facilitated our initial conversations. Semela told me that she relied on the Church's cooperation and support not only because it was the primary source of authority and means of communication among Syriac Orthodox communities across northern Europe, but also because it was the bishop's office that facilitated connections with local Dutch Protestant, Catholic, and secular human rights organizations. Representatives from these agencies saw the bishop as the community's de facto leader and spokesperson, which, she said, she found problematic. With a pained expression, she chose her words carefully:

> So . . . yes . . . it is tricky . . . the Church is the "location" of our culture, in a sense, and in the past, the church has always protected our culture's identity . . . but now . . . it seems to me that the Church is keeping people ignorant . . . we are so focused on the religious side of things that not many of us are politically aware . . . and ironically that might be what causes us to disappear.

Semela returned to this theme frequently in our subsequent conversations, pointing out that a strong sense of religious identity was not enough to keep Syriac Christianity from disappearing from the world. In today's world, she said, you cannot stake a public claim to political autonomy on religious identity alone. For that, you need an ethnicity, with all the ties to land and blood the secularist concept of "ethnicity" is presumed to entail. For Semela, it was important to make clear to outsiders that she was Assyrian because her family's history was both "Syriac" in terms of the language of the liturgy performed at their church and "Christian" in terms of a social and cultural belonging organized by and through that church. Ethnic ties to ancient Mesopotamia and to the Assyrian Empire whose ruins dot the landscape of northern Iraq were, in her analysis, reproduced over the centuries by and through the church and the language of its liturgy. The church was therefore essential, but also not enough. To compound matters, she disliked attending Mass now as an adult despite her love for the hymns. This she told me with a defiant air that only made sense to me once I discovered that many of her constituents were growing increasingly incensed by what they perceived as her public displays of impiety (such as admitting in an interview with a local newspaper her discomfort with how the church characterized God). For many of my research participants, this admission of doubt constituted a grave breach of one of the unshakeable norms of diasporic Syriac Orthodox social life.

Such reactions could provoke her frustration, as could the visiting anthropologist's naive questioning. But Semela was well-versed in social scientific theory and equipped to answer my skeptical questions in terms I could wrap my brain around. Stuck on the fact that ancient Assyria had ended in the 600s BCE, I asked her to explain how exactly she linked her Christian upbringing to an empire that was destroyed six hundred years before the birth of Christ. She threw up her hands and switched to English to bellow at me: "Everyone else gets to invent their tradition—why can't we? Our identity is no more or less constructed than every single other ethnic group in the world! That doesn't make us any less *a people*! Why should we be the exception?!"

While the West Syriac Rite of the Syriac Orthodox Church is genealogically and linguistically linked to the East Syriac Rite of the Assyrian Church of the East, it is very different in form and content. Yet, in both cases, political identity is inescapably Christian because Christianity is an inherent, rather than an optional, dimension of Syriac personhood—the overarching difference between them is in how the Syriac Orthodox person positions his or herself in different spatiotemporal configurations of the broader Syriac world. These competing configurations are not reducible to a secularization narrative, but they do bear traces of secularism's effects in how secularism elevates the predicament of legibility to a full-blown crisis when it makes conflicting demands on invisible minorities as they engage different scales of governance.

Not Just Suryoyo!

Despite proliferating diasporic debates about what to make legible and how best to do so using the terms "Assyrian" and "Aramaean," nearly all of my research participants happily referred to themselves as Suryoyo when speaking among themselves. Yet this would suggest a certain emic neutrality that is misleading: it, too, is heavy with the weight of explanation to outsiders, especially at the municipal scale of governance in Enschede and Hengelo where the Syriac Orthodox *are* well-known locally as "Suryoye." Community frustrations around the term "Suryoyo" became particularly apparent to me during a women's committee meeting in March 2010 at an Aramaean cultural organization the day before scheduled regional and national elections in the Netherlands. At this meeting, fifteen women gathered to meet Myra Koomen, the alderwoman responsible for Work and Income for the Enschede municipal government and the head of the local Christian Democrat party (CDA). The meeting, which was organized by Ayfer Koç, a Syriac Orthodox councilwoman for the CDA, took place in a large hall where the organization hosts social gatherings, soccer viewing parties, and public lectures. Alderwoman Koomen was there to promote immigrant women's economic, social, and political participation and to encourage her constituents to vote for the CDA in the next day's elections. During the meeting, the alderwoman admonished the women for failing to organize their community effectively. The women around the table nodded in agreement; they acknowledged their difficulties in organizing to make the most of the resources for minority accommodation available from the Dutch government. Their greatest failure was their inability to form a single, overarching umbrella organization to represent all Syriac Orthodox in the Netherlands, they admitted. At the table that evening, the conversation began to heat up as the women struggled to explain to the alderwoman why they have difficulty forming such an organization until finally someone burst out:

> It is because there are two different cultural organizations in the neighborhood; we cannot organize successfully with the other women in the church. Women from one side will not sit on a committee with women from the other side!

Councilwoman Koç spoke up to explain just how fraught the situation had gotten. She herself was frequently attacked, she said, because she refused to use either the words "Aramaean" or "Assyrian." She instead used the word "Suryoye" because she thought it was neutral and would hurt no one. Another woman at the table nodded: "Exactly! It is crazy to talk about the divisions in church because we are all just Suryoyo, end of story!"

But then someone else spoke up: "No! We are not *just* Syriac (*Syrische*)—we are Syriac Orthodox as religion! Syriac-Aramaic is the language we speak because we have Aramaean identity!" Interestingly, she rendered the word "Suryoyo" into the Dutch word "Syrische," which the councilwoman countered with another complication that unsettled the other woman's implicit focus on the classical language used in liturgy, Syriac, by assuming that "Syrische" referred to Ṭuroyo, the spoken vernacular of Tur Abdin, which she did not speak: "But what about this? My family is from Mardin, so we speak Arabic, not *Syrische*. Does that make me not 'Suryoyo'? I had never even heard the word 'Suryoyo' until I came to the Netherlands as a child!" But another woman immediately spoke up in defense of her friend: "*Geloof* (faith/belief) and *afkomst* (ancestry/descent/lineage) are different! If you go to America and you are Catholic, you do not tell people you come from the country of Catholicism! Your *afkomst* is Turkey, your *geloof* is Syriac Orthodox!" And so the discussion went until someone said with an embarrassed laugh, "As you see, there is a lot of confusion!"

The group's uncertainty about whether *Suryoyo* references *geloof* or *afkomst* reflected, I suggest, a situation in which the complex regional history described above comes to bear in a novel political context. In this context, newer forces are woven into older ones and global discourses are refracted through nationally specific histories. While these women attested to having experienced the bureaucratic distinction between ethnic background (collapsed into the notion of nationality) and religious identity as a problem for international border-crossing, many of them nonetheless refused to let that distinction set the terms of their self-understanding. Becoming legible to the Dutch state at the municipal level meant that Syriac Orthodox Christians now had to contend with the legacies of Dutch religious and political history. Unlike at the supranational level of the United Nations where the political salience of religion is defined in terms of freedom from discrimination, in the Dutch case, religious difference *has* legitimately furnished the ground of communal political identity and aspiration. A history of anti-Enlightenment Calvinist theocracy remains very much in play in the secular politics of minority recognition despite the common story that Dutch society is thoroughly secular, a tension I examine more closely in Chapter 6. For Dutch Suryoye, these legacies reverberate in intra-communal theological discussions about what it means to be a "people," as in the community discussion at the monastery about Christian freedom above.

The Solitude of the Soul

Elena, Marta, and Rebekah are, each in their own way, worried about the ruptures inherent to the reproductive work in which they are engaged. Some they fear and hope to forestall, some they welcome, and some they know they cannot avoid. So, too, the continuities. Rupture and continuity intertwine in new configurations in every act of reproduction. This dance of heredity and novelty, materiality and imagination, mirrors the abductive relation within the heart of the iconic sign. These uncertainties, debates, and outright fights about secular legibility flow out of the perforations torn open by iconicity.

Arguably, *all* Christian identity entails such a fraught entanglement of continuity and rupture, found in many different possible configurations. Analytically, scholars working in the anthropology of Christianity have established that one of the few shared premises of Christian identity across traditions is a certain anxiety about the relationship between the historical family of the church and the solitude of the soul seeking God. As scholars such as Austin-Broos (1997), Cannell (2006), Coleman (2006), Keane (2006, 2007, 2008), and many others have argued, a genealogy of Western Protestant Christianity, particularly that which has been influenced by Calvinist and Arminian theologies, emphasizes the private, individual, and interior process of *becoming Christian* over Christianity's embodied and communal character,[5] the very process of becoming the young philosopher spoke of at the public lecture at the monastery. Anthropologists working on the globalization of evangelical and other Protestant forms of Christianity have documented an array of possibilities in how the rupture of conversion can be understood and experienced, but there is a shared sense among scholars of the centrality of conversion to Protestant notions of Christian identity. In the meantime, scholars working on different branches of Eastern Orthodoxy have examined the centrality of continuity in Orthodox self-representations, often in order to explain the frequent correlation between ethnic identity and national orthodox churches (e.g., Hann and Goltz 2010). This is not, however, to suggest an easy characterization of the "Latin" / "Orthodox" split as an oppositional binary between rupture and continuity. Fenella Cannell's study of Mormon genealogy is instructive, for example, in how it has cast light on the labor involved in creating and recreating the links that constitute continuity and how spiritual temporality can be reworked so that conversion or spiritual recom-

Syriac Orthodox mosaic in a converted Roman Catholic Church in Amsterdam (photo by author).

mitment reveals an always-already spiritual-genealogical relationship (Cannell 2005).

As important as this conversation is, I am less concerned here with the cross-cultural definitional exercise concerning Christian identity than I am with a tiny yet recurring detail. In each story described so far, either explicitly or implicitly, my interlocutors convey a deep well of fear or grief about inter-generational conflict; that is, fighting, or being afraid of fighting, with parents and grandparents about how to talk about Christianity. The being/becoming dichotomy is not just a conceptual problem but an emotional one that shapes the dynamics of everyday family life. In the lecture on Kierkegaard and Christian freedom, audience members admitted to fights with parents and grandparents; Marta and Rebekah were terrified of arguments with their parents and took pains to avoid them; Elena's aunt learned the hard way what walking a different spiritual path meant for her relationship with her kin, as did the aunt of Nicme, the choir girl and

Aramaean activist I interview in Chapter 6. Fear of angering or hurting one's parents was a common refrain among every single one of my research participants, without exception. Though, at first glance, this may seem the most banal of observations, given the theological and sociopolitical stakes of a communally and intergenerationally agreed-upon criterion for establishing one's public identity as Christian, it is worth understanding where, literally, my research participants' parents and grandparents were coming from. How, in other words, has history—including histories of violence, dispossession, displacement, migration, and trauma—brought them to this moment where Christianity feels non-optional?

Maryam and the Saint

The dynamics of religious freedom, obligation, and authority in elder Syriac Orthodox conceptions of kin-relatedness were explained to me by Maryam, mother of Philippa, one of my choir friends. Maryam was the wife of the priest at the parish church in central Enschede, where I often sang on Sunday mornings and attended evening madrashto. After Holy Mass one day, I sat with Maryam on the women's side of the coffee hall (*koffiezaal*), where she told me the story of how her son Gabriel was conceived. Like many Christians and Muslims in the area around the Mor Gabriel Monastery in Tur Abdin,[6] she had once held an all-night vigil praying to the saint in hopes of becoming pregnant. She was successful, as is everyone who talks about their experience, and with proper gratitude, eventually named her child after the saint. She explained to me, with fervent animation, that "you cannot just name your child following your fantasy . . . you have to honor the saint, or he will be angry." She knew a woman who did not name her son after the saint, so St. Gabriel took him away in a car accident when he turned eighteen. To Maryam, this was a sad but predictable outcome.

From one perspective, there is a complicated entanglement of kinship, authority, and moral obligation built into the ritual structure of St. Gabriel's role in Maryam's family life that highlights a point of tension between Syriac Christian and Western Christian, particularly Calvinist, conceptions of the religious subject. This tension turns on differently conceived notions of transcendence and immanence as constitutive of the relationships among Christians and the divine. Keane reminds us that the problem of transcendence, as defined and refined by Calvinist Christians, has come to haunt the very condition of secular modernity: the modern sub-ject desires "a self freed of its body, . . . meanings freed of semiotic media-tion, and . . . agency freed of the press of other people" (2006, 320). The problem of transcendence assures an eternal paradox and ambiguity in the status of subjects and objects, of words and things, and all material mediations of the ontological gap between the invisible and the visible worlds (Keane 2006, 312). This classically Calvinist distinction between human subjects and nonhuman objects is fundamental to many secular-modern conceptions of personhood (Cannell 2006, 14–22; Mauss 1985) and exerts a normative—but not necessarily inevitable—pressure on sub-jects whose theories of personhood are otherwise configured.

For Maryam and many of her peers, there is no ontological gap between the visible and invisible worlds, as long as the Christian subject has the ca-pacity for poetic thought necessary to grasp this unity (see also den Biesen 2010; McVey 1989). This is captured in Syriac liturgical theology by the no-tion of *rozo*, or "mystery." Rozo, as Dr. den Biesen explained to me one day when I visited him and his American wife (my good friend Catherine) for dinner, is like a symbol in a way but more so: rozo materializes the mystery by making it accessible to human experience. This is a notion, he said, of immanent transcendence, in which "now" becomes "eternity," and the visi-ble reveals the invisible.[7] Such a principle operates in a universe in which there is no opposition between sacred and profane and in which holiness is a condition of moral personhood conveyed in the notion of *qadishto*. In this same conversation, Dr. den Biesen explained that liturgical chant itself is meant, formally, to be an emotional state of participating in this mystery. Such a view of the immanence of singing is an embodied theology that ap-proaches cosmological salvation holistically. Maryam's understanding of the relationships among herself, her children, and the saint thus rests on the assumption of the invisible's immanent presence in the visible world. In this single, unified reality, humans and angels interact, albeit within a certain asymmetrical structure of authority and obligation. This ontological unity gives a different valence to the "value" in exchange than that bestowed by the logic of transcendence. For Maryam, a name quite rightly bears the same value as a life. Its value is in the way it materializes her submission to the immanent power and moral authority of the saint. For this reason, the sonorous materiality of the name, Gabriel or Gabriela, matters.

The historically Dutch Calvinist Christian discourse of materiality and interiority, which posits an opposition between material value and social value (i.e., the worth of the human subject over and against the worth of objects), looks askance at the relation of exchange between Maryam and the saint. The structure of authority is wrong, both from a secular humanist point of view and from a Calvinist Christian point of view. The metaphysical order of the universe, the collapsing of "immanence" and "transcendence" into a singular reality, is wrong. The modern subject must be the source of her own value and authority, authenticated by the sincerity of her individual will. The moral authority of the modern Christian subject's will derives from a sincere relationship with its own interiority (Keane 2006, 315–316; see also Seligman 2009). Maryam repudiates this logic of will as a "fantasy," and she warns of its lethal consequences for the Syriac Christian family. This embodied theology structures Syriac Christianity as a kinship practice. Maryam is ethically entangled with the divine through her non-optional kin relations, in complete transgression of the categorical distinctions of modern secular and Western Christian thought.

But Maryam lives in the Netherlands, so the saint coexists uneasily with other powerful forces and logics. Maryam inhabits the interstices of competing and overlapping authorities. The lines run right through the middle of her everyday family life. She is deeply pious and concerned for the preservation of the spiritual community according to correct norms. Her husband, soon to be promoted to the highest rank in the ecclesiastical hierarchy available to a married priest, is a widely admired paragon of moderate Syriac conservativism. At the same time, she is extremely proud of her daughter, Philippa, a law student at a Dutch university, who is clearly living a life unrecognizable to Maryam in a world governed by logics that classify her own cosmological common sense as superstitious and absurd. Maryam sighs and shakes her head over how hard Philippa has to work. Maryam cannot imagine Philippa's life herself, but she beams with pride touched by sadness when she speaks of her daughter. "So many big books! All of the time!" she tells me. Sometimes Philippa is so busy studying that she cannot come to church on Sundays, even though she was for a long time a core member of the women's choir (and during the course of my fieldwork, Philippa often returned to sing in the choir when her schedule allowed, comfortably embodying her authority as the priest's daughter to correct my posture when I sang next to her in the gudo). The logic of Maryam's ritual relation of obligation to the saint is, in part, a reflection of her full-bodied and whole-hearted habitation of Syriac Orthodox liturgical life, which organizes social and familial relations. But this ritual obligation is mingled with her love and respect for her daughter and her recognition that her daughter *must*, for the sake of Syriac political viability and visibility in the Dutch public sphere, fulfill her ambitions for a career practicing Dutch law, even though this requires submission to other structures of authority (none the least the textualized authority of academic credentials) that make an almost all-consuming claim on Philippa's time and energy. The ambivalently proud yet tearful expression on Maryam's face and the catch in her throat as she says "so many big books!" suggest her uneasy acceptance of a competing authoritative claim on her daughter. The bridge between liturgical kinship and secular power is Maryam's affective labor.

Ethical Ruptures

How do young women of Philippa's generation relate to the immanent transcendence in Syriac liturgical kinship characterized by Maryam's dutiful submission to the saint? In my observation, they focus explicitly on moral behavior and emphasize the importance of submitting to the patriarchal authority of church and family. An intimate overlap between home and church was, in my informants' view, an ethically necessary and distinctive part of Syriac Orthodox life both before migration to Europe and after. My friend Elizabeta, for example, wondered aloud during Sunday night madrashto whether it was proper that she was training to become a secular social worker. Matthias, her malphono, told her: "I think it is alright for you to be a social worker because you can help others who are not Suryoye that way, as long as you yourself turn to the church for guidance if you have family problems."

The question of morality, along with its complex relationship with the ethics of recognition and the sociopolitical legibility of liturgical kinship, became especially apparent to me during another day spent with the sisters Elizabeta and Mariane Mansur and their extended family. Because it was a Sunday afternoon, over a dozen relatives, including Ilona and Karin, the oldest married Mansur sisters and their families, were there for their weekly Sunday visit. During the afternoon's meandering conversations, someone mentioned a vicious rumor circulating through the Dutch- and German-Syriac communities. According to the rumor, a Syriac Orthodox girl in Germany had been disgraced for making a sex tape with her boyfriend several years prior. Someone, presumably the boyfriend, had put the tape on the Internet for all to see. The day before my visit, the sisters had heard that the girl in Germany had attempted suicide. During the course of the afternoon, over tea and snacks, the women in the family discussed the news with varying levels of dismay, disapproval, and skepticism. They all agreed that no one could say for sure whether the rumor of the girl's suicide was true, but Karin assured them that the original allegation, at least, *was* true, claiming to have seen the tape for herself. Elizabeta, the youngest sister, wondered out loud at the fact that she had never heard anyone say anything bad about the boy involved in the affair. With indignation, she reminded the women in her family that the boy was also Suryoyo and, therefore, just as guilty.

"Why is he not spoken of the same way?" she asked. "Is that not a double standard?" Her aunt and her sister Karin then both said, at the same time: "No! It would be better if she were dead!"

As she registered what her aunt and sister had just said—that it would have been better for the girl to have died in her alleged suicide attempt—Elizabeta's face fell. She began to protest. Karin turned to her and said, voice rising in fury: "You do not know what she did, on that tape, with every possible hole from every possible angle! She cannot present (*vertonen*, exhibit) herself as Surayto after what she did! She is *not Suryayto!*"

Beyond this, no one had much to contribute but headshaking, tongue-clucking, and an attempt to change the subject, especially, I think, because they were aware of my presence in the room. During this exchange with her sister, Elizabeta frequently looked at me out of the corner of her eye with what I interpreted was an expression of nervous self-consciousness. Being well experienced with secularist university goers in the Netherlands, she had every reason to suspect I would not be an approving audience for this kind of talk. Whether Elizabeta moderated her own opinions for my benefit, I do not know, but based on my subsequent conversations with her over the years, I think that even then she disagreed with her sister and aunt. Worse yet, from Elizabeta's perspective, the kind of repressive social control that is achieved through vicious gossip is precisely that which secularist audiences attribute to illiberal religion—of, in the language of Dutch anti-Muslim hardliners, a "backward religious village mentality." But this is not just an image problem. Many young Syriac Orthodox women I knew complained of the repressive social control that they were subjected to by their extended families and social networks. In the tightly knit enclaves of suburban Enschede and Hengelo, everyone was watching and everyone was commenting. This tension presents a deeper ethical predicament for young women like Elizabeta as they try to determine who and how they should be in the midst of conflicting discourses about sexuality, self-exposure, and gender. What role *should* women's moral comportment play in defining the public dimensions of Suryoyo-ness socially, culturally, and politically? This is an electrically charged question—as distressing as it is unavoidable—as Syriac Orthodox women contend with Western European debates about honor killing and other practices that defy easy categorization as "religious," "cultural," or "ethnic" and are easy fodder for the anti-immigrant sentiments of their neighbors.

A Suryoyo from the Village of Maastricht

Moral comportment is one dimension of Syriac Orthodox anxieties about the tension between *becoming Christian* and *being Christian*, tensions which are as theological as they are sociological. A certain common sense about the hereditary requirements of being Suryoyo prevails, perforated in complex patterns by engagement with global discourses of indigeneity and minority recognition as well as Protestant rupture thinking and religious freedom. One development in particular that causes many of my Syriac Orthodox interlocutors to furrow their brows is the case of Dr. den Biesen, a native-born Dutchman who was raised devoutly Roman Catholic in the southern Dutch city of Maastricht. He had taught himself classical Syriac as a young man and has written books about the poetry and theology of St. Ephrem, the fourth-century founding saint and poet-theologian associated with the ancient Syriac women's choirs.

A middle-aged, soft-spoken man of gentle humor, Dr. den Biesen writes widely on mystical poetry, from Ephrem to Dante to Blake. In addition to his university teaching and publishing schedule, he worked, for the duration of my fieldwork, part-time for the monastery to develop an educational program for the diocese. Dr. den Biesen is also distinguished as one among a tiny handful of outsiders who have converted to Syriac Orthodoxy, despite the insistence among many in the community that conversion to Syriac Orthodoxy simply is not possible. He frequently introduced himself, with a mischievous laugh, as "a Suryoyo from the village of Maastricht." At this, even his closest friends in the church raised their eyebrows, to his endless amusement.

And yet no one ever said outright, at least not in front of me, that Dr. den Biesen was kidding himself. The reason for this is that he was in possession of one thing that is in short supply and conveys a status of moral authority akin to the highest ranks of the priesthood. Dr. den Biesen is a malphono's malphono—one of the world's foremost authorities on ancient Syriac theology whose knowledge of St. Ephrem is matched only by Syriac studies professors at elite universities. His claim to conversion carries a certain weight and opens up another perforating space of uncertainty because of his privileged scholarly access to the founding saint's writings and wisdom, which, as we have seen in earlier chapters, my interlocutors see as fundamental to crafting Syriac Orthodox liturgical kinship. His intellectual authority serves as a bridge, offering a potential strategy for addressing the complex question of freedom and obligation that so confounded the audience members of the New Year's event described at the beginning of this chapter.

Later in that very same New Year's lecture described above, Dr. den Biesen also addressed the monastery audience, presenting them with his interpretation of St. Ephrem's symbolic thought. According to Dr. den Biesen, the path out of the morass, the path to becoming a whole person—a fully integrated, ethical human being—is to return to the founding texts with an open mind and a creative spirit. "Christianity is like an atlas," he told the audience:

> You can decide where you want to go—it is not a closed system. The church, and our Christian identity, exists to help us to grow in responsibility. Yes, we go to church because our parents did, but we also have the responsibility, now, to decide what that means for us. The church is there to help us grow into adulthood. Western culture has lost the capacity for culture, and so it fails to cultivate mature adults. Mor Ephrem's message is that the church enables us to be faithful in our own unique way, and to help us make our faith personal. We have to learn how to discern the difference between things you cannot choose and the possibilities you can choose from, and we have to learn how to handle freedom and cultivate ourselves to learn to live with other people with freedom [leren omgaan met vrijheid].

Thus, in Dr. den Biesen's view, the church is a school. According to him, Western countries are in the midst of a massive identity crisis because of a breakdown in upbringing and education [opvoeding en onderwijs]. The question of what to do with ancient tradition is resolved by true spiritual maturity. The goal is not to reject the past but to use the past in a creative way to give form to the future and the present. His words left an impression on his audience. When I spoke with some of my friends and acquaintances after the event, some were overwhelmed by the intellectual complexity of his ideas, but others were intrigued and wanted to hear more.

At the time of my research, it was too early to know whether Dr. den Biesen's ideas would be taken up by members of the church community, but his theologically and historically grounded approach addressed head-on my interlocutors' theological anxieties about the relationship of the past to the present and how to think about Christianity as a process of moral becoming that encompasses faithfulness to the history of past relations that resound in the liturgy—without adopting a Calvinist model of ruptured individuality and indifference to relational histories. Dr. den Biesen's approach to thinking about the relationship between freedom and ethical cultivation suggested a possibility for recuperating the pastoral and educational role of the church and the liturgical tradition in the relations of care and authority in the community while reconfiguring them to be more flexible, inclusive, and less authoritarian. Implicitly, his approach nodded to the growing sense that the tightly knit relationship between kinship and ecclesial identity is a political problem. Addressing this problem requires an ethical reconfiguration of the bonds of relatedness, their underlying patterns of social obligation and authority, and possibly their moral and spiritual foundations. The challenge is to do so without losing Syriac Orthodoxy's tradition of interpreting and practicing historical diversity and cosmopolitan complexity as part of the mystery of Christ's Incarnation. This mode of interpreting and practicing history constitutes the Iconic economy—earthly and divine matters are intimately interwoven and extend into domains conventionally considered "secular" in dominant Western Christian traditions—and remains central to liturgical practice.

An Imperceptible Iconic Economy

Maryam, the priest's wife, exemplifies how an embodied Incarnational theology is lived out in kin relations: her all-night vigil, her conception, giving birth and raising her child, naming her child after the saint, caring for the priest who cares for the parish. When I described Maryam's explanation of her relationship to the saint to an (ex)Calvinist Dutch family member of mine who had studied theology at seminary, he was astonished.[8] He said: "That's not Christianity—that's animism!" To Maryam, these practices are what make her Christian. To my Calvinist kin, they are unrecognizable. Maryam's liturgical subjectivity is audible to Dr. den Biesen because he has spent his life immersed in the theological poetry of St. Ephrem. To mainstream secularist and Western Christian audiences, Maryam is entirely inaudible, illegible, and incomprehensible. The inaudibility of her liturgical subjectivity makes dialogical recognition for her generation all but impossible. This compounds the hurt caused by intergenerational trauma and lack of political recognition for the Sayfo, inflamed by subsequent, regularly recurring experiences of mass violence, dispossession, and migration.

The absence of dialogical recognition blocks Suryoye efforts to engage the Dutch state and its proxies in their efforts to "integrate" them. In the examples I have provided so far, the failure of dialogical recognition turns on differently understood conceptions of responsibility in the secular Dutch citizen-subject and in the Syriac liturgical subject. In the New Year's public lecture, the audience was asked to adopt a Western Christian view of taking individual responsibility for *becoming Christian* from a voice that came from within their liturgical community. The echoes of Calvinist theology in secularist and Western Christian discourses of minority recognition and integration would disentangle their immanent relations with saints, angels, and divine authority. The distress triggered in the monastery event described above hinged on the complexity of the notion of responsibility implicit in secular Dutch "minority integration" policies as well as in the modern Protestant strands of Western Christian theology favored by intellectually inclined Dutch Christians today. Responsibility was invoked through a notion of freedom understood as the burden of an individual's relationship to the divine—or phrased even more precisely, freedom is the individual's *chosen relation to their obligation* to the divine. Individual responsibility stands in stark contrast to the Iconic economy of young Syriac Orthodox Christians' liturgical practices of relating, both inside and outside of church. Yet because this economy is imperceptible to Dutch interlocutors, it rarely comes up for explicit discussion. This leaves an open, unspeakable wound of anxiety and confusion among second- and third-generation Syriac Orthodox when contemplating the possibility of severing the "ethnic," or the non-optional dimensions of liturgical kinship inherited from family, from the "religious," or the optional dimensions of liturgical kinship cultivated through reflection and experimentation. The unspeakability of these matters is one of the perforating forces at work in their lives.

The Subject of Responsibility

This discussion raises two questions for understanding the ethics of recognition and iconicity as reproductive power. In *The Gift of Death* (2008), Derrida devotes a chapter to the "Secrets of European Responsibility," in which he argues that the history of sovereign power in Europe is bound up with the joint history of (Western) Christianity and of the free self as the subject of responsibility (Derrida 2008, 4). The management of life that animates modern state power is—in this perspective—rooted in a submerged religious history of subjecting the subject of responsibility "to the wholly and infinite other that sees without being seen" (Derrida 2008, 5), such that secular discourses of political responsibility echo Western Christian discourses of religious responsibility. Another way to put this is that the Christian soul is answerable to God for the caring management of earthly life: though free, the soul is responsible because it is ultimately subject to God's sovereignty. Similarly, citizens are free, although responsible, because they are ultimately subject to the sovereign state. Thus, political arguments in Europe over the incompatibility of religious traditions with secular democracy emerge from uncertainty over the quality and character of the "unseen other" that shapes cultural and political conceptions of the relationship between the free self and sovereign power, what Derrida describes as a relationship of responsibility (Derrida 2008, 7–8). The sovereign in a Western theopolitical imaginary is, in this narrative, transcendent and inaccessible like the Calvinist God. A government is not its people; a people are not their government. This model of sovereign power rests upon a paradox: a responsible subject is a subject who exists in a relationship to power in which the reproductive relations that produce that subject are effaced.[9] This view of sovereign power is rooted in a belief in "a 'radical separation' between man and God" (Cannell 2006, 17–18). This belief recurs as tropes—e.g., "the mediation of the power of a God withdrawn from the world of mortal men" and "spirit and matter as irreconcilable opposites" used to define a normative secular category of "religion" (Asad 1992, 2003; Cannell 2006, 18).[10] Yet these tropes contain variations that illuminate the interpretive difficulties of the Incarnational theological politics undergirding them.

Anthropologists such as Simon Coleman (2000, 2006), for example, have shown the diversity of relations that can exist between even the most modernist of Protestant persons and the divine. He analyzes the Swedish Charismatic Protestant economy of salvation in which Faith Christians gave gifts to strangers not in order to create social bonds (which contrasts significantly with Mauss's theory of gift exchange), but with the idea that the spiritual self would be materialized in the gift and sent out "into a world where the unknown other could be the apparent recipient of the donation, but where the greatest beneficiary would be herself" (Coleman 2006, 180). Thus, Coleman writes, "the charismatic self is constituted by becoming a materialized self through the agency of words and things" (Coleman 2006, 182). The agency of words and things in Swedish Charismatic Protestantism suggests a different configuration of subject-object relations, as well as a different attitude toward agency and materiality, than that of Webb Keane's Dutch Calvinist missionaries in colonized Indonesia, whose views of freedom and agency tend to be taken as paradigmatic of secular modernity.

The Swedish Charismatic materialization of the self in the exchange of words and things (rendering the invisible visible) resonates surprisingly with the materialization of mystery conveyed by the West Syriac conception of rozo, as exemplified in Maryam's relation with the saint. The crucial difference is that while Protestants and other Western Christians materialize selves, Maryam materializes a relation animated by the Orthodox Iconic economy. The relation between Swedish Charismatic Christian and their God is *contractual*, resonating with the possessive individualism of liberal and capitalist notions of personhood (Locke 2004; see Macpherson 2011 [1964]). This Christian self, like other modern selves, is first and foremost a property owner whose primary property is his own individual self. This individual self elects to enter into relations with others, and these relations are governed by the law and logic of contracts. In modern liberal states, a relation of legitimate responsibility is one that has been ratified by a contract. A contractual obligation is enforced by the law of the sovereign state. More importantly still, state sovereignty is a function of its status as enforcer and protector of property rights and contractual relations (Macpherson 2011 [1964]). The subject of contractual relations is the self-possessing individual. The subject of responsibility is he who holds property and honors a contract. The Swedish Charismatics of Coleman's study render their understanding of their relation to God in these liberal economic terms. God may be sovereign but the person that exists in relation to that sovereignty is individuated and self-possessed.

Although the individuated and self-possessed person is ubiquitous in a world shaped by capitalism, Marilyn Strathern (1988, 2005) has shown in her work on Melanesian kinship that "the individual" is far from a universal model of personhood. A self may instead be understood, for example, as the intersection of multiple relations (2005, 13). In the Melanesian model, intersecting relations produce a self (the "dividual"). This is in contrast to the "individual" of Western thought, a pre-constituted self who willfully elects to enter into relations with others. One of the only areas in which the Melanesian "dividual" is thinkable and translatable into liberal terms is in the reproductive dimensions of Euro-American kinship. I do not elect to be a sister or daughter, but the intersection of these kin relations produces vital parts of my sense of who I am. When I elected to become a mother, this, too, produced a vital sense of selfhood that cannot now be undone. There are very few things in modern liberal life that stick like this (although it is a testament to the limits of this life that the gendered and sexualized dimensions of liberal personhood are not easy to square with the legal and public identity of the abstract, bounded, individual citizen-subject) (see also Scott 2007).

However, the self that is produced by the West Syriac conception of rozo and by Maryam's relation with the saint is different yet again. It is possible to catastrophically disrupt the kin relations that produce Syriac selves by irresponsible behaviors, such as failing to name your child after the saint, being filmed while having sex, or joining a Western evangelical Christian church. The divine power to take away a parent's child if the parent does not materialize gratitude, respect, and submission through embodied practice is immanent within kin relations. This is precisely why, when persons who are born Syriac Christian cease to believe in God, they cease to be Suryoye. The entangled relation with God and kin produces the Syriac Orthodox self. Disrupting those relations destroys that self. To translate into secularist Euro-American terms, the day I cease to be a daughter or a sister or a mother is the day I will have died.

Although Rebekah the choir leader foresees that in thirty years' time this Syriac Orthodox conception of a relational self will have radically altered, for now, the sense of existential and political crisis is exacerbated by its inaudibility. When the perspicacious young man at the New Year's event invoked the figure of Henry Ford and his famous dictum "you can choose any color you like as long as it's black," he was laughed at and then ignored. I suggest this was because he was beginning to articulate something that is in fact very difficult and dangerous to articulate within the politics of minority recognition in Europe, especially in the Netherlands, where norms are explicit and overtly enforced. The laughter, I would argue, betrayed uneasiness rather than dismissal. The humorous way the young man formulated the question and the inability of his peers to engage him points to the excess of meanings contained within the problem he identified. For West Syriac Christians in the Netherlands, there is but one God and one relation to that God, and one is born into it so there is nothing to choose. For the European Christian heirs of Chalcedon, there may be but one model of personhood, but its relations with the divine may be variously configured. One might choose one's relation to God, but monotheism entails an exclusive truth-claim and one cannot choose what is true in itself.

Second- and third-generation Syriac Orthodox find themselves in a situation one might call a "relational impossibility." As Ashley Lebner argues, writing of Catholicism and the secular in Brazil, "distinctions between religion and politics never just happen by themselves. They are always lived and negotiated by persons through relations, variously conceived, experienced, and problematized" (Lebner 2021). Whether a secular distinction between "ethnicity" and "religion" will become naturalized to a degree that one may be a secular Suryoyo who openly does not believe in God or disregards patriarchal norms of moral comportment without being disowned by family or experiencing a destabilizing degree of loss remains to be seen. The perforating processes in my interlocutors' lives may take that shape, or not, depending on how their reproductive labor unfolds in the coming years. What is clear, however, is that how others perceive them affects how they perceive themselves and each other, with consequences for their modes of relating. The ethics of recognition integrates their political activism with their explicit theological explorations of what disarticulating ethnicity from liturgical kinship might mean for their future. In the next chapter, I turn to an implicit, yet even more unsettling, theopolitical problem for their liturgical activism and political aspirations: racism.

CHAPTER

6

BLOOD IN MY VEINS

The icon sets the visible and the invisible into a relation with each other. . . . (Mondzain 2005, 85)

*   *   *

As the saying goes: now you see me, now you don't. (Fanon 1952, 65)

H eleen confounds Dutch perceptions of Middle Eastern migrants with her long blonde hair, vivid blue eyes, and provincial Dutch accent. Like many of her peers, she came to the Netherlands as a child in the 1980s, when her parents fled their mountain village to escape violent conflict between Kurdish separatists and the Turkish government. And, like many other Suryoye of her generation, she is deeply committed to her parish community, her extended family, and speaking Turoyo. Every week, Heleen drives with her sister and cousin into the city of Enschede from Glanerbrug, their village on the Dutch-German border, to sing in church on Sunday mornings and to attend weekly *madrashto*, the church's evening classes on classical Syriac language and liturgy. One mid-summer's day, Heleen and I met for lunch at a bagel-shop-meets-café-terrace in Enschede's city center. A place where one can study or talk undisturbed for hours, the café appealed to a certain class of urban Dutch cosmopolitan concerned with the quality of their cappuccinos and a taste for American-style baked

goods. Eating our bagels and drinking our tea and coffee, our cheerful conversation turned glum, and Heleen lowered her voice to a near-whisper
as she began to tell me about a number of upsetting interactions she had
recently with some of her "ordinary" or *gewoon*—by which she meant
"white"—neighbors.

Just yesterday, she said, she'd had an encounter with the butcher at the
grocery store during which she felt a strange submerged hostility:

> There was a sale on meat, and, you know, we are Middle Eastern . . .
> we have big get-togethers and eat a lot of meat! I went with my aunt
> to the store for a dinner we were going to prepare, and when my aunt
> approached a store clerk about getting more meat from the back, he
> told her there was no more. My aunt looks like most of us . . . she
> looks like she is from the Middle East, so I think that is why he would
> not give her the meat. So I went up and asked him for the meat my-
> self. And, you know . . . I have blonde hair and blue eyes, so . . . the
> clerk just thought I was an ordinary Dutch girl (*een gewone Neder-
> landse*). So he told me it was no problem and went to go get me more
> meat. When he came back, I asked him, "Can I get some for my aunt
> over there as well?"—and when the man saw we were related, he was
> embarrassed and turned red.

This conversation prompted an older memory, which she then recounted:

> Now that I'm thinking about this, I remember something that hap-
> pened in high school that really upset me. I had a friend from school,
> just an ordinary girl from the village, who said something to me
> once. You remember how we all go to the monastery to visit our
> dead in the cemetery on the day after Easter? You remember how
> many of us come—from all over the Netherlands and Germany—
> there are thousands of us. The street is full of cars and bikes and
> people—it gets very busy! Well, the day after, I met my friend on
> the street in Glanerbrug, and she started to complain to me about
> "all those Moroccans crowding up the street." I told her, "No!
> Those were not Moroccans! They were Syriac Orthodox people like
> me! I was there myself!" And then my friend said, "Ach, it is all the
> same." I could not believe she said that—the difference didn't matter
> to her at all!

She paused and sighed. She did not get visibly angry as she told this story, but she could not explain it, and it made her feel confused and sad. As the Dutch server in the bagel shop approached us to ask whether we wanted more tea and coffee, we both instinctively lowered our voices, and the look of self-consciousness on her face mirrored the self-consciousness I felt, as if our conversation transgressed against the cheerfully cosmopolitan-Dutch space of the bagel shop. This transgressive feeling was familiar—I have gone through the same routine with other interlocutors when the subject drifts toward the subject of Dutch discrimination. Voices lowered, facial expressions closed up, and conversations stopped when white Dutch people came within earshot, as if something very embarrassing or offensive was being discussed.

Since 2007, I have heard or witnessed countless such stories while conducting fieldwork in the Netherlands. Friends, neighbors, and acquaintances have trouble registering the conspicuous Christianity that my research interlocutors put on display, with their oversize gold cross necklaces, Jesus bracelets, headscarves embroidered with images of the Virgin Mary, and tattoos in classical Syriac script.

There is the story of the elderly man in Amsterdam whose neighbor asks him every year, for thirty years without fail, how Ramadan is going, and every year he responds: "I am not Muslim, remember? I am Christian, I don't celebrate Ramadan." There are the students at the local secondary school where Syriac Orthodox youth are nearly as numerous as the white Dutch majority and yet were denied their request for accommodation for a major religious festival because they "were just given time off for the Sugar Feast [the three-day Muslim festival of Eid al-Fitr]." There was the moment the contractor finished erecting a giant cross at the entrance to St. Ephrem Monastery and triumphantly presented it to the archbishop with the words, "Congratulations, Your Excellency— your mosque is finished!" My interlocutors would retell these stories with a laugh but also a sense of injury. Amidst their struggle with the intergenerational traumas of unrecognized genocide, dispossession, and displacement, these refusals to register Syriac Orthodox ethnoreligious difference stung. For those of us concerned with the damage done to Muslims and Christians alike by reductive binaries equating Europe with Christianity and the Middle East with Islam, these stories ask us not only to pay attention to the racialized dimensions of Syriac Orthodox Christian historical experience in the Netherlands, but also to interrogate the role of race-thinking in constructions of religious difference in Western Europe more broadly.

Since 9/11, European debate over immigration and minority accommodation has often been framed as a matter of Islam's distance from Europe's "Judeo-Christian" *ethical* tradition and, therefore, a matter of neither explicitly racial nor religious animus. For example, in an influential tract, former Pope Benedict XVI makes explicit what is usually implicit in more Liberal and secularist framings when he grounds the "moral-spiritual" foundations that distinguish Europe as an "autonomous cultural unit" in Incarnational theology, a Christologically specific theorization of personhood from which all ethics and politics flow (Ratzinger 2007, 43). In this formulation, human reproduction is inflected with theological significance, as the sexual, social, and spiritual formation of individual souls together comprise the Church, the Body of Christ in the world, whose historical inheritances separate a "European" ethico-political identity from other "autonomous cultural units" like the Islamic World whose mere presence within Europe "cannot help but undermin[e] it" (Ratzinger 2007, 24).

In this worldview, theology undergirds ethics, and ethics undergirds culture. How then do we account for the claim by Heleen's school friend, echoed by many of her neighbors, that Syriac Christian difference is no different than Moroccan Muslim difference in the social imaginary of a Western European nation like the Netherlands, where the fraught relationship among Roman Catholicism, Calvinism, and Liberalism has shaped a normative twenty-first-century secularity? Why is it that in my research participants' accounts, it is skin, eye, and hair color, as well as accent, comportment, and other embodied traits, that register in their neighbors' attention, while visual symbols like crosses and tattoos of the Holy Family—symbols that could index a shared Christological "moral-spiritual foundation"—do not? What precisely is the nature of the "difference" perceived in these encounters? Approaching these moments of misrecognition from another angle, what does it mean that "Moroccans" and "Muslims" are invoked interchangeably throughout these stories? Given the ostensibly secular national context in which "race" and "religion" tend to be seen as separate ontological objects, what do we make of this collapsing of racial, national, ethnic, and religious histories in establishing which differences matter, and which differences do not?

In this chapter, I explore these questions by examining how racial and religious "difference" is constructed in the Netherlands through a commonsense, albeit complex, belief in the power of the body to communicate "ethical" difference. As I have suggested throughout preceding chapters, ethics is enmeshed in sites of social reproduction in that people generate, organize, and reproduce relations among selves and others through inherited evaluative hierarchies, which they may or may not reexamine as they proceed through life. As such, our intersensorial and social relations— the history of relations that form us as individual subjects—are imbued with power, reinforced by judgments. This understanding of "ethics" entails relational differentiation of the sort that inscribes moral hierarchies onto unequal power relations. That is, perceptions of moral superiority ascribed not to individuals but to groups reproduce social hierarchies. Racialization, in this analysis, operates on the basis of heritable (in that it is socially reproduced) moral difference rather than heritable biological difference. Considering that this racialization process and such judgments must be communicated in order to work, this chapter explores how a racializing regime of ethical differentiation plays out through everyday and bureaucratic misrecognition. These misrecognitions shape the conditions in which Dutch Suryoye try to make themselves politically recognizable to their neighbors, and so they weave themselves into the story of what it means to be Syriac and Orthodox and Christian in this setting. In the Dutch context, ethical misrecognitions occur when the body communicates a relational history that challenges the autonomous, Liberal, ethical subject. More specifically, miscommunication arises when the perceiver refuses their own implication in the history of relations that makes the communication possible. Here, I turn the logic of the icon onto Dutch secularity in order to understand this communicative process, and its breakdown.

As I elaborated in Chapter 3, an icon is a communicative sign in which a signifier resembles what it represents (e.g., a road sign with an image of a bicycle indicating the bicycle lane). Unlike symbolic and indexical signs, an iconic sign's meaning depends upon connections among form, experience, context, and memory. When the communicator and the recipient of a communication create meaning together in a dialogical encounter, they do so through abduction, a process of inference that requires an interplay of materiality and imagination between the perceivable and the imperceptible. In conversation with her friend, a central piece of who Heleen is and aspires to become in an ethical sense—that is, the evaluative hierarchy undergirding the communal practices she undertakes to rededicate herself daily, weekly, and annually to the liturgical life of the Syriac Orthodox

Church and its ancestors—was obscured by her friend's inability to see these practices as anything other than social disruption. In seeing her liturgical identity as socially disruptive, her friend, in turn, constructed it as fundamentally *unethical*—a violation of what is popularly called Dutch *normen en waarden* [norms and values]. Her friend de-historicized Heleen's ethical life, disarticulating its public form from experience, context, and memory in the very moment that she observed its social implications. In so doing, she invoked the figure of the Muslim-Moroccan body as a template for racial and religious differentiation and classification. In the same breath, she collapsed the complexity of Moroccan[1] and Muslim ethnicities, religiosities, histories, and ethical lives by linking even minor disruptions of the social order to certain kinds of ethical embodiment.[2] In this racializing regime, Moroccan Muslim and Syriac Christian bodies are made into icons of ethical difference through an iconoclasm that refuses to see the very relational histories that produce them as ethical subjects. At stake in this racializing regime is a question of reproductive power. As we have seen, reproductive power entails interpretive, material, and political control over sites of social reproduction (over, in other words, the care-taking practices that socialize human persons into the body politic). This is a kind of control that is implicated in but does not necessarily have to include sexual reproduction. As I explained in Chapters 2 and 3, disputes between ecclesiastical and state authorities over reproductive power have shaped the history of Christian theological politics and the secular political cultures influenced by them since the first Iconoclastic Controversies in eighth-century Byzantium (see also Mondzain 2005).

In this chapter, I examine one thread of the iconoclastic inheritance shaping a process of racial-religious differentiation and classification in the Netherlands in the obscured link between the "ethical" and the "social." The outline of this chapter's argument is thus: In moments of racial-religious misrecognition when Muslims are interpellated, in the Althusserian (1970) sense of *the hail*, as the archetype of ethical difference and Syriac Christians are hailed as either "Moroccan," as in this example, or as "Turkish" or "Muslim" elsewhere, the human body is read as an iconic sign to communicate an invisible difference. The constellation of form, experience, context, and memory that makes this meaning-making process possible constitutes a Dutch racial-religious imagination. The logic of the icon reveals an interplay of visibility and invisibility shaping Dutch perceptions of new minorities as ethically Other when they take the human body to be a vehicle of

ethical communication while refusing to account for the history of reproductive relations that generate the body's form and bestow it with signifying
power. In cases where this results in racializing and frankly racist moments
of misrecognition, I theorize this configuration of ethical thought, practice,
and embodiment as "sensory politics." Sensory politics can illuminate
how race is "made and unmade in specific constellations" (Balkenhol and
Schramm 2019; M'Charek 2008, 2013; M'Charek et al. 2014) rooted in
"implicit colonial afterlives in everyday life" (Balkenhol 2014, 2016). The
colonial afterlives of everyday life are especially pronounced in the enduring
entanglement of reproduction and racialization, as black feminist scholars
have long shown (Bridges 2011; Davis 2019; Shange 2019; Mullings and
Wali 2001). This entanglement problematizes the concept of "freedom" at
the heart of the Liberal ethical tradition and its theorization of personhood,
which rests on a "false presumption that the right to choose is contained
entirely within the individual and not circumscribed by the material conditions of the individual's life" (Roberts 2017 [1997], 309).[3]

One crucial dimension of my analysis derives from the fact that neither
my interlocutors nor I ever intended to talk about race in our work with
each other. And yet, it surfaced again and again in our conversations during my fieldwork. As a novice ethnographer, I went looking for something
I think of as religion, not race; that I found complex "racial" formations
embedded in conversations about "religious" life destabilized my own commonsense notions of what my analytical categories ought to be. Thus, the
empirical material this chapter is based on only emerged as my interlocutors began to grasp my ambivalent relationship with Dutch national identity as a white (aspirationally ex-) Calvinist Dutch-American researcher who
had lived in the Netherlands as a child. The evidence I examine in this
chapter thus comes from moments that I either witnessed in person or were
recounted by my interlocutors over the course of a decade, in which some
perceived violation of the social order had registered in someone's attention as a "cultural"—and thus, by definition in the Dutch context, an
"ethical"—difference. I argue that in Dutch commonsense, "Syriac Christian difference is no different than Moroccan Muslim difference" because
the state's distributed management of reproductive power among its minoritized subjects rearticulates Calvinism's iconoclasm; by erasing the relational histories, whether those of Moroccans or Suryoye, that produce
subjects capable of ethical judgment or action, this iconoclasm subjects
minoritized populations to a theological knot of an evaluative hierarchy,

producing "race" and "religion" as inextricably entwined effects of ethical differentiation, classification, and control.

I develop this argument by tracing the interplay of visibility and invisibility in political and popular efforts to establish *which differences matter* across historical, ethnographic, and bureaucratic domains, efforts that mark reproduction as the contentious center of sociopolitical life. I first elaborate "the racial-religious imagination" as an analytic for approaching the fraught relation between ethical life and reproductive power in Western Christian political history, tracing the generation of modern biological essentialism to long-running battles over heresy, "purity of blood," maternal embodiment, language, and the *ethos* of an *ethnos*. Then, I explore an ethnographic scene in which Syriac Orthodox are misrecognized by the Dutch state's bureaucratic/social work/"minority integration" apparatus and are interpellated as Muslim. The Orthodox icon here becomes an analytical tool for unpacking the shifting and unstable meanings contained within the Dutch concept of "allochthony," a term drawn from ancient Greek meaning "of foreign earth." As a key technique of minority differentiation and classification, the concept of allochthony links up with "culture," "religion," "race," or "ethnicity" in complex, overlapping ways. The allochthony concept, in turn, perforates Syriac Orthodox understandings and experiences of liturgical kinship.

The pervasive influence of allochthony discourse accounts for why, in Chapter 1, the young Dutch-speaking Suryoyo boy at the monastery asked me about my "culture" when he wanted to know which branch of Christianity I had been raised in. Consistently at stake in these varying usages of "allochthony" is an underlying effort to control sites of reproductive power where "the ethical" inflects public conceptions of sociality, in effect politicizing and publicizing "private" morality. I conclude with a reflection on how background assumptions about personhood and materiality—in this case, semiotic ideologies that try to obscure or theorize iconicity away— shape the sensory and theological politics of racial-religious imaginations in ways that can either reinforce or destabilize sovereign states and ethical subjects alike.

A Racial-Religious Imagination

To understand the intractability of racial-thinking in postcolonial European imaginations, even in situations where "religious difference" is what is ostensibly at stake, ethnographic perspectives rooted in political-economy are necessary but insufficient. Inchoate anxieties about access to the welfare state (cf. Geschiere 2009) or sentimental attachments to blood-and-soil metaphors of national or regional belonging that can be corroded by fast-capitalism (cf. Holmes 2000) require an imagination primed to assign criteria of inclusion or exclusion in destabilizing times.[4] Such criteria are unavoidably entangled with Christian theopolitics (e.g., McAllister and Napolitano 2020). As many scholars have pointed out, "religion is always operational in the study of race" (Husain 2017; see also Hage 2010; Khabeer 2017; Khan 2004; Özyürek 2015; Rogozen-Soltar 2017; Tamarkin 2014) in that several European Christianities furnished the moral reasoning required to perceive the embodied difference of non-Europeans as objects available for conquest, enslavement, and conversion. Historical scholarship on race, ethnicity, and ecclesial power has shown the extent to which these criteria emerge from late antique imperial Christianity's fixation on the physical embodiment, territorial inscription, and social reproduction of heresy (Berzon 2016). Out of this ancient repertoire, early modern Christians fashioned a theologically ordered "scale of existence" classifying the spiritual distance of racially marked bodies from Divine power to legitimize the trans-Atlantic slave trade, exclude Jews from sociopolitical life, and construct Muslims as civilizational threats (Arendt 2004 [1968]; Asad 2003; Jennings 2010).

Verena Stolcke (1993), reflecting on the intersection of gender and class in the European history of racialization, traces the global circulation of *limpieza de sangre*, the imperial Spanish Catholic doctrine of blood purity. This doctrine was deployed against Jewish and Muslim converts to Christianity to deprive them of access to public and ecclesiastical office in the sixteenth century. A lineage with no Jewish or heretical antecedents signaled "purity," as blood became a vehicle of faith and then a marker of social condition (Stolcke 1993, 31). Mediating among imperial state, church, and sociopolitical life were the blood and milk of the maternal body, such that descent from heretics, Jews, or Muslims became a "permanent, indelible stain." This physical sign of original sin naturalized unequal power relations (Stolcke 1993, 32). Anxiety over reproductive power circulated within and beyond Europe in a colonial communicative order that "operated through an 'episteme of resemblance' in which similitude dominated the organization of symbols and interpretations and representations of the universe" (Martinez 2008, 13). Here, anti-Semitism, Islamophobia, and colonial racism share joint descent in Western Christian theological anxieties, perpetuated iconically, about the relationship between reproduction and power.[5] This global formation endures, setting the parameters for endlessly refracted variations contained within it.

Yet this period coincided with equally significant transformations of European understandings of "religion" and its proper role in organizing public life (Asad 1993; Connolly 1999; Markell 2003). As Anya Topolski (2018) argues, theology serves as the horizon of past and present forms of racism in Europe, from anti-Semitism to Islamophobia. In this constellation, earlier religious categories ("Christians," "Jews," "Mohammedans," and "the Rest," e.g., pagans and polytheists) were transformed in the seventeenth and eighteenth centuries into philological categories (Hamito-Semitic, Aryan/Indo-European, Turanian, etc.). These categorical transformations shifted the imagined locus of a "people's" essential, defining, hereditary *ethos* from a Scripture-based discursive tradition to language. Philology lent the category of "Semite," which included Jews, Arabs, and Aramaic-speaking Christians of the Middle East (Gross 2020), a veneer of scientific neutrality that bridged earlier heresiological classifications with nineteenth-century scientific racism's "biological" classifications. This constituted a racializing process that culminated in the Holocaust (Topolski 2018). Across these transformations, however, a theopolitical link between *ethos* and *ethnos*, an "imperial economy of Christian kinship," as Candace Lukasik (2021) describes it, endured.

In grappling with the aftermath of World War II, the Netherlands turned toward a discourse of "norms and values" (de Koning 2016, 173) in a public moral project to silence "race" and "culturalize" citizenship. This moral project reforged imagined connections among genealogy, culture, and the body as sites of power for producing ethical citizen-subjects capable of the independence of thought necessary to prevent another Holocaust. And yet, against the historical backdrop of four hundred years of the Dutch slave trade (Oostindie 2009) and contentious relations among Dutch Calvinists and Roman Catholics (Kennedy 1995), the emerging political culture of the twentieth century was defined by a distinct sensory politics. This sensory politics was founded upon pervasive ambivalence toward the theological questions of mediacy and immediacy posed human bodies and religious icons alike.

Europeanist ethnographers have identified what is often at stake in the sensory politics of racial and religious difference in Western Europe, as in Halleh Ghorashi's (2010) study of the pendulum swing between invisibility and hypervisibility of migrant women in the Netherlands, Mayanthi L. Fernando's (2014) study of the French state's "secular cunning" inciting Muslim women to make their "private" religious and sexual lives public, or Elayne Oliphant's study of Catholic art and architecture as the banal background of everyday life in France (2020). In each of these cases political secularism and cultural secularity reassert dominant religious norms at the expense of minoritized subjects by controlling what is visible and what is invisible in ever-shifting configurations. Only through this unstable push-pull effect can white and secularist Europeans construct a narrative of European identity as "ethical." In her study of Dutch cultural amnesia around the slave trade and colonialism in Indonesia, Gloria Wekker links this push-pull effect to a racialized identity narrative she calls "white innocence" (2016).

The Orthodox icon makes explicit the interplay between visibility and invisibility in these histories of racialization, drawing our attention to sites of reproductive power where invisible relations generate visible forms, which is the process through which, in Christian Incarnational theology, an iconic sign becomes meaningful (Mondzain 2005). In the Dutch case, iconicity's theological undercurrents, historically submerged by the Protestant Reformation's iconoclastic suspicion of the materiality of meaning—that is, the question of mediacy and immediacy—not only enable a variant of European racism but safeguard its continuing purchase in twenty-first-century debates over immigration. This is because in post-Calvinist commonsense views of the body, it is difficult to speak directly about the ethical evaluation of embodied forms taking place in any given interpersonal interaction.

Syriac Christian encounters with the Dutch racial-religious imagination illuminate how post-Calvinist theological politics, in obscuring its own dependence on iconic thought, produces "race" and "racial-thinking" by construing bodies as dangerous semiotic forms. In the Dutch politics of minority accommodation, Calvinist anxiety over the materiality of meaning meets Liberal suspicion of the relationship between reproductive power and ethical life. As Kimberly Arkin argues in her study of the self-racializing practices of Parisian Sephardic youth, materialist Liberal and secular understandings of ethnic identity obscure the centrality of maternal reproductive power in fashioning Jewish communal life (2013).[6] In the Dutch situation, the theological politics undergirding the tension between Liberal *and* Calvinist understandings of reproductive power does not obscure the role of reproduction in ethical life so much as it ambivalently distributes responsibility for it over a network of state-funded social welfare organizations, as in the ethnographic situations I describe below. This distribution of responsibility poses a set of ethical dilemmas for diasporic Syriac Orthodox whose desire for recognition is conditioned by the sociopolitical histories of non-Chalcedonian Christianity. In these ethnographic scenes, Syriac Orthodox Christians are explicitly charged by both the state and by their neighbors with adapting to Dutch "norms and values" in ways that, intentionally or no, target the ethical dimensions of Syriac Orthodox Christian liturgical kinship.

Organizing this national project for minority "integration" for much of the late twentieth and early twenty-first century is a distinctively Dutch conception of "allochthony." Until 2017, allochthony was an official state category used by bureaucrats and social workers to denote residents and citizens of "non-Western" descent. Derived from the ancient Greek *allo-* meaning "other" and *chthon-* meaning "earth," *een allochtoon* is a person who lives permanently and may have parents and grandparents who were born in the Netherlands. Nonetheless, they are understood by others to be visibly marked as descended from a "non-Western" part of the world (van Schie 2018). This visible mark is rooted in an explicitly religious understanding of territorial belonging. As early as 1959, a government report for the southern province of Brabant used the word *allochtoon* to refer to Dutch workers migrating from the northern provinces, highlighting the religious and economic difference of these mostly Protestant, middle-class migrants from the mostly Catholic, working-class southerners among whom they settled. The essentialist discourse of allochthony, according to Yanow and van der Haar (2013), is deeply rooted in ancient Hippocratic thought, basing "differentiations among persons and groups on 'socioeconomic and cultural differences'" tied to place and behavior (2013, 246–247). Whether a subgroup was designated "allochthonous" depended on perceptions of their relative likelihood to "integrate" into a social fabric whose local organization fell along sectarian lines. While in some respects these sectarian lines have since been subsumed within a secular ethics of cosmopolitan-nationalism[7] (Lechner 1999, 2008), many commentators nonetheless claim this cosmopolitan-nationalism as a major achievement of the "Judeo-Christian" ethical tradition that was, as Pope Benedict XVI reminds us, produced in large part by political tension between European Protestants and Catholics. And yet my interlocutors' Christianity, it turns out, is insufficient to ensure smooth assimilation into this tradition, as the following story demonstrates.

"Living Between Two 'Cultures'"

One of the moments in my fieldwork when I first discerned the sensory and theological politics undergirding Dutch anxieties over new minorities' "norms and values" took place one Saturday afternoon in 2010, when the niece of the abbot of the Mor Ephrem Monastery organized a public lecture and panel discussion on "Living Between Two Cultures." The expert panel included an alderman from the city of Enschede; a police officer responsible for liaising with the Syriac Orthodox community; a Syriac Orthodox jurist working in Amsterdam; Dr. den Biesen, the monastery's resident theologian described in Chapter 5; and a senior researcher from a nonprofit policy, research, and training organization located in the far-away city of Utrecht. This researcher, one Dr. Eemers, was the keynote speaker of the event; it was her speech—and her audience's outraged response to her words—that began to trouble my understanding of the boundaries between racial and religious discourse in my field site.

Dr. Eemers introduced herself to the at-capacity crowd as an academic criminologist and professional expert in social pedagogy.[8] As the "Interculturalization" project leader at a Youth Care [*Jeugdzorg*] Organization's Study Center on Migrants and Refugees, she had been invited by the abbot's niece to address their community's growing problem with young Syriac boys causing trouble on the streets of Enschede. These "menacing" [*straatkwaad*] Syriac adolescents were a growing problem for criminologists, she said, and she was there to help the community understand the behavior of what she called "these so-called street terrorists." She informed her audience that the roots of young male Syriac aggression were as much "cultural" as they were "social" and "psychological." Based on studies conducted by her organization among Turkish, Moroccan, and Surinamese youth in the cities of central Holland, she explained that it had been scientifically established that young migrant boys are susceptible to developing a problematic image of masculinity defined by a lack of empathy, which could lead to problems with drugs, alcohol, the wrong friends, and eventually street violence. The source of this unhappy version of masculinity, she explained, was the "coercive dynamic" of many "allochthonous" families.

In her "Living Between Two Cultures" lecture, Dr. Eemers explicitly hailed her Syriac Orthodox audience as *allochtonen*. Their families were not alone, she told them, in experiencing problems with physical and verbal abuse, but the susceptibility of their young men to grow into the criminal element had everything to do with cultural resistance to receiving expert help from pedagogues, social workers, psychologists, and other professional caregivers [*zorggevers*]. She admitted that while some other experts claim that lack of integration causes criminality among allochthonous communities in the Netherlands, she believed that the source of the trouble was that the uneven process of emancipation from "traditional" norms and values itself causes intergenerational conflict within families and communities. Without specifying what kind of norms and values she meant, she explained that "Moroccans are much too quickly integrated," while "Turks remain more isolated and subject to social control within their communities, so that the emancipation process leads to family conflict." The real problems arise, she said, when families do not avail themselves of the support offered by youth-care organizations. Addressing the audience with emphasis on the English phrase "*er is absoluut geen* case management" [there is absolutely no case management], she began to plead: "Let the professional caregivers do their job—let them intervene in all the problems that arise in your family! They have specially trained caregivers for every member of the family, many from the same ethnic group, who can act as a go-between with the relevant care-organizations; please, make use of them!"

By the end of her speech, the churning anger in the room was palpable. Her audience was appalled. The question-and-answer session did not go well—at one point, with an embarrassed laugh, Dr. Eemers admitted that she could not understand the local Twents accent of many of her questioners, which did little to soothe the crowd's disquiet. Their questions betrayed varying degrees of indignation and skepticism: "We are not the ones who need to hear this—and the people who need to hear it would not come to something like this anyway!" "We are not Turks, we are not Moroccans, we are not Surinamese! What does any of this have to do with us? How can you come speak to us without knowing the first thing about who we are?" One audience member of my acquaintance, a trained schoolteacher from Syria named Farida, raised her hand to comment: "You cannot deny that more and more there are 'black' schools and 'white' schools. Discrimination and exclusion really happen here, and that makes it hard for people like us to even want to integrate. It would make a huge difference if Dutch people could work on integrating themselves a little too [*een beetje mee integreren*]!" A rare moment of audible approval and visible head-nodding occurred when Dr. den Biesen, the resident theologian, spoke up to ask the panel: "So why have we not asked the most important question of all yet? What does it mean to be a Christian in all of this? We are having this meeting in a monastery for a reason!" But despite the audience's applause at his intervention, the panel discussion veered off in another direction. After the meeting ended, I asked my friends and acquaintances what they made of it, and they shared a general sense that the event had been a failure.

From where I was sitting, the encounter between the criminologist and her audience began to unravel when Dr. Eemers named "culture" as the source of young, male Suryoyo criminality. While pathologizing "culture" is a familiar strategy of colonial power the world over, what the Syriac Orthodox audience reacted to in that moment was when Dr. Eemers diagnosed the problem with their "culture" as the "coercive dynamic" of allochthonous family life. While her characterization of Moroccan, Turkish, and Surinamese family life as culturally deficient was troubling enough, the audience's outrage at having their family life hailed as culturally indistinguishable from that of families from other backgrounds was inflamed by their understanding that it was their liturgical tradition—their "culture" and its "norms and values"—that had brought them all together for this meeting in the first place. Here, the reader might reasonably wonder whether the audience's response was not a classic "model minority" refusal of solidarity with other marginalized groups in order to secure for themselves the privileges of closer proximity to Whiteness. This would be a plausible explanation had not so many of my interlocutors been preoccupied with safeguarding their ethical difference as a recognizable form of ethnic difference in opposition to their secularist and Western Christian Dutch neighbors. Given their insistence on publicly flouting the expectations of Dutch model minorityhood whenever the obligations of Orthodox liturgical life demanded it, even when it comes at a social cost, and given how often I heard veiled and not-so-veiled criticisms of the spiritual and ethical lethargy of their Christian and secularist Dutch neighbors, I suggest the primary source of their outrage lay elsewhere, in the desire to adapt the tools of Dutch social work to non-Chalcedonian liturgical theology, and to have that theology recognized as sociopolitically salient by municipal and national authorities.

Much like Heleen's friend in the village, however, Dr. Eemers worked within a discourse in which cultural, ethical, religious, national, and ethnic differences were effectively synonyms—as evidenced by her vagueness about what, precisely, any of her research subjects needed to be "emancipated" from. She was left with no frame of reference, then, for integrating non-Chalcedonian theology into the category of allochthony, much less discerning the kind of ethical demand it might make of her audience to violate Dutch "normen en waarden." Instead, she identified Syriac Orthodox difference with Muslim difference, which she, in turn, constructed as a psychological problem to be solved by surrendering "traditional" parental authority over individual socialization to the state. For all my research participants described in earlier chapters, socialization is a crucial dimension of the reproduction of Syriac Orthodox tradition and Suryoyo ethnocultural identity. Parental authority over social reproduction is grounded in a soteriological system in which kin relations are integrally and intimately intertwined with ecclesiastical authority and monastic life. For my interlocutors, Dr. Eemers's suggestion that they surrender authority over family life to secular social workers was a dagger in the heart of their efforts to innovate theologically acceptable configurations of liturgically ordered family life in a Dutch context.

The "Two Cultures" confrontation rearticulated two long-standing questions in Dutch political history: (1) *Who is responsible for the reproduction of social life?*—one of the key controversies bedeviling nineteenth and twentieth-century negotiations between Calvinists and Liberals over the role of the family and of religious education in mediating a child's relationship with the state (e.g., Kuyper 1943), and (2) *Who mediates relations among competing sites of reproductive power?* Here, reproduction and mediation are mutually entangled theological problems. In the process of forming the modern state, Calvinists and Liberals worked out their theological differences through an institution called *verzuiling*, or "pillarization," a rigid, vertically organized, and self-reproducing system of segregation among Protestants, Catholics, Liberal Humanists, and, later, Socialists, that is widely understood to have ended in the 1960s, although scholars have noted pillarization's lingering structural legacies (Bracke 2013; Blom and Talsma 2000). The Calvinist-led movement to maintain boundaries between religious and comparable ideological blocs developed throughout the nineteenth century as part of a backlash against French Enlightenment values, which was itself linked to resentment against Napoleonic incursions into the Low Countries. Never a formal doctrine of state per se, pillarization was the outcome of compromises in which differences across the populace were not to be transcended through individualistic, abstract citizenship as in secular Liberal regimes, but rather by crystallizing those differences into self-reproducing corporate entities. When the Dutch Constitution was reformed in 1848 to formalize the separation of church and state, Calvinists insisted that religious institutions mediate the integration of new groups of citizens into public life. This dynamic, in which multiple religious and ideological differences were collapsed into four overarching categories, has had several notable effects on the conditions in which other ethnoreligious minorities have come to be incorporated into Dutch society. One consequence was that Dutch Jews were absorbed into the Liberal and especially Socialist pillars because changes in municipal governance policy forced them so often to migrate from city to city for work that they came to rely on national labor unions for political representation and solidarity. This, in turn, diminished the public visibility of the religious dimensions of Jewish identity (Knippenberg 2001), contributing to a national sensory politics of kinship in which labor and class became important criteria for affiliation within the tightly policed boundaries of a pillar. Meanwhile, the dimensions of communal ritual life that historically constituted the Jewish community as a "nation apart" receded from public view—until, that is, the Nazi occupation in World War II reactivated and reauthorized latent anti-Semitic sentiment among willing Dutch collaborators who required little prompting to remember and reframe Jewish religious difference as intolerable racial difference (Hirschfeld 1988).

Central to these historical debates was the status of schools and families: Should, as the Liberals demanded, a secular authority oversee the relationship between children and society, or should parents? For Abraham Kuyper, the nineteenth-century architect of Dutch political Calvinism and founder of the Anti-Revolutionary Party, the father was the mediator of a family's relation with the state because his authority within the family structure mirrored that of the earthly Church's relation to the Holy Trinity; rooted in the primal blood relation, the family was the basis for all human social relations (1943). In my interpretation, Kuyper's Christian political philosophy rested upon a logic of iconicity that had been meticulously theorized away: the relation of iconic resemblance inspired by Divine Providence communicates a family's holiness directly to God. Dutch

Liberals, unsurprisingly, strongly rejected the premise of such an arrangement. To resolve the impasse, the Anti-Revolutionary Party (ARP) formulated the principle of *souvereniteit in eigen kring*, "sphere sovereignty"—the
same political theology used by white South African political elites to justify racial *apartheid*. In this system, Liberal Humanism and Socialism
constituted pillars of communal difference commensurable with the religious difference of Catholics and Protestants, and boundaries were maintained as much by private kinship practices like marriage endogamy and
exclusive burial grounds as by public-facing institutions such as denominational schools, newspapers, labor unions, and drinking establishments.
In state-funded denominational schools especially, religious authorities
gained significant power over how children were taught. While this tension between Dutch Calvinists and Liberals created the structural conditions through which new minorities must find their way into Dutch social
life, it also created a set of concepts through which they know and are
known by the state and their neighbors. As I show in the following section, these theologically grounded concepts produce racializing effects
because, while currently clustered into the word *allochtonen*, they are fundamentally concerned with the very questions of ethical relatedness, reproduction, and differentiation/classification on which earlier controversies
over schools and families turned.

The Shifting Frames of "Allochthony": Culture, Ethnicity, Religion, Race?

One reason the Syriac Orthodox audience was so frustrated with the
criminologist that day at the monastery was what they saw as a missed
opportunity to talk through with each other what was meant and what was
demanded by the "two cultures" referenced in the event's name. Plagu-
ing their efforts to know and make themselves known to the Dutch state
and their neighbors was a contentious debate over which meta-categories
properly apply to being Syriac Orthodox in the Netherlands. The term
"culture" was often privileged in these conversations because they ac-
commodated my interlocutors' diverse political aspirations; "culture"
functioned as a polysemic container for a host of differences deemed politically salient enough to garner disciplinary attention (and thus funding
for community programs) from the state. My friend Eva, for example,
pointedly used the Dutch word *kultuur* over and against the term "reli-

gion," when she told me, "We are not *just religious*. Syriac Orthodoxy is a *culture*." Meanwhile, a Dutch-Syriac anthropologist friend, objecting to scholarly definitions of Syriac Orthodoxy that reduce it to an "ecclesial community" used the Dutch word *volk* ["people"; "ethnic group"] to insist that "just because we gather in a church does not mean we are *not* a people in a political sense." And yet, despite "culture's" strategic value, it also silenced Syriac Orthodox efforts to convey the sociopolitical salience of their non-Chalcedonian Christianity. In this silence, the question of "race" lurked awkwardly at the edge of our attention. Race was a problem no one quite knew what to do with, as conversations died and facial expressions closed up whenever the subject veered toward communal relations with white Dutch neighbors. It took many years for me to make sense of race's unspeakability in these situations, except for uncomfortable references to "black schools" and "white schools," until I came to discern its roots in the ethical demands of Dutch cosmopolitan-nationalism, a discourse that defines Dutch national identity in terms of a sophisticated sort of worldliness: well-traveled, well-informed, and speaking multiple (European) languages fluently.

Twenty-first-century Dutch cosmopolitan-nationalism is today explicitly staked upon the public discourse of "norms and values," reasserted by Prime Minister J. P. Balkenende in 2002 in an effort to restabilize Dutch social relations after the assassination of anti-Islamic provocateur and politician Pim Fortuyn. In silencing "race," Dutch cosmopolitan-nationalism links perceptions of public-facing, politically salient ethical difference to the category of "culture"; as a category, "culture" *invites* a particular kind of engagement with the state and its funding programs (cf. Duyvendak et al. 2016; Mepschen 2016). This partially accounts for why Eva and other Syriac Orthodox explain their commitments in culturalist terms: their ethical obligations as Orthodox Christians are communal, "public," and political *as well as* individual, "private," and spiritual, and thus require the engagement of interested outsiders like the municipal government to secure spaces in which to reproduce these ethical commitments. And yet the durably racializing logic of "culture" is evident in the very ambiguity it generates, particularly among public commentators who explain social friction in terms of Islamic "norms and values," as in this opinion piece by Dirk Vlasblom, published in November 2017 in the national center-left newspaper NRC Handelsblad for an online feature called "Dossier: Racism":

There is some confusion in the heated Western debate over migration. Newcomers tend to call every expression of discontent with their arrival and every form of discrimination "racism." This is incorrect. The fact that application letters signed with Islamic sounding names are often ignored is not a matter of racism. The applicant is discriminated against for his/her culture or religion, not on the basis of appearance, like skin color, eye shape, or hair type. (November 17, 2017; translation by author)

Here, the journalist insists on distinguishing between perceptions of religious difference signified by a person's name and the perception of some unnamed difference signified by a person's phenotype, as if cultural/religious identity were in no way embodied, material, or relational. What Vlasblom thinks "skin color, eye shape, or hair type" signifies in a racist schema is left unexplained, but his writing invokes a sensory politics of its own, one that differentiates among varieties of visuality in the interplay between visibility and invisibility, such that a written name signifies what the unseen body cannot: a genealogical, and therefore an embodied, material, and reproductive relation to intolerable ethical difference.

What remains unexamined in commentary such as Vlasblom's is why new minorities in the Netherlands, especially those from the Middle East and North Africa, might think of themselves as subject to "racist" discrimination in situations where only their "religious" or "cultural" background is perceptible in the first place (see also Özdil 2014). This is because, in insisting on the body's invisibility in a chain of reasoning that infers Islamic difference from a job-seeker's family, which is in turn inferred from a job-seeker's visible name, the journalist elides how any inference drawn from names, religions, cultures, nationalities, and families is only made possible by taking these as iconic of an embodied relationality in the first place. Ethical difference, whether named "cultural" or "religious," is inferred through the logic of reproduction, genealogy, and inheritance. This is a mode of reasoning grounded in iconic thought: the signifying practice (a name) constitutes the relation that it signifies (genealogy). But—and this is the crucial part—the author disavows the relationality to which he obliquely refers in the very process of referring to it. "Culture" produces "race" by erasing the historical social relations—the reproductive powers—through which "old" and "new" European subjects were formed in relation to each other through globalized processes of colonial domination, missionary work, labor migration, trade relations, and economic extraction.

To return to the question of terminology, however, Syriac Christianity does not technically exist in Dutch legal-bureaucratic terms, so in the state's management apparatus, their perceived differences are yoked to a moralized perception of Muslim difference. Bureaucratically, the state has formulated "national origin" into a signifier of "allochthonous norms and values," which it then renders into a biopolitical category called "religion." This process is evident in documents like the WRR's (Scientific Council for Government Policy's) 2004 report by G. van den Brink, entitled "Sketch of a Civilization Offensive: On Norms, Normalcy, and Normalization in the Netherlands." This document mirrors the categorical collapse of ethnic, national, religious, linguistic, and racial histories in Heleen's high school friend's reference to "Moroccans" as the archetype of ethical otherness. In section 4.3, devoted to "Migrants and Modernity," the author explains his approach to analyzing the differences among citizens of migrant descent:

> [I]n the past few years there has been increasing debate over whether these ideas hinder successful integration. I rely on a survey taken among a large number of allochthonous citizens in the Netherlands in 1998. This survey distinguished between five groups: Turks, Moroccans, Surinamese, Antilleans, and authochthonous citizens. Because the differences between Turks and Moroccans are minimal, I will treat them as a single category and refer to them as Dutch citizens with an *Islamic* background (emphasis in original). (van den Brink 2004, 110)

Although no longer an official category, in everyday conversation allochthony remains a powerful tool of ethical differentiation, classification, and control in how it evokes a kaleidoscopic sensory politics with both spatial and temporal dimensions. Spatially, it refracts perceptions of difference across shifting boundaries of north/south and east/west, as it extends to "white" Eastern Europeans, especially those from Poland, as well as to people from Africa and the Middle East. At the same time, allochthony works in a temporal dimension to produce religion as an artifact of a past that the Dutch allegedly overcame when they dismantled pillarization. Allochthony embeds a religious imaginary—religion-as-atmospheric-museum-piece—within an embodied ethic of secular emancipation, which, for many, is a defining feature of twenty-first-century Dutch cosmopolitan-nationalism. And yet Calvinist theocratic norms persist in this embodied ethic and aesthetic atmosphere. Nineteenth-century notions of "'personal self-discipline' as well as collective moral control" (Stoler 1994, 119) circulate in twenty-first-century common sense about how properly to orient one's life trajectory toward the pool of collective energy that sociologists Coenders and Chauvin call Dutch "emotional democracy" (2017), forming subjects who might engage religious music, architecture, and church bells aestheti-cally while policing the reach of more ethically demanding sensory forms like the daily Muslim call to prayer (e.g., Tamimi Arab 2017, 111–149).

In her research on genetic counseling in the Netherlands, Karen-Sue Taussig found that the pillarization system continues to be integral to a nationally cultivated worldview despite having been formally dismantled. She observes that for mainstream Dutch society, there are "different kinds of difference" that require explicit management by credentialed experts (Taussig 2009, 28). It is an enduring legacy of pillarization that difference must be bound and managed, on the one hand, while on the other, the story of de-pillarization, in which boundaries have been overcome, pro-duces the image of the average Dutch person as the archetype of abstract secular liberal citizenship (cf. Gauchet 1997; Scott 1996, 2007).

In Dutch genetic centers—as elsewhere, Taussig observes—normal-ization is explicit, openly acknowledged, and deliberately pursued (2009, 86). The concern shared by her geneticist interlocutors is to render genetic differences *gewoon* ("ordinary") by categorizing them. The notion of ordi-nariness is ubiquitous in the Dutch language: unusual only in that it is used constantly, everywhere, to reaffirm what is supposed to be unmarked in everyday Dutch society. *Gewone Nederlanders* are everything Gloria Wekker described above: white, post-Christian, and inclined to believe in their own universality. Rendering difference "ordinary" through processes of classification, Taussig argues, is an essential technique of tolerance: the social ideal of ordinariness is achieved by managing difference (2009, 87). While categories themselves may be contestable, the imperative to catego-rize is never contested, while building consensus is essential to the process of producing categories. Thus, Dutch cosmopolitan-nationalism demands that citizens of color accommodate white sensibilities by submitting to the normalization consensus to ensure the Netherlands remains an ethical, "anti-racist" society—because ethics, in Liberal tradition, is marked by reflexive freedom from "tradition." For Dr. Eemers, this entailed allowing social workers to "intervene in every part of family life" to correct parents when they were not appropriately socializing their children according to Dutch "norms and values." Every "axis of othering" (de Koning 2016) that "allochthony" touches, it touches in order to assert interpretive control over sites of reproductive power, whether social pedagogy, job applications, genetic testing centers, community funding programs, genealogical practices, mosque-building projects, or indeed, raising children—anywhere, really, where the formation of ethical subjects intersects with public sociality.

Irritation and the Social

The intersection of the ethical and the social in the national political landscape hit me like a brick in the elections of 2010, when the far-right, anti-immigrant PVV (Freedom Party) picked up enough seats in the *Tweede Kamer*, the Dutch parliament, that the then-dominant centrist CDA (Christian Democratic Appeal) was forced to publicly countenance the thought of forming a governing coalition with them. This prospect threw the CDA into crisis and prompted a televised national conference in which delegates from across the country gathered to debate whether cooperating with the Freedom Party was not a gross violation of Christian Democratic values. Watching the debate on television with my Dutch-Iranian family, I observed a generational fault line among those party officials who supported the accord and those who were against it, as a long line of elderly Christian Democrats gave impassioned speeches against the PVV's Islamophobia, declaring it morally anathema to Dutch norms and values, which was rooted, many said, in the Dutch Calvinist tradition of respecting the integrity of religious differences.[9] Meanwhile, many of the speeches given in support of the coalition hinged on what was described as the indignities of suffering the *asociale gedrag van allochthonen*, or the "anti-social behavior of allochtones," in public spaces like trains and buses. "Religious freedom is all well and good," several young CDA'ers said to the assembly with visible indignation, "but this public unruliness is too much!" In one of the most densely populated, consciously designed, and meticulously engineered countries in the world, public unruliness was, according to many of the speakers, unacceptable. The indignation on the speakers' faces spoke volumes: their irritation had accumulated over years and tipped over into outrage.

Whether on village streets or national television, there are few moral sentiments more banal than irritation, yet it is powerful enough that delegates of a prominent centrist political party with a commitment to protecting religious minorities would cite it as their reason to cooperate with anti-Muslim hardliners. Irritation is an inchoate response to the perception that someone has transgressed socially: this transgression becomes subject to moral appraisal. There is something about irritation that cannot be fully situated in most scholarly accounts of anti-immigrant sentiment, whether the anxieties of neoliberalism or theopolitical genealogies of European Christendom's antagonism toward Islam. Irritation is not an ideological or economic or theological problem. Irritation is visceral. It's *itchy. Someone did something wrong.* Not *to* me exactly, just *around me.* This moral feeling arrives sensorially—it is a function of noticing. It indexes that moment where moral acuity folds into sensory perception: it fudges and blurs and mutes reflexive ethical reasoning. Irritation, pooling at the nexus between the social body and the sensory body, is not anger, but it can accumulate to the point where it tips over into anger, when a series of slights coalesce into an injury.

Irritation evokes something of the "affective elements of historical consciousness" that Raymond Williams called a structure of feeling (1954), but in a more particular sense, it is the effect of a structure of inattention, which is a more limited concept yoked to actual bodies and their perceptual capacities—a trained sensorium replete with invisibilities and inaudibilities. This sensorium, in the Dutch case, is an ethical habitus in which the Dutch state invests heavily in order to secure a particular set of "norms and values" among the population. Irritation as a moral sentiment selectively interweaves personal and collective histories, activating substrates of consciousness with half-forgotten memories and metonymic associations. Irritation is amorphous enough to fill whatever vessel is at hand. *Is this* really *about race? Is this* really *about religion?* Both and neither—the vessels are made of flexible material too. The question facing the CDA leadership that day in 2010 was whether their junior delegates' irritation justified compromising their deeply held commitments to religious freedom for all, including Muslims.

My Syriac Orthodox research participants watched the CDA's conference at home too; many were not pleased. Later that week, my friend Mariane told me that she was furious at the CDA's decision to work with Wilders and his people. She and her family were committed supporters of the Christian Democrats, with the exception of her uncle, who voted for the Freedom Party. She said:

> My uncle insists that Wilders can distinguish between Middle Eastern Christians and Middle Eastern Muslims . . . and I did hear someone challenge Wilders once by asking about Middle Eastern Christian women who still wear the headscarf, and Wilders said "well . . . it is okay when Christians wear a headscarf because it means something different." Although, to be honest, my sister and I argue about what the headscarf means all the time . . . so . . . does he actually know what it means? My sister does not like it but . . . Paul is clear in the New Testament that it is a requirement, so. . . .

She trailed off, shook her head, and then resumed her diatribe:

> But still . . . voting for the Freedom Party is so stupid! If they get rid of all the Muslims tomorrow, they will come after us next. Wilders may say he knows the difference, but I promise you, Sarah, that his supporters do not, and even if they did, they *would not care.*
>
> Here is an example of what I mean. I work at a grocery store where if you have a large bag, you need to leave it with the information desk before you enter to do your shopping. A little while ago, I saw a Syriac Orthodox woman I know who did not want to leave her bag with strangers. She wanted to leave it with me. But it is against the rules, so I could not allow it, and so she got angry with me and walked into the store through the cash register area rather than through the proper entrance. A Dutch woman, a customer in line, said to me, "You should tell her she is doing something wrong!" And I told her, "Don't worry . . . I plan to." Then the woman behind her said, "No . . . all those people should just go back to their own country!" This is the Wilders' mentality! It does not *actually* matter what you look like or what your religion is, it is just about how you act. Do what you want as long as no one can see it or hear it or smell it. But if you enter the grocery store through the wrong entrance, well, then you deserve to be kicked out of the country!

As Mariane points out, sometimes Middle Eastern Christian difference *does* register in the Dutch public sphere, when it is convenient to making the political claim that a ban on Muslims is about intolerable religious values rather than race.

Really Living with the Other

These ethico-political tensions resonate within young Suryoye self-understandings and introduce a host of perforating challenges. A young woman named Nicme explained her difficulties with these questions very precisely one day. Nicme grew up in Oldenzaal, a small town in Twente, near Enschede and Hengelo, but had been living in Amsterdam for several years, where she studied at university to be a dentist. When we met, she was twenty-four years old and had her last ever exam the day before our meeting. Despite living hours away from home, she was still a regular member of the women's choir at her parents' church and took the train every weekend to ensure she did not miss the Holy Qurbono on Sunday mornings.

As we walked from the station to a café terrace in the city center, she spoke eagerly, full of ideas, feelings, and passion, telling me that she is entering a phase in her life where she feels she is having an identity crisis because she is trying to figure out what it means to be Dutch and to be Suryayto at the same time. She finds it very difficult, she said. Over and over again, she referred to it as a struggle.

Our conversation flowed seamlessly between Dutch and English, as English sometimes provided expressions she needed that were difficult to convey in Dutch. She is irritated with Dutch attitudes about integration, she said; she is irritated with Dutch irritation:

> The problem is not minorities' failure to integrate, but the Dutch inability to really respect difference, that minorities absolutely *cannot* and *must not* be themselves, if they want to be accepted in Dutch society. Dutch people think, "It is fine to be different over there, but not where we can see it or be affected by it!"

Here race suddenly became an unexpected part of the conversation: we were sitting at a rather nice café in Hilversum, which is the center point of a posh region called 't Gooi. She pointed out that in this wealthy area, everyone is blond, and no one looks like her. She knew immediately that this is not a place where she could safely speak Ṭuroyo. Her predicament, she said, is that she feels she cannot be part-Dutch or part-Suryayto; partial identity in one means an entire rejection of the other, and she does not know what to do about it. It does not make sense in the Netherlands that "Christian" is her identity, something she was born with and that comes with family and social obligations, not something she chooses—even though, at the same time, she says, if she were to cease to believe in God, she would cease to be Suryoyo. She knows she would no longer be accepted in the community.

"If someone who had been involved with the church and was an active Suryoyo for fifty years were to have a spiritual crisis when they were older, what would happen?" I asked.

She replied: "It would have to be kept secret and brushed under the rug, or you would be shunned by the community and would be seen as no longer Suryoyo. It happened to my aunt. She has left the community and has been completely ostracized. She has become completely Dutch and has no contact with the family or anyone else in the community."

"The expectations in the community are intense," Nicme said. "You are expected to marry another Suryoyo, and that, far too young." She raised her voice, passionately striking her hand on the arm of her chair: "*Maar dat kan toch niet?! Het kan gewoon niet! Zo werkt de wereld niet!*" [But that cannot be, can it?! It just cannot be! The world does not work like that!] She says, "I had to tell my parents . . . it just was not going to work out that way. I have done everything I could have and should have done. I have been a dedicated member of all the organizations and have gone to all the events, but it has not happened and it probably will not."

Fortunately, her parents are understanding, she said. Although they were somewhat fearful when she moved to Amsterdam and became depressed following her departure, her parents have been supportive of her efforts to develop herself, grow, and make her own decisions. But, she said, there are some problems in the larger family, and part of why she decided to leave originally was because she needed to extricate herself from what she sees as the dysfunction of her relatives.

"The problems in my extended family are typical of the community, to be honest. The community is so insular. By not looking outward, and by not opening themselves up to the world and the society they are in, they are trapped in immature habits of mind and behavior," she said. "They are so competitive, they feud, they nurse resentments over minor slights and grievances!" In the years she has been living in Amsterdam, making Dutch friends, going to school, and learning about the world, she has noticed she has outgrown her age-mate cousin who stayed home and went to the University of Twente. Where once they responded in the same way to things, now she is perplexed by her cousin's attitudes, reactions, and the way she handles her relationships with other people. Even though they both went to VWO (*Voorbereidend wetenschappelijk onderwijs*), the highest level of university prep high school, and both went to university, their outlook and emotional development have taken different trajectories, because she physically removed herself from the tight-knit community and her cousin did not.

When I asked about the village politics that seem to affect the community's ability to organize and communicate with each other, Nicme sighed with evident exasperation: "They want to recreate Tur Abdin in Holland, and they do not understand that it is not possible!" She said, "They should not preoccupy themselves with going back to a place that has nothing, no people, nothing going on to offer themselves or their children! We have to accept what we have lost and not try to get it back. What we still have, yes, we should protect and take care of, but we should not waste energy and resources trying to recreate something that does not and cannot exist anymore."

In Nicme's view, this mindset is not good for the community: it keeps them small-minded, parochial, and disengaged from the world. Nicme feels the community is stuck partially because of this unwillingness to move on. It is hurting the community and their ability to be recognized or accepted in the Netherlands. She tells me that when she was young, she and her sister made a pact with each other to never speak Ṭuroyo outside the house or at school:

> Dutch people judge you for it. I would never do this interview with someone in Ṭuroyo, in a public space like this. People would look at me and I would be *afgekeurd* (rejected) immediately. On the outside, I have to be Dutch, and 100 percent so, even though I am not on the inside. It is difficult. I do not know what to do about it. I do not know what to think about it.

Throughout our conversation, Nicme raised numerous questions about the tensions of living as a racial-religious minority in the Netherlands, facing pressures from within her community as well as pressures from without. She awkwardly inhabited the borderlands between liturgical kinship and the secular, cosmopolitan Dutch nation, although her participation in the liturgical choir at her parents' church continued to be the one non-negotiable dimension of her existence. The first question Nicme raised concerns the dialectical relationship between externally imposed ghettoization and an impulse within the community to keep to themselves. This relationship, as we have seen, emerged from complex transformations in the way Dutch society has historically organized pluralism through the pillarization system.

The second issue is produced by the first: Nicme feels that the Syriac Orthodox community maintains its difference by not engaging with others around them and that, in the long run, this will hurt both the community and society at large. Keeping together in an insular way and reenacting the social dynamics of life in a rural Turkish village cannot and should not be sustained. But this pushes up against the third tension, which is that Suryoyo sociality is bound up with Christian liturgical identity and, as such, is the ethical core of being Syriac. To lose that sociality risks losing the qualities that make Syriac Christians ethically recognizable to themselves: the spoken and sung dialects of the Aramaic language and the tightly knit bonds that connect families to each other through the Church. As a highly educated citizen who has left certain elements of these behaviors behind her, she can still be painfully rejected by her white Dutch peers if she expresses any part of herself that is not normative of white-middle-class Dutch identity. When she and I sat together in a white-middle-class Dutch space, it was perfectly acceptable (even a sign of prestige) for us to switch occasionally into English to capture some elusive thought, but it would not have been acceptable to switch into neo-Aramaic or a related language like Arabic.

This final issue—not being able to speak what she feels is an important part of who she is—is connected to a crucial point she made in another part of the conversation that day:

> Really living with the Other is the great problem of society. It is a problem for me too. My neighbor is gay. Publicly, of course, it is no problem; he is my neighbor. It is fine. But deep down inside, I know the Bible says being gay is not okay, and I am a Christian before anything else. So that makes me a hypocrite . . . I am just as bad as anyone else.

Language and moral identity are impossible for Nicme to disentangle in her sense of what it is to be a Syriac Christian, but it is precisely these parts of herself that she must silence to achieve the secular civilized *habitus* of a respected Dutch citizen. Nicme's crisis has to do with how hard she must work at cross-purposes with herself. Laboring to exhaustion to

protect and preserve an endangered ethnoreligious identity, she simultaneously works to silence and suppress the very religious subjectivity that is
shaped by and gives shape to that identity. The affective and ethical reach
of her liturgical identity—in its entanglement with insular kin relations,
in the effort to preserve Ţuroyo and revive classical Syriac, and in the cultivation of a moral disposition—is not simply inaudible to her secular
Dutch environment: she must actively work to keep it silent. This suggests
a distinction between "speaking" and "audibility" within mainstream
Dutch norms of secular cosmopolitan citizenship. It is a conundrum, and
she sees no clear way forward. She focused efforts, instead, on advocat-
ing for a distinction between being Suryoye (Syriac) and being *Oromoye*
(Aramaean).

At the time of our interview, Nicme was secretary of the nationwide Aramaean cultural organization that coordinates the activities of local Aramaean organizations; sometime later, she was appointed its national
director. She supported the establishment in Hengelo of Aram House, a
building that would be both a museum and a conference center for the
community, which would have nothing to do with the Church. When she
spoke of *geloof* (literally "belief" but used functionally like the English word
"faith" or "religion," as in "What is your religion?"), she meant it as something different from being *Oromoye*. What remains to be seen is how many
of her peers will follow her logic in perforating Suryoyeness—linked as it
is to Oromoyeness in the very name of her organization—into separable
religious and ethnic dimensions. Racialization and ethnicization operate
as two distinct yet intersecting registers of recognition through which
Nicme reshapes her sense of herself as an ethical, religious, and political
subject, and the work is ongoing and unfinished.

Sovereignty, Ethics, and the Reproductive Future

Structuring Dutch cosmopolitan-nationalism's moral project, in which
disparate sites of reproductive power generate the ethics that generate sociality, is a set of background assumptions about materiality and personhood.
These assumptions shape communicative practice, what linguistic anthropologists call semiotic ideology. One key feature of a Calvinist semiotic
ideology, reinforced in the colonial missionary encounter (Keane 2007), is
the "dematerialization of meaning" that contains a seed of ambivalence over
the inescapable materiality of all communicative practice, whether linguis-

tic or extra-linguistic. In Calvinism, materiality is mistrusted; human persons are persons because they communicate without mediation. This ideal of immediacy, of direct communication without relying on intermediary sensory forms to transmit or facilitate the connection between human persons and God, and between persons and other persons, is a hallmark of Calvinist-inflected varieties of secularity. This dematerialization of meaning divorces secularist Dutch responses to religious aesthetics from any sense of ethical demand. The seed of ambivalence reaches crisis point when confronted with the human body *as* semiotic form. But this semiotic form is not "expressive." Rather, it is the durable outcome of the history of reproductive relations that produced a person. In Calvinist semiotic ideologies, a person may intentionally express themselves through their body in a way that demonstrates their agentive self-mastery, as with the normative Calvinist family's mimesis of the Holy Family. Yet there is a perception of danger when the body communicates not the intentional spirit of the person "inside" but invisible forces beyond the person and their intentions. This is the ever-recurring crisis of Christian iconoclasm since the seventh century: all bodies are formed through the history of social relations that precondition any person's individual capacity for self-mastery, a capacity that the modern Liberal tradition identifies with "ethics" as long as a person can prove their independence from those relations when deciding how to act.

In a twenty-first-century Calvinist semiotic ideology, and in the ethical regime staked upon it, confronting the postcolonial history of reproductive relations communicated by the bodies of others disrupts the story of ethical self-mastery. "Race," according to philosopher Reid Miller (2017), is the name "we" (in this case, white Euro-Americans) bestow upon our perception of persons whose histories we cannot assimilate into our own self-image while remaining intelligible to ourselves as ethical subjects. In the twenty-first century, this is a characteristic problem of Whiteness-as-sociopolitical-formation and of imperial Christianity, linked by a global political economy built on slavery and colonial extraction. The descendants of white European Christian missionaries, colonizers, and slave traders mark others as ethically different in order to remain stable, ethical subjects to themselves. This requires a unique interplay of visibility and invisibility: *I must erase that part of my history that I share with you, a history that produced both of us, in order to mark you as visibly, ethically, distinct from me.* This is not a universal habit of thought. Its condition of possibility is that it partakes of the logic of iconicity while denying it.

An Orthodox understanding of iconicity, on the other hand, acknowledges that all forms are semiotic, in the sense that they communicate *because* their material existence is the outcome of a history of socially significant reproductive relations. Whether the human body or a painted icon, everything that exists in material form takes its shape via a relational act of Divine creation or human reproduction, where the invisible intersects the visible. On one end of the Christian imagination, Orthodox semiotic ideologies acknowledge the icon's power to materialize the relationship between viewer and invisible power. This relationship *is* a history of relations and it produced both the icon and the viewer as intimately interconnected parts of an Incarnational economy (Mondzain 2005). In a Calvinist-inflected theological politics, such acknowledgment can be difficult, at best. This means that in addition to everything else it is, racism is the denial of the history of relations that have made us all who we are and a denial of the invisible forces of reproduction that generate our material and ethical existence. Just as secular ethnicity is a theological proposition about the ontological foundation of relatedness, so racism is a theological error that denies the ontological foundation of relatedness. In this view, the materiality of the body communicates these histories of reproductive relations because it is an outcome of these histories. Bodily materiality renders the invisible "history of responsibility," which Miller (2017) identifies as the implicit link between race and ethics in European philosophical tradition, perceptible. In this sense, as Eboni Marshall Turman (2013) argues, racism is constituted through unequal power relations originating in the theological failure to recognize the Incarnational economy through which persons are formed relationally. This is where the dematerialization of meaning can lead—to a sensory politics dedicated to obscuring the history of reproductive relations as a tool for asserting interpretive control over future sites of reproductive power.

With this in mind, consider again Heleen's misrecognition by her friend on the streets of Glanerbrug. I, too, have attended the day-after Easter festivities at the monastery and have seen for myself the vocal outrage expressed by Dutch passersby at the monastery's chaotic crowd control and diminished capacity to operate according to Dutch conventions of regulating public space. Although their passage by the monastery was only briefly delayed, I observed the voluble irritation of numerous cyclists and drivers shouting at the devout coming to honor their dead, calling them "ridiculous" [*belachelijk*], in outraged tones that struck me as out of proportion to such a minor inconvenience. Although Dutch-born Suryoye often speak of themselves as "model minorities," their liturgical obligations, especially where they concern ancestors and kin relations, tend to take precedence over other concerns. This will often prompt public displays of ritual mourning that transgress local Dutch norms, such as spontaneously processing by foot and *en masse* through city streets to attend a funeral. The collective, affective dimensions of such liturgical obligations are inscrutable to their neighbors, my interlocutors tell me, because "even our Roman Catholic friends are so Calvinist in how they think and act that they have forgotten how to be Christian."

For Syriac Orthodox Christians in the Netherlands, what is seen and what remains unseen, what registers viscerally in their neighbors' impressions of their difference and what escapes attention entirely, illuminates a race-producing evaluative hierarchy. This hierarchy emerges from a history of contested interpretive control over sites of reproductive power, the formation of ethical subjects, and their interface with public sociality. An outcome of Calvinist-Liberal compromise, this theological politics bureaucratizes European Christian ambivalence toward the communicative and reproductive power of the human body/icon. The religious icon offers an analytical tool for making sense of this ethical economy, in which the anxieties provoked by encounters with bodies-deemed-heretical draw attention to the crux of the matter: conflicting views of sovereignty over the reproductive future. The body/icon threatens to destabilize the sovereignty of states and subjects because it shows us where the past becomes the future, now, in the present, whether we will it to or not.

POSTLUDE

LIFE POURS OUT

Clear distinctions between the categories of race, ethnicity, religion, and secularity form the bedrock of political life in modernity. These words, we believe, name different kinds of relatedness, although we are rarely explicit about the nature of the relatedness we mean. Our coyness hides the fact that we place these relations in a hierarchy of value. Some kinds of relatedness grant some of us the rights of citizenship, sovereignty over territory, access and mobility, protection or aid, and some measure of social power over the sites where we reproduce our relations. But these rights are often withheld from those participating in other kinds of relatedness. For example, when one group claims sovereign rights to a territory at the expense of another whose history on that land has been shaped by a different kind of relatedness, global powers will support one claim over another, with bombs when necessary, based on the perceived "realness" of their relations. Recognition, in these moments, is an ethical question before it is political.

The force of these distinctions stems, in large part, from a near-ubiquitous belief in their inescapability as outcomes of modernization. The view of secular modernity as a universal, impersonal, and inexorable force is embedded in the foundations of the social sciences. It is discernable in Émile Durkheim's conception of social solidarity, which he contrasted with *anomie,* the alienation felt when community norms break down in encounters with others who do and think differently. It is in Max Weber's "iron cage," in which Calvinist Christianity played an outsize role in forming the modern individual subject and which similarly projects a temporal rupture onto the history of human consciousness. Weber saw this rupture, imagined as a distinct *before* and *after* catalyzed by the rise of capitalist rationalization and bureaucratization, as necessarily inducing secularization on a mass scale (see also Hughes 2003, 2, 32–33). While many scholars have corrected, refined, or refuted much of the empirical basis of these early theoretical accounts, their premise that modernization—a process that entails secularization and individualization in some form or at some stage—*comes for everyone* has survived in introductory social theory textbooks and become a part of a globalized common sense.

A presumption of impersonal inevitability underlies nearly all influential theories of the secular. This is so whether theorists approach it as a process in which cultural secularity conceptually precedes political secularism or as a process in which political secularism insists upon and thus unavoidably produces cultural secularity. Whoever fails to be caught in its net is marked as modernity's abject Other. Despite their otherwise critical assessments, this sense of inevitability is evident in both Talal Asad's (2003) and Charles Taylor's (2007) accounts as they discern secular sensibilities and practices of personhood in poetry and drama before they manifest as practices of state governance. In their accounts, early modern art expressed a rupture in consciousness as Europeans learned to live with the uncertainty and contingency of experience and materialized that uncertainty in aesthetic form. Asad, following Benjamin, located this emergence in Baroque allegory, in which the fundamental subject/object relationship is between persons and social relations. The uncertainty and contingency of these relations generate, and are the substance of, artistic representation (2003, 63–66). Taylor, on the other hand, located this historical moment in Romantic poetry, which conveyed a hardening of the boundaries between self and nature (2007, 353). In each case, the conception of the human was recalibrated in relation to a broader context: nature, the universe, or the intellectual frame of human experience.

In such accounts, the prime mover of the secular is *difference* and the cognitive shock of the Other on human self-understanding. In Peter L. Berger's (2014) equally influential sociological argument, modern life is modern and secular discourse is secular because knowledge of difference produces a phenomenological condition of living with uncertainty. This is a condition that the philosopher, the sociologist, and the anthropologist all see as fundamentally rooted in a cognitive state, as a person's or people's worldview and authorizing framework become relativized by awareness of others who think and do otherwise. This uncertainty mirrors the arbitrary space between signified and signifier in Saussure's referential view of the linguistic sign.

But why? Why do we so easily presume this is so? When, I wonder, have humans ever really lived without difference?

For some theorists, it is the European Enlightenment, with its viral notions of progress, rationality, and emancipation from the past, that drives secularization, infecting everyone with whom it comes into contact. In this framework, even those forms of religious life that do not fit the Protestant ideal-type of state-regulable religion (including those practiced by some actual Protestants) are living in a state of radical disjuncture from the premodern version of their traditions because secularism/secularity/secularization has ruptured reality comprehensively, for everyone, forever. Projects of purification, definition, and regulation are what make secular modernity both secular and modern, we are told. Again, why? Does this mean that *before*, there were only impure, undefined, and unregulated forms of life? When was this? When have humans ever lived in a state *without* constant rupture, exactly? When have humans ever *not* tried to coordinate their efforts at managing the unruly dimensions of social life?

Other scholars have told me that to ask these questions is to indulge in a banal Latourianism. In *We Have Never Been Modern*, Bruno Latour famously argued that even properly scientific "Moderns" constantly transgress their carefully erected distinctions between science/religion, nature/society, and reason/unreason in the course of their scientific pursuits. Our modernity, therefore, is a conceit in every sense of the word. But I am saying something else: I am not sure that anyone was ever *pre*modern because we have always been making and living with distinctions. Making distinctions is a prerequisite for establishing relations. And at no point in the history of our species have we been relation-less. This is the brute fact of sexual and social reproduction. Alterity within the parent-child dyad is the first principle of human life. When philosophers and social scientists insist on the modern/premodern binary, even in order to critique it, a temporal distinction masquerades as a conceptual distinction. This presumed temporal distinction, this imaginary before and after, explains little, obscures much, and assumes everything.

That said, it may be imprudent to try to rebut theories generated in other disciplines in terms that proponents of those theories would find satisfactory. For the philosopher thinking on so vast a temporal scale as the Axial

Age and for the sociologist seeking parsimony on a global scale (although Berger also situates the origins of secular discourse in the Axial Age), ethnographic description might not amount to a rebuttal because it attends to different scales of temporal experience and spatial practice. And yet, I cannot *not* be bothered ethnographically by the claim that there's something uniquely modern about *knowing difference* that catalyzes the constitutive rupture of the modern subject. In the cosmopolitan and continent-spanning late antique and medieval worlds, Christians, Muslims, Jews, and (for lack of a better word) pagans of all stripes constantly grappled with the problem of people doing and thinking otherwise. The boundaries between these traditions only emerged *because* of this grappling. In the context of multilingual imperial theocracies, *people knowing differently* was an intellectual, theological, translational, and political problem of near-global proportions. As such, it produced all manner of complex disciplining institutional configurations, media forms, epistemic practices, and political projects to deal with this uncertainty (for just two examples, see Brown 2008 and Wood 2021). Some of these, such as the linearization and visualization of chronological history, first constructed by the imperial Byzantine historian Eusebius of Ceasarea in the fifth century (Johnson and Schott 2013), we should hesitate to identify with "modernity," "secularity," or "the West" exclusively. To do so distorts our understanding of how and why such inherited practices maintain their purchase when they are innovated in new political situations. The history of media forms in late antiquity here serves not as another philosophical abstraction akin to the Axial Age but as the horizon of our ethnographic present. This is to enable critical inquiry into the relational preconditions of Euro-American social scientific practices and to produce less distorted descriptions of the temporal and spatial boundaries of our field sites. In the traces of our history's histories, we might see with greater clarity how power and knowledge move through and, in so doing, transform the relations that make and remake worlds.

The Suryoye in my study demonstrate that nothing is inevitable, not even secularity. It is very hard work to secularize, just as it is very hard work to do this kind of communal self-fashioning. The future is an open question, reopened in every moment and act of reproduction. This is not a banal observation, or ultra-right-wing political factions the world over would not be battling for interpretive control over female bodily autonomy, gender and sexual identity, public education, and other sites of reproductive power, and then framing alternate interpretations of these sites as threats to Western civilization. According to my Syriac Orthodox interlocutors, as it happens, the greatest threats to Syriac liturgical kinship are the demands of capitalism and the allures of consumerism that come with them. Coordinated collective labor, organizing in defense against work shifts at the grocery store scheduled on Sunday mornings or being permitted to miss school for religious holidays are all the more important. My research participants, including the ones with PhDs and their own IT consulting firms, tell me that secularity is something to ward off not simply for its Godlessness but for its threat to the rhythms of the liturgical world order that makes being Syriac Orthodox possible in a sense they understand to be, in the secular social scientist's terms, as ethnic and cultural as it is religious.

For me, the architectural metaphor through which Saba Mahmood approached theorizing personhood is indispensable for clarifying that even when "religion" *is* a set of propositional truth-claims to which believers cognitively assent, it is also, for Christians, Muslims, Jews, and many, many others, a set of relationships and powers that shape us. It is common to describe this process as cultivating the self's sensory capacities and ethical dispositions, and I add to this the generation of that kin-relatedness that forms the self's sense of *to whom I am related* and *on whom I am dependent* and thus *who, as a consequence of these relations and dependencies, I am.* How these relations are recognized and named depends on the particular grammar of power operating in a given social and political context. There are some Syriac Orthodox in the Netherlands who do not believe in God, to be sure. My interlocutors suggested as much when they spoke of how carefully the community brushes these instances under the collective rug. When these irreligious Suryoye marry non-Suryoye and baptize their children outside the Syriac Orthodox Church without risking disinheritance from their families, then I will be convinced that something has changed in how Suryoyeness is reproduced in this corner of the Syriac world. But for now, the capacity to imagine a universe without a God does not logically dictate that these relations will be dislodged from the architecture of the self in a way that would make it possible for a Suryoyo to go cheerfully through the human life cycle without any reference to the rhythms, sounds, emotions, flavors, scents, and social demands of the Syriac Orthodox liturgy.

The metaphor of perforation describes how the attachments constituting dominant conceptions of Euro-American kinship are shot through with racial and religious discourses at the same time, to an extent that reveals the racial as belonging to a religious imagination and the religious as belonging to a racial imagination. Perforation suggests the vulnerability and permeability of the icon as a site of reproductive power. To think in these terms is to ask about the ethical and sensory forms of training entailed in making kin and erecting boundaries around who we believe counts as kin. The aim is to generate better descriptions of the modes, intensities, etiologies, and stakes of different varieties of relatedness and also, I hope, to interrogate our knee-jerk assumptions about who does not belong and why. This, I also hope, makes it possible for us to discern multiple modalities of power at work in the same sets of relations, but to do so will require some historical humility. Here, the icon can help, as it directs our attention to the possibilities for pluralism within relatedness itself.

The Syriac world is shot through with multimodal power relations generated by distinct trajectories of state secularism in the twentieth century and by an ethics of recognition shaped in relation to imperial theocracies in earlier centuries. There is never a clear-cut "inside" and "outside" to the conversations that produce a community's sense of itself. The past is no more settled or uniform than the present, as past conflicts resurface in the present because we are still living with their world-making effects.

Ultimately, whether Syriac Christianity is characterized as a "religious" or an "ethnic" group, it is a global kinship network made up of people who talk to each other and seek to account for each other's experiences in their interpretations of their own experience, and these experiences are inflected by countless conversations with others, past and present. As Bakhtin observed long ago, external voices have a way of becoming a part of our inner voice. In these spirited conversations, I recognize not only secular power refracted across scales of governance but other powers that the state tries yet sometimes fails to co-opt, if it notices them at all: these are the powers that animate interwoven relations of economic dependency, domestic intimacy, ecclesiastical authority, ethico-aesthetic docility, reproductive agency, embodied theology, and the generative rhythms of liturgical worlds forged and dissolved with great labor and at a high cost.

* * *

In 2013, Dutch-Syriac novelist Stire Kaya-Cirik published *Echo uit een onverwerkt verleden* (*Echo of an Unresolved Past*), an account of her family's memories of the Sayfo, the genocide of 1915, and her own experiences growing up in their fear and trauma. The main character of the novel, Meryem, a lightly fictionalized version of the author, addresses the cycle of intergenerational trauma causing her chronic illness and pain in adulthood by returning to her family's ancestral village in Tur Abdin. There, she encounters a monk whose story is modeled on the true story of a priest, Melke Tok, in southeast Turkey who had been kidnapped, tortured, and almost murdered in 1994. The scene in which she describes the monk's escape and return to his community is striking:

> When the monk saw his friends, he choked up. The scene of the group of men emotionally meeting each other calmed the crowd. After the initial excitement died down, the prominent local men—Turkish, Kurdish, and Syriac Orthodox—led everyone to a celebration feast that seemed like it would never end. All the women in the community had, immediately and en masse, started cooking when the message [of the monk's return] arrived. Even for such a massive gathering, this was a job that could be safely entrusted to the Syriac Orthodox women. (Kaya-Cirik 2013, 240, translation by author)

After a day of celebration with hundreds of people, Meryem sits with the monk at the monastery nearby. After he describes his ordeal, she asks him: "Are you angry? Do you hate the people who did this to you?" The monk responds, "No. I feel no resentment. Because love is the essence of my belief."

Days later, Meryem flies home to the Netherlands, meditating on his words, and feels the chronic pain, the lifelong weight and pressure in her body, begin to dissipate. Suddenly, she longs for her life back in the Netherlands with her friends, her husband, her children, her home. Like Elena in the opening chapter of this ethnography, who felt born again spending time with the nuns of Mor Gabriel, she carries something home with her. She describes her elders' world, their memories of Tur Abdin, as something she embraces physically with her arms and carries with her, coexisting with her own memories, and together they make a new world that rests on her chest. This world is pain, and loss, and death, but also life.

ACKNOWLEDGMENTS

This book was made possible by the care and attention of many, many people. Melissa Caldwell, best of advisors, guided me through the early years of this project's development with uncommon commonsense and compassion, and it is not an exaggeration to say the book would never have been completed without her unwavering support. Similarly, without Don Brenneis's instruction and encouragement in the ethnography of sound, I would never have been able to imagine, much less execute, it. Mayanthi Fernando challenged me to deeper critical self-reflection as I sought an ethical place to speak about religion as a secular social scientist. Whether I found that place, time will tell. I will always be grateful for the serendipity that put me on a cross-country train in the Netherlands with Susan Ashbrook Harvey in the summer of 2008. As my mentor in all things Syriac, her empathy and concern for this project have kept me going in tough times, while her expertise has saved me from error again and again. Her indispensable work on the ancient Syriac women's choirs was my guiding light in more ways than one.

In my pre-PhD years, Arzoo Osanloo and Vicente Rafael planted the seeds of this project at the University of Washington and made it possible for me to pursue an academic career. I am grateful for everything I have learned since then from Dan Linger, Carolyn Martin-Shaw, Susan Harding, Jim Clifford, Danilyn Rutherford, Megan Moodie, Anna Tsing, Lisa Rofel, Donna Haraway, Mark Anderson, Triloki Pandey, and many others among the faculty at UC Santa Cruz, each of whom shaped this book in a specific, significant way. I am also thankful for my Santa Cruz friends and colleagues, who I will always view as true kin: Nellie Chu, Patricia Alvarez Astacio, Sarah Chee, Carla Takaki-Richardson, Peter Leykam, Aimee Villareal, Noah Tamarkin, Juno Parreñas, Heather Swanson, Sarah Kelman, Stephie McCallum, Colin Hoag, Celina Callahan-Kapoor, Nishita Trisal, Heath Cabot, Danny Soloman, Xochitl Chavez, Rebecca Feinberg, Kim Cameron-Dominguez, Bettina Stoetzer, Jeffrey Omari, Kali Rubaii, and many others who have left their mark on the pages of this book. Neither in Santa Cruz nor in the Netherlands would I have gotten anywhere without Bregje van Eekelen, while Josh Brahinsky's friendship as a long-term writing partner, reading and commenting on nearly everything I have ever written over the years, has been one of my most important lifelines.

I was fortunate to have early versions of this project read and responded to by many brilliant scholars across different fields. Andrea Muehlenbach, Jillian Cavanaugh, and Neringa Klumbyte of the Society for the Anthropology of Europe honored me with the 2010 Graduate Student Paper Prize, which led to transformative discussions with Michael Herzfeld, Susan Gal, Matti Bunzl, Elif Babul, and Rachel Caesar—with Michael Herzfeld doing double duty as a caring, intellectual grandfather. I also benefited from important conversations with Lihi Ben Shitrit, Matt Ellis, Fahad Bishara, and other colleagues in the Austin 2011 cohort of the Social Science Research Council's International Dissertation Research Fellows' Workshop.

I am grateful for preliminary fieldwork grants provided by the Institute of European Studies at UC Berkeley and the UC Santa Cruz anthropology department. I received generous funding for extended fieldwork from the Wenner-Gren Foundation and from the Social Science Research Council's International Dissertation Research Fellowship. I was able to complete my dissertation with a writing fellowship from the Charlotte W. Newcombe Foundation, and my time as a graduate student at UC Santa Cruz was supported with an early Regent's Fellowship, teaching fellowships in the anthropology department and the Writing Program, and teaching assistantships in the politics and anthropology departments.

In the postdoctoral phase of research and writing, I received support from the Hunt Postdoctoral Fellowship, courtesy of the Wenner-Gren Foundation, and the Jay P. Young Excellence Award, courtesy of the anthropology department at San Francisco State University. I began developing the core of this text as a visiting scholar in the music department and at the Center for the Study of Religion at the University of California, Berkeley. During this disoriented and disorientating period, I made it through with the support of Charles Hirschkind, Jocelyne Guilbault, and Jonathan Sheehan, as well as from extended, transformational conversations with Martin Stokes, Rachel Colwell, Christina Azahar, Arathi Govind, Yunus Telliel, Mary McCann, Tripp Hudgins, and Ruth Meyers. Tala Jarjour became an essential interlocutor in this period, and this book would have been far harder, if not outright impossible, to write without her visionary scholarship.

One of the great joys of being an ethnographer of Christianity is that it means being able to talk to and think with a remarkable community of scholars, including Candace Lukasik, Ashley Lebner, Sarah Riccardi-Swartz, Chris Sheklian, Diego Maria Malara, Valentina Napolitano, Jon Bialecki, Naomi Haynes, Lena Rose, Mark Calder, Clayton Goodgame, Gaetan du Roy, Heather Mellquist, Jan Gehm, Habtom Yohannes, Jeffers Engelhardt, Nicholas Harkness, Maria Jose de Abreu, and Angie Heo, among many, many others. Core elements of my argument began to take shape in dialogue with Chris Hann, Pooyan Tamimi Arab, Ramazan Turgut, Vlad Naumescu, Heleen Murre-van den Berg, and especially the late Sonja Luehrmann. This book is an extended conversation with her memory, and I regret not being able to have it with her in person. In Syriac Studies and its adjacent fields, I have benefited immeasurably from years of delightful and stimulating conversation with Andreas Schmoller, Marta Woźniak-Bobińska, Gabriel Bar-Sawme, Fiona McCallum, Önver Cetrez, Magdalena Nordin, Andreas Westergren, Henrik Johnsen, Adam Becker, George Kiraz, Anna Hager, Gabriel Aydin, Henry Clements, and Sonja Thomas. Although we never spoke in person, Sebastian Brock's life's work infuses this project, as does the thought of the late Saba Mahmood.

At San Francisco State University, I have been glad to be part of an intellectual community where scholarship, teaching, and community engagement are equally valued not only in marketing materials but also in practice. I am thankful for the camaraderie and support of Rita Melendez, Chris Bettinger, Ikaika Gleisberg, Hülya Gürtuna, Alexis Martinez, Ryan Moore, Jen Reck, Clare Sears, Valerie A Francisco-Menchavez, Andreana Clay, Karen Hossfeld, Sahar Khoury, James Quesada, Aviva Sinervo, Peter Biella, Jeff Schonberg, Martha Lincoln, Katherine Young, Cynthia Wilczak, Thao Pham, and Erik Hidalgo.

At Fordham University Press, I have been so fortunate to have John Garza as an editor, who guided this first-time author with patience and humor, as well as the support of Aristotle Papanikolaou and Ashley M. Purpura. My anonymous reviewers, who later revealed themselves to be Grant White and Heleen Murre-van den Berg, gifted me with incredible, incisive feedback that improved the manuscript in significant ways.

During my fieldwork in the Netherlands, I would have been lost without the kindness and generosity of scholars working in my area. Dr. Naures Atto has been a good friend and confidante, while her path-clearing research is an essential prerequisite to my own. Dr. Jan Schukkink provided an invaluable introduction to the local history of the Syriac Orthodox community in his city. Dr. Heleen Murre-van den Berg gamely allowed herself to become the object of ethnographic inquiry and has since become an indispensable interlocutor. Dr. Kees den Biesen exceeded the bounds of intellectual generosity and, with Catherine Lombard, provided me a haven from the cold and the loneliness of fieldwork. By feeding me, caring for me, and letting me work in their garden and rest in their home, they sustained me through hard times, and I cherish the memory of my time with them.

My ability to work with the Syriac Orthodox community in the Netherlands would not have been possible without the gracious hospitality of His Excellency Mor Polycarpus Augin Aydin. He facilitated my introduction to the local parish choirs, housed and fed me in his monastery, and encouraged his flock to welcome me into their homes. The monks and nuns of the Mor Ephrem Monastery were my glad companions for many a long, dark Dutch afternoon. Without fail, they always made me feel welcome and at home.

I am grateful to the members of each parish where I conducted research, as well as the members of Platform Aram and the Assyrian Mesopotamian Cultural Association, for facilitating my efforts to understand Syriac Orthodox experience from every possible angle. I am grateful for the friendship of Nahrin Malki-Atto, a liturgical singer who is quietly and powerfully making the world a better, kinder, and more forgiving place. My deepest, and frankly most unpayable, debt goes to the women and men who are hidden behind pseudonyms in these pages for their privacy. That they were willing to share their stories, thoughts, and feelings with me when so many times in the past their community has been harmed by people from the outside is a testament to their bravery, open-heartedness, and ethical commitment to a living relationship with the unseen other. They will always have my love and gratitude.

I am endlessly thankful for the congregation and clergy of All Soul's Episcopal Parish in Berkeley, California, who daily demonstrate that theology is a practical family affair, and the whole world counts as family. Time and time again I have been encouraged, consoled, and mentored by a rowdy, brilliant, and endlessly caring community of academic parents, especially Sarah McKibben and the much-missed Elizabeth Freeman. Finally, I thank my Dutch, American, and Iranian families for their encouragement, hospitality, and unceasing faith in me. I am grateful for my always-inspiring sisters Carolien and Ashley and my stalwart brothers-in-law Kevin and Mark, and my sweet nephew Jack. My mother, Beth, and my father, Dingeman, are the reason for this book. They taught me to ask questions from a very young age about the most difficult questions of faith, family, culture, and identity and to relate to the pain of the past with both compassion and hope. Their stories and struggles—as much as their love and support—set me and kept me on this path.

Sean Bakker Kellogg has been there every step of the way, keeping me and this project alive through countless acts of love and care. Milo Bakker Kellogg teaches me daily about the joyful, terrifying dance of power and powerlessness that is reproducing kinship, and the mysterious interplay of sameness and difference, materiality and imagination, at the heart of a relation like ours.

This book is dedicated to the memory of my grandmothers, Aaltje Bakker-Toornstra and Leona M. Boyd, whose voices resound on every page.

GLOSSARY OF FREQUENTLY
USED SYRIAC WORDS

ʾ**Estrangelo.** The dominant classical Syriac script of antiquity, later displaced by the Serṭo script among West Syriac Rite traditions. It is commonly transliterated as *Estrangela* among religious studies and Syriac studies scholars.

gudo (pl. gude). The space or spaces in front of the altar in a Syriac Orthodox Church, positioned around a lectern, where students, singers, and ordained members of the diaconate gather to read or chant their parts in the liturgy. The word *gudo* is also commonly used to refer to groups of singers themselves and is often glossed as "choir," although it does not always exhibit the same formal features associated with the English-language word.

ʾ**ihidoyutho.** A Christological concept meaning "Only Begotten One," and evoking various shades of "singleness" as a moral discourse. A person who embodies the qualities of singleness by imitating Christ in their moral conduct might be called an ʾ*ihidoyo*.

kthobonoyo. The book language; a common term for classical Syriac in ordinary usage. It is usually used to specify the written liturgical language as opposed to spoken Ṭuroyo (see *Ṭuroyo*).

madrashto. A church school, similar to a Western Christian concept of Sunday School but might take place any day or night of the week. The content, purpose, and pedagogical structure of lessons learned at madrashto vary widely.

malphonitho (pl. malphonithe). A teacher who is a woman, usually indicating someone knowledgeable about Syriac language, liturgy, music, theology, history, or some other aspect of tradition. In practice, a malphonitho tends to have a more circumscribed role than that of a malphono, or male teacher.

malphono (pl. malphone). A teacher who is a man, usually indicating someone knowledgeable about Syriac language, liturgy, music, theology, history, or some other aspect of tradition; an important and respected figure in most parishes, often tasked with teaching younger Syriac Orthodox the language and melodies of the liturgy, either through modeling or explicit instruction.

mshamshonitho. A deaconess, historically an ordained female member of the diaconate. If there are women in the Syriac Orthodox Church today who have been ordained as a full deacon beyond the level of child Reader, I have yet to hear of them. However, the word is in colloquial use today, informally and inconsistently, to refer to those women who are regular and committed members of their parish gudo.

mshamshono. A deacon, an officially ordained senior member of the diaconate. This usually denotes a level of technical mastery over the sonic forms of liturgical melody; proficiency in classical Syriac, its pronunciation, and grammar; and/or understanding of theological meanings. A position of social esteem; always male.

Qurbono. The Divine Liturgy performed on Sunday mornings centered on the Eucharistic celebration and denotes the dimension of offering, oblation, or gift-giving as an act of drawing near to the Divine. For a step-by-step description of the ritual shape of Holy Qurbono as currently practiced among Syriac Orthodox parishes of the northern European diaspora, see Bar-Sawme 2021.

rozo. Mystery, from the ancient Greek *mysterion*, a term drawn from Incarnational theology associated with the Divine Liturgy. It describes the double process of materialization, when a spiritual reality takes on material form, and symbolization, when a material form becomes the symbol of a spiritual reality.

Serṭo. The name of the cursive classical Syriac script associated with the West Syriac Rite, likely originating as an everyday form of writing in third-century Edessa and later elevated in the eighth century to literary and liturgical uses west of the Euphrates River. It is now used predominantly by the Syriac Orthodox and Maronite Churches for writing liturgical Syriac. For a detailed overview, see Francoise Briquel-Chatonnet's contribution to King 2019.

Suryoyo. The Syriac word for "Syriac," or "Syriac Orthodox." It is frequently used to designate "the people" of the Syriac Orthodox Church in an unhyphenated ethnoreligious sense; its cognate is *Suryānī* in Arabic and *Süryânî* in Ottoman Turkish. Historically, Suryoyo was translated as "Syrian" in English, but in the early twentieth century, it became standard practice to translate it as "Syriac" to avoid confusing associations with the modern state of Syria. See Chapter 2 for a detailed discussion of Assyrian/Syriac name debates and relation to the ʿamo, the ʾumtho, and different senses of "the people."

Ṭuroyo. "The mountain language," the Central Neo-Aramaic subgroup of dialects spoken among Christian communities in the Tur Abdin region of southeast Turkey, between the town of Mardin in the west and the Tigris River in the north and east. It is commonly spoken among diasporic Syriac Orthodox Christians in the Netherlands, along with Arabic, Turkish, or Kurdish, depending on their village of origin. It is also referred to as *Surayt* or *Surayth* among Ṭuroyo speakers themselves, or *Syrische* when they are speaking Dutch. For a detailed overview of Ṭuroyo's geographical and historical origins, see Geoffrey Khan's contribution to King 2019.

NOTES

1. Incarnations of the Word

1. *Suryoye* is the plural form of the *Suryoyo*, the neo-Aramaic cognate of *Suryānī*, the name that the Syriac Orthodox are known by in much of Syria and Turkey. In the Netherlands, the majority of local Syriac Orthodox Christians' first language is *Surayt,* a non-standardized dialect of Central neo-Aramaic that developed in the highlands of Tur Abdin, a poor and rural region in southeastern Turkey considered by many to be the heartland of Syriac Orthodoxy. Surayt is commonly referred to in the diaspora as *Ṭuroyo,* "the mountain language," whereas classical Syriac, the second century dialect of Aramaic used in the liturgy, is *Suryoyo kthobonoyo,* "the book language." In the global diaspora, Syriac Orthodox are predominantly either Ṭuroyo speakers if they are from Tur Abdin, Arabic-speakers if they are from Syria, Iraq, Lebanon or the Arabic-speaking cities of southeast Turkey like Mardin, Turkish-speakers if they are from major urban areas in Turkey like Istanbul, or Kurdish-speakers if they are from any of the smaller towns or villages where Kurdish clans dominated local politics.

2. Pseudonyms have been used to protect research participants' privacy and anonymity, with the exception of certain well-known figures whose identities cannot be obscured, or otherwise indicated.

3. State-driven efforts to erase Syriac Christians from national records have made demographic data notoriously difficult to establish, but see Gaunt, Atto, and Barthoma 2017 for one of the best available accounts of the *Sayfo's* long-term demographic effect.

4. While the term "Assyrian" has been an official census category in the United States since the nineteenth century, on account of political advocacy by

early Assyrian immigrants from Iran, neither this term nor any other ethnic labels associated with Syriac Christianity are legally recognized in Turkey nor in most of the European countries to which Syriac Christians have migrated over the past fifty years.

5. Both West and East Syriac Rites also continue to be used, with adaptations, among congregations who have adopted Protestant theologies, such as the Reformed Eastern Malankara Mar Thoma Church and the Assyrian Pentecostal Church. Generally speaking, I understand a congregation to be "Syriac" if it maintains a commemorative relationship with the language of ancient Edessa in its liturgical practices.

6. Many Syriac Orthodox Christians who identify as Aramaean tend to focus on historical ties to Roman Syria in the "West," where city-states like Greek-speaking Antioch and Syriac-speaking Edessa were among the very first converts to Christianity. Assyrian Syriac Orthodox Christians, on the other hand, tend to emphasize the historical continuities connecting the Syriac-speakers of ancient Edessa and Nisibis to the Mesopotamian "East" in what is now the borderland areas of Syria, southeast Turkey, Iran, and especially northern Iraq, where the material remains of the ancient empires (Old Assyrian Empire 2025–1364 BCE, Middle Assyrian Empire 1363–912 BCE, and Neo-Assyrian Empire 911–609 BCE) are located. There is considerable debate over whether Assyrian ethnicity is a modernist construct introduced by colonial powers to the neo-Aramaic-speaking Christians of northern Iraq in a deliberate effort to undermine pan-Arab nationalism; this debate misses the point that Syriac Christians themselves have been debating whether they are descended from ancient Assyria or the biblical city-states of Aram since at least the ninth century CE. The issue is not whether one or the other narrative is "correct" in naive primordialist terms but rather how imperial and state powers establish or transform the terms of political recognition through which minoritized communities can secure for themselves the space needed to reproduce socially. Irrespective of whatever name they are known by others in a given historical moment, they are "a people" in both an "ethnic" and a "religious" sense.

7. As I make clear in the coming chapters, Assyrian identity is a broader ethnonational category linked to both West and East Syriac Rites, while Aramaean identity is more narrowly linked to the West Syriac Rite. For detailed examination of the Chaldean Catholic Church and its ethnopolitical articulations see Hanoosh 2019.

8. Demonstrating the global scope of the Syriac Orthodox Church's commitment to liturgical training from a young age, Vlad Naumescu has also documented and analyzed the rigor and centrality of such formal education (what he calls "enskillment") to Syriac Orthodox Christian models of communal and individual personhood, but his study takes place in the south Indian

context, where class and colonialism have shaped its practical application in locally distinctive ways (2018, 2019).

9. I thank Ozan Aksoy for this detail and his insights into the professionalization of ethno-religious diasporic music scenes.

10. For an official Church authorized account, see Aydin 2017. For an ethnomusicological assessment, see Jarjour 2018.

11. Hirschkind's analysis of how pious Muslims cultivate an ethically responsive sensorium draws upon Walter Benjamin's reflections on the epochal transformations of sensory experience under capitalism in the early twentieth century. Such training renders "worlds perceptible," in Hirschkind's words, and as such is a key site for understanding how historical constructs like "modernity," "tradition," "secularity" or "religion" become integrated into individual subjects' self-understandings and embodied modes of living in the world (see also Alibhai 2023; Amir-Moazami 2016; Brahinsky 2012; Farman 2013; Hirschkind 2006, 2011; Scheer, Fadil, and Johansen 2020; Selby 2020; Vliek 2020; Wiering 2017).

12. An example of this rhetoric is found in the words of Deacon Epiphanios at the second Council of Nicaea against Severus, Peter the Fuller, Philoxenos of Mabbug, and "their many headed but head-less (*Akephaloi*) hydra" (Brock 1978, cited in Vesa 2017, 386). The accusation went generally like this: the monophysite, or one-nature, Christology so overemphasizes Christ's divinity that his humanity is effectively swallowed up within it. This leads to iconoclasm, according to iconophile logic, because it is by definition impossible to represent divinity pictorially (Vesa 2017, 386). That dogma was only ever accurately attributed to a group called the Euthychians, however, who were condemned by Chalcedonians and non-Chalcedonians alike. Early followers of Severus, on the other hand, held that the incarnate nature of Christ was *one* coming 'from' (*ek*) two natures, human and divine, in perfect union of the two, in contrast to a Chalcedonian formulation, which insisted that the Incarnate Christ was 'in' (*en*) two natures" (Vesa 2017, 386).

13. Over the past thirty years, the rise of mass media technologies has coincided with a scholarly perception of religion's "return" globally, inspiring a vast body of research on media and religion—especially Islam and Pentecostal Christianity. While this scholarly literature is far too extensive to cite adequately here, much of it is organized by an analytical focus on interiority, sincerity, and especially mediation, conceptual concerns that Niloofer Haeri has identified as rooted in theological anxieties most strongly associated with Calvinist Christianity, which has had an outsized influence on liberal theories of bounded, self-willed personhood. She sums up the anxiety thus: "What, if anything, should be allowed to mediate and matter in constructing a relationship to God? Should images, statues, saints, deceased kin, things, pilgrimages, other people's

words, music, the Internet, offerings, vows, devotional poetry, different languages of prayer, and so on, mediate that relationship?" (Haeri 2017, 130; see also Keane 2002; 2007). Marking a notable break with this literature, Maria Jesus de Abreu (2021) has written that the concept of mediation is insufficiently Christological for her ethnography of Brazilian Catholic Charismatics whose practices are inspired by Byzantine Orthodoxy; for my own study, I find the concept of mediation too imprecise to provide any analytical purchase on the specific interior qualities that constitute a given relation.

14. Peircean philosophers find evidence of C.S. Peirce's theological imagination not only in the occasional off-hand comment in his unpublished papers (e.g. Robinson 2010, 61) but also in the evolution of his writings on the fundamentally triadic nature of his metaphysics and the influence of 13th century Scottish theologian Duns Scotus (e.g. Conway 2014; Thellefsen and Sorensen 2014).

15. For an analysis of the political theory of possessive individualism in Western democratic traditions, see MacPherson 1964.

16. My use of Bakhtin here builds on Susan Harding's dialogical analysis of the linguistic practices through which religious subjects are fashioned in fundamentalist American Christianity (2001), but where her non-denominational American Christians deploy specific narrative and rhetorical techniques in sermons and witnessing, my research participants use liturgical sound.

17. Where a Wittgensteinan approach understands meaning to be defined by and through use, a Peircean approach understands meaning *through* and *beyond* use.

18. Scholars working outside of Abrahamic traditions have been making a similar argument for a long time. See for example Yang 1991; Guo 2023.

19. For more on the complexity of relations between Non-Chalcedonian Orthodox Christianity and Protestantism as "breaking with the Protestant break with the past," see Diego Maria Malara 2022.

20. For a useful assessment of these historical studies on Syriac Christianity as sociopolitical identity see Durmaz 2021.

21. For a sense of the range of scholarly efforts to conceptualize liturgy both theologically and sociologically, see Bradshaw 2002; Hughes 2003; Meyers 2010; Schmemann 1990; Spinks 2008.

22. See Goodgame 2023 for a resonant example of Palestinian Greek Orthodox Christians' liturgical use of olive oil to fashion sacral relations of lineage and descent from and with the land.

23. For further examples of feminist anthropology's long tradition of demonstrating the limited cross-cultural applicability of normative liberal theories of personhood as a bounded, self-willed subject see Abu-Lughod 1990,

2002; Collier, Rosaldo, and Yanagisako 1981; Fernando 2010; Gal 2002; Martin-Shaw 1995; Ortner 1975; Oyewumi 1997; Rapp and Ross 1981; Rubin 1975; Rosaldo 1980; Strathern 1987; see also Truth 1851.

2. Liturgical Memory

1. In late antiquity, women liturgical singers are referenced in a variety of Syriac-language sources—hymns, sermons, ecclesiastical canons, hagiography, chronicles, and liturgical commentaries—but they are not always called Daughters of the Covenant. In some sources they are referred to as "consecrated virgins" and in others as "the order of sisters." In still other sources they are sometimes identified as deaconesses. Historical references to women's choirs seem to disappear altogether by the tenth century, however, and by the fifteenth century a *bnoth qyomo,* Daughter of the Covenant, means "the priest's wife." Usage of the term "Daughters of the Covenant" began in my own field site when someone from Marta and Rebekah's church in Hengelo translated a research article by the historian Susan Ashbrook Harvey, who not coincidentally was my own mentor in Syriac Studies, about the ancient choirs and posted it on the church's official website before I arrived for fieldwork. My research participants are enthusiastic consumers of historical research on their tradition.

2. For an overview of the extensive body of anthropological scholarship on the global scope of non-binary gender and sexual-social reproductive systems, see Nanda 2014. For examples of gender's complex interweaving with diverse cosmological systems see Jacobs, Thomas, and Lang 1997; Reddy 2005; Ramberg 2014.

3. For a beginner's level introduction to microtones in Middle Eastern modal systems, see https://taqs.im/scales/. For an introduction to the specifics of Syriac Orthodox microtonality, which involves even narrower sonic intervals than those used in Arabic and Turkish maqam, see Aydin 2017 and Jarjour 2018.

4. Being able to read and sing in *kthobonoyo* was not so unusual for someone of the contractor's class position. The life trajectories and migration stories of many Suryoyo men who are highly educated in classical language and liturgy and thus socially respected in the community have led them to working-class professions in the Netherlands.

5. The *'amo* refers to "the people" of the Syriac Orthodox Church in a narrower, less politicized sense than Peter's preferred term, *'umtho,* which carries more explicitly nationalist connotations.

6. See also Garriott and O'Neill 2008.

7. For another way of conceptualizing the interplay of complexity, rupture, continuity, and context that shapes Christianity as an ethnographic formation, see Jon Bialecki's discussion of the Deleuzian diagram, which describes a set of

relations or "abstract maps of how forces play out that point as much toward the different potentials in outcome as they do toward a similarity in relations or constitution" (Bialecki 2017, 69).

8. The word *miaphysite* is a twentieth century neologism, derived from the ancient Greek words *mia-* "one" and *phusis,* conventionally translated in theological discourses as "nature" but which in its earliest usage was a verbal noun meaning growth or development.

9. The councils' purpose was to curtail the proliferation of theological discourses raging throughout the empire, and the political strife in which they were entangled. In 429 CE, Nestorius, briefly Bishop of Constantinople and himself a Greek-speaking monk born in the province of Syria, delivered a sermon claiming that while he could refer to Mary as *Christotokos,* the mother of Jesus's humanity, he could not call her *Theotokos* because "no mother can bear what is not consubstantial to herself" (quoted in Marshall Turman 2013, 31). By implication, this called into question Jesus's identity: could he be both consubstantial with God and with humanity? Cyril took exception to this sermon, publicly complaining that Nestorius's comment constituted a dualistic Christology that fragmented Jesus' identity and "led to the complete separation of the divine and human natures, and thus threatened the efficacy of salvation" (Marshall Turman 2013, 32–33).

10. While "miaphysite" is widely used today, it is worth recalling that it is a neologism. As Millar writes, "It is not only that there is no evidence for the contemporary use of 'miaphysite' in our sources, either in Greek or in Syriac transliteration. It is also that . . . no compound nouns formed from μία + feminine noun + ending are found in either Classical or Patristic Greek" (Millar 2013, 52).

11. This was also true of the Bnay Qyomo, or Sons of the Covenant, men in the community who similarly served the community in partnership and sang in dialogical call-and-response with their consecrated sisters, the Daughters of the Covenant.

12. In this first modern instance of mass population removal in the region, the Russian Empire expelled 800,000 people from Circassia and Abkhazia, and then 900,000 ethnic Turks (Chatty 2010, 61).

13. Assyrian historian Aryo Makko (2010) argues that ethnonationalists throughout the region rendered the English term "Assyrian" into neo-Aramaic as *Aturāyā* (in keeping with the phonetic conventions of East Syriac Sureth-speakers) when speaking of members of the Church of the East exclusively, and as *Othuroyo* (in keeping with the phonetic conventions of West Syriac Ṭuroyo/ Surayt-speakers) when speaking of a broader ecumenical nation that encompasses all branches of the Syriac liturgical tree. Turkish-speaking Assyrian nationalists, on the other hand, rendered "Assyrian" into the term

Süryânî to speak solely of the Syriac Orthodox branch. However, other historians see this term not as a translation of "Assyrian" but as adherence to millet nomenclature for the sake of recognizability within an Ottoman and later Turkish context. Armenian speakers, meanwhile, used the term *Asouri* to speak of the Syriac traditions' shared historical descent (Makko 2010, 7).

14. In 1932, a period of disquiet in relations between Assyrian refugees from the Hakkari Mountains and the Iraqi government culminated in a massive outbreak of violence known as the Massacre of Simele, in which the military murdered more than six thousand Assyrian civilians and destroyed nearly two hundred villages. A number of survivors fled to the Khabur River Valley in the eastern part of Syria, where they built new towns and eventually founded the Assyrian Democratic Association.

15. For the history of modern Assyrian popular music and its complex relationship with liturgical memories of the West and East Syriac Rite, see Zeitoune 2015.

16. As Martin Stokes has written, the Turkish situation exemplifies the notion that "the nation-state is committed to co-opt or eradicate plurality in the pursuit of a unitary national culture; this process renders unthinkable the fractured, partial worlds that many, if not most, people inhabit within the categories that it propagates" (Stokes 1994, 264).

3. The Voice in the Icon

1. In the Coptic Orthodox context, Angie Heo conceptualizes the paradox of the icon as a communicative genre called "mystical publicity," in which "to be visible, holiness must be invisible; to be revealed, holiness must be hidden" (Heo 2018, 212).

2. The Syriac Orthodox Church's appreciation for the diversity its liturgical practices is long-standing, and, according to Fr. Baby Varghese, the twelfth-century writings of Bishop Dionysius Bar Salibi reflect a broader consensus: "That fact that people of every country pray differently, and have something which singles them out from the rest, goes to their credit, first because it indicates the wealth of their devotions and spiritual vigor, and secondly because it is a sign of the incomprehensibility of God, who wishes to be glorified in different ways in different countries and towns" (Bar Salibi, *Against the Melchites,* 34, cited in Varghese 2004, 3).

3. The fracture among my interlocutors concerning how to name their relationship to history—Assyrian or Aramaean—thus emerges from conflicting understandings of *how much* history they could claim through liturgical memory.

4. As I argued in Chapter 1, where one stands on the question of the secular rupture of language in modernity will influence whether Wittgensteinian or Peircean thought is more useful to making sense of these vocal practices as

ethical. From a Wittgensteinian perspective, ethics relies on a correspondence between ritual and ordinary speech (Lambek 2010, see also Rappaport 2010 [1999]). Both ritual and speech rely on "the conjunction of the indexical and the canonical" (Lambek 2010, 45): the "canonical" dimension of an utterance or act is its conventional, patterned, repetitive elements—that which must be repeated in order for the utterance or act to be intelligible. So, to elaborate on a commonly cited example, breaking bread and pouring wine are essential elements without which most Christians would not recognize communion on a Sunday morning as the Holy Eucharist. The "indexical" dimension, in anthropologist Lambek's sense, meanwhile, would be *today's instance of breaking the bread and pouring the wine,* by this priest or deacon, who perhaps spills some of the wine while pouring it, and so must take care in wiping up the spill, and then in disposing of the rag used to wipe up the spill, because the consecrated wine saturating the rag must be discarded in consecrated fashion. While something old and established happens every time, each happening is an occasion for some new development—the indexical—which must proceed and be judged according to the criteria established by earlier canonical dimensions of the performance. *The wine has been consecrated so you cannot just throw the rag out in the trash.* These new developments may, with repetition, come to be seen as canonical, part of the authority of the tradition. The priest or deacon may pour less wine in the cup next time, or decide to develop a new sacral strategy for disposing of wine-stained cloths. My research participants engaged in just such a practice of ethical discernment in debating how and by what criteria they and their peers should reproduce the sounds of their liturgical tradition, and themselves as Syriac Christians: what should stay, what should go, and why? In the process, they reproduce their tradition and the kin relations staked upon that tradition. So, a Wittgensteinian approach to ethics makes partial sense of their efforts, but reaches its limits in grappling with the theological dimensions of my research participants' ethical and aesthetic practices.

5. For a very different use of Peircean semiotics to theorize liturgy in a Protestant setting, see Hughes 2003. The key distinction between Hughes' approach to the iconic meanings of liturgy and my own is in his background assumption of a "virtual frontier," a state of secular rupture that defines the space and time of the Protestant perspective he writes of and from, and which emphasizes the role of the imagination in the work of interpretation, and de-emphasizes its reproductive dimensions.

6. For more on Ephrem and his legacy, see Amar 2011; den Biesen 2006; Brock 1995; McVey 1989, 26–30; Palmer 2015.

7. As Archimandrite Benedict Vesa writes, Christ "is the image/icon of the Father and, in consequence, the human is created in 'the image of the image' / in the 'icon of the icon' (of Christ)" (2017, 386).

8. As Vesa observes, this reinforces the point that "(t)he Syriac icon was rooted in the written Word of God" (2017, 390).

9. See Klomp et al. 2018 for more on the complexity of Calvinism's legacy in secular Dutch aesthetic cultures.

4. Daughters of the Covenant

1. For feminist theories of "voice" and the politics of the speaking subject, see Gal 1991; Sinha 1996; Spivak 1999; Weidman 2003, 2006.

2. Other members of the community have suggested to me that more was going on behind the scenes of the patriarchal decision to excommunicate these monks than was generally understood by average parishioners like the Mansurs. According to someone close to the situation, the decision was officially rooted in the monks' repeated violation of their vows of obedience to the previous bishop. This official reasoning covered a number of transgressions.

3. That Father Yaqub did not find it unseemly to speak to me, a young woman, about this subject had to do with my ambiguous status in the community at that point in my fieldwork. At the monastery, the bishop made it clear that I was a visiting scholar, so in nonliturgical situations I was often treated as if I were a man. This was not always the case, however. For good measure, my father happened to be visiting me that day, and so Father Yaqub was speaking as much to my father as to me when this conversation took place.

4. As Jarjour also notes at St. George's parish in Aleppo, women's voices may be audible but their bodies must not be visible. In some parishes in the global diaspora, this continues to be the case, as in one of the Syriac Orthodox parishes in Amsterdam I regularly visited, where for major events the girl's choir is positioned out of sight in a loft above and behind the sanctuary. In the parishes in Hengelo, Enschede, and the cathedral at the Mor Ephrem monastery, on the other hand, the women's choirs would often be permitted to stand at the front of the sanctuary for special events.

5. The Theology of Ethnicity

1. See also Collier and Yanagisako 1987; Hylland Eriksen 2002; McKinnon and Cannell 2013, 29.

2. Such are the idioms in which the eighteenth-century European philosopher Johan Herder thought as he developed the conceptual apparatus of both modern nationalism and secular social science (see also Holmes 2000; Markell 2003).

3. For more on aesthetic conditions of political legibility, see Cabot 2013 and Tambar 2010.

4. See http://www.wca-ngo.org/about-us/name-change-sua-wca. Last accessed January 9, 2014.

5. What is less clear in Keane's analyses, in particular, is the tension among and across modern Protestant denominations between Calvinist doctrines of unconditional predestination and Arminian doctrines of conditional election and justification contingent upon the individual's decision to believe. This debate among seventeenth-century Dutch Reformed Protestants continues to be among the most globally widespread doctrinal debates over free will versus divine will. This debate has characterized Western Christianity since Augustine argued against the Pelagians. The tension between Calvinist and Arminian doctrine is thus of a different character than the tension between Protestant concerns for the faith of an individual and Orthodox concerns for the hereditary, kin-based formulations of religious community.

6. See also Dalrymple 1997 for further accounts from Muslims and Christians who have used Mor Gabriel monastery for these purposes.

7. See also Varghese 2004; for a similar notion among Brazilian Charismatic Catholics explicitly borrowing from an Orthodox Christian theological imagination see de Abreu 2021.

8. This family member also happens to be an adamant supporter of inclusive multiculturalism policy and for many years worked professionally to fight Islamophobia and help the Muslim community in his city gain access to improved employment opportunities. It is worth remembering that sympathy for religious minorities (or its lack) is not the key issue in the Dutch politics of minority recognition.

9. This is a move in which European secular powers misrecognize and misrepresent themselves, as anthropologist Mayanthi Fernando has similarly diagnosed in the case of the French state's relationship with Muslim French (2014).

10. See also Mauss [1938] 1985, 20; Foucault 1976.

6. Blood in My Veins

1. Not all Moroccans or Dutch people of Moroccan descent are Arab or Arabic speakers, nor even, for that matter, Muslim. Many Dutch-Moroccan families identify not as Arab but as Amazigh, hailing originally from the Rif Mountains in Morocco where the Tamazight language is preeminent over Arabic and economically marginalized from the rest of Morocco (van Amersfoort and van Heelsum 2007).

2. Feminist and disability studies scholars have shown the link between trained bodily capacities for sensory perception and hegemonic power relations within a society. Sachi Sekimoto, for example, argues that "individuals incorporate social values and orientations into their bodies, as the embodied sensory orientations shape and inform their social and physical experiences" (Sekimoto 2018, 87).

3. In her study of ethical striving among black Brazilian *lesbicas*, for example, Nessette Falu (2015) develops an expansive conception of "modes of freedom" as reformulating the Self's relation to the Self and to Others by seeking recognition as ethical subjects against the grain of racial and sexual domination (see also Falu 2023).

4. For a comparative example of this political genealogy in the contemporary Spanish context, where criteria for inclusion and exclusion are translated into the language of sentiment, rather than "norms and values," see McDonald 2021.

5. As Stolcke reminds us (1993), racism reinforces women's maternal role by naturalizing social inequalities. In capitalism, this naturalization reconciles equality of opportunity with inequality in reality; prior to and beyond capitalism, this naturalization reconciles any model of ethical personhood that poses reproductive power as a problem for the constitution of autonomous ethical subjects.

6. Looking beyond Europe, Adeola Oni-Orisan (2017) similarly argues that a secularism formed through complex tensions among Liberal and Pentecostal Christian traditions shapes the biopolitical field where racialization, maternal health, development discourse, and reproductive desire intersect in postcolonial Nigeria.

7. Ethnographic studies of Dutch cosmopolitan-nationalism have diagnosed a gap between what Oscar Verkaaik and Pooyan Tamimi Arab (2016) term "constitutionalist secularism" and "culturalist secularism." In this formulation, secular political practices, cultural self-images, and perceptions of religious difference are equally integral to Dutch attitudes towards immigration in both official commitments to pluralism and its nativist rejection. These practices and self-images rest upon the hard-won discursive silence around both "religion" and "race" (Essed and Trienekens 2008; Tamimi Arab 2012; Wekker 2004). Driven from both the top-down and the bottom-up after World War Two, political leaders worked to eradicate anti-Semitism and colonial racism by eliminating "race" as an official category. Meanwhile, Dutch religious culture was transformed by swift and widespread rejection of pillarization (Houkes 2009).

8. In the Netherlands as in much of Europe, "social pedagogy" is both a field of research and a professional practice akin to "social work" in the U.S., with some significant differences that lie beyond the scope of this chapter.

9. There is a tension among diverse accounts of Dutch historical attitudes toward difference that reflects the tensions within those historical attitudes themselves. Sam Cherribi, a Moroccan-born, French-educated, and self-avowed secular Muslim sociologist who served for awhile among the first cohort of Dutch-Moroccan Members of Parliament in the 1990s, attributes late

twentieth-century multicultural policies to a historical Dutch spirit of tolerance. This, he writes, is the spirit inherited from both Spinoza and from Snouk Hurgronje, the nineteenth-century attaché for the colonial government in the East Indies who converted to Islam and argued that interfering with the affairs of Muslim locals would be bad for trade (Cherribi 2010). But this secularist configuration of "tolerance" reflects a different set of social concerns than those implicit in the careful policing of the boundary between the bourgeois white Christian European colonizers and the racial-religious colonized Others that Ann Stoler has described in her work on Dutch missionaries in the East Indies. It is also not the tolerance expressed by the Dutch Protestant and Catholic Churches who have since the 1960s been on the vanguard of protecting minority religious identities from secular silencing in the name of a meaningful religious pluralism. Led by the *Raad van Kerken* [the Council of Churches], devout Dutch Christians have lobbied and organized in defense of Muslim and other religious minority rights under the motto of *Samen Leven, Samen Bidden* ("Living Together, Praying Together"). First opening up their churches to Muslim immigrants to use for prayer, these churches played a central role in shaping early Moroccan and Turkish community organizing along religious lines. Sam Cherribi wrote of these efforts as misguided, however, because he attributed them with influencing the "non-secular dynamic" of Islamic community formation in the Netherlands (2010).

BIBLIOGRAPHY

Abdul Khabeer, Su'ad. "Citizens and Suspects: Race, Gender, and the Making of American Muslim Citizenship." *Transforming Anthropology* 25, no. 2 (October 2017): 103–19. https://doi.org/10.1111/traa.12098.

Abreu, Maria José A. de. *The Charismatic Gymnasium: Breath, Media, and Religious Revivalism in Contemporary Brazil*. Durham, NC: Duke University Press, 2021.

Agamben, Giorgio. *Opus Dei: An Archaeology of Duty*. Stanford, CA: Stanford University Press, 2020. https://doi.org/10.1515/9780804788564.

Agamben, Giorgio, and Adam Kotsko. *The Highest Poverty: Monastic Rules and Form-of-Life*. Meridian, Crossing Aesthetics. Stanford, CA: Stanford University Press, 2013.

Agrama, Hussein Ali. "Ethics, Tradition, Authority: Toward an Anthropology of the Fatwa." *American Ethnologist* 37, no. 1 (February 2010): 2–18. https://doi.org/10.1111/j.1548-1425.2010.01238.x.

———. *Questioning Secularism: Islam, Sovereignty, and the Rule of Law in Modern Egypt*. Chicago Studies in Practices of Meaning. Chicago: University of Chicago Press, 2012.

Alibhai, Zaheeda. "Bodies of Becoming: The Regulation of Religion and Gender and the Subjectivation of the Secular Body." In *The Routledge Handbook of Religion and the Body*, edited by Yudit Kornberg Greenberg and George Pati. London: Routledge, 2023.

Al-Mohammad, Hayder. "Poverty beyond Disaster in Postinvasion Iraq: Ethics and the 'Rough Ground' of the Everyday." *Current Anthropology* 56, no. S11 (October 2015): S108–15. https://doi.org/10.1086/681800.

Al-Mohammad, Hayder, and Daniela Peluso. "Ethics and the 'Rough Ground' of the Everyday: The Overlappings of Life in Postinvasion Iraq." *HAU:*

Journal of Ethnographic Theory 2, no. 2 (September 2012): 42–58. https://doi
.org/10.14318/hau2.2.004.

Althusser, Louis. "Ideology and Ideological State Apparatuses: Notes Toward
and Investigation." In *Lenin and Philosophy and Other Essays*. Monthly
Review, 1970.

Amar, Joseph. "Christianity at the Crossroads: The Legacy of Ephrem the
Syrian." *Religion and Literature* 43, no. 2 (2011): 1–21.

Amir-Moazami, Schirin. "Investigating the Secular Body: The Politics of the
Male Circumcision Debate in Germany." *ReOrient* 1, no. 2 (April 1, 2016).
https://doi.org/10.13169/reorient.1.2.0147.

Anderson, Benedict. *Imagined Communities: Reflections on the Origin and
Spread of Nationalism*. Rev. and Extended ed. London: Verso, 1991.

Arendt, Hannah. *The Origins of Totalitarianism*. 1st ed. New York: Schocken,
2004.

Arkin, Kimberly A. *Rhinestones, Religion, and the Republic: Fashioning Jewishness
in France*. Stanford Studies in Jewish History and Culture. Stanford, CA:
Stanford University Press, 2014.

Armbruster, Heidi. "Linked Biographies in Changing Times. Syriac Christians
in Vienna." *Ethnologie Française* 44, no. 3 (July 1, 2014): 469–78. https://doi
.org/10.3917/ethn.143.0469.

Asad, Talal. *Formations of the Secular: Christianity, Islam, Modernity*. Cultural
Memory in the Present. Stanford, CA: Stanford University Press, 2003.

———. *Genealogies of Religion: Discipline and Reasons of Power in Christianity
and Islam*. Baltimore: Johns Hopkins University Press, 1993.

Ashbrook Harvey, Susan. *Asceticism and Society in Crisis: John of Ephesus and
The Lives of the Eastern Saints*. The Transformation of the Classical
Heritage 18. Berkeley: University of California Press, 1990.

———. "Revisiting the Daughters of the Covenant." *Hugoye: Journal of Syriac
Studies* 8, no. 1 (February 1, 2011): 125–50. https://doi.org/10.31826/hug-2011
-080111.

———. *Song and Memory: Biblical Women in Syriac Tradition*. Milwaukee, WI:
Marquette University Press, 2010.

———. "Women and Children in Syriac Christianity: Sounding Voices." In
The Syriac World, edited by Daniel King. London: Routledge, 2019.

Atto, Naures. "Hostages in the Homeland, Orphans in the Diaspora: Identity
Discourses among the Assyrian/Syriac Elites in the European Diaspora."
Leiden: Leiden University, 2011.

Austin-Broos, Diane J. *Jamaica Genesis: Religion and the Politics of Moral
Orders*. Chicago: University of Chicago Press, 1997.

Aydin, Gabriel, ed. *Syriac Hymnal According to the Rite of the Syriac Orthodox
Church of Antioch*. Cumberland, RI: Syriac Music Institute, 2017.

Bakir, Sarah. "New Massive Assault on Christian Villages in Syria." World Council of Aramaeans, 2015. https://wca-ngo.org/humanrightsfiles/the-syria-crises/509-new-massive-assault-on-christian-villages-in-syria.

Bakker Kellogg, Sarah. "Perforating Kinship: Syriac Christianity, Ethnicity, and Secular Legibility." *Current Anthropology* 60, no. 4 (August 2, 2019): 475–98. https://doi.org/10.1086/705233.

———. "A Racial-Religious Imagination: Syriac Christians, Iconic Bodies, and the Sensory Politics of Ethical Difference in the Netherlands." *Cultural Anthropology* 36, no. 4 (November 18, 2021): 618–48. https://doi.org/10.14506/ca36.4.08.

———. "Ritual Sounds, Political Echoes: Vocal Agency and the Sensory Cultures of Secularism in the Dutch-Syriac Diaspora." *American Ethnologist* 42, no. 3 (August 2015): 431–45. https://doi.org/10.1111/amet.12139.

Balkenhol, Markus. "Silence and the Politics of Compassion. Commemorating Slavery in the Netherlands: Silence and the Politics of Compassion." *Social Anthropology* 24, no. 3 (August 2016): 278–93. https://doi.org/10.1111/1469-8676.12328.

———. "Tracing Slavery: An Ethnography of Diaspora, Affect, and Cultural Heritage in Amsterdam." PhD dissertation, Vrije Universiteit, 2014.

Balkenhol, Markus, and Katharina Schramm. "Doing Race in Europe: Contested Pasts and Contemporary Practices." *Social Anthropology* 27, no. 4 (November 2019): 585–93. https://doi.org/10.1111/1469-8676.12721.

Ballinger, Pamela. *History in Exile: Memory and Identity at the Borders of the Balkans.* Princeton, NJ: Princeton University Press, 2003.

Bandak, Andreas, and Tom Boylston. "The 'Orthodoxy' of Orthodoxy: On Moral Imperfection, Correctness, and Deferral in Religious Worlds." *Religion and Society* 5, no. 1 (January 1, 2014). https://doi.org/10.3167/arrs.2014.050103.

Barnard, Anne. "Isis Onslaught Engulfs Assyrian Christians as Militants Destroy Ancient Art." *New York Times*, February 26, 2015. http://www.nytimes.com/2015/02/27/world/middleeast/more-assyrian-christians-captured-as-isis-attacks-villages-in-syria.html.

Bar-Sawme, Gabriel. "Entering the Holy Place in Syriac Orthodox Liturgy: A Ritual and Theological Analysis." PhD dissertation, Uppsala University, 2021.

Barsoum, Mor Ignatius Ephrem I. *The Syrian Church of Antioch: Its Name and History.* Glane, the Netherlands: Mor Ephrem Monastery, 1983.

Becker, Adam H. *Revival and Awakening: American Evangelical Missionaries in Iran and the Origins of Assyrian Nationalism.* Chicago: University of Chicago Press, 2015.

Begbie, Jeremy. *Music, Modernity, and God: Essays in Listening.* 1st ed. Oxford: Oxford University Press, 2013.

————. *Theology, Music and Time*. Repr. Cambridge Studies in Christian Doctrine 4. Cambridge: Cambridge University Press, 2008.

Benjamen, Alda. *Assyrians in Modern Iraq: Negotiating Political and Cultural Space*. 1st ed. Cambridge: Cambridge University Press, 2021.

Benjamin, Walter. "The Work of Art in the Age of Mechanical Reproduction." In *Illuminations*, edited by Hannah Arendt, translated by Harry Zohn. New York: Harcourt, Brace, and World, 1968.

Berger, Peter L. *The Many Altars of Modernity: Toward a Paradigm for Religion in a Pluralist Age*. Boston Berlin: De Gruyter, 2014.

————. *The Sacred Canopy: Elements of a Sociological Theory of Religion*. New York: Anchor Books, 1990.

Berger, Teresa. *Gender Differences and the Making of Liturgical History: Lifting a Veil on Liturgy's Past*. Liturgy, Worship, and Society. Farnham: Ashgate, 2011.

Berlin, Isaiah. *Against the Current: Essays in the History of Ideas*. Edited by Henry Hardy. 2nd ed. Princeton, NJ: Princeton University Press, 2013.

————. *Vico and Herder: Two Studies in the History of Ideas*. New York: Viking, 1976.

Berzon, Todd S. *Classifying Christians: Ethnography, Heresiology, and the Limits of Knowledge in Late Antiquity*. Oakland: University of California Press, 2016.

Bet-Shlimon, Arbella. *City of Black Gold: Oil, Ethnicity, and the Making of Modern Kirkuk*. Stanford, CA: Stanford University Press, 2019.

Bialecki, Jon. "Religion after Religion, 'Ritual' after Ritual." In *The Routledge Companion to Contemporary Anthropology*. London: Routledge, 2017.

Biesen, Kees den. *Simple and Bold: Ephrem's Art of Symbolic Thought*. Repr. from the 2006 Gorgias Press ed. *Gorgias Dissertations Early Christian Studies* 26, no. 6. Piscataway, NJ: Gorgias Press, 2014.

Björklund, Ulf. *North to Another Country: The Formation of a Suryoyo Community in Sweden*. Stockholm Studies in Social Anthropology 9. Stockholm: Dept. of Social Anthropology, University of Stockholm, 1981.

Blom, J. C. H., and J. Talsma, eds. *De Verzuiling Voorbij: Godsdienst, Stand En Natie in de Lange Negentiende Eeuw*. Amsterdam: Het Spinhuis, 2000.

Boehmer, Elleke, and Sarah de Mul, eds. *The Postcolonial Low Countries: Literature, Colonialism, and Multiculturalism*. Lanham, MD: Lexington Books, 2012.

Borneman, John. *Belonging in the Two Berlins: Kin, State, Nation*. Cambridge Studies in Social and Cultural Anthropology 86. New York: Cambridge University Press, 1992.

Bowen, John R. *Why the French Don't like Headscarves: Islam, the State, and Public Space*. Princeton, NJ: Princeton University Press, 2007.

Boylston, Tom. *The Stranger at the Feast: Prohibition and Mediation in an Ethiopian Orthodox Christian Community.* Oakland, CA: University of California Press, 2018.

Bracke, Sarah. "Transformations of the Secular and the 'Muslim Question.' Revisiting the Historical Coincidence of Depillarisation and the Institutionalisation of Islam in the Netherlands." *Journal of Muslims in Europe* 2, no. 2 (2013): 208–26. https://doi.org/10.1163/22117954-12341264.

Bradshaw, Paul F. *The Search for the Origins of Christian Worship: Sources and Methods for the Study of Early Liturgy.* 2nd edition. Oxford: Oxford University Press, 2002.

Brahinsky, Josh. "Pentecostal Body Logics: Cultivating a Modern Sensorium." *Cultural Anthropology* 27, no. 2 (May 2012): 215–38. https://doi.org/10.1111/j .1548-1360.2012.01141.x.

Bridges, Khiara M. *Reproducing Race: An Ethnography of Pregnancy as a Site of Racialization.* Berkeley: University of California Press, 2011.

Briggs, Charles L. "The Politics of Discursive Authority in Research on the 'Invention of Tradition.'" *Cultural Anthropology* 11, no. 4 (November 1996): 435–69. https://doi.org/10.1525/can.1996.11.4.02a00020.

Brink, G. J. M. van den. *Schets van Een Beschavingsoffensief: Over Normen, Normaliteit En Normalisatie in Nederland.* WRR Verkenningen 3. Amsterdam: Amsterdam University Press, 2004.

Brock, Sebastian. "The Holy Spirit as Feminine in Early Syriac Literature." In *After Eve*, edited by Janet Martin Soskice. Basingstoke, UK: Collins Marshall Pickering, 1990.

———. *The Luminous Eye: The Spiritual World Vision of Saint Ephrem.* Rev. ed. Cistercian Studies Series, no. 124. Kalamazoo, MI: Cistercian Publications, 1992.

Brown, Peter. *The Body and Society: Men, Women, and Sexual Renunciation in Early Christianity.* Lectures on the History of Religions, new ser., no. 13. 1988. Reprint, New York: Columbia University Press, 2008.

Bryant, Rebecca. "The Soul Danced into the Body: Nation and Improvization in Istanbul." *American Ethnologist* 32, no. 2 (2005): 222–38.

Buell, Denise Kimber. *Why This New Race: Ethnic Reasoning in Early Christianity.* Gender, Theory, and Religion. New York: Columbia University Press, 2005.

Bull, Michael, and Les Back, eds. *The Auditory Culture Reader.* Paperback ed., Reprinted. Sensory Formations Series. Oxford: Berg, 2006.

Butler, Judith. 2006. *Gender Trouble: Feminism and the Subversion of Identity.* New York: Routledge.

Butts, Aaron Michael, and Simcha Gross, eds. *Jews and Syriac Christians: Intersections across the First Millenium.* Texts and Studies in Ancient Judaism,

Texte Und Studien Zum Antiken Judentum, 180. Tübingen: Mohr Siebeck, 2020.

Bynum, Caroline Walker. *Wonderful Blood: Theology and Practice in Late Medieval Northern Germany and Beyond*. The Middle Ages Series. Philadelphia: University of Pennsylvania Press, 2007.

Calder, Mark D. *Bethlehem's Syriac Christians: Self, Nation, and Church in Dialogue and Practice*. The Modern Muslim World 4. Piscataway, NJ: Gorgias Press, 2017.

———. "Syrian Identity in Bethlehem: From Ethnoreligion to Ecclesiology." *Iran and the Caucasus* 20, nos. 3–4 (December 19, 2016): 297–323. https://doi.org/10.1163/1573384X-20160304.

Caldwell, Melissa L. *Living Faithfully in an Unjust World: Compassionate Care in Russia*. Oakland, CA: University of California Press, 2017.

———. *Not by Bread Alone: Social Support in the New Russia*. Berkeley: University of California Press, 2004.

Campbell, Elizabeth, and Luke E. Lassiter. *Doing Ethnography Today: Theories, Methods, Exercises*. Malden, MA: Wiley-Blackwell, 2014.

Cannell, Fenella, ed. *The Anthropology of Christianity*. Durham, NC: Duke University Press, 2006.

———. "The Christianity of Anthropology." *Journal of the Royal Anthropological Institute* 11, no. 2 (June 2005): 335–56. https://doi.org/10.1111/j.1467-9655.2005.00239.x.

Caputo, John D. *The Prayers and Tears of Jacques Derrida: Religion without Religion*. Indiana Series in the Philosophy of Religion. Bloomington: Indiana University Press, 2006.

Certeau, Michel de. *The Mystic Fable. Vol. 1: The Sixteenth and Seventeenth Centuries/Michel de Certeau*. Translated by Michael B. Smith. Paperback ed. Vol. 1. Religion and Postmodernism. Chicago: University of Chicago Press, 1995.

Cetrez, Önver. "The Next Generation of Assyrians in Sweden: Religiosity as Functioning System of Meaning within the Process of Acculturation." *Mental Health, Religion, and Culture* 14, no. 5 (2011): 473–87.

Chaillot, Christine. *The Role of Images and the Veneration of Icons in the Oriental Orthodox Churches: Syrian Orthodox, Armenian, Coptic, and Ethiopian Traditions*. Studien Zur Orientalischen Kirchengeschichte, Band 55. Zürich: Lit, 2018.

Chatty, Dawn. *Displacement and Dispossession in the Modern Middle East*. The Contemporary Middle East 5. New York: Cambridge University Press, 2010.

Clements, Henry. "Documenting Community in the Late Ottoman Empire." *International Journal of Middle East Studies* 51, no. 3 (August 2019): 423–43. https://doi.org/10.1017/S0020743819000369.

Coenders, Yannick, and Sébastien Chauvin. "Race and the Pitfalls of Emotional Democracy: Primary Schools and the Critique of Black Pete in the Netherlands: Race and the Pitfalls of Emotional Democracy." *Antipode* 49, no. 5 (November 2017): 1244–62. https://doi.org/10.1111/anti.12328.

Coleman, Simon. "Materializing the Self: Words and Gifts in the Construction of Charismatic Protestant Identity." In *The Anthropology of Christianity*, edited by Fenella Cannell. Durham, NC: Duke University Press, 2006.

Connolly, William E. *Why I Am Not a Secularist*. Minneapolis: University of Minnesota Press, 1999.

Dağtaş, Seçil. "The Civilizations Choir of Antakya: The Politics of Religious Tolerance and Minority Representation at the National Margins of Turkey." *Cultural Anthropology* 35, no. 1 (February 13, 2020). https://doi.org/10.14506/ca35.1.11.

Das, Veena. "Ordinary Ethics." In *A Companion to Moral Anthropology*, edited by Didier Fassin, 133–49. Malden, MA: Wiley-Blackwell, 2012.

Davis, Dána-Ain. *Reproductive Injustice: Racism, Pregnancy, and Premature Birth*. Anthropologies of American Medicine: Culture, Power, and Practice. New York: New York University Press, 2019.

De Koning, Martijn. "'You Need to Present a Counter-Message': The Racialisation of Dutch Muslims and Anti-Islamophobia Initiatives." *Journal of Muslims in Europe* 5, no. 2 (October 28, 2016): 170–89. https://doi.org/10.1163/22117954-12341325.

Derrida, Jacques, and Jacques Derrida. *The Gift of Death*, 2nd ed. and *Literature in Secret*. Religion and Postmodernism. Chicago: University of Chicago Press, 2008.

Donabed, Sargon. *Reforging a Forgotten History: Iraq and the Assyrians in the Twentieth Century*. Edinburgh: Edinburgh University Press, 2015.

———. "Rethinking Nationalism and an Appellative Conundrum: Historiography and Politics in Iraq." *National Identities* 14, no. 4 (December 2012): 407–31. https://doi.org/10.1080/14608944.2012.733208.

Donabed, Sargon George, and Shamiran Mako. "Ethno-Cultural and Religious Identity of Syrian Orthodox Christians." *Chronos* 19 (April 11, 2019): 71–113. https://doi.org/10.31377/chr.v19i0.457.

Durkheim, Émile. *The Division of Labor in Society*. 13. Translated by Wilfred D. Halls. New York: Free Press, 2008.

———. *The Elementary Forms of Religious Life*. Translated by Carol Cosman. Oxford World's Classics. Oxford University Press, 2001 [1912].

Duyvendak, Jan Willem, Peter Geschiere, and Evelien H. Tonkens, eds. *The Culturalization of Citizenship: Belonging and Polarization in a Globalizing World*. London: Palgrave Macmillan, 2016.

Eisenlohr, Patrick. "The Anthropology of Media and the Question of Ethnic and Religious Pluralism." *Social Anthropology* 19, no. 1 (February 2011): 40–55. https://doi.org/10.1111/j.1469-8676.2010.00136.x.

———. "As Makkah Is Sweet and Beloved, So Is Madina: Islam, Devotional Genres, and Electronic Mediation in Mauritius." *American Ethnologist* 33, no. 2 (May 2006): 230–45. https://doi.org/10.1525/ae.2006.33.2.230.

———. *Sounding Islam: Voice, Media, and Sonic Atmospheres in an Indian Ocean World*. Oakland: University of California Press, 2018.

———. "Technologies of the Spirit: Devotional Islam, Sound Reproduction and the Dialectics of Mediation and Immediacy in Mauritius." *Anthropological Theory* 9, no. 3 (September 2009): 273–96. https://doi.org/10.1177/1463499609346983.

Engelhardt, Jeffers. "Right Singing in Estonian Orthodox Christianity: A Study of Music, Theology, and Religious Ideology." *Ethnomusicology* 53, no. 1 (January 1, 2009): 32–57. https://doi.org/10.2307/25653046.

———. *Singing the Right Way: Orthodox Christians and Secular Enchantment in Estonia*. Oxford: Oxford University Press, 2015.

Engelke, Matthew. "Angels in Swindon: Public Religion and Ambient Faith in England." *American Ethnologist* 39, no. 1 (February 2012): 155–70. https://doi.org/10.1111/j.1548-1425.2011.01355.x.

Ephrem. *The Harp of the Spirit: Poems of Saint Ephrem the Syrian*. Introduction and translation by Sebastian P. Brock. 3rd enlarged edition. Cambridge: Aquila Books; The Institute for Orthodox Christian Studies, 2013.

———. *Hymns on Paradise*. Introduction and translation by Sebastian Brock, 240. Popular Patristics. Crestwood, NJ: St. Vladimir's Seminary Press, 1990.

Erlmann, Veit, ed. *Hearing Cultures: Essays on Sound, Listening, and Modernity*. Wenner-Gren International Symposium Series. Oxford: Berg, 2004.

Erol, Su. "The Syriacs of Turkey: A Religious Community on the Path of Recognition." *Archives de Sciences Sociales des Religions*, no. 171 (September 1, 2015): 59–80. https://doi.org/10.4000/assr.27027.

Essed, Philomena, and Sandra Trienekens. "'Who Wants to Feel White?' Race, Dutch Culture, and Contested Identities." *Ethnic and Racial Studies* 31, no. 1 (January 2008): 52–72. https://doi.org/10.1080/01419870701538885.

Falu, Nessette. "Lèsbicas Negras' Ethics and the Scales of Racialized Sexual Recognitions in Gynecology and Public Discourses in Salvador-Bahia." PhD dissertation, Rice University, 2014.

———. *Unseen Flesh: Gynecology and Black Queer Worth-Making in Brazil*. Durham, NC: Duke University Press, 2023.

Fanon, Frantz. *Black Skin, White Masks*. Translated by Richard Philcox. New York: Grove Press, 1952.

Farag, Lois. "Review of Missionary Stories and the Formation of the Syriac Churches, by Jeanne-Nicole Mellon Saint-Laurent." *Journal of Early Christian Studies* 25, no. 2 (2017): 329–30.

Farman, Abou. "Speculative Matter: Secular Bodies, Minds, and Persons." *Cultural Anthropology* 28, no. 4 (November 2013): 737–59. https://doi.org/10.1111/cuan.12035.

Faubion, James D. *An Anthropology of Ethics*. New Departures in Anthropology. Cambridge: Cambridge University Press, 2011.

Feld, Steven. *Sound and Sentiment: Birds, Weeping, Poetics, and Song in Kaluli Expression*. 3rd ed.; 30th anniversary ed. with a new introduction. Durham, NC: Duke University Press, 2012.

Feld, Steven, and Donald Brenneis. "Doing Anthropology in Sound." *American Ethnologist* 31, no. 4 (November 2004): 461–74. https://doi.org/10.1525/ae.2004.31.4.461.

Ferguson, Everett. "Sacraments in the Pre-Nicene Era." In *The Oxford Handbook of Sacramental Theology*, edited by Hans Boersma and Matthew Levering. Oxford: Oxford University Press, 2015.

Fernando, Mayanthi L. "Belief and/in the Law." *Method and Theory in the Study of Religion* 24, no. 1 (2012): 71–80. https://doi.org/10.1163/157006812X634520.

———. "Intimacy Surveilled: Religion, Sex, and Secular Cunning." *Signs: Journal of Women in Culture and Society* 39, no. 3 (March 2014): 685–708. https://doi.org/10.1086/674207.

Fessenden, Tracy. *Culture and Redemption: Religion, the Secular, and American Literature*. Princeton, NJ: Princeton University Press, 2007.

Foucault, Michel, Michel Senellart, François Ewald, and Alessandro Fontana. *Security, Territory, Population: Lectures at the Collège de France, 1977–1978*. New York: Palgrave Macmillan, 2007.

Fox, Aaron A. *Real Country: Music and Language in Working-Class Culture*. Durham, NC: Duke University Press, 2004.

Freeman, Elizabeth. *Time Binds: Queer Temporalities, Queer Histories*. Perverse Modernities. Durham, NC: Duke University Press, 2010.

Gal, Susan. "Between Speech and Silence: The Problematics of Research on Language and Gender." In *Gender at the Crossroads of Knowledge: Feminist Anthropology in the Postmodern Era*, edited by Micaela di Leonardo, 175–203. Berkeley: University of California, 1991.

Garriott, William, and Kevin Lewis O'Neill. "Who Is a Christian?: Toward a Dialogic Approach in the Anthropology of Christianity." *Anthropological Theory* 8, no. 4 (December 2008): 381–98. https://doi.org/10.1177/1463499608096645.

Gauchet, Marcel. *The Disenchantment of the World: A Political History of Religion.* New French Thought. Princeton, NJ: Princeton University Press, 1997.

Gaunt, David, Naures Atto, and Soner O. Barthoma, eds. *Let Them Not Return. Sayfo: The Genocide against the Assyrian, Syriac and Chaldean Christians in the Ottoman Empire.* War and Genocide, vol. 26. New York: Berghahn, 2017.

Geschiere, Peter. *The Perils of Belonging: Autochthony, Citizenship, and Exclusion in Africa and Europe.* Chicago: University of Chicago Press, 2009.

Geschiere, Peter, and Stephen Jackson. "Autochthony and the Crisis of Citizenship: Democratization, Decentralization, and the Politics of Belonging." *African Studies Review* 49, no. 2 (September 2006): 1–8. https://doi.org/10.1353/arw.2006.0104.

Ghorashi, Halleh. "From Absolute Invisibility to Extreme Visibility: Emancipation Trajectory of Migrant Women in the Netherlands." *Feminist Review* 94, no. 1 (March 2010): 75–92. https://doi.org/10.1057/fr.2009.38.

Ghorashi, Halleh, and Maria Van Tilburg. "'When Is My Dutch Good Enough?' Experiences of Refugee Women with Dutch Labour Organizations." *Journal of International Migration and Integration/Revue de l'integration et de La Migration Internationale* 7, no. 1 (December 2006): 51–70. https://doi.org/10.1007/s12134-006-1002-4.

Göle, Nilufer. "The Civilizational, Spatial, and Sexual Powers of the Secular." In *Varieties of Secularism in a Secular Age,* edited by Michael Warner, Jonathan VanAntwerpen, and Craig Calhoun. Cambridge, MA: Harvard University Press, 2010.

Green, Ben. "Nestorius and Cyril: Fifth-Century Christological Division and Recent Progress in Reconciliation." *Concept* 28 (2004).

Griffith, Sidney Harrison. *The Church in the Shadow of the Mosque: Christians and Muslims in the World of Islam.* Jews, Christians, and Muslims from the Ancient to the Modern World. Princeton, NJ: Princeton University Press, 2008.

Griffith, Sydney. "'Singles' in God's Service: Thoughts on the Ihidaye from the Works of Aphrahat and Ephraem the Syrian." *The Harp* 4, nos. 1–3 (1991): 145–59.

Haar Romeny, R. B. ter, ed. *Religious Origins of Nations? The Christian Communities of the Middle East.* Leiden: Brill, 2010.

Haeri, Niloofar. "Unbundling Sincerity: Language, Mediation, and Interiority in Comparative Perspective." *HAU: Journal of Ethnographic Theory* 7, no. 1 (March 2017): 123–38. https://doi.org/10.14318/hau7.1.013.

Hage, Ghassan. "The Affective Politics of Racial Mis-Interpellation." *Theory, Culture and Society* 27, nos. 7–8 (December 2010): 112–29. https://doi.org/10.1177/0263276410383713.

Hager, Anna. "When Ephrem Meets the Maya: Defining and Adapting the Syriac Orthodox Tradition in Guatemala." *Hugoye: Journal of Syriac Studies*

23, no. 1 (January 1, 2020): 215–62. https://doi.org/10.31826/hug-2020 -230108.

Hainthaler, Theresia. "Theological Doctrines and Debates within Syriac Christianity." In *The Syriac World*, edited by Daniel King. London: Routledge, 2019.

Hall, David W., and Peter A. Lillback. *A Theological Guide to Calvin's Institutes.* Phillipsburg, NJ: P and R Publishing, 2008.

Handler, Richard, and Jocelyn Linnekin. "Tradition, Genuine, or Spurious." *The Journal of American Folklore* 97, no. 385 (July 1984): 273. https://doi.org /10.2307/540610.

Hanish, Shak. "The Chaldean Assyrian Syriac People of Iraq: An Ethnic Identity Problem." *Digest of Middle East Studies* 17, no. 1 (April 2008): 32–47. https://doi.org/10.1111/j.1949-3606.2008.tb00145.x.

Hann, Chris, and Hermann Goltz, eds. *Eastern Christians in Anthropological Perspective: A Conference at the Max Planck Institute for Social Anthropology, Halle/Saale in September 2005.* The Anthropology of Christianity 9. Berkeley: University of California Press, 2010.

Hanoosh, Yasmeen S. *The Chaldeans: Politics and Identity in Iraq and the American Diaspora.* Library of Modern Middle East Studies. London: I. B. Tauris, 2019.

Harding, Susan Friend. *The Book of Jerry Falwell: Fundamentalist Language and Politics.* Princeton, NJ: Princeton University Press, 2000.

Harkness, Nicholas. *Songs of Seoul: An Ethnography of Voice and Voicing in Christian South Korea.* Berkeley: University of California Press, 2014.

Hayden, Corinne P. "Gender, Genetics, and Generation: Reformulating Biology in Lesbian Kinship." *Cultural Anthropology* 10, no. 1 (February 1995): 41–63. https://doi.org/10.1525/can.1995.10.1.02a00020.

Heo, Angie. *The Political Lives of Saints: Christian-Muslim Mediation in Egypt.* Oakland: University of California Press, 2018.

Heron, Nicholas. *Liturgical Power: Between Economic and Political Theology.* 1st ed. Commonalities. New York: Fordham University Press, 2018.

Herzfeld, Michael. *The Body Impolitic: Artisans and Artifice in the Global Hierarchy of Value.* Chicago: University of Chicago Press, 2004.

———. *Ours Once More: Folklore, Ideology, and the Making of Modern Greece.* 1st ed. The Dan Danciger Publication Series. Austin: University of Texas Press, 1982.

———. *A Place in History: Social and Monumental Time in a Cretan Town.* Princeton Studies in Culture/Power/History. Princeton, NJ: Princeton University Press, 1991.

Hirschfeld, Gerhard. *Nazi Rule and Dutch Collaboration: The Netherlands under German Occupation, 1940–1945.* Oxford: Berg, 1988.

Hirschkind, Charles. *The Ethical Soundscape: Cassette Sermons and Islamic Counterpublics*. Cultures of History. New York: Columbia University Press, 2006.

———. "The Ethics of Listening: Cassette-Sermon Audition in Contemporary Egypt." *American Ethnologist* 28, no. 3 (August 2001): 623–49. https://doi.org/10.1525/ae.2001.28.3.623.

———. *The Feeling of History: Islam, Romanticism, and Andalusia*. Chicago: University of Chicago Press, 2021.

———. "Is There a Secular Body?" *Cultural Anthropology* 26, no. 4 (November 2011): 633–47. https://doi.org/10.1111/j.1548-1360.2011.01116.x.

Hobsbawm, E. J., and T. O. Ranger, eds. *The Invention of Tradition*. Past and Present Publications. Cambridge: Cambridge University Press, 1983.

Hollywood, Amy. "Love Speaks Here: Michel de Certeau's *Mystic Fable*." *Spiritus: A Journal of Christian Spirituality* 12, no. 2 (2012): 198–206. https://doi.org/10.1353/scs.2012.0047.

Holmes, Douglas R. *Integral Europe: Fast-Capitalism, Multiculturalism, Neofascism*. Princeton, NJ: Princeton University Press, 2000.

Holquist, Michael. *Dialogism: Bakhtin and His World*. 2nd ed. New Accents. London: Routledge, 2002.

Houkes, Annemarie. *Christelijke Vaderlanders: Godsdienst, Burgerschap En de Nederlandse Natie (1850–1900)*. Amsterdam: Wereldbibliotheek, 2009.

Hughes, Graham. *Worship as Meaning: A Liturgical Theology for Late Modernity*. Cambridge: Cambridge University Press, 2003.

Husain, Atiya. "Retrieving the Religion in Racialization: A Critical Review." *Sociology Compass* 11, no. 9 (September 2017): e12507. https://doi.org/10.1111/soc4.12507.

Ignatius III, Yacoub. *History of the Syrian Church of Antioch: Tarīkh al-Kanīsa Āl-Suryāniyya al-Antākiyya*. Piscataway, NJ: Gorgias Press, 2010. https://doi.org/10.31826/9781463228644.

Jacobs, Sue-Ellen, Wesley Thomas, and Sabine Lang, eds. *Two-Spirit People: Native American Gender Identity, Sexuality, and Spirituality*. Urbana: University of Illinois Press, 1997.

Jacobsen-Bia, Kristina. "Radmilla's Voice: Music Genre, Blood Quantum, and Belonging on the Navajo Nation." *Cultural Anthropology* 29, no. 2 (May 19, 2014): 385–410. https://doi.org/10.14506/ca29.2.11.

Jakobsen, Janet R., and Ann Pellegrini, eds. *Secularisms*. Social Text Books. Durham, NC: Duke University Press, 2008.

Jarjour, Tala. *Sense and Sadness: Syriac Chant in Aleppo*. New York: Oxford University Press, 2018.

Jennings, Willie James. *The Christian Imagination: Theology and the Origins of Race*. New Haven, CT: Yale University Press, 2010.

Johnson, Aaron P., and Jeremy M. Schott, eds. *Eusebius of Caesarea: Tradition and Innovations.* Hellenic Studies 60. Washington, DC: Center for Hellenic Studies, 2013.

Kapchan, Deborah A. "The Promise of Sonic Translation: Performing the Festive Sacred in Morocco." *American Anthropologist* 110, no. 4 (December 2008): 467–83. https://doi.org/10.1111/j.1548-1433.2008.00079.x.

Kathanar Koonammakkal, Thomas. "Ephrem's Ideas on Singleness." *Hugoye: Journal of Syriac Studies* 2, no. 1 (February 1, 2010): 57–66. https://doi.org/10.31826/hug-2010-020107.

Keane, Webb. "Anxious Transcendence." In *The Anthropology of Christianity,* edited by Fenella Cannell. Durham, NC: Duke University Press, 2006.

———. *Christian Moderns: Freedom and Fetish in the Mission Encounter.* The Anthropology of Christianity 1. Berkeley: University of California Press, 2007.

———. "The Evidence of the Senses and the Materiality of Religion." *Journal of the Royal Anthropological Institute* 14, no. s1 (April 2008): S110–27. https://doi.org/10.1111/j.1467-9655.2008.00496.x.

———. "On Semiotic Ideology." *Signs and Society* 6, no. 1 (January 2018): 64–87. https://doi.org/10.1086/695387.

———. "Sincerity, 'Modernity,' and the Protestants." *Cultural Anthropology* 17, no. 1 (February 2002): 65–92.

Keil, Charles, Dick Blau, Angeliki V. Keil, and Steven Feld. *Bright Balkan Morning: Romani Lives and the Power of Music in Greek Macedonia.* Middletown, CT: Wesleyan University Press, 2002.

Keil, Charles, and Steven Feld. *Music Grooves: Essays and Dialogues.* 2nd ed. Tucson, AZ: Fenestra, 2005.

Kennedy, James. "Building New Babylon: Cultural Change in the Netherlands during the 1960s." PhD dissertation, University of Iowa, 1995.

Khan, Aisha. *Callaloo Nation: Metaphors of Race and Religious Identity among South Asians in Trinidad.* Latin America Otherwise. Durham, NC: Duke University Press, 2004.

King, Daniel, ed. *The Syriac World.* 1st ed. New York: Routledge, 2019. https://doi.org/10.4324/9781315708195.

Kiraz, George. *The Syriac Orthodox in North America (1895–1995): A Short History.* Piscataway, NJ: Gorgias Press, 2019.

Knippenberg, Hans. "Assimilating Jews in Dutch Nation-Building: The Missing 'Pillar.'" *Tijdschrift Voor Economische En Sociale Geografie* 93, no. 2 (May 2002): 191–207. https://doi.org/10.1111/1467-9663.00194.

Koltun-Fromm, Naomi. *Hermeneutics of Holiness: Ancient Jewish and Christian Notions of Sexuality and Religious Community.* New York: Oxford University Press, 2010.

Kuyper, Abraham. *Calvinism: Six Stone Foundation Lectures*. Grand Rapids, MI: Eerdmans, 1943.

Laarse, Rob van der. "De Deugd En Het Kwaad: Liberalisme, Conservatisme, En de Erfenis van de Verlichting." In *De Verzuiling Voorbij: Godsdienst, Stand En Natie in de Lange Negentiende Eeuw*, edited by J. C. H. Blom and Talsma. Amsterdam: Spinhuis, 2000.

Lambek, Michael, ed. *Ordinary Ethics: Anthropology, Language, and Action*. 1st ed. New York: Fordham University Press, 2010.

Lambek, Michael, Veena Das, Didier Fassin, and Webb Keane. *Four Lectures on Ethics: Anthropological Perspectives*. Masterclass Series, vol. 3. Chicago: Hau Books, 2015.

Latour, Bruno. *We Have Never Been Modern*. 5th pr. Harlow, Essex: Pearson Education, 2000.

Lebner, Ashley. "On Secularity: Marxism, Reality, and the Messiah in Brazil." *Journal of the Royal Anthropological Institute* 25, no. 1 (March 2019): 123–47. https://doi.org/10.1111/1467-9655.13000.

———. "The Work of Impossibility in Brazil: Friendship, Kinship, Secularity." *Current Anthropology* 62, no. 4 (August 1, 2021): 452–83. https://doi.org/10.1086/716466.

Lechner, Frank. "Managing Others: Minorities Policy and National Identity in the Netherlands." In *Halle Institute Occasional Paper*. Emory, Atlanta: Claus M. Halle Institute for Global Learning, 1999.

Lechner, Frank J. *The Netherlands: Globalization and National Identity*. Globalizing Regions. London: Routledge, 2008.

Linke, Uli. *Blood and Nation: The European Aesthetics of Race*. Contemporary Ethnography. Philadelphia: University of Pennsylvania Press, 1999.

Locke, John. *Two Treatises of Government and a Letter Concerning Toleration*. Rethinking the Western Tradition, edited by Ian Shapiro. New Haven, CT: Yale University Press, 2003.

Loosley, Emma. "After the Ottomans: The Renewal of the Syrian Orthodox Church in the Twentieth and Twenty-First Centuries." *Studies in World Christianity* 15, no. 3 (December 2009): 236–47. https://doi.org/10.3366/E1354990109000598.

Luehrmann, Sonja, ed. *Praying with the Senses: Contemporary Orthodox Christian Spirituality in Practice*. Bloomington: Indiana University Press, 2018.

Lukasik, Candace. "Economy of Blood: The Persecuted Church and the Racialization of American Copts." *American Anthropologist* 123, no. 3 (September 2021): 565–77. https://doi.org/10.1111/aman.13602.

———. "Postcolonial Solidarities: Oriental Orthodox Kinship in an Age of Migration." *Journal of Ecumenical Studies* 55, no. 4 (2020): 484–517. https://doi.org/10.1353/ecu.2020.0043.

Mack, Jennifer. *The Construction of Equality: Syriac Immigration and the Swedish City*. Minneapolis: University of Minnesota Press, 2017.

Macpherson, C. B.. *The Political Theory of Possessive Individualism: Hobbes to Locke*, with introduction by Frank Cunningham. Wynford edition. The Wynford Project. 1964. Reprint, Don Mills, ON: Oxford University Press, 2011.

Mahmood, Saba. "Feminist Theory, Embodiment, and the Docile Agent: Some Reflections on the Egyptian Islamic Revival." *Cultural Anthropology* 16, no. 2 (May 2001): 202–36. https://doi.org/10.1525/can.2001.16.2.202.

———. *Politics of Piety: The Islamic Revival and the Feminist Subject*. Princeton, NJ: Princeton University Press, 2005.

———. *Religious Difference in a Secular Age: A Minority Report*. Princeton, NJ: Princeton University Press, 2016.

———. "Religious Freedom, the Minority Question, and Geopolitics in the Middle East." *Comparative Studies in Society and History* 54, no. 2 (April 2012): 418–46.

Makdisi, Ussama Samir. *Age of Coexistence: The Ecumenical Frame and the Making of the Modern Arab World*. Oakland: University of California Press, 2019.

Makko, Aryo. "The Historical Roots of Contemporary Controversies: National Revival and the Assyrian 'Concept of Unity.'" *The Journal of Assyrian Academic Studies* 24, no. 1 (2010): 1–29.

Malara, Diego Maria. "Exorcizing the Spirit of Protestantism: Ambiguity and Spirit Possession in an Ethiopian Orthodox Ritual." *Ethnos* 87, no. 4 (August 8, 2022): 749–70. https://doi.org/10.1080/00141844.2019.1631871.

Malinowski, Bronislaw. *Argonauts of the Western Pacific: An Account of Native Enterprise and Adventure in the Archipelagos of Melanesian New Guinea*. Routledge Classics. London: Routledge, 2014.

Markell, Patchen. *Bound by Recognition*. Princeton, NJ: Princeton University Press, 2003.

Martínez, María Elena. *Genealogical Fictions: Limpieza de Sangre, Religion, and Gender in Colonial Mexico*. Stanford, CA: Stanford University Press, 2008.

Masters, Bruce Alan. *Christians and Jews in the Ottoman Arab World: The Roots of Sectarianism*. Cambridge Studies in Islamic Civilization. New York: Cambridge University Press, 2001.

Masuzawa, Tomoko. *The Invention of World Religions; or, How European Universalism Was Preserved in the Language of Pluralism*. Chicago: University of Chicago Press, 2005.

Mattingly, Cheryl, and Jason Throop. "The Anthropology of Ethics and Morality." *Annual Review of Anthropology* 47 (2018): 475–92.

Mauss, Marcel. "A Category of the Human Mind: The Notion of Person; the Notion of Self." In *The Category of the Person: Anthropology, Philosophy, History*, edited by Michael Carrithers, Steven Collins, and Steven Lukes. Cambridge: Cambridge University Press, 1985.

Mayblin, Maya. "The Untold Sacrifice: The Monotony and Incompleteness of Self-Sacrifice in Northeast Brazil." *Ethnos* 79, no. 3 (May 27, 2014): 342–64. https://doi.org/10.1080/00141844.2013.821513.

McAllister, Carlota, and Valentina Napolitano. "Introduction: Incarnate Politics beyond the Cross and the Sword." *Social Analysis* 64, no. 4 (December 1, 2020): 1–20. https://doi.org/10.3167/sa.2020.640401.

———. "Political Theology/Theopolitics: The Thresholds and Vulnerabilities of Sovereignty." *Annual Review of Anthropology* 50, no. 1 (October 21, 2021): 109–24. https://doi.org/10.1146/annurev-anthro-101819-110334.

McCarthy, Justin. *The Ottoman Peoples and the End of Empire*. Historical Endings. London: St. Martin's Press, 2001.

McCullough, W. Stewart. *A Short History of Syriac Christianity to the Rise of Islam*. Scholars Press General Series, no. 4. Chico, CA: Scholars Press, 1982.

McDonald, Charles A. "Rancor: Sephardi Jews, Spanish Citizenship, and the Politics of Sentiment." *Comparative Studies in Society and History* 63, no. 3 (July 2021): 722–51. https://doi.org/10.1017/S0010417521000190.

McGuckin, John. "St. Cyril of Alexandria's Miaphysite Christology and Chalcedonian Dyophysitism." *Ortodoksia* 53 (n.d.): 33–57.

M'Charek, Amade. "On the Materiality of Race in Practice: Beyond Fact or Fiction." *Cultural Anthropology* 28, no. 3 (August 2013): 420–42. https://doi.org/10.1111/cuan.12012.

———. "Silent Witness, Articulate Collective: DNA Evidence and the Inference of Visible Traits." *Bioethics* 22, no. 9 (November 2008): 519–28. https://doi.org/10.1111/j.1467-8519.2008.00699.x.

M'Charek, Amade, Katharina Schramm, and David Skinner. "Technologies of Belonging: The Absent Presence of Race in Europe." *Science, Technology, and Human Values* 39, no. 4 (July 2014): 459–67. https://doi.org/10.1177/0162243914531149.

McNay, Lois. *Against Recognition*. Cambridge: Polity, 2008.

McVey, Kathleen, trans. *Ephrem the Syrian: Hymns*. Mahwah, NK: Paulist Press, 1989.

Mcvey, Kathleen E. "Images of Joy in Ephrem's Hymns on Paradise: Returning to the Womb and the Breast." *Journal of the Canadian Society for Syriac Studies* 3, no. 1 (March 1, 2009): 59–77. https://doi.org/10.31826/jcsss-2009-030106.

Mepschen, Paul, Jan Willem Duyvendak, and Evelien H. Tonkens. "Sexual Politics, Orientalism and Multicultural Citizenship in the Netherlands."

Sociology 44, no. 5 (October 2010): 962–79. https://doi.org/10.1177 /0038038510375740.

Merdjanova, Ina, ed. *Women and Religiosity in Orthodox Christianity.* Orthodox Christianity and Contemporary Thought. New York: Fordham University Press, 2021.

Meyer, Birgit, ed. *Aesthetic Formations: Media, Religion, and the Senses.* 1st ed. Religion/Culture/Critique. New York: Palgrave Macmillan, 2009.

Meyer, Birgit, and Jojada Verrips. "Aesthetics." In *Key Words in Religion, Media, and Culture,* edited by David Morgan. London: Routledge, 2008.

Meyers, Ruth A. "Missional Church, Missional Liturgy." *Theology Today* 67, no. 1 (2010): 36–50.

Milbank, J. "Against Human Rights: Liberty in the Western Tradition." *Oxford Journal of Law and Religion* 1, no. 1 (April 1, 2012): 203–34. https://doi.org /10.1093/ojlr/rwr014.

Millar, Fergus. "The Evolution of the Syrian Orthodox Church in the Pre-Islamic Period: From Greek to Syriac?" *Journal of Early Christian Studies* 21, no. 1 (2013): 43–92. https://doi.org/10.1353/earl.2013.0002.

Miller, J. Reid. *Stain Removal: Ethics and Race.* New York: Oxford University Press, 2017.

Moll, Yasmin. "Television Is Not Radio: Theologies of Mediation in the Egyptian Islamic Revival." *Cultural Anthropology* 33, no. 2 (May 21, 2018): 233–65. https://doi.org/10.14506/ca33.2.07.

Mondzain, Marie-José. *Image, Icon, Economy: The Byzantine Origins of the Contemporary Imaginary.* Cultural Memory in the Present. Stanford, CA: Stanford University Press, 2005.

Morgan, David, ed. *Key Words in Religion, Media, and Culture.* New York: Routledge, 2008.

Mosher, Rhiannon. "Speaking Together: Exploring Discourses of 'Dutchness' in Language Learning, Voluntarism, and Active Citizenship." PhD dissertation, York University, 2016. York Institutional Repository.

Mullings, Leith, and Alaka Wali. *Stress and Resilience: The Social Context of Reproduction in Central Harlem.* New York: Kluwer Academic/Plenum Publishers, 2001.

Murdoch, Iris. *The Sea, the Sea.* Penguin Twentieth-Century Classics. New York: Penguin, 2001.

Murre-van den Berg, Heleen. "Syriac Identity in the Modern Era." In *The Syriac World,* edited by Daniel King. London: Routledge, 2019.

Napolitano, Valentina. "Anthropology and Traces." *Anthropological Theory* 15, no. 1 (March 2015): 47–67. https://doi.org/10.1177/1463499614554239.

Naumescu, Vlad. "Becoming Orthodox: The Mystery and Mastery of a Christian Tradition." In *Praying with the Senses: Contemporary Orthodox*

Christian Spirituality in Practice, edited by Sonja Luehrmann. Bloomington: Indiana University Press, 2018.

———. "Pedagogies of Prayer: Teaching Orthodoxy in South India." *Comparative Studies in Society and History* 61, no. 2 (April 2019): 389–418. https://doi.org/10.1017/S0010417519000094.

Navaro-Yashin, Yael. *Faces of the State: Secularism and Public Life in Turkey*. Princeton, NJ: Princeton University Press, 2002.

Nordin, Magdalena. "Family and the Transmission of Traditions in the Syriac Orthodox Church in Sweden." *Nordic Journal of Religion and Society* 36, no. 1 (June 2023): 19–32.

Oliphant, Elayne. *The Privilege of Being Banal: Art, Secularism, and Catholicism in Paris*. Class 200 New Studies in Religion. Chicago: University of Chicago Press, 2021.

Oni-Orisan, Adeola. "Church and (Re)Birth: Legacies of Christianity for Maternal Care in Nigeria." *Transforming Anthropology* 25, no. 2 (October 2017): 120–29. https://doi.org/10.1111/traa.12099.

Oostindie, Gert. *Postkoloniaal Nederland: Vijfenzestig Jaar Vergeten, Herdenken, Verdringen*. Postkoloniale Geschiedenis in Nederland 3. Amsterdam: Bert Bakker, 2010.

Özdil, Zihni. "'Racism Is an American Problem': Dutch Exceptionalism and the Politics of Denial." *Frame* 27, no. 2 (2014): 49–64.

Özyürek, Esra. *Being German, Becoming Muslim: Race, Religion, and Conversion in the New Europe*. Princeton Studies in Muslim Politics. Princeton, NJ: Princeton University Press, 2015.

———. *Nostalgia for the Modern: State Secularism and Everyday Politics in Turkey*. Politics, History, and Culture. Durham, NC: Duke University Press, 2006.

Palmer, Andrew. "Ephrem of Nisibis." In *The Wiley Blackwell Companion to Patristics*, edited by Ken Parry. Hoboken, NJ: John Wiley and Sons, 2015.

Porcello, Thomas, Louise Meintjes, Ana Maria Ochoa, and David W. Samuels. "The Reorganization of the Sensory World." *Annual Review of Anthropology* 39, no. 1 (October 21, 2010): 51–66. https://doi.org/10.1146/annurev.anthro .012809.105042.

Quataert, Donald. *The Ottoman Empire, 1700–1922*. 2nd ed. New Approaches to European History. Cambridge: Cambridge University Press, 2005.

Qureshi, Regula. "How Does Music Mean? Embodied Memories and the Politics of Affect in the Indian *Sarangi*." *American Ethnologist* 27, no. 4 (November 2000): 805–38. https://doi.org/10.1525/ae.2000.27.4.805.

Ramberg, Lucinda. *Given to the Goddess: South Indian Devadasis and the Sexuality of Religion*. Durham, NC: Duke University Press, 2014. https://doi .org/10.1215/9780822376415.

Rancière, Jacques. *Aesthetics and Its Discontents*. Cambridge: Polity, 2009.

Rappaport, Roy A. *Ritual and Religion in the Making of Humanity.* Cambridge Studies in Social and Cultural Anthropology 110. 1999. Reprint, Cambridge: Cambridge University Press, 2010.

Ratzinger, Joseph (Pope Benedict). *Europe: Today and Tomorrow.* San Francisco: Ignatius, 2007.

Richardson, Tanya. *Kaleidoscopic Odessa: History and Place in Contemporary Ukraine.* Anthropological Horizons. Toronto: University of Toronto Press, 2008.

Robbins, Joel. "Between Reproduction and Freedom: Morality, Value, and Radical Cultural Change." *Ethnos* 72, no. 3 (September 2007): 293–314. https://doi.org/10.1080/00141840701576919.

Roberts, Dorothy E. *Killing the Black Body: Race, Reproduction, and the Meaning of Liberty.* 2nd ed. New York: Vintage, 2017.

Robinson, Andrew. *God and the World of Signs: Trinity, Evolution, and the Metaphysical Semiotics of C.S. Peirce.* Philosophical Studies in Science and Religion, v. 2. Leiden: Brill, 2010.

Robson, Laura, ed. *Minorities and the Modern Arab World: New Perspectives.* 1st ed. Middle East Studies beyond Dominant Paradigms. Syracuse, New York: Syracuse University Press, 2016.

———. *States of Separation: Transfer, Partition, and the Making of the Modern Middle East.* Oakland: University of California Press, 2017.

Rogozen-Soltar, Mikaela H. *Spain Unmoored: Migration, Conversion, and the Politics of Islam.* New Anthropologies of Europe. Bloomington: Indiana University Press, 2017.

Rutherford, Danilyn. "Kinky Empiricism." *Cultural Anthropology* 27, no. 3 (August 2012): 465–79. https://doi.org/10.1111/j.1548-1360.2012.01154.x.

Saint-Laurent, Jeanne-Nicole Mellon. *Missionary Stories and the Formation of the Syriac Churches.* Transformation of the Classical Heritage 55. Oakland: University of California Press, 2015.

Samuels, David W., Louise Meintjes, Ana Maria Ochoa, and Thomas Porcello. "Soundscapes: Toward a Sounded Anthropology." *Annual Review of Anthropology* 39, no. 1 (October 21, 2010): 329–45. https://doi.org/10.1146/annurev-anthro-022510-132230.

Scheer, Monique, Nadia Fadil, and Birgitte Schepelern Johansen, eds. *Secular Bodies, Affects, and Emotions: European Configurations.* New York: Bloomsbury Academic, 2019.

Sahlins, Marshall. *The New Science of the Enchanted Universe: An Anthropology of Most Humanity.* Princeton, NJ: Princeton University Press, 2022.

Schmemann, Alexander. "Theology and Liturgical Tradition." In *Liturgy and Tradition: Theological Reflections of Alexander Schmemann,* edited by Thomas Fisch. Crestwood, NY: St. Vladimir's Seminary Press, 1990.

Schmitt, Carl. *Political Theology: Four Chapters on the Concept of Sovereignty.* Chicago: University of Chicago Press, 2005.

Schmoller, Andreas, ed. *Middle Eastern Christians and Europe: Historical Legacies and Present Challenges.* Orientalia—Patristica—Oecumenica, vol. 13. Wien: Lit, 2018.

Schukkink, A. J. "De Suryoye: Een Verborgen Gemeenschap." PhD Dissertation, Vrije Universiteit, 2003.

Scott, Joan Wallach. *The Politics of the Veil.* The Public Square Book Series. Princeton, NJ: Princeton University Press, 2007.

Sekimoto, Sachi. "Race and the Senses: Toward Articulating the Sensory Apparatus of Race." *Critical Philosophy of Race* 6, no. 1 (January 1, 2018): 82–100. https://doi.org/10.5325/critphilrace.6.1.0082.

Seligman, Adam B. "Ritual, the Self, and Sincerity." *Social Research* 76, no. 4 (2009): 1073–96. https://www.jstor.org/stable/40972203.

Seremetakis, Constantina Nadia, ed. *The Senses Still: Perception and Memory as Material Culture in Modernity.* Chicago: University of Chicago Press, 1996.

Shange, Savannah. *Progressive Dystopia: Abolition, Antiblackness, + Schooling in San Francisco.* Durham, NC: Duke University Press, 2019.

Shannon, Jonathan H. "The Aesthetics of Spiritual Practice and the Creation of Moral and Musical Subjectivities in Aleppo, Syria." *Ethnology* 43, no. 4 (October 1, 2004): 381. https://doi.org/10.2307/3774034.

———. *Among the Jasmine Trees: Music and Modernity in Contemporary Syria.* Music/Culture. Middletown, CT: Wesleyan University Press, 2006.

Sheklian, Christopher. "Theology and the Community: The Armenian Minority, Tradition, and Secularism in Turkey." Chicago: University of Chicago Press, 2017.

Shepherd, Massey H. *The Worship of the Church.* Greenwich, CT: Seabury, 1952.

Starrett, Gregory. "The Varieties of Secular Experience." *Comparative Studies in Society and History* 52, no. 3 (July 2010): 626–51. https://doi.org/10.1017/S0010417510000332.

Stokes, Martin. *The Arabesk Debate: Music and Musicians in Modern Turkey.* Oxford Studies in Social and Cultural Anthropology. Oxford: Oxford University Press, 1992.

Stokes, Martin, ed. *Ethnicity, Identity, and Music: The Musical Construction of Place.* Berg Ethnic Identities Series. Oxford: Berg, 1994.

Stolcke, Verena. "Is Sex to Gender as Race Is to Ethnicity?" In *Gendered Anthropology*, edited by Teresa del Valle, 17–37. London: Routledge, 1993.

Stoler, Ann Laura. *Race and the Education of Desire: Foucault's History of Sexuality and the Colonial Order of Things.* Durham, NC: Duke University Press, 1995.

Stoller, Paul. *Sensuous Scholarship*. Contemporary Ethnography. Philadelphia: University of Pennsylvania Press, 1997.

Spinks, Brian D., ed. *The Place of Christ in Liturgical Prayer: Trinity, Christology, and Liturgical Theology*. Collegeville, MN: Liturgical Press, 2008.

Strathern, Marilyn. *The Gender of the Gift: Problems with Women and Problems with Society in Melanesia*. Studies in Melanesian Anthropology 6. Berkeley: University of California Press, 1988.

———. *Kinship, Law, and the Unexpected: Relatives Are Always a Surprise*. Cambridge: Cambridge University Press, 2005.

Syriac Orthodox Resources. "Worship in the Syriac Orthodox Church." Syriac Orthodox Resources, n.d. https://syriacorthodoxresources.org/Worship/index.html.

Syrian Orthodox Church of Antioch Archdiocese of the Western U.S. "Our Faith," n.d. http://www.soc-wus.org/ourchurch/ourfaith.html.

TallBear, Kim. *Native American DNA: Tribal Belonging and the False Promise of Genetic Science*. Minneapolis: University of Minnesota Press, 2013.

Tamarkin, Noah. "Genetic Diaspora: Producing Knowledge of Genes and Jews in Rural South Africa." *Cultural Anthropology* 29, no. 3 (August 11, 2014): 552–74. https://doi.org/10.14506/ca29.3.06.

Tambar, Kabir. "The Aesthetics of Public Visibility: Alevi *Semah* and the Paradoxes of Pluralism in Turkey." *Comparative Studies in Society and History* 52, no. 3 (July 2010): 652–79. https://doi.org/10.1017/S0010417510000344.

———. *The Reckoning of Pluralism: Political Belonging and the Demands of History in Turkey*. Stanford Studies in Middle Eastern and Islamic Societies and Cultures. Stanford, CA: Stanford University Press, 2014.

Tamimi Arab, Pooyan. *Amplifying Islam in the European Soundscape: Religious Pluralism and Secularism in the Netherlands*. Islam of the Global West. London: Bloomsbury, 2017.

———. "(Dis)Entangling Culturalism, Nativism, Racism." *Krisis* 2 (2012): 68–74.

Taussig, Karen-Sue. "Calvinism and Chromosomes: Religion, the Geographical Imaginary, and Medical Genetics in the Netherlands." *Science as Culture* 6, no. 4 (January 1997): 495–524. https://doi.org/10.1080/09505439709526483.

———. *Ordinary Genomes: Science, Citizenship, and Genetic Identities*. Experimental Futures: Technological Lives, Scientific Arts, Anthropological Voices. Durham, NC: Duke University Press, 2009.

Taylor, Charles. *Modern Social Imaginaries*. Public Planet Books. Durham, NC: Duke University Press, 2004.

———. *A Secular Age*. Cambridge, MA: The Belknap Press of Harvard University Press, 2007.

————. *Sources of the Self: The Making of the Modern Identity*. Cambridge, MA: Harvard University Press, 1989.

Taylor, Charles, et al. *Multiculturalism: Examining the Politics of Recognition*. Edited by Amy Gutmann. Princeton, NJ: Princeton University Press, 1994.

The Syriac Orthodox Patriarchate of Antioch. "Syriac Orthodox Resources." 2001. http://sor.cua.edu/Patriarchate.

Thellefsen, Torkild, and Bent Sørensen, eds. *Charles Sanders Peirce in His Own Words: 100 Years of Semiotics, Communication and Cognition*. Semiotics, Communication and Cognition, vol. 14. Boston: De Gruyter Mouton, 2014.

Thomas, Todne. *Kincraft: The Making of Black Evangelical Sociality*. Religious Cultures of African and African Diaspora People. Durham, NC: Duke University Press, 2021.

Throop, C. Jason. "'Becoming Beautiful in the Dance': On the Formation of Ethical Modalities of Being in Yap, Federated States of Micronesia." *Oceania* 79, no. 2 (July 2009): 179–201. https://doi.org/10.1002/j.1834-4461.2009 .tb00058.x.

Topolski, Anya. "The Race-Religion Constellation: A European Contribution to the Critical Philosophy of Race." *Critical Philosophy of Race* 6, no. 1 (January 1, 2018): 58–81. https://doi.org/10.5325/critphilrace.6.1.0058.

Turino, Thomas. *Music as Social Life: The Politics of Participation*. Chicago Studies in Ethnomusicology. Chicago: University of Chicago Press, 2008.

Turman, Eboni Marshall. *Toward a Womanist Ethic of Incarnation: Black Bodies, the Black Church, and the Council of Chalcedon*. New York: Palgrave Macmillan, 2013.

Valenta, Markha G. "How to Recognize a Moslem When You See One: Western Secularism and the Politics of Conversion." In *Political Theologies: Public Religions in a Post-Secular World*, edited by Hent de Vries and Lawrence E. Sullivan, 444–74. New York: Fordham University Press, 2006.

Van Amersfoort, Hans, and Anja Van Heelsum. "Moroccan Berber Immigrants in The Netherlands, Their Associations, and Transnational Ties: A Quest for Identity and Recognition." *Immigrants and Minorities* 25, no. 3 (November 2007): 234–62. https://doi.org/10.1080/02619280802407343.

Van Den Berg, Marguerite, and Jan Willem Duyvendak. "Paternalizing Mothers: Feminist Repertoires in Contemporary Dutch Civilizing Offensives." *Critical Social Policy* 32, no. 4 (November 2012): 556–76. https://doi.org/10.1177/0261018312439360.

Van den Berg, Mariecke, et al., eds. *Transforming Bodies and Religions: Powers and Agencies in Europe*. Routledge Critical Studies in Religion, Gender and Sexuality. Abingdon: Routledge, 2021.

Van Reekum, Rogier, and Jan Willem Duyvendak. "Running from Our Shadows: The Performative Impact of Policy Diagnoses in Dutch Debates on

Immigrant Integration." *Patterns of Prejudice* 46, no. 5 (December 2012): 445–66. https://doi.org/10.1080/0031322X.2012.718164.

Van Schie, Gerwin. "Origins: A History of Race-Ethnic Categorisation in the Dutch Governmental Data Ontology (1899–2018)." *TMG Journal for Media History* 21, no. 2 (November 1, 2018): 67. https://doi.org/10.18146/2213-7653 .2018.367.

Varghese, Baby. *The Early History of the Syriac Liturgy: Growth, Adaptation and Inculturation*. Go? Ttinger Orientforschungen, Band 62. Wiesbaden: Harrassowitz Verlag, 2021.

———. *West Syrian Liturgical Theology*. Liturgy, Worship and Society. Aldershot: Ashgate, 2004.

Vasta, Ellie. "The Politics of Avoidance—the Netherlands in Perspective." In *Dutch Racism*, edited by Philomena Essed and Isabel Hoving, 387–95. Leiden: Brill, 2014.

Verkaaik, Oskar. "The Cachet Dilemma: Ritual and Agency in New Dutch Nationalism." *American Ethnologist* 37, no. 1 (February 2010): 69–82. https://doi.org/10.1111/j.1548-1425.2010.01242.x.

Verkaaik, Oskar, and Pooyan Tamimi Arab. "Managing Mosques in the Netherlands: Constitutional versus Culturalist Secularism." *Journal of Muslims in Europe* 5, no. 2 (October 28, 2016): 251–68. https://doi.org/10 .1163/22117954-12341331.

Vesa, Benedict. "Icons and Iconography in the West Syriac Church." *Altarul Reîntregirii*, no. Suplim. 1 (2017): 385–99. https://doi.org/10.29302/AR.2017 .Suplim.1.28.

"Vijf Eeuwen Migratie." Centrum voor de Geschiedenis van Migranten, 2010.

Vlasblom, Dirk. "Hoe Sorteren van de Soort Uitdraaide Op Rassenwaan." *NRC Handeslblad, Dossier: Racisme*, n.d. https://www.nrc.nl/nieuws/2017/11/17 /hoe-sorteren-van-de-soort-uitdraaide-op-rassenwaan-14075192-a1581607.

Vliek, Maria. "'It's Not Just about Faith': Narratives of Transformation When Moving Out of Islam in the Netherlands and Britain." *Islam and Christian– Muslim Relations* 30, no. 3 (July 3, 2019): 323–44. https://doi.org/10.1080 /09596410.2019.1628459.

Vogel, Henk, Mirella Klomp, and Marcel Barnard. "Competing Authenticities: The Appropriation of Psalms in the Festival '150 Psalms.'" *Journal of Contemporary Religion* 37, no. 3 (September 2, 2022): 535–52. https://doi.org /10.1080/13537903.2022.2094114.

———. "Making Sense of the Psalms: Aesthetics and Embodied Experience in the Performance of Psalms." *Religion and the Arts* 26, no. 1–2 (March 24, 2022): 136–63. https://doi.org/10.1163/15685292-02601006.

Vries, Hent de, ed. *Religion: Beyond a Concept*. New York: Fordham University Press, 2008.

Vries, Hent de, and Lawrence E. Sullivan, eds. *Political Theologies: Public Religions in a Post-Secular World.* 1st ed. New York: Fordham University Press, 2006.

Weber, Max. *Economy and Society: An Outline of Interpretive Sociology.* Berkeley: University of California Press, 1978.

———. *Max Weber: Essays in Sociology.* Edited by H. H. Gerth and C. W. Mills. London: Routledge, 1974.

———. *The Protestant Ethic and the Spirit of Capitalism: The Relationships between Religion and the Economic and Social Life in Modern Culture.* Tr. Talcott Parsons. New York: Charles Scribner's Sons, 1958.

Weidman, Amanda. "Gender and the Politics of Voice: Colonial Modernity and Classical Music in South India." *Cultural Anthropology* 18, no. 2 (May 2003): 194–232. https://doi.org/10.1525/can.2003.18.2.194.

———. *Singing the Classical, Voicing the Modern: The Postcolonial Politics of Music in South India.* Durham, NC: Duke University Press, 2006.

Wekker, Gloria. "Still Crazy after All Those Years . . . : Feminism for the New Millennium." *European Journal of Women's Studies* 11, no. 4 (November 2004): 487–500. https://doi.org/10.1177/1350506804046822.

———. *White Innocence: Paradoxes of Colonialism and Race.* Durham, NC: Duke University Press, 2016.

Weltecke, Dorothea. "Bar 'Ebroyo on Identity: Remarks on His Historical Writing." *Hugoye: Journal of Syriac Studies* 19, no. 1 (January 1, 2018): 303–32. https://doi.org/10.31826/hug-2018-190107.

White, Benjamin. "The Nation-State Form and the Emergence of 'Minorities' in Syria." *Studies in Ethnicity and Nationalism* 7, no. 1 (March 2007): 64–85. https://doi.org/10.1111/j.1754-9469.2007.tb00108.x.

Wiering, Jelle. "There Is a Sexular Body: Introducing a Material Approach to the Secular." *Secularism and Nonreligion* 6 (May 12, 2017): 8. https://doi.org/10.5334/snr.78.

Wilf, Eitan. "Swinging within the Iron Cage: Modernity, Creativity, and Embodied Practice in American Postsecondary Jazz Education." *American Ethnologist* 37 no. 3 (2010): 563–82.

Williams, Brackette. "A Class Act: Anthropology and the Race to Nation Across Ethnic Terrain." *Annual Review of Anthropology* 18, no. 1 (October 1989): 401–44. https://doi.org/10.1146/annurev.an.18.100189.002153.

Wood, Philip. *The Chronicle of Seert: Christian Historical Imagination in Late Antique Iraq.* 1st ed. Oxford Early Christian Studies. Oxford: Oxford University Press, 2013.

———. *The Imam of the Christians: The World of Dionysius of Tel-Mahre, c. 750–850.* Princeton, NJ: Princeton University Press, 2021.

Woźniak-Bobińska, Marta. "Big Fat Assyrian/Syriac Weddings: Rituals and Marriage Traditions among Middle Eastern Christians in Sweden." *Journal of Ethnic and Migration Studies* 44, no. 16 (December 10, 2018): 2684–2700. https://doi.org/10.1080/1369183X.2017.1389036.

———. "Intergenerational Relations: Exploring Ambivalence Within Assyrian/ Syriac Families in Sweden." *Parole de l'Orient* 45 (2019): 393–417.

Yanow, Dvora, and Marleen Van Der Haar. "People out of Place: Allochthony and Autochthony in the Netherlands' Identity Discourse—Metaphors and Categories in Action." *Journal of International Relations and Development* 16, no. 2 (April 2013): 227–61. https://doi.org/10.1057/jird.2012.13.

Young, Frances M. *From Nicaea to Chalcedon: A Guide to the Literature and Its Background.* 2nd edition. Grand Rapids, MI: Baker Academic, 2010.

Zeitoune, Abboud. *Music Pearls of Beth-Nahrin: An Assyrian/Syriac Discography.* 1st ed. Wiesbaden: Assyrische Demokratische Organisation, 2015 [2007].

Zigon, Jarrett. "Moral Breakdown and the Ethical Demand: A Theoretical Framework for an Anthropology of Moralities." *Anthropological Theory* 7, no. 2 (June 2007): 131–50. https://doi.org/10.1177/1463499607077295.

———. "On Love: Remaking Moral Subjectivity in Postrehabilitation Russia." *American Ethnologist* 40, no. 1 (February 2013): 201–15. https://doi.org/10.1111 /amet.12014.

———. "Within a Range of Possibilities: Morality and Ethics in Social Life." *Ethnos* 74, no. 2 (June 2009): 251–76. https://doi.org/10.1080 /00141840902940492.

INDEX

vocality, 9, 116
voice: dialogical effect of others', 164, 231; liturgical, 16, 17, 18, 2, 105, 133, 134, 149, 154,
  251n4; material, 2, 12, 50, 51, 76, 89, 91,
  97, 102, 104, 115, 161, 184, 194, 195, 219; as
  phonosonic nexus, 27; as *qolo*, 14; sociopolitical sense of, 151, 171, 188, 251n1; as sonic
  icon, 80, 83, 85, 87, 89, 91, 92, 93, 95, 105,
  107, 114–117, 129, 132, 133, 160
volk, 110, 211

wall paintings, 70, 95
Weber, Max, 28, 99, 226, 227
Wekker, Gloria, 203, 214, 253n7

Weltecke, Dorothea, 6, 69, 80
Wesselerbrink, 6, 54, 118
West Syriac Rite, 4, 6, 7, 10, 18, 22, 38, 47, 50, 53,
  70, 72, 74, 76, 78, 79, 83, 89, 91, 102, 109, 110,
  115, 131, 139, 173, 175. *See also* Syriac Orthodox
Wilders, Geert, 157, 216, 217
Whiteness, 207, 223
World Council of Aramaeans (Syriacs), 110,
  161, 162

yoldath aloho, 5, 15, 65. *See also* Mary, Mother
  of Jesus

Zeitoune, Abboud, 89, 249n15

An anthropologist by training, Sarah Bakker Kellogg teaches courses on religion, gender, and ethnography at San Francisco State University. As an interdisciplinary and publicly engaged scholar, she bridges North American, European, and Middle Eastern conversations about racism, religious difference, gender, and global migration politics. She has presented and published work on secularism and aesthetics, racism and racialization, and the transnational politics of minority recognition in flagship social science journals like *American Ethnologist*, *Current Anthropology*, and *Cultural Anthropology*.

ORTHODOX CHRISTIANITY
AND CONTEMPORARY THOUGHT

SERIES EDITORS
Aristotle Papanikolaou and Ashley M. Purpura

Sarah Bakker Kellogg, *Sonic Icons: Relation, Recognition, and Revival in a Syriac World*

A. G. Roeber, *Orthodox Christianity and the Rights Revolution in America*

Bryce E. Rich, *Gender Essentialism and Orthodoxy: Beyond Male and Female*

Kristina Stoeckl and Dmitry Uzlaner, *The Moralist International: Russia in the Global Culture Wars*

Sarah Riccardi-Swartz, *Between Heaven and Russia: Religious Conversion and Political Apostasy in Appalachia*

Thomas Arentzen, Ashley M. Purpura, and Aristotle Papanikolaou (eds.), *Orthodox Tradition and Human Sexuality*

Christina M. Gschwandtner, *Welcoming Finitude: Toward a Phenomenology of Orthodox Liturgy*

George E. Demacopoulos, *Colonizing Christianity: Greek and Latin Religious Identity in the Era of the Fourth Crusade.*

Pia Sophia Chaudhari, *Dynamis of Healing: Patristic Theology and the Psyche*

Brian A. Butcher, *Liturgical Theology after Schmemann: An Orthodox Reading of Paul Ricoeur*. Foreword by Andrew Louth.

Ashley M. Purpura, *God, Hierarchy, and Power: Orthodox Theologies of Authority from Byzantium*.

Aristotle and George E. Demacopoulos (eds.), *Faith, Reason, and Theosis*

Aristotle Papanikolaou and George E. Demacopoulos (eds.), *Fundamentalism or Tradition: Christianity after Secularism*

George E. Demacopoulos and Aristotle Papanikolaou (eds.), *Christianity, Democracy, and the Shadow of Constantine.*

George E. Demacopoulos and Aristotle Papanikolaou (eds.), *Orthodox Constructions of the West.*

George E. Demacopoulos and Aristotle Papanikolaou (eds.), *Orthodox Readings of Augustine* [available 2020]

John Chryssavgis and Bruce V. Foltz (eds.), *Toward an Ecology of Transfiguration: Orthodox Christian Perspectives on Environment, Nature, and Creation.* Foreword by Bill McKibben. Prefatory Letter by Ecumenical Patriarch Bartholomew.

Lucian N. Leustean (ed.), *Orthodox Christianity and Nationalism in Nineteenth-Century Southeastern Europe.*

Georgia Frank, Susan R. Holman, and Andrew S. Jacobs (eds.), *The Garb of Being: Embodiment and the Pursuit of Holiness in Late Ancient Christianity*

John Chryssavgis (ed.), *Dialogue of Love: Breaking the Silence of Centuries.* Contributions by Brian E. Daley, S.J., and Georges Florovsky

A. G. Roeber, *Orthodox Christians and the Rights Revolution in America*

Ecumenical Patriarch Bartholomew, *In the World, Yet Not of the World: Social and Global Initiatives of Ecumenical Patriarch Bartholomew.* Edited by John Chryssavgis. Foreword by Jose Manuel Barroso

Ecumenical Patriarch Bartholomew, *Speaking the Truth in Love: Theological and Spiritual Exhortations of Ecumenical Patriarch Bartholomew.* Edited by John Chryssavgis. Foreword by Dr. Rowan Williams, Archbishop of Canterbury.

Ecumenical Patriarch Bartholomew, *On Earth as in Heaven: Ecological Vision and Initiatives of Ecumenical Patriarch Bartholomew.* Edited by John Chryssavgis. Foreword by His Royal Highness, the Duke of Edinburgh.

www.ingramcontent.com/pod-product-compliance
Lightning Source LLC
Chambersburg PA
CBHW031142020426
42333CB00013B/479